# Good Neighbours: Itteringham, Norfolk in the 18<sup>th</sup> Century

*William and Maggie Vaughan-Lewis*

For
Ann and Martin MacKeown
who loved the Manor House

*ITTERINGHAM HISTORY*

Published 2010 by Itteringham History

ISBN: 978-0-9561795-1-7

Printed in the UK by The Lavenham Press Ltd, Lavenham, Suffolk

Cover photographs by the authors. Front cover: the Manor House of Thomas Robins. Rear cover: White House farm; Thomas Robins's 1765 summer house on Broom hill; dogs on the Manor House staircase; enclosure map of 1823 marking domestic buildings in red, outbuildings and farm buildings in grey.

# Contents

## Acknowledgments

Our thanks go to all the residents of the villages of Itteringham and Irmingland for their encouragement and help with special thanks to Mr and Mrs Michael Rogers, Mr and Mrs Jonathan Seaman, Mr and Mrs Peter McVeigh, Ann McKeown and Dawn Maiden for allowing us to explore and photograph their houses.

As ever, all the Norfolk Record Office staff have been endlessly helpful and patient; our thanks are due to Dr John Alban for permission to use extracts from so many original letters, parish accounts and inventories; and to reproduce the illustrations of handwriting (Chapter 14), the 1823 enclosure map (Chapters 2, 7, 10 and 15), the 1809 Orford estate plan (Chapter 6), the 1778 Road Order plan (Chapters 2, 7, and 10), the Itteringham Hall plan 1748 (Chapter 7), the print of Oulton Meeting House (Chapter 9) and Aylmerton tithe map (Chapter 19).

Very particular acknowledgement must go to Lord and Lady Walpole and Elizabeth Rutledge for the use of, and expert help with, the Wolterton archive from which so much of the village story has been drawn.

Thanks also to Dr Elizabeth Griffiths for her knowledge of the Blickling estate, permission to use her drawing of the 1729 map and her work on farming to halves. We are grateful to the National Trust and their tenants for allowing the use of external photographs of their properties.

Thanks to Mr and Mrs C Shippam for permission to use the 19th century water colours of Mannington. The Wolterton Hall images (Chapter 15) are courtesy of Norfolk County Council Library and Information Service.

For their kind help and support with the Rebecca Robins/Emes story, we must thank members of The Silver Society especially Jane Ewart, John Fallon and Lucy Morton.

For the only known photograph of a Robins, acknowledgements and thanks are due to Rod Hodgson and the Hudson Historical Society; for background on the Hudson Bay Company thanks go to the Ontario Heritage Foundation, Canada and the website of the Archives of Manitoba.

Thanks to Jonathan Neville for additional material from his Norfolk Mills website and the photographs of the bricklayer's mark in the mill, Keepers Cottage, and of the 1595 and 1742 maps.

And to Bill Byford and Lisa Spiking at Lavenham Press for helping us through the production process.

## Abbreviations, footnotes, style and transcription

| | |
|---|---|
| NRO | Norfolk Record Office at the Archives Centre, County Hall. The catalogue is available online. |
| TNA | The National Archives, Kew, Surrey |
| Wolterton archive | Private collection of Lord and Lady Walpole |
| Newspapers | *Norwich Mercury* and *Norfolk Chronicle* on microfilm at the Heritage Library, The Forum, Norwich |
| IGI | International Genealogical Index (Familysearch.org) has been used extensively - but with caution - as a research tool and where possible confirmed by original registers and wills (generally not footnoted being readily findable in online catalogues). |
| *See You in Court* | W & M Vaughan-Lewis, *See You in Court: The Potts Family of Mannington, Norfolk 1584 -1737*, 2009 |
| *NA* | *Norfolk Archaeology* |
| NAHRG | Norfolk Archaeological and Historical Research Group |
| *ODNB* | *Oxford Dictionary of National Biography* |

Transcriptions have been modernised for easier reading where necessary except for instances where the original is relevant to the text. Dates before 1752 have been given as modern years, ie January-March 1748 is shown as January-March 1749. Sums of money are shown as £ - pounds, s - shillings and d - pence. Capitalisation has been kept to a minimum except in quotations (eg dissenters, rector, chancery). Family surnames inevitably were found spelt in many variations. For each a standard form has been selected but other forms may be discussed at first occurrence of the name and shown in index entries.

The details given in this book are taken from contemporary sources and information from secondary sources has been checked with original documents where possible. If we could not prove a statement absolutely - such as where parish registers or deeds have not survived - we have said 'probably' or similar wording. To keep the text clear, no footnotes have been used but short summaries of key sources are shown at the end of each chapter. If any reader wishes to obtain a specific reference, we shall be delighted to assist.

## Introduction

For such a small village, the story of Itteringham in the 18th century is surprisingly complex. As with all communities, events and influences do not sit neatly in an artificial time-frame nor in a geographical island. Here the 'long' 18th century - we start in the 1660s and end about 1820 - is more appropriate. No community was able to exist or change without networks of inter-relationships - both at each class level and in other spheres including trade and religious affiliations. On the one hand therefore, the story is one of the influence of local estates and families who vied for the land and economic value of the village; on the other it is the tale of ordinary families linked to neighbouring villages and towns making a life through trade and useful marriages. As property was the lifeblood of development as well as the basis of everyday life - where one lived, worked, shopped, passed the time of day   a history of those buildings which were then in existence, has also been attempted. No coverage would be complete without a look at how people lived – poor and rich, old and young, sick and healthy. Glimpses of their lives are to be found in a wide range of records – we have used as many as possible to bring Itteringham and its surroundings alive.

The central story that emerged, interwoven in every aspect of village life and society, was the rise and decline of a family called Robins. Now largely forgotten - save for some initials in ironwork and tombs in the church - the Robinses exemplified how success was often achieved through a mixture of a puritan work ethic, a tightly-knit extended family network which traded together and looked after its own, and that entrepreneurial streak which seized and maximised opportunities. In the end, as so often happened in families, both genes and character changed. All was lost and between 1799 and 1801 their two estates were sold to the Blickling and Wolterton estates; in the 19th century, barring a few freeholds, most of the village was shared between the Earl of Orford (Wolterton) and Lord Suffield (Blickling). That very different century must await a later book.

*Good Neighbours* is divided into five parts. The first sets the scene and introduces the village, the local estates and the Robins family. Their links with the Bell family of Oulton, who were similarly successful in the adjoining parish, are given here. In the second part, local farms and farming practices are discussed giving a feeling for the nature of the soil and the difficulties faced. The third looks in detail at the properties, their uses and ownership. Here in the 'heart of the village', the trades are examined followed by the 'soul of the village' where the relationship of the church and the early dissenters are discussed. As the Robinses were major players in the building of Oulton meeting house - a good example of the need to take the holistic view of the way village life interlinked with a greater area - this is discussed in detail. Also included here is the life-blood – the villagers and the rows of small cottages. The fourth section looks at the day-to-day lifestyle of the people – with an emphasis on the poor and disease. Death and taxes, as ever, loomed large in their lives.

And finally the last part of the book takes the Robins story forward – to the last of the line at Itteringham Hall, now White House farm. Their fascinating finales take place far from the village, in very different worlds. The Robinses, like the Bells in Oulton, filled the local power vacuum for a few generations; their story deserves to be told.

# Part 1

## ITTERINGHAM AND ITS NEIGHBOURS:
## ORIGINS OF ESTATES AND FAMILIES

*Abundance of Pretty Wenches; An Exceeding good Neighbourhood, good Roads, very few Poachers, No Beggars, And not within sixteen Miles of a Lord!*

*1727 description of Heydon estate*

The development of Itteringham village; local estates and farms - dominance and opportunity; the Robins and Bell families

# Chapter 1

## *Itteringham Village Development*

---

*In order to understand Itteringham in the 18th century, a wider view of how the village developed must be taken. Fortunately a map of the Mannington estate - which covered the northern half of the parish - has survived from 1595. By using this as a base and adding 17th century documentation, the story starts to unfold.*

In late Elizabethan times Itteringham was a very small village and its neighbour Mannington no longer had any village centre. The Mannington estate map of 1595 shows much of the centre of Itteringham where there were few houses or cottages. A listing of inhabitants of 1589 shows only one tradesman (Edmund Buck, a carpenter) whereas Wickmere had a number of different trades. At this point there was almost certainly no shop, no inn, probably no tannery at Bintry and few cottages outside the main tenant farms and their farmyards. This was a small farming community with one or two weavers and few other artisans. The owners of the larger houses were not, as yet, sufficiently wealthy to create additional employment and growth.

It seems likely that the village started to develop from the 1620s when Sir John Potts, the 1st Baronet, came into his inheritance of the Mannington estate, which covered a large part of Itteringham parish. This would be in line with the known surge in rural house building in the early decades of the century. A barber surgeon, Tobias Johnson, moved into the neighbourhood in the 1630s and other trades appeared. The first mention of a grocer of Itteringham comes in 1637 and by the 1650s there was a blacksmith at work. The surviving tax assessment of 1660 shows four significant tradesmen assessed at upwards of £100 worth of stock. Edmund Chapman the tanner (whose lands were in Aldborough and Saxthorpe) was assessed on £200 of stock. Richard Robins the blacksmith, James Jempson a glover (working with fine leathers) and Robert Empson had £100 worth each. Empson may have been the shopkeeper, perhaps the son of Thomas Empson, a grocer in Aylsham at the time. As grocer he would have carried a large stock which would have been taxable. His administration of 1667 was signed by his widow and William Jackson then grocer of Itteringham. Jackson had appeared on the list as worth less than £100 so may have later taken over running the business. Similarly the miller, John Browne, operating a service, would not have carried much stock and so was only taxable at the lower general adult rate. Of the 41 adult male names listed for the lower rate, smaller tradesmen such as the carpenter cannot be identified.

At this time there were 87 adults on the list, including widows. By taking the 23 married couples and other obvious households (surname clusters) there would seem to have been at least 29 homes in the parish. Of the single women no doubt many were in service and living with their employers. Some others may have been widows living in the almshouses. The 14 single men again may have been lodging with the farmers who were no doubt their employers, although some may have been sharing cottages. Taking standard ratios for numbers of children per couple it is likely that there were about 150 people in the parish by 1660.

A reasonable estimate for the number of buildings would be about 35 houses or cottages, including the almshouses. This is supported by the hearth tax returns with their exemption certificates of the 1660s and 1670s. These show that there were between 17 and 19 tax-paying homes and typically about 15 poor people exempted from paying in Itteringham. (Exemption was based on value and income; those having one or two hearths were often included if they had a modest living.) Assuming all the latter were in separate dwellings there may have been just over 30 homes, again including almshouses.

It has been suggested by Margaret Spufford that in rural Cambridgeshire, one hearth correlates to 2-4 rooms, two hearths to 4-6 rooms, 3-4 hearths to 6-11 rooms and 5 or more hearths to 10 or more rooms. These of course include fires in brewhouses and washhouses and allow for other unheated services and other rooms. In 1664 those in the larger houses or cottages in Itteringham were listed as Daniel Muddiclift 6 hearths, William Jackson 5, Robert Empson 5, Edmund Chapman 4, Richard Robins 3, Robert Jackson 3, James Jempson 3, William Earle 3, and Henry Williams 3. Of these, only three can be firmly identified. Muddiclift was the Potts family steward, probably living in what is now the Old Rectory; Chapman was the tanner leasing Bintry from the Gay family; and Richard Robins was the blacksmith, in the cottage (later part of the Manor House) and Love's Messuage in the yard. As either Empson or William Jackson may have been the grocer, one of them might have been living on the current shop site. At 5 hearths however, this substantial house might have been Larwood's Messuage or a house at the site of Hill farm. The Jacksons were also farming at either Hill farm or West Field farm. Where Jempson the glover lived is unknown. The last three may have included Meadow House and the

Atwood/shop house site if not held by Empson. Given the number of their hearths, Earle and Williams were more likely tradesmen rather than agricultural labourers.

This list does not seem to include Itteringham Hall, now White House farm, which would probably have had 10 or so hearths. There are a couple of entries with the number of hearths omitted which might account for the problem. Alternatively the hall could have been unoccupied at the time. Of the other entries, five people had one hearth and another, the widow of a land-owning farmer, had two.

For the most part the Itteringham cottages had just one hearth. The poorer, exempted, villagers lived in small cottages which had just one downstairs and one upstairs room. By contrast, Mannington Hall was shown with 20 hearths. Given the likely floor plan, this figure seems high and may include another dwelling in the farmyard and even Mere farm, neither of which was separately listed. In Wolterton there were 13 taxable dwellings. Thomas Jackson the rector of both Itteringham and Wolterton was in the 5-hearth parsonage house there. Matthew Bacon, of the former Wolterton cleric's family, also had five hearths. Two other families, Wenn and Johnson, had large cottages with several hearths, possibly all on the village green to the north-east of the church. The largest of course was the old Wolterton Hall where James Scamler had 14 hearths. Even allowing for kitchen and backhouse service fireplaces this was a substantial house. From these returns, it is clear that Mannington did not contain an identifiable village and at Wolterton the village community was already on the wane; Itteringham and Wickmere, as a result, had started to rise in importance.

Helpfully in one of the returns, for 1674, Itteringham was shown as having seven almshouses. Five of these were probably in Church Row (now the modern rectory's parking area). Before demolition in 1969 Church Row definitely comprised five tiny one-up one-down cottages. In 1733 on a visit to the village, Thomas Martin noted them as bearing the Potts arms on one gable end. It seems likely that Sir John Potts and his wife Dame Ursula had them built, perhaps in the 1630s or 1640s. They were run by the parish poor overseers on a rent-free basis but remained part of the Mannington estate. It is hard to see how this site could have had seven dwellings. The other two, now long gone, were almost certainly on the Common standing in front of Orchard farm. So the size and layout of the village was largely settled by the 1670s.

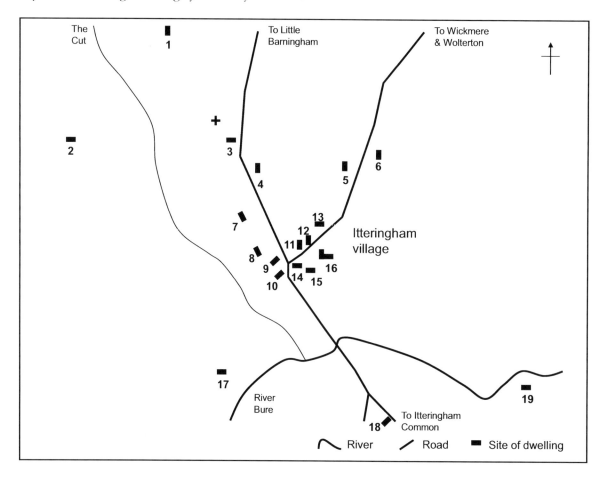

Central dwelling sites

| 1 | The Old Rectory | Pre-1595 high status house, later attached to farm. 1857 conversion to rectory house after exchange with **8**. With site in adjoining field, Larwood's Messuage |
|---|---|---|
| 2 | West Field farm | Pre-1595 tenant farmstead on enclosure of west open field, originally called Diers. Farm merged with **1** mid-18th century. Buildings disappeared by mid-19th century. |
| 3 | Church Row | Almshouses for the poor probably built mid-17th century. Demolished 20th century to make way for new rectory. |
| 4 | The Street east side, now 98-100 | Pre-1595 cottages. Originally freehold. Extended from 2 to 3 cottages in 18th century. Acquired by William Creasey and sold to Blickling in 1799. |
| 5 | Wolterton Rd W | Probably built 17th century - not on 1595 map. Freehold. |
| 6 | Wolterton Rd E | Pre-1595 house. Acquired by Thomas Robins. |
| 7 | John Bell's House | Pre-1595 house. Sold by Bell family to Walpole mid-18th century. Now Meadow House. |
| 8 | Parsonage Cottage | Pre-1595 house - originally glebe. Parsonage sometimes let to tenant farmer or curate. 1857 exchanged to Walpole for **1**. Now Glebe House. |
| 9 | Big Yard (part) | Freehold created out of part of **10** probably late 17th century. Probably became 2 cottages and barns or workshops during 18th century. |
| 10 | Front of Big Yard | Pre-1595 house and land of Richardson family. Acquired by Thomas Robins. |
| 11 | Old Smithy & Cottage | Built early 18th century when smithy moved from Manor House site. Now outhouses at rear of Wingfield House |
| 12 | The Shop & House | Pre-1595 house. First grocer 1630s. House probably upgraded early 18th century, with tiny extra cottage in the shop building. Continuous use as shop since 1630s. |
| 13 | Cottage behind shop | Set back behind shop. Unclear exactly when built in 17th century. Conveyed with shop by early 18th century. Acquired by Thomas Robins. |
| 14 | Love's messuage | Pre-1595 high status house. Acquired by Thomas Robins. Became cottages. Disappeared 19th century. (Possibly **15** was Love's) |
| 15 | Manor farm cottages | Probably built 18th century by Thomas Robins – present in 1778. Disappeared 19th century. |
| 16 | Manor House | First 2 cottages in east wing probably built c1640s (not on 1595 map). Site of first smithy. Thomas Robins built front part of Manor House 1707. |
| 17 | Bintry farm | Land here had manorial status. Tannery probably started early 17th century. Uncertain if house here earlier, but possible. Acquired by Thomas Robins. |
| 18 | The Artichoke | Pre-1595 2 cottages. Market garden. Pub (with bowling green) named this by 1760s when bought by Walpole and later became The Walpole Arms. |
| 19 | Mill House | Pre-1595 house for the miller. Now Mill Cottage. The mill was purely a working building in 18th century. |
| 20 | Mossymere | Pre-1595 small cottage – perhaps for shepherd on large area of Mannington heath. Later gamekeeper's cottage. Now Mossymere House. |
| 21 | Dairy farm house | Built 18th century (possibly early 1750s) – present in 1778. Became 2 cottages by 19th century. Demolished 20th century on erection of new barn. |
| 22 | Daniel Robins's House | Probably built by c1630s as tenant farm – Purdy & Daniel Robins. Acquired by Thomas Robins. Demolished mid to late 18th century on acquisition by Walpole. |
| 23 | Itteringham Hall | Built 16th century. Fine E-shaped Hall still evident on 1748 estate map. Dilapidated and rebuilt to smaller size in 1790s. Sold to Walpole. Now White House farm |
| 24 | Hill farm | Present house built 1704, but probably a dwelling here or nearby dating back at least to 16th century. However, housing before 1704 not identified. |
| 25 | Broom Hill cottage | Possibly a dwelling here in 16th century and prior. Land owned by Blickling estate then Bells & Pitmans of Oulton. Cottage likely in 18th century. |
| 26 | Itteringham Common | Some freehold cottages here definitely by 1750s (where the chapel now stands), more added in mid-century and 1790s. Other cottages 19th century. |
| 27 | Common poor house | Small cottage for the poor here by 1740s and probably since 1660s or earlier. Most cottages and chapel on east of New Road are 19th century. |
| 28 | Common farm | Farm house and barn here on 1729 Blickling estate map. Possibly 17th century build and gone by 1756. |
| 29 | Blickling Lodge | Site just within Itteringham parish beside drive into Blickling Park. Probably built mid-late 18th century. Demolished soon after 1823. |

**Itteringham dwelling-sites existing in the 18th century**

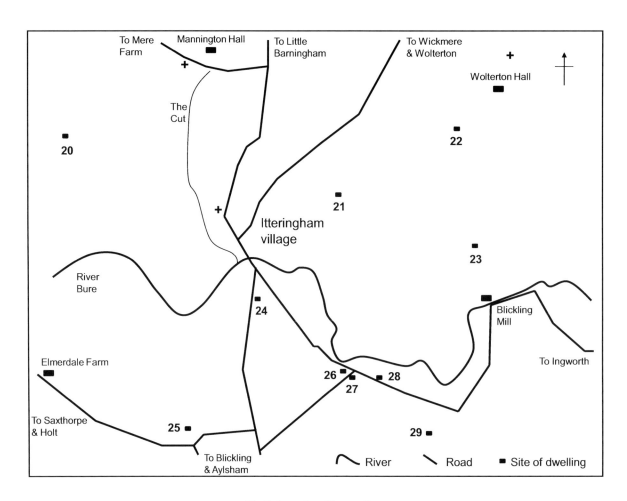

Outlying dwelling sites

The village population gradually increased in the 18th century, as it did nationwide. A few more houses or cottages were built but many sites became homes to two or more families rather than one. By the late 18th century 29 sites with dwelling houses can be identified – several now with multiple cottages on them. At the 1801 census Itteringham had 36 inhabited houses occupied by 64 families. These numbers are not straightforward. For example at this time 98-100 The Street was three distinct cottages, but it had at peak eight different tenants. At the 1801 census it was probably counted as three houses. There were 139 men and 160 women (including both adults and children), with 59 employed in agriculture and 31 in trades. Mannington by contrast was down to two houses (the Hall and Mere farm) with 12 men and 12 women. In Wolterton the houses around the green had all gone; now there remained six houses, 8 families with 18 men and 16 women. The green itself had become part of Wolterton Hall park.

A little more detail is needed for Itteringham Common (26-29), which was not developed until the mid-17th century. The Blickling estate had a cottage and barn (28) by 1729 and a lodge house into the park (29) at some point during the 18th century. The almshouse total for 1674 makes it highly likely that two small cottages for the poor were by then on the Common. The Thorn and Lound families built small cottage encroachments on the Common by about 1750; these may have been there for some years before as both families were well-established in Itteringham in the 17th century. At some point before 1756, the Blickling estate had abandoned the old cottage and barn and built new cottages near the poor houses. Thomas Plaford built several small cottages in the middle of the 18th century, by which point this would have been a distinct hamlet. Thomas Hurrell added a couple more at the end of the century. The Plaford and Hurrell cottages do not seem ever to have been lived in by their builders – build to rent was an old idea. As the rent of poor tenants would be paid by the parish, a return was guaranteed as long as the buildings were cheaply built.

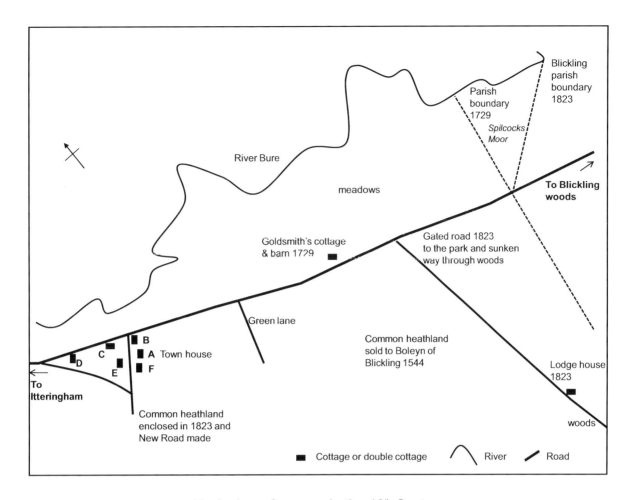

## Itteringham Common in the 18th Century

**A**  Town houses for parish poor, present by 1740 and probably included in the 1674 almshouses total, now demolished

**B**  Thorn and Lound, 2 small cottages present by 1749, now the chapel site

**C**  2 cottages built by Thomas Plaford, perhaps in 1750s, now 89 & 90 The Common

**D**  2 cottages built by Thomas Hurrell in 1792 &1796, now Bure Cottage

**E**  2 cottages built by Thomas Plaford, perhaps in 1750s, now Sunnyside & Flint Cottage

**F**  Cottages built by the Blickling estate, possibly in 1740s or early 1750s when Goldsmith's farm demolished. Now themselves demolished with Orchard farm on new site set back from road

The numbering for the main 29 sites shown on the table and sketch maps is used throughout the book eg Bintry farm (**17**). For brevity and ease, premises may be referred to by modern names: the Old Rectory (**1**) for example. This is shorthand for: 'Site number **1**, where an old house stood from before 1595, sometimes with farmland, which was converted in the mid-19th century for use as a rectory, until the 1960s. It was not church property before 1857.'

### Sources

NRO: AYL 202/1; NRO, RYE MS 17, Thomas Martin notebook

Wolterton archive

Norfolk Record Society vol 54; British Records Society, Hearth Tax series for Norfolk and Cambridgeshire (Spufford reference) and *Norfolk Genealogy* vols 15 & 20

# Chapter 2

## *Local Estates Around Itteringham*

---

*Having looked at the early development of the village, an overview of the farms and major properties in and immediately around Itteringham follows. The Itteringham area was dominated by the big estates of Wolterton and Mannington, with the Blickling estate holding a modest section of land at the southern end of the parish. Four surviving estate maps provide the details: Blickling's estate in 1729, Wolterton's lands in 1732, Mannington in 1742 and Lord Orford's holdings in 1809.*

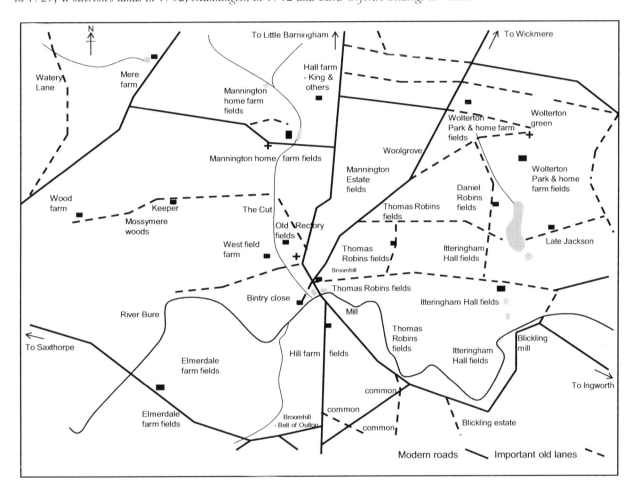

Farm areas in the 18th Century

## Wolterton

Emerging from a complex manorial history in the middle ages, Wolterton manor with its relatively modest demesne lands was in the hands of the Moore family in the middle of the 16th century. By the 1580s Gregory Houghton, a Norwich merchant and younger son of the Houghton family of Gunthorpe, had acquired it as his country seat. It stayed in the family in the ownership of his son Robert and grandson Richard until sold in 1660 to James Scamler senior, the husband of Sir John Potts's eldest daughter Anne. He and his son James, both London lawyers, held it for the next 50 years. In 1714 James Scamler junior left Wolterton and other properties to his nephew James Grey, son of his sister Elizabeth. In April 1714 James Grey of Wolterton sold 1 ½ acres of the 'manor meadow' of Wolterton to Thomas Robins for £15 – adjacent to brick kiln close and right on the parish boundary. In October 1717 the arrangement was confirmed and a three way deal between Grey, Thomas Robins and his cousin William Robins of Heydon was agreed to rationalise each others' meadows on the parish boundary and in a small piece of arable by the Stulps. As we shall see this would bring the Robins family in close proximity to Wolterton. Grey died just a few years later leaving Wolterton to his sister Penelope Grey on condition she provided for their mother and their sister Anne Crissell. (Their other sister Deborah died in 1717 the same year as James.) In December 1722 Penelope Grey completed the sale of the Wolterton estate to Horatio Walpole for £4,300. With the mansion house and park came 3 small farms. Together with parkland, the whole estate was only about 290 acres. It took the acquisition of the Wickmere property to create a good-sized estate.

---

## Wolterton estate 1732

| Tenant | Acres | Location |
|---|---|---|
| Wolterton Hall | 99 | Part of original purchase in 1722 - gardens, lakes and meadows |
| Late Richard Jackson's | 120 | Part of original purchase to south-east of Hall, later keeper's cottage. Jackson, a grandson of the rector, died in 1728 |
| Thomas Partridge | 69 | Wolterton Hall's dairy farm, lands largely in the west part of the parish |
| Henry Bayfield | 119 | Lands scattered particularly around north-east Wolterton. Own lands in Wickmere. Not clear if related to Thomas Bayfield the Wolterton steward |
| Thomas Page | 62 | Wolterton – immediately to west of the Green and Hall |
| Nicholas Wayt | 294 | Wickmere Hall and lands scattered around estate, including windmill close by present main gates to Wolterton Hall |
| Mrs Jane Cook | 170 | Wickmere – opposite Wickmere Hall |
| Henry Purdy | 26 | Wickmere – lands around present 'Purdy House' |
| Jeremiah Marshall | 58 | Wickmere – mostly strips in the 2 open fields |
| Henry Gunton | 65 | Wickmere – lands around Squallham |
| Matthew Woolmer | 70 | Calthorpe – Hook Hall farm in eastern end of parish by Scarrow Beck. Farmyard now AJ Cooper's yard |
| Dennis Gunton | 18 | Wickmere – east end of parish |
| Richard Smith | 26 | Wickmere – near the Common |
| Fring Wood | 8 | Presumably in Walpole's use. Adjacent Hospital farm, not then owned by the estate |
| 8 small tenants | 20 | In Wolterton and Wickmere – Grange, Curston, Brown, Jackson, Cubitt, Gay, Sutton, Bussel |
| Wolterton estate | 289 | |
| Wickmere estate | 924 | |
| | 1213 | |
| Mrs Neale | 19 | Lands in Wickmere, acquired after the 2 main estates purchased |
| Total | 1232 | |

---

Horatio Walpole clearly saw Wolterton as having the potential for a good house and garden and the possibility of building a large landed estate by acquisition. About two years after the purchase, workmen were in the Hall starting on major renovation and extension work. The precise appearance and location of the old hall is not known. However, it seems likely that it was an old house which had undergone some significant improvement by Richard Houghton in the 1640s. The pattern of lanes in the vicinity and descriptions in earlier deeds of its location place it just to the east of the present hall. In order to create the enlarged park and fine views, the cottage tenants and freeholders in Wolterton were progressively displaced. Rather than wholesale removal, Horatio carried out a sustained campaign of only purchasing properties on the death of a resident and there can be no doubt that Walpole had to pay a premium to achieve his goal. Deeds survive for James Dawson's cottage in Wickmere in 1733, Ann Neale's in Wickmere purchased from Mr Mickleburgh in 1734 and Thomas Burton's cottage and pightle on the old lane to Itteringham near the parsonage house in Wolterton in 1742. The Burton purchase was for £85 10s but presumably the cottage was in a poor state since there were only farm buildings on its site in 1809.

The last of the important deals were done in the 1740s when Walpole was particularly focussed on completing buying out the property holders around Wolterton green. In December 1742 Ann Johnson was paid £16 19s for a meadow which was then exchanged away to Richard Robins. She was also paid 5s for 'one year's acknowledgement for her common right on Wolterton green' – another indication of Walpole's very proper approach to freeholders' rights. In September 1746 Walpole bought the Wolterton property of the recently deceased Andrew Fiddyman, yeoman and thatcher of Wolterton, from his son William Fiddyman, a thatcher of Trunch. This was a complicated deal which made provision for Andrew's widow Hannah and William's sister Elizabeth Fortescue in addition to a payment of £35 to William. Perhaps Fiddyman's was the unnamed house shown on the 1732 map on the southern edge of Wolterton green. It was essential to clear the view north and east from the Hall to achieve Walpole's vision for his park.

Earlier in 1746 Richard Ness, Walpole's steward, had to ensure that Purdy's house on Wolterton green was not sold to Wickes of Blickling, a tanner who had a partial mortgage on it. He understood 'that the old man [Purdy] is determined to sell it outright and ... is made to believe that it will be most for his advantage so to do'. The freehold house, which had some ground and an orchard, was not named on the 1732 map but may have been one of those at the northern end of the green. Walpole was anxious to prevent Wickes trying to re-sell it to him at an inflated price. He authorised Ness to pay £100 or even £150 for it. There is no indication there was any material amount of land with it, so this was a big sum to be prepared to pay for a property that would immediately be knocked down.

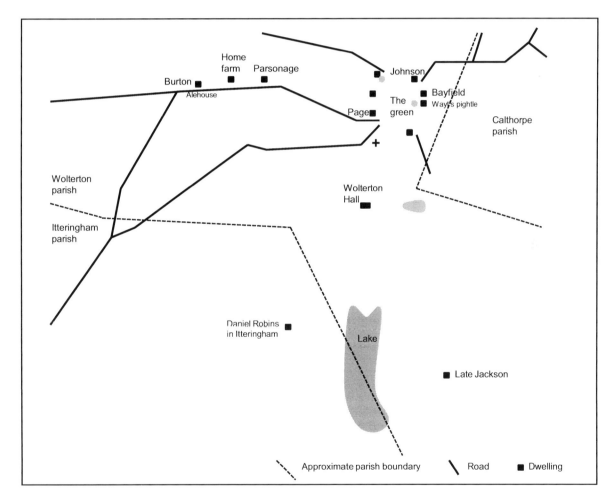

Dwellings in Wolterton 1732

By mid-century the small holdings around the old green had been swallowed up and by the time of the estate map of 1809 a mature landscape had been achieved with park grazing, trees and all the roads moved into the far distance.

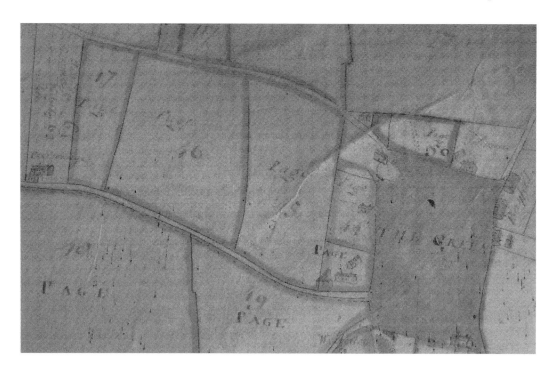

Wolterton green in 1732

| Wolterton estate 1809 | | Acres |
|---|---|---|
| Horatio Walpole | Wolterton park, Wolterton home farm and estate woods | 805 |
| John Beane | Wickmere Hall farm opposite the old Wickmere Hall | 269 |
| Wickmere glebe | In occupation of John Beane & William Symonds | 35 |
| John Middleton | Fring Wood farm | 157 |
| James Earl | Small farm in Calthorpe behind Fring Wood (since gone) | 42 |
| Henry Soame | Calthorpe | 360 |
| Smallholdings | In Calthorpe: William Brown, John Elden, Rev Marsh, total | 27 |
| John Murrell | Church farm Wickmere | 109 |
| Wickmere cottages | 12 cottages all with very small gardens & Wickmere Poor | 4 |
| John Partridge | Mannington Hall farm | 168 |
| Richard Pratt | Itteringham Hall | 225 |
| Itteringham glebe | | 23 |
| [Thomas] Roberts | Itteringham mill | 16 |
| John Smith | The Artichoke/Walpole Arms in Itteringham | 12 |
| Thomas Platord | Meadow House in Itteringham | 3 |
| Widow Cook | Thwaite Hall | 300 |
| Sayer | Thwaite | 10 |
| John Jarvis | Itteringham Old Rectory | 218 |
| W Ward | Keeper's cottage Mossymere | 12 |
| Widow Oakes | Mannington Hall & home farm | 321 |
| Widow Plaford | Mannington Mere farm & Wood farm Saxthorpe | 319 |
| Wenham | Little Barningham between Church farm and Mannington | 103 |
| W Rivett & R Ward | 2 cottages by Coldham manor, now Barningham Lowes | 5 |
| Thomas Partridge | Old Wickmere Hall now demolished | 306 |
| Widow Elden | Purdy House Wickmere | 2 |
| Amiss, Wingfield, King | 3 cottages opposite Old Wickmere Hall, Squallham hospital for poor | 2 |
| William Symonds | Squallham house & smallholding | 31 |
| John Barnes | Little Barningham Church farm & lime kilns area | 248 |
| James Mack | Elmerdale farm in Irmingland & Oulton | 305 |
| | | |
| Totals including woods and | Arable total | 3364 |
| glebe | Pasture total | 1089 |

## Mannington

The history of the Mannington estate in Potts family ownership has been described in *See You in Court: the Potts Family of Mannington*, but the location and size of the farms at the end of the 17th and start of the 18th centuries have not been covered in any detail. The first Sir John Potts had started adding to the estate as soon as he came of age in 1614 with the purchase of the small manor of Coldham's on the Little Barningham boundary close to Mannington Hall. More minor acquisitions extended the edges of the estate. The 1595 estate map suggests that much of the estate was then in sheep closes run by the home farm. In addition tenant farms were already clearly established at Mere farm, Wood farm and Itteringham West Field farm (then known as Dier's). A substantial acreage of grazing was later turned into parkland with avenue walks – perhaps laid out by Sir John or his son the second Sir John. Major changes were made in the 1660s to try to make the estate more financially productive for the family. Also, as will be seen, from the 1670s small parcels of more marginal land were sold off to raise cash badly needed by three generations of the Potts family. By the later part of the century the estate had settled into a stable group of tenant farms.

### The farms

An undated rental included in the 1710 family settlement papers of Sir Roger Potts and his son Algernon showed Mannington 'mansion house' and 110 acres of gardens, woods and park as a tenancy which was unlet at that time. The farm tenants were listed and their rents given.

| Mannington tenants and rents about 1710 | | |
|---|---|---|
| Tenants | £ | s |
| Matthew Digby (now somebody else ...) | 105 | |
| Thomas Blogg | 42 | |
| Richard Hill | 90 | |
| Thomas Dewing | 120 | |
| Robert Jackson | 53 | |
| Robert Rose | 37 | |
| John Leake, a mill and 2 tenements | 35 | 10 |
| John Bond | 94 | |
| William Empson | 90 | |
| Edward Plane, with a lime kiln | 31 | 10 |
| John Empson, all land | 4 | 10 |
| Total | 711 | 10 |

Mannington Hall farm (not to be confused with the home farm and yard at the Hall) was created from a farm in the ownership of the Cooke family of Little Barningham in 1595 but the house and much of the farm land lay in Wolterton parish. It has not proved possible to identify the early tenants here – in 1710 it might have been John Bond. Itteringham mill and its house is readily identifiable. The lime kiln was on the Wolterton/Little Barningham parish boundary to the east of the Little Barningham road out of Itteringham. John Empson's small piece of land was in Little Barningham. Thomas Dewing was in Elmerdale, then the largest farm (which was mapped in 1729 as 'Duen's farm'). At this time Mere farm was the second largest estate farm, probably that shown as leased by Matthew Digby. Rose and Blogg would have been in either Itteringham West Field farm or Wood farm Saxthorpe: Thomas Blogg and his wife Emma Perry, both earlier of Edgefield were baptising their children in Saxthorpe, making Wood farm their likely home. Richard Hill and his wife Susan Kendall, buried his daughter Sarah in Saxthorpe in 1708; he was probably running the Mossymere Wood farm which was disbanded in 1737 38 when new farm areas were set out for the home farm of the Hall and those bordering it. On this evidence, Bond and Empson were in Mannington Hall farm and the Hall's home farm, although which was in each is not clear.

Surviving documentation improves after Horatio Walpole finally purchased the Mannington estate in 1737 from Dame Mary Potts's heirs, having failed to persuade Sir Charles or his widow to sell earlier. The farms gradually changed in the 18th century as, under Walpole ownership, farm sizes were increased to attract and reward better tenants. In 1742 the Mannington estate was mapped with the tenants and their acreages clearly shown. Mannington Hall farm was held by William King and had much of the old halving lands farm in Wolterton added to its lands in Barningham. This included the field named Stulps (for the parish boundary posts nearby) still known as Stulps Plantation. Beside the road down to Mannington Hall King had the Old Brick Kiln Close – local brick-making was a feature of Mannington, Itteringham and Wolterton.

| Mannington tenants in 1742 | Pieces | Acres | Location |
|---|---|---|---|
| George Copland | 41 | 331 | Mannington Hall and home farm |
| William King | 19 | 207 | Mannington Hall farm and Wolterton Woolgrove area |
| John Willamott jnr | 24 | 224 | Mannington Mere farm |
| William Riches | 22 | 71 | Barningham Road area based on the lime kilns (land only) |
| Cornelius Graver | 15 | 102 | Itteringham 'Old Rectory' farm and closes by Barningham road |
| Henry Breese | 15 | 129 | Itteringham West Field farm |
| Robert Breese | 16 | 105 | Mannington/Saxthorpe Wood farm |
| Edward Edwards | 7 | 99 | Mossymere, keeper's cottage – 16 acres of wood in Walpole's use |
| Martha Starling | 21 | 310 | Irmingland Elmerdale farm |
| Robert Colls | 9 | 17 | Itteringham mill and meadows around |
| 3 small tenants | 9 | 25 | Willamott snr, Spurrell & Carr in Little Barningham & Hickling |
| Total | | 1627 | |

After the immediate changes to farms and tenants in 1737-38, the rent from the Mannington estate in the year to November 1738 totalled £752 with George Copland in Mannington Hall and Simon Starling in Elmerdale as the two biggest tenants. This was not much of an improvement on the tail end of the Potts management of the estate and rents would not increase materially for many years. But this was also the case at Wolterton and Wickmere and reflects the long period of relatively poor agricultural prices in the 18th century. It is noticeable, however, that the tenants were far more stable in the next fifty years than the large number of short lease and very mobile tenants of the previous fifty years.

## The Hall

The Hall itself had had a rather chequered history since its heyday in the mid-17th century. Unlike his father and grandfather, Sir Roger Potts did not live in Mannington and for part of his time as head of the family it was probably empty. There is no evidence for a tenant in the Hall in the 1680s and the tenant of the home farm cannot be identified. In the 1690s Oliver le Neve rented the Hall and the lands around it and baptised some of his children in Mannington. After he moved out to his new house at Witchingham it seems likely that Mannington Hall was unoccupied until after Sir Roger's death in 1711 when his son Sir Algernon moved in and made much needed repairs to the Hall, church and gardens. He was succeeded in 1717 by his brother Sir Charles who died in 1732 followed by his widow Dame Mary in February 1737, after which their heirs sold the estate to Horatio Walpole.

Walpole acted immediately when Mary died as he knew he was not the only interested party. The previous autumn his gardener, John Bradshaw, had written to tell his master what he had heard from a visitor at Wolterton, probably Thomas Vaughan, a London lawyer friend of the Potts. Vaughan had told him that 'most gentlemen hereabouts are against your Honour having Mannington, which I believe'. John Turner, the husband of Dame Mary Potts's niece and heir, was at that time living at Mannington and had been wined and dined at 'Mr Morden's'. William Morden was Robert Britiffe's son-in-law. By implication the occasion had allowed Lord Hobart of Blickling privileged access to Turner. Bradshaw continued: 'I have heard Mr Turner was advised to apply to Mr Britiffe for he was not in Mr Walpole's interest in that affair but for Lord Hobart. This is the country talk which

I thought it my duty to let your Honour know'. It seems that John Hobart's father-in-law Robert Britiffe, more usually cast as an aide to Walpole, was supporting a Blickling estate push to acquire Mannington. This would go a long way to explain why Walpole acted with almost indecent haste and paid such a high multiple of the annual rents to win the deal from John Turner and his fellow heir-at-law.

For the estate was then described as somewhat underlet. It seems that Sir Charles, a London merchant, had not managed the estate well. A handful of letters from around the time of the purchase show how close Walpole came to pulling down Mannington Hall because of the poor state of repair. On 20th March 1737 Walpole's estate steward, Thomas Bayfield wrote:

> I received your honour's of the 12th instant and was yesterday at Mannington and talked with Mr Fearer [Hammond Farrer of Plumstead, acting for Turner] but he had not then received any letter from Mr Turner nor had any orders with respect to selling the stock on the farme in Turner's own use, but he and I rod all over the farme to see the stock and what order the farme is in. Mr Fearer was very swell and kind and told me how every piece of land belonging to the farm shall or should be sown this year and I thinke if Mr Turner think fit it will be altogether as proper for Mr Turner to pay your honour rent for that farm till Michaelmas next and come in to covenant to leave the ground in order for a tenant to take at Michaelmas next by which time perhaps we may meet with a good tenant for it, but if the worst should come up, that we cant let it by that time it will be a more proper time to buy the stock when harvest is over and the corne lay into the barne, and Mr Fearer is wholly of my minde there being many ill covenantes in takeing it now booth for your honour and Mr Turner both, there being a dairy let on the premises and I suppose they will expect to be paid for plowing the land to this time in order for summer corne turnip etc which I can't say but is reasonable, then there is wheat now sown on the premises which must be valued and no body can say how it will prove at harvest, neither have your honour's servants provided to goe on with the plowing and sowing the summer corne etc: And if your honour thinke to have the whole cropp of corne view before harvest and laid into the barnes and if your honour and Mr Turner think fit buy it then, if your honour dont, to pay the threshing and clensing and have the straw chaff and colder for the same which is the usall way between landlord and tenent and if we can meet with a goode tenent for the farme and let against Michaelmas then your honour will have no accation to buy any of the stock and the tenant take the straw chaff and colder and pay the threshing.

In his not very articulate way Bayfield was pointing out that leases changed hands at Michaelmas (late September) for good reasons. Before that date it was hard to ensure an orderly handover of a farm from one tenant to another, particularly given the difficulty of valuing growing crops. He went on to the poor state of the contents of the Hall itself:

> As to the goods in the Hall they are very indeferent. There is some old hanging which when taken down will be of no value but [if] it can be bought cheap it will be proper to buy them because when puled down will make the house looke very naket and the walls very bad. Mr Fearer have promised me to give me a list of what tax every farme pay and what out goeing rent and a rentall of the quit rents. He say he is willing to oblidge your honour in any thing he can or me, but will not have any thing to doe with Mr Riches, for he know he know nothing of those affairs and indeed I knowe not how he should being browt up a weaver.
>
> I believe the housel stuff at the Hall is very indeferent that your honour will buy very little of it the boat and some other things abroad may be proper for your honour's use if can be bought worth the money, Mr Fearer have promised me that as soone as he have a letter from Mr Turner he will let me know and then I will forthwith goe to him and make my report to your honour.

The letter continued about making hurdles and fence railings from the 'great many scruby trees which are dead on the tops and never will be better' at Mannington. He finished with a postscript that he had just heard that Farrer had received a letter from Turner. Presumably Walpole was being offered first refusal on whatever goods he wanted to buy at Mannington as well as, no doubt, a response on how to treat the in-hand farm. In March Bayfield sent Walpole a detailed inventory of all the goods in the Hall, which ended with one boat on the moat (see Chapter 11). On 3rd April 1737 Bayfield returned to the Mannington situation, where the Hall and other buildings were not weather proof:

Mr Fearer and I have talked about the affair of the farme in Mr Turner's use for him to become your honour's tenent till Michaelmas next and Tuesday next is the day appointed to finish the agreement and signe an article, but there is some land belonging to the Hall in all about 14 or 15 acres but not above 4 acre of plow land which is now turnips and is to be sown with barley. I want your honour's advice whether I am to let Mr Turner the Hall and the land which belong to that till Michaelmas next or not and whether your honour determine that I or Mr Riches should take ceare of the repair at the Hall and elsewhere, there is a great deele to be don at the Hall the great barne in the yard is all most naket and the tenent's house and stables a very long houss want to be new tyled or they will shoot down and spile the tyle which will be a greater loss, and a good deele of tyle on the Hall and sparrs to keep it wind and water thit, and some plomers work on the flat form of lead the water comeing through and rot the house.

Bayfield later in the letter returned to the Hall and potential tenants, referring to Walpole's wish to pull the Hall down. It is clear from this that, despite some recent writers' comments, Walpole had not bought the estate with any intention of using the Hall as a residence for family members:

I think Mr Fearer and I shall agree about the boote [*the boat on the moat which Walpole wanted*], tymbrells [*carts*], brick, tyles, board, spars, etc, and also let Mr Fearer the ground and Hall till Michaelmas next if I can, he is a little cold for he thinks Mr Turner will turne the farme into his hand till Michaelmas next which he have agreed with me for. I am of your honour's opinion at present to pull down all the Hall and make some addition to the tenent's house which is in the yard and use the materialls for that purpose and repairs, there is a good quantity of lead which is worth a good sume of money, the front next the long walke to the west being a flat forme and all laid with lead, and the whole house very much decayde but will further view the premises and consider the surcomstances of that affair and give your honour my thoughts and opinion in every particular.

The front by the walk to the west seems to refer to the main west facing part of the house and indicates the whole of this old range was then flat roofed and leaded. Then only two days later, he wrote again with a complete change of heart on what to do at Mannington:

I was yesterday at Mannington and took another view of the old Hall and farme house in the yard which is a very bad one and as inconvenient as it well can be being a very long house more than is necessary yet impossible to make it convenient but thinke one ½ of it may be pulled down and leave enough for a workman to live in, and if it stand it must be all new tyled and all new planchers. There is a prity good flore of joyce and is of no use but for a granary to lay corne on when new planchered, but if pulled down for about 60 feet long will save a greate deele of money which must be constantly laid out to keep it in repair and there is in it flores of joyce which may be put up in the coach house which is allmost a new house and in very good repair which will answer the end for a granary to lay corne on. And if two parts of the Hall be pulled down the other third part will make a very convenient and good farm house, it will cost some money to repair that part which must be left for a farm house but there will be materialls anough to repair it, and the lead which come off the flat form will I thinke pay all the charges. The brewhouse where Mr Turners great copper hang and brewing vessels stand may be pulled down there being brewhouse and dairy anough besides for a tenant. There is a very fine barne which part was kept in Sir Charles Potts use and part the tenent had which the farmers, whose names are Copland the father and son, and are very honest and industrious persons and I am in hopes to get them to take the farm which is in Mr Turner's hand at Michaelmas next and lay it to that farm the houses being very bad and not any ways conveant for a tenent of a farm of £100 per annum and was let at £105 but never paid the rent and so I told Sir Charles Potts when your honour ordered me to looke it over for him, but fear I must trow in the land which belong now to the Hall, If I can come to agreement with them Mr Fearer assure me that there surcomstances are suffitient to hold boot the farmes if laid together. There is one Graver which hold a farm of your honour's at £53 per annum who is son in law to Copland senior, the three farmes joyne together, and I find that if your honour aprove of such agreement what lands joyne to him they will agree together and lay to that farm and make the old house on the farm now in Mr Turner's use only to set a dairy or put in a cupple of workemen ... The barne which I said before was part in Mr Turner's use and part in the tenents is all roten and worne out and is a very good oake ruff and will beare a coat of tyle very well, and straw is not to be had, and reed so very dear and far off that tyle will be cheapest and if the part of the tenents house be taken down there will be a good many tyles and the brewhouse there will be more, and if that part of the granary store then must be new tyled and the barne must be cear taken of it or the tenent cant lay his corne and the ruff will take damage and the winds will blow it all off. There is a great deele of repairs to be don at Mannington estate. My Lady Potts and Sir Charles before did very little and what was done was in a bad manner but cant all be don at once but what require most haste must be done first.

So Mannington Hall was saved. The service wings to the rear were substantially reduced in size at this time and over the following years. The farmyard buildings and house were presumably also reduced in scale as suggested. For the next 100 years and more Mannington Hall was simply a house for a tenant farmer with a very good sized 330 acre farm. The farmyard was adjacent to the Hall and the large barn was still there in the 1830s when water colour sketches of the, rather dilapidated, Hall were made.

Mannington Hall in the 1830s

From 1737 onwards, the combined Wolterton/Mannington estate dominated the area of Itteringham to the west, north and north-east. The southern part of the parish was in part still common heathland; the meadow and arable lands were split between what is now Hill Farm (**24**) and the Blickling estate.

## Blickling

The Hobart family of Blickling had not acquired much land to the north of their estate but their holdings in Itteringham (**25, 28, 29**) comprised a farm and a cottage and barn which may have been at (**28**) for a long time. During the 16th century the estate acquired a large area of meadow and common land from the lords of Itteringham's manors. These fields between Itteringham Common and Blickling woods still remain in the Blickling estate. In the 18th century they were split between two farms. One was a group of ten pasture and meadow fields next to Itteringham Common, which in 1729 was let to Samuel Goldsmith.

The Blickling estate map of 1729 shows very clearly Goldsmith's cottage and barn on the water meadows just along the lane towards Blickling woods – an early resident of Itteringham Common. This may have been what was earlier called the wood barn. The other land was part of the large farm of Thomas Fiddy which covered much of the open parkland in Blickling along the present main Holt to Aylsham road.

A later feature, not mentioned in a survey of the Blickling estate made in 1756, was a lodge into Blickling park near the woods. The 1823 enclosure map shows very clearly a small lodge house and 'lodge plantation' just in Itteringham on the edge of the park. A road, gated at either end, ran from Blickling mill lane to the lodge, diagonally across what is now the last large field before wood gate. The lodge was just in the arable field by what is now the corner of the woods. In dry years crop marks of the house site and driveway to it can be seen and the road into the park is still marked in the woods by a very pronounced sunken way – this was a very old way from Itteringham to Blickling and Aylsham. It seems most likely that the lodge was built by the 2$^{nd}$ Earl of Buckinghamshire (d 1793) who was responsible during his long tenure for rejuvenating the park, building the tower as a viewing spot for horse races and generally turning Blickling into a much more fashionable place. The lodge had a relatively short life. Only built in the 1760s or 1770s the building was destined to go when the estate blocked up the road through this corner of the park shortly after the enclosure map was drawn up.

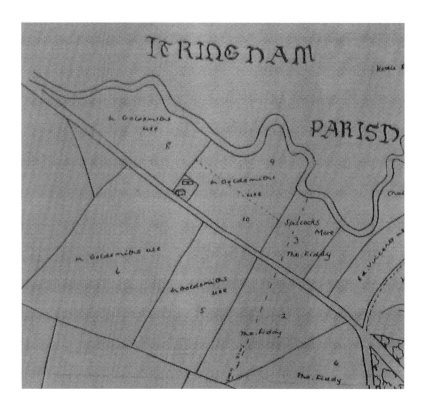

A modern drawing of part of the 1729 Blickling estate map

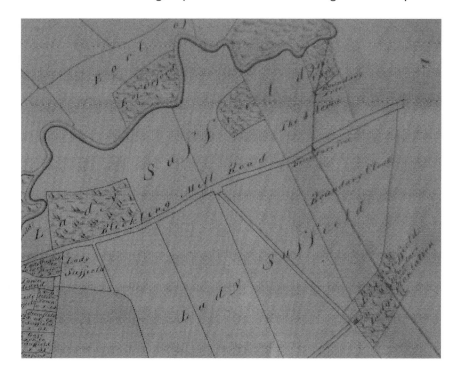

The Blickling estate in Itteringham in 1823: the park drive and lodge were removed

## Other landholders and new opportunities

As well as the big three, there was a fourth estate, albeit much smaller, covering what is today Hill farm's core land (**24**); this was held by a series of absent landowners and will be covered later. With these four estates dominating the parish, there was little opportunity for other independent freeholders to build up landholdings. However, one such family made the most of the chances opening up in the village at the end of the 17th century. As the Potts family declined and before Walpole's arrival, a brief vacuum of power allowed the Robins family to create two smaller but very influential estates occupying much of the land and property in the centre of the village. That of Thomas Robins, based at the Manor House, was compiled by determined purchase of small parcels over many years; the other, Richard Robins's estate at Itteringham Hall (**23**), came by a single purchase of the old manor of Nowers. Had either the Scamler or Potts families survived and enlarged their estates, the opportunity would not have arisen; once Walpole was established the window would close. By the end of the 18th century, Walpole and the Robins clan between them not only held most of the farms and tied cottages but also owned the mill, the tannery, the smithy, the shop and the pub. In the centre of the village there were just two separately owned freehold sites with cottages – at Big Yard and on the west side of the Wolterton road. On Itteringham Common there was a small handful of tiny cottages and gardens, built as encroachments on the common land.

The story of Itteringham in the long 18th century is in many ways the story of the Robins family, their rise to a significant position in the village and their almost total disappearance by 1800. They were not gentry or aristocracy like their neighbours. We shall see how they created a foothold here through trade when Richard became the first blacksmith. But who were the Robinses and where were they from?

### Sources

NRO: WAL collection deeds show the ownership from the 1580s. WAL 337, 272x6; WAL 375, 273x2; WAL 1148, 286x4; WAL 1441/8, 290x3; WAL 1448/1-8, 290x4; WAL 1504, 292x5; FX 257/1, drawing of the Blickling estate map by Dr Elizabeth Griffiths; COL/13/14; MC3/252, 468x4; MC 3/845; NRS 11993-5, 27A5; NRS 21029, 73x4; NRS 20994, 69x3; C/Sca 2/178; C/Sce 1/11; 1809 Wolterton estate map and survey Acc MJ Sayer 26/2/1970

Wolterton archive: 3/1/1; 8/2; estate maps of 1595, 1732 and 1742

NAHRG articles, 2008 & 2009 by W & M Vaughan-Lewis

# Chapter 3

## *The Robins and Bell Families*

---

*Firmly outside the big estates, two local families rose to become increasingly important landowners in and around Itteringham. Closely linked to the Robins family, by marriage, attitude and religion, was the Bell family of Oulton. Both families had their origins in north-east Norfolk. Both gradually accumulated landed estates through earnings from weaving and other trades. Both were dissenting families that saw themselves apart from the senior establishment figures of north Norfolk at least until the middle of the 18th century. Neither family ever applied for a coat of arms although both later borrowed devices. Both were intensely loyal to their own – for the most part. Both families had strong genes for fertility and longevity and produced many sons in the 17th century creating complex clans. This chapter introduces the two families and gives summary family trees so that when the characters appear later their interrelationships will be clear.*

### The Robins family of Heydon

Robins (sometimes Robbins or Robyns) is a common name across Norfolk, which has made it difficult to be certain of the Itteringham family's origins before the early 1590s when William Robins, a yeoman of Heydon, started having children by the first of his two wives. He may have been a son of Peter Robins of Saxthorpe, born there in 1566. Peter was the second son but apparently ultimate heir of John Robins, a husbandman of Hethersett who, in his will made in 1576, left his house and tenement (part of it freehold) in Saxthorpe to his son Simon, defaulting if he had no heirs to his second son Peter. John mentioned his grandsons, Peter's sons William and his brothers Robert and John, whereas Simon appeared to be unmarried and childless. The proximity of Saxthorpe and Heydon supports the possibility. It is also interesting that Peter's wife was Mary King whom he married in Saxthorpe in 1565. Later Richard Robins, Itteringham's blacksmith, took over land in Itteringham leased by the widow Mary King – was she a relation or was this just a coincidence? A Robins family continued in Saxthorpe through several generations, but we have no definite proof of the connection. The name Peter was used by William of Heydon's eldest son for one of his children.

Whatever his background, William Robins of Heydon had been able to purchase a reasonable estate in Heydon from William Buggins, the MP cousin of John Potts of Mannington (the father of the 1st baronet). This was to prove useful as security for what was to be a very large family. William Robins married twice – both times to Heydon girls named Agnes. In September 1593 he married Agnes Frost and the Heydon (with Irmingland) register recorded eleven baptisms of their children between 1594 and 1610. Two of them will have some relevance to the Itteringham story: William the heir in Heydon born in 1598 and John, born in 1604, later to be found in the weaving trade in Norwich.

### *William Robins of Heydon*

We do not know when the first Agnes died, but in June 1613 William remarried to Agnes Starkes and she produced another five children for him. Of these, two were vital to the Itteringham story: Thomas the eldest (born in 1614) although he stayed in Heydon as a weaver, would be a role-model for success. He was to inherit the main Buggins property after his mother's death. The furniture and household goods descended to Thomas's children William, Anne and Katherine, after Agnes's death. As we shall see his brother Richard, born in April 1619, started the Itteringham line. Showing that Richard was quite favoured by his father, he was left (after his mother's death) a posted bedstead from the parlour chamber, with all its trappings including his best coverlet lying on it. This was clearly William's own best bed. Of the other twelve children less is known and many may not have survived childhood. Robert, Francis, Bridget and Clement were all mentioned in their father's will and two of the boys certainly married. Clement, born in 1625 married Helena (probably Eston or Easton of Cawston) and had sons Andrew and Isaac. At his untimely death in 1662, he was a woolcomber of Heydon with a house and 4 acres. In his will Clement made arrangements for his wife and young children: his brothers Thomas and Richard were to call in the various monies owing to him to purchase land for their benefit. His brother Francis had daughters Anne and Sarah by his wife Dorothy; after her burial in Heydon in 1646 he may have moved to Norwich. Bridget, the only daughter of William's to be mentioned in his will - either the only unmarried one or the only surviving girl - received money as did Robert and Francis.

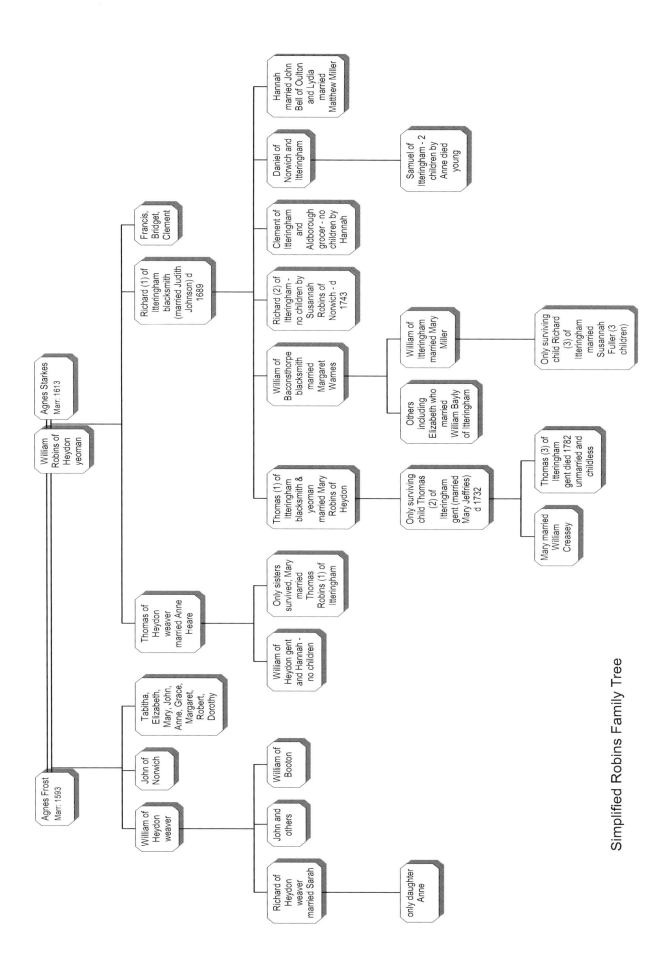

Simplified Robins Family Tree

William senior died in 1649 at the good age of 83. Despite featuring heavily in his will, his family by his second wife did not include his heir. William junior, born in 1598, was already 51 when his father died; he had waited a long time to inherit his 26 acres in Heydon. He seems to have been the William who married Anne 'Beall' (Beale or possibly Bell) on 18th December 1624 at St George Colegate in Norwich. They baptised eleven children in Heydon between January 1626 and April 1645. Unfortunately three years after his inheritance William junior died in July 1652. As he did not leave a will and his wife died during the same month, an infectious disease may have been to blame.

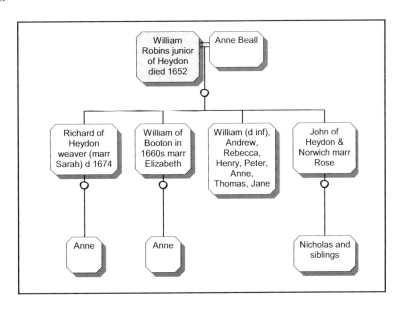

**William Robins junior of Heydon and family**

Their eldest surviving son Richard became a worsted weaver in Heydon, married Sarah (buried in Heydon in October 1664) and had a daughter Anne born in April 1663. His brother John and wife Rose can be found in Heydon and Norwich. As well as the Heydon property, Richard held lands in Great and Little Melton near Hethersett, and in Wood Dalling and Corpusty. With no wife alive and just one daughter to provide for, his will, made and proved in late 1674, is a very useful source of information on his many brothers and sisters. Anne, not yet 21, was left a messuage and lands in Lamas and Scottow (perhaps where Sarah came from) and provision for her education was made with the rents from Great and Little Melton. If Anne were to die, brother John's son Nicholas would inherit her lands. Richard left various small legacies to all the children of his brothers William and John, as well as his brothers John and Henry and his sisters Rebecca and Jane. He also left small bequests to his kinsman Richard Fulcher of Heydon and his godson Richard Fulcher junior.

Rather more complicated were the arrangements involving his 60 year-old step-uncle Thomas Robins of Heydon, also a weaver. Thomas was to inherit Richard's Heydon, Wood Dalling and Corpusty real estate contingent on fulfilling their prior agreement for Thomas to pay £530 to Richard and a further £120 plus interest to Amy Drake widow of Heacham. Amy may have had a mortgage on one of the properties. Thomas's wife Anne was to have the 'chest' that stood in the dairy: this was a cheese press valued at 10s. Richard's inventory, which was signed by Thomas, valued his personal estate at £141, with £88 of debts due to him being by far the largest single item.

## Jacob Robins

Jacob Robins the blacksmith will appear later as one of the prime movers in building the meeting house at Oulton. He was probably a grandson of John Robins the Norwich weaver, the second son of William of Heydon. Jacob was about 11 years old in 1683 when his father, also Jacob, died. Being a younger son he was put to a trade and it is likely he was apprenticed to one of his blacksmith cousins.

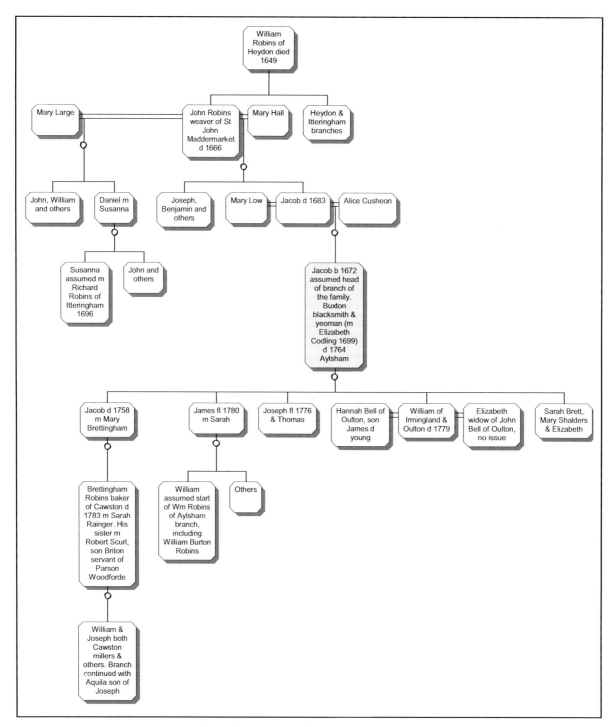

**Simplified Jacob Robins family tree**

He and his wife Elizabeth Codling appear to have brought up their family in Baconsthorpe after he took over the smithy there on his cousin William's death. Jacob seems to have inherited his great-grandfather's genes as he was 92 when he died in 1764 by which time he had moved to Aylsham. His son William lived at Irmingland where he married twice into the Bell family of Oulton. In his will of 1732 Thomas Robins of Itteringham made his 'kinsman' William Robins of Irmingland one of his executors and guardian of his young children, showing how intimate Jacob and his family were with the Itteringham family. Both William of Irmingland and Jacob of Aylsham were in Thomas's long list of default heirs if his son Thomas did not survive. All Jacob's children were left a legacy. In 1741 Jacob Robins 'yeoman of Aylsham' was named as the default heir - if all the other male Robinses in the Itteringham families were to die - to the estate of Richard Robins 2 of Itteringham. This again demonstrates how Jacob was treated as very close kin. Since Richard had married another grandchild of John Robins of Norwich, the linkage looks robust. Subsequent generations of Jacob's branch of the family produced the Aylsham and Cawston farming, milling and baking families. They remained involved in the dissenting movement for many generations.

## *Thomas Robins of Heydon*

As we have said Thomas of Heydon, and his lands, are important to the Itteringham story. Thomas, William's first son by Agnes Starkes, married Anne Heare (or Hare) in December 1639. Both were to live to a good age, Thomas dying in 1698 at 84 and Anne in 1706 when nearly 93 years old. Anne had shown an early adherence to the dissenting Independents and her membership at Guestwick began the long association of the Robins family with the local meeting house congregations.

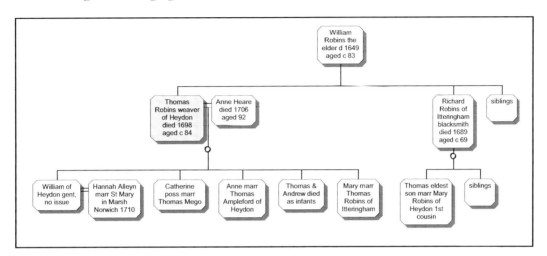

Family of Thomas Robins of Heydon

Thomas's wealth - he had property in Colkirk as well as his business in Heydon before inheriting his nephew's lands - should have continued through his son William but he and his wife Hannah Alleyn were childless. As Thomas's other two sons had died as infants, William left his inheritance to his sister Mary's husband and their son. As Mary had married her first cousin Thomas Robins 1 of Itteringham, the eldest son and heir of Richard 1 the blacksmith, the property was neatly kept in the family. Mary had died in 1725, the year before her brother; her husband Thomas died a month after him. Thomas Robins 2, their only surviving child, was now extremely well set up. So the Robins family of Itteringham evolved from Heydon but retained extremely strong family ties to their Heydon and Norwich relations. But who were the other major local family - the Bells - that William of Irmingland had married into?

## The Bell family

The Bell family appear in medieval deeds of Oulton and all the main branches of the clan in Oulton and Itteringham can be traced back to William Bell who died there in 1547. They were not linked to the grander, armigerous family of Bell of Outwell as the Victorian pedigrees suggest. Despite the lack of parish registers for Oulton before 1706, a number of key members of the family leaving no wills, and a number of old family documents of Oulton Hall not surviving, the basic interrelationships can be worked out. These are shown in the summary tree which recreates the descent of the main properties through the lines. Two of William's sons, Nicholas and William, produced an Itteringham land-owning branch and by the 18th century several lines in Oulton. Many other Bell families were scattered around the neighbourhood, but only the main families are of relevance to the Itteringham story. As we will see, several branches of the family were committed dissenting protestants and were involved with the Robins clan in funding and building Oulton Meeting House.

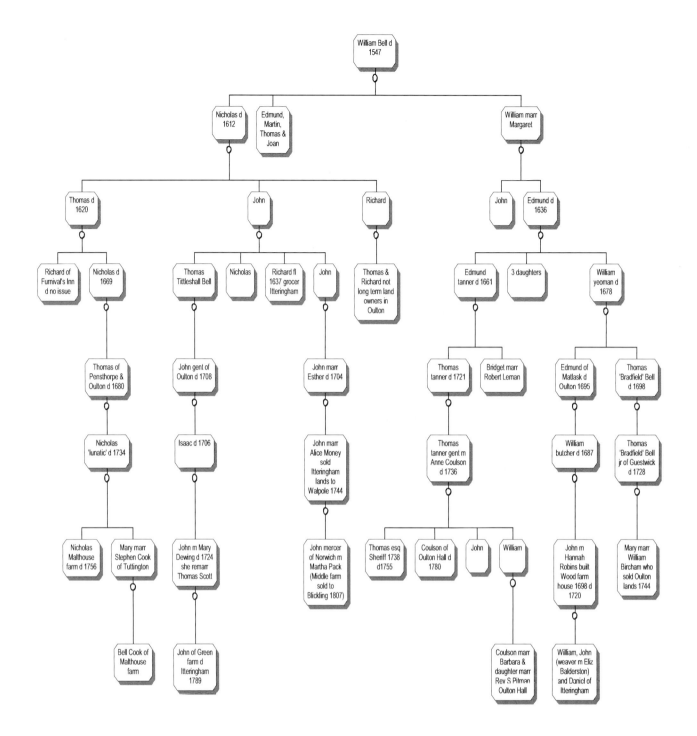

## Summary Bell family tree

From two of Nicholas's sons came three major lines. His own core property was at what is now known as Malthouse farm in Oulton Street (one of the oldest houses in the National Trust's Blickling estate). When he died in 1612 this passed to his eldest son Thomas and, through a number of other Nicholas and Thomas Bells, eventually ended up with Bell Cook who inherited from his unmarried uncle in 1756. At this time he had a survey and map prepared of his estate. Nicholas's second son, John, had a part of his father's holdings which passed down the line of his eldest son Thomas and is now known as Green farm Oulton Street (see below). John's third son, Richard, was Itteringham's first resident grocer; he had been given the shop site by his father in 1637 while his brother, John junior, had the remainder of the lands in Itteringham that had been acquired from the modest estates of the Jarvis and Langdon families. John junior's grandson John and his wife Alice sold them to Horatio Walpole in 1744. John had also inherited Middle farm, Oulton (see below).

Nicholas's brother William also produced three further lines in Oulton, initially the more junior part of the family. His son Edmund died in 1636 (remembered by a brass in the church) and his son Edmund junior was the tanner in Oulton when he died in 1661. At this period the tanner's house was a modest 3-hearth building near the beck in the middle of the village, nothing like the present Oulton Hall. In parallel to the Robins family, they built up a degree of economic momentum and Thomas 'Tanner' Bell (as he was known in the meeting house) energetically added significant real estate to the family acreage. He lived to the splendid age of 89 years and 8 months, dying in 1721. He retired in 1703, aged about 73, and conveyed the house with its surrounding 14 acres to his son Thomas who was running the tannery. Thomas junior had recently married Anne Coulson of Aylsham, the only daughter of Thomas and Martha Coulson, carpenter and property owners in the town. Needing more space for his growing family, Thomas Bell junior probably created a new fine front on the older building – as Thomas Robins was to do in Itteringham. His father would have lived comfortably off after the sale and may have retained his rooms in the house. Thomas junior had raised the family status: he died a gentleman in 1736. Through his wife, the Bell family became lessees of the Rectory (the living) of Aylsham which was owned by the Dean and Chapter of Canterbury. The tithes and rental stream from the property would have been very useful. Two years later his son, also Thomas Bell, was High Sheriff of Norfolk - with Edmund Jewell as his undersheriff - and he may well have continued enlarging the Hall. The property (and the lay impropriation) eventually descended to a last remaining Bell daughter, Barbara, who married the Reverend Samuel Pitman. She died in 1832.

Edmund Bell senior (d 1636) also had a son William whose two sons were Edmund of Matlaske and Thomas 'Bradfield' Bell. Edmund died in Oulton in 1695 having outlived his butcher son William. They held the predecessor of Wood farm in Oulton Street. William's son John built the current house there in 1698 (see below). John's wife was Hannah Robins of Itteringham, one of the earliest Bell/Robins marriages. As it was her brother Thomas who built the manor house in Itteringham in 1707, perhaps there was an element of sibling rivalry. Edmund's brother Thomas 'Bradfield' Bell (a great supporter of the Bradfield and Guestwick meeting houses) had lands in Oulton near the boundary with Blickling parish but his son lived in Guestwick and his granddaughter's husband sold their Oulton lands.

Various of the Oulton Street properties were later sold to the Blickling estate: Erasmus Buck (in an earlier generation related by marriage to the Bells) sold his farm at what is now Oulton Lodge farm in 1747; the Bradfield Bell lands went to William Bircham at his marriage who then sold them on to Blickling; Green and Wood farms went in the 1760s; and Malthouse farm in 1772 when Bell Cook left for Aylsham. At the other end of the parish the Bell family gradually consolidated the land around Oulton Hall including the old Page family lands – a process which carried on into the 19th century. But during the 18th century a very large area of the parish was controlled by the Bells who, like their neighbours the Robins family, had gradually built themselves up by hard work from yeomen farmers and tradesmen.

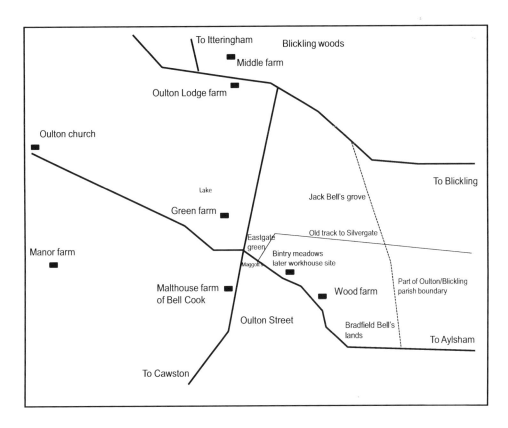

Oulton Street farms in the 18th century

Wood farm Oulton Street

The farm, now known as Wood farm, and the cottages on the road leading from Eastgate green (Oulton Street main crossroads) to Aylsham were owned by John or Jack Bell, a butcher and yeoman of Oulton. He had inherited them from his father, William Bell also a butcher, who died in 1687. The farmland lay largely to the north of the road – William's will mentioned two closes called Drury's Croft and closes called 'the meadows'. The wood across the fields to the north is still known as Jack Bell's Grove. He was married to Hannah Robins of Itteringham and they had four children William, John, Daniel, Lydia and Hannah. Jack died relatively young in 1720 and in his will, described his 'new built tenement or dwelling house' which Hannah was to have for life and which then should go to their eldest son William, subsequently a founder trustee of Oulton Meeting House. His fine house has its build date of 1698 still showing in large iron numbers on the gable end. William duly lived in Wood farm and was buried in Oulton in 1747. He died intestate so the farm passed to his brother John who died soon after in 1750, without any children by his wife Elizabeth. In 1751 she became the second wife of William Robins of Irmingland and in 1756 they were using the farm property, in which she had effective jointure rights. The couple may have lived here or in a part of Irmingland Hall. The full ownership of the farm had passed to Jack's third son Daniel, a peruke or wig-maker of Itteringham who used it as security in 1756 to borrow £300 from Edmund Jewell of Aylsham. Three years later he sold the estate (totalling about 75 acres), with Samuel Robins of Itteringham as trustee, to the 2nd Earl of Buckinghamshire of Blickling. The sale compensated Elizabeth and Daniel's two sisters for their interests by creating life-time annuities.

John Bell's end of Green farm at Eastgate green Oulton

The farm, now known as Green farm, lay almost next to Jack Bell's farm but to the north and west of the Oulton Street main crossroads. When John Bell, gentleman, died in 1708, his grandson John inherited all his property. From John, who died in 1724, it came to his son John. In 1761, in a parallel style of transaction to Daniel's, John Bell, gentleman and his wife Mary sold the estate with its 'capital messuage' to the Earl of Buckinghamshire for £4,200 payable either in cash or in annuities. In particular he provided £20 a year for his mother Mary (Dewing) who had remarried to Thomas Scott the dissenting preacher. It appears that Bell then loaned £3,000 back to the Earl of Buckinghamshire, to produce an annuity of £180 per year for his wife Mary for her life. The same year the farm was leased, at £135 rent, to William Gedge. Gedge had been a tenant farmer of the Blickling estate, running the neighbouring Oulton Lodge farm on the Blickling/Itteringham borders until 1753. He knew the fields well and may even have leased both farms for several years. In the sale, John Bell had retained for life the best rooms, the hall, parlour and chamber, with Gedge living in the remainder, facing onto part of the yard. In Gedge's lease, Bell also kept the gardens and summer house and the right to kill game on the estate. The property also had a 'wood close' next door and it may well be that the gardens extended through wood close down to the lake. John Bell and his family apparently stayed in the house until around 1774. In 1782, after the death of Thomas Robins 3, they moved into the Manor House in Itteringham.

Interestingly, the Green farm estate also had a malthouse in 1761, then in the occupation of John Stockings. The location is not clear; but, because of the different ownership, it seems it was probably not the malthouse in Bell Cook's farm just down the street. While it may have been elsewhere in Oulton, it was probably in the yard of Green farm. The farms of this area had been formed out of the old heathland. The light soils would have been best suited for barley and it is likely that all or most of Oulton's farms were integrated businesses, growing barley and malting it.

## *John Bell and Alice of Middle farm Oulton*

The house now at Middle farm was built in the 1860s by the Blickling estate, but just like its near neighbour at Oulton Lodge, both were very long standing farmsteads. The line of John Bells descending from Nicholas (d 1612) held Middle farm, Oulton (adjacent to both Oulton Mill common and Itteringham heath) and its 50 acres by the 18th century. It is probable that they had held it throughout the previous century, just as other members of the Bell clan had owned almost all the other farms making up the eastern half of the parish. Certainly both John (d 1693) and his son John (d 1704) held land and a house in Oulton. The next John Bell was described as of Oulton or Itteringham and his main property was the long-held family estate in Itteringham, centred on what is now Meadow House. In June 1731 in Great Yarmouth, John Bell married 17 year-old Alice the daughter of John and Anne Money. Born in Oulton in 1714, she was of a family with Cawston, Heydon and Saxthorpe connections. Her marriage settlement gave Alice jointure rights in the Oulton property in exchange for the portion she brought to the marriage. Although their son John was baptised in Oulton in 1732 where they lived at this time is unclear, as both Meadow House and Middle farm were usually let to tenants. Bell may have been operating as a merchant in Great Yarmouth as by 1744 he had become insolvent and sold the Itteringham estate to Walpole. He and Alice moved to Broome, where he was described as a yeoman. Even after the proceeds from the sale to Walpole, Bell owed £60 plus interest to a Norwich brasier named John Smith and £100 to his father-in-law. That same year he conveyed his Middle farm property to John Money, now living in Trowse. The family arrangement was to clear the debts by transferring Middle farm to Money in return for an annuity of £10 to John Bell and all other benefits from the premises to be for the sole benefit of Alice and their only surviving son John.

At the end of 1758 young John, by now a mercer and woollen-draper of Norwich, was betrothed to Martha the daughter of William Pack gent of West Raynham. They married in East Raynham in January 1759. In their marriage settlement John Bell and Alice conveyed to them lands and houses in Oulton, Cawston and Norwich, giving John junior the rental stream for life and the reversion of the properties to any children of John and Martha. It seems that John Money had honoured the spirit of the deal and had returned the ownership of Middle farm to John senior, who was now living with Alice in Egmere near Walsingham.

From the early 1730s to at least the late 1750s, the Middle farm tenant was John Baxter. Interestingly a Jonathan Baxter, perhaps his son, was for a time owner of the windmill on Oulton Common in the 1780s. Perhaps the Baxter family had suffered the cold winds on their exposed site at Middle farm for so long that eventually one of them decided to harness the wind power. The exact site of the mill is not known, but with Middle farm lands immediately adjoining the common it is tempting to believe that it was sited very close to the road and so at no great distance from their farmhouse. In 1758 William Chapman was tenant of Middle farm.

John Bell senior died in about 1765, it seems without leaving a will, and Alice returned to live in Oulton where she lived until her death in December 1793. In 1768 she bought 2 ½ acres of land from the Bulwer estate in Heydon – land entirely surrounded by her own and beside the Saxthorpe to Aylsham road. Alice seems to have fallen out with her son or at least his wife Martha. In 1759 John had been made bankrupt when the Newman family of Melksham Wiltshire, his wholesale wool and silk trading partners, had called in their debts. It seems he had inherited his father's lack of business competence. In July 1765 Alice Bell, with husband John's active support (then still alive in Egmere), made a deal with the Norfolk bankruptcy commissioners. She offered the best price to buy out his interest in the Oulton property and £60 was paid over to go towards his debts. This deed would have removed John junior's rights in the property but not his wife's. No more is heard of John junior and when his mother made her will in 1788, she left all her property in Oulton, Cawston and on the castle ditches in Norwich to the Reverend Charles Mann of Denver, her executor. No explanation was given and no link has been found. Mann was the only child of George Mann and Mary Codd, a hotpresser and mercer in Norwich who died in 1788. He and his first wife Lucia MacGuire lived in Denver Hall as tenants from the 1770s and he eventually bought the Hall outright in 1803, before marrying again in 1807 to Susannah McDougall of Catton. His wives seem to have no linkage to the Bell or Money families. Perhaps John Bell junior had been apprenticed to George, or maybe he had owed him significant sums at his bankruptcy.

Yet Alice's daughter-in-law Martha was still alive. In 1794, by now widowed, she sold all her rights in the Middle farm house, farm buildings and 50 acres to Mann for £300. By the end of the century William Clarke was tenant at Middle farm where he remained many years. In 1807 Mann sold the farm to William Harbord, later Lord Suffield of Blickling which completed the Blickling estate consolidation of the whole eastern end of Oulton parish.

Itteringham's farms have more complex histories than their Oulton counterparts. In Part Two we shall look at the role of estate stewards and the farming practices of the time before moving to study the farms themselves.

**Sources**

NRO: MC 310/12; NAS 1/1/5/4; NRS 13028, 13030, 13033-13038 & 13059, 13455, 13460-61, 13467, 17228, 23289; ANW inventory 1674, 23/3/206; HEA 9/1, 9/14, 9/16, relate to bonds and surrenders in 1683 involving Thomas Robins and Robert Blake single previously of Heacham and a 1687 quitclaim by Robins to Francis Crampe of Snettisham, presumably honouring the arrangement with the widow Drake's heir; PRA 96, 376x4

The poor survival of Cawston registers makes it hard to clarify the Easton relationship. For more on William Buggins see *See You in Court*. Freeholder list in 1734 poll book. J Venn, *Alumni of Gonville & Caius*, 1897 (Venn G & C)

# Part 2

## FARMS AND FARMING

*From Aylsham to North Walsham good land; better than to Holt. Around Wolterton good; and the first four miles to Cromer. It is bad to Cawston; and much of it indifferent to Norwich. ... Wickmere and Wolterton have very good land.*

Arthur Young, *A General View of the Agriculture of the County of Norfolk,* 1799

Estate stewards; farming practices; the farms in Itteringham

# Chapter 4

## *Estate Stewards: Walpole and Ness*

---

*In many respects the local estate stewards were the most important people in Itteringham and nearby in the 18th century. So much of the land and so many of the cottages were owned by the large estates that the steward was involved with most of the community on a regular basis. He negotiated leases, collected rents, provided work for key staff on annual contracts and for many more as day labourers on the home farms. For many of the tradesmen the big houses were their most important customers. At both Blickling and Wolterton there were bailiffs or stewards responsible for day-to-day matters with family lawyers often managing property affairs.*

### Blickling

In 1707 John Brewster was bailiff to the 14-year old John Hobart at Blickling. Although few estate records survive, there can be no doubt that Robert Britiffe, the lawyer, also played some part at Blickling. Britiffe was a man of many parts and very influential both in Norwich and, as Lord Townshend's legal advisor, in Norfolk more widely. He represented Norwich as a Whig MP for many years from 1715. His two daughters married the heads of the Hobart family at Blickling and Harbord at Gunton – then the two largest local estates. He was clearly a friend of John Hobart the 1st Earl of Buckinghamshire, not just his father-in-law.

The everyday estate management was conducted by two generations of the Sendall family from at least the early 1730s to around 1760. Martin Sendall senior, the gentleman farmer at Irmingland had probably been steward for the Fleetwood family of Irmingland Hall until his death in 1725. His son John, also a gentleman, having learned the business there, moved to Blickling where by 1731 he was well-established. Stewards had to be well-educated and able to communicate with other gentlemen on behalf of their employers. A good example of John's excellent hand, good spelling and use of appropriate social language has survived in a letter of January 1731 that he wrote to Ashe Windham at Felbrigg, to whom Hobart owed rent:

> Blickling Jan 16 1731
>
> Honoured Sir
> I would have waited on you before this time but upon my Lords going away I have been very busy that I could not well get out but hope your Honour will excuse me for my Lord have given me orders to pay you all the arrears of Rent that is due for w$^{ch}$ I will wait upon you and pay the same within a very few days w$^{ch}$ is from your Honours most Dutifull and Obedient Servant
>
> Ju$^n$ Sendall

By contrast Windham's endorsement - 'Mr Sendal came in a day or two & pd the rent (at 11s 4d a year) up to Mich 1731 A. Windham' - is written in a markedly less good hand!

At his death in January 1749, John was buried in the chancel of Blickling church - unusual for all but the grander residents of the parish. His son, Martin junior, took over as steward and like his father was also a churchwarden. An estate survey made in 1756 (by a Londoner) noted 'the house and garden Mr Sendry [sic] lives in and also a good close [of] 6 acres formerly Bullemurs ... £8 annual value, although Mr Sendry has never paid any rent for these'. This house can be identified from the 1729 map as the fair-sized house in Silvergate, the one nearest the Hall on the lane leading to Blickling church. The family also farmed the old Thomas Fiddy farm which had part of its land in Itteringham. Martin's first wife Mary died young in 1747 leaving him with four children; in 1753 he married Jane, the only child of the Irmingland preacher Abraham Coveney. At some point 'by the most unkind advantage taken by the common Law' he had lost a great part of his property. Fortunately in 1760 Jane inherited a substantial estate from her Athill aunts enabling them to end their days in comfort at Foulsham. By 1780 the 2nd Lord Buckinghamshire's land agent was Robert Copeman who lived nearby in The Old Hall Aylsham, a very fine house which the estate had purchased in 1751. His surviving letters show how difficult the relationships between a master (especially when elderly and suffering from gout) and his man on site often were. Stewards had to be masters of tact.

## Wolterton and Mannington

Mannington seems not to have had a strong steward after Daniel Muddiclift who had the role for most of the second half of the 17th century. In 1737 when John Turner was negotiating the sale of Mannington to Horatio Walpole, Hammond Farrer a tenant farmer then of Plumstead acted for him. Farrer may have collected rents for Dame Mary in the 1730s but before that it seems that the Potts family themselves were managing the estate, relying on one of their senior tenants for farming advice. After 1737 the estate was run together with Wolterton.

### *Wolterton: Britiffe and Bayfield*

Britiffe was also heavily engaged in the Norfolk affairs of Sir Robert Walpole at Houghton and at least in the 1720s was probably in overall charge of his brother Horatio's affairs in Wolterton. As a local man by origin, from a Baconsthorpe and Stody family, Robert Britiffe knew the area and was well placed to oversee manorial court, farming and house building activities. Surviving letters show he was closely involved in Walpole's early purchases in Wolterton and Wickmere.

In August 1722 Britiffe wrote to Walpole to congratulate him on the purchase of Wolterton. He had been to see the place and had met the gardener and the bailiff. Penelope Grey, the vendor, had recommended both of them but Britiffe said 'I did not like either'. He wrote again the following month reporting that Mr Rice, the bailiff, was too ill to show him round and he could not get a key to enter the house. The gardens however were in better order than at his last visit. Other letters of 1722-24 show that Britiffe, despite his parliamentary and legal business, was then heavily engaged in estate management tasks for Walpole and materially involved in supervising garden and park improvements. No doubt he was also keeping an eye on the major building work that Walpole started under the leadership of his architect Thomas Ripley, whom Britiffe knew from his work at Houghton and Raynham. Britiffe may also have been first to tell Walpole that the old house had burned down. On 19th November 1724 he wrote that there had been a fire at about 11 o'clock at night and the house was entirely demolished. The servants had been woken up by the fall of the roof and fortunately had got out; only the gardener's boy had received burns. Little furniture had been saved. He assumed that the workmen had been careless, possibly having made a fire in the nursery since the flames appeared to have started in a garret.

On 17th December Ripley wrote to Walpole:

> I am very sorry for your loss; but since this has happened I think you should put an entire stop to all your works at Woollerton; because I believe you will find a more convenient place to set your house in than were it now is; and to answer your present gardens ... I am going to Houghton and intend to go from thence to Woolterton.

Ripley knew that moving the site of the Hall just a short distance to the west would place it precisely at the head of the shallow valley and give a stunning view from the main rooms of the Hall down the lake and across to Blickling woods in the far distance. The construction of the new Hall went ahead over the next few years – a long drawn out affair given the scale of the building and all the fitting-out work involved. In April 1726 Samuel Underwood and Thomas 'Haukings' were paid for taking down the burnt walls of the old hall and at around the same time huge quantities of furze were being carted to Wolterton to fuel the new kiln making bricks for the new hall.

In early January 1725 Britiffe suggested that Walpole hired a house in the neighbourhood:

> ... there is one thing which I know not whether you may think it a conveniency to you; I got a friend to speak to Lady Potts to know if Sir Charles would be willing to let Mannington House with its furniture And I was told he would, you may consider of it and let me know whether you shold like it till your own be built and finished, it is very near your own.

Walpole did not take up the offer of renting but the idea of owning Mannington took root.

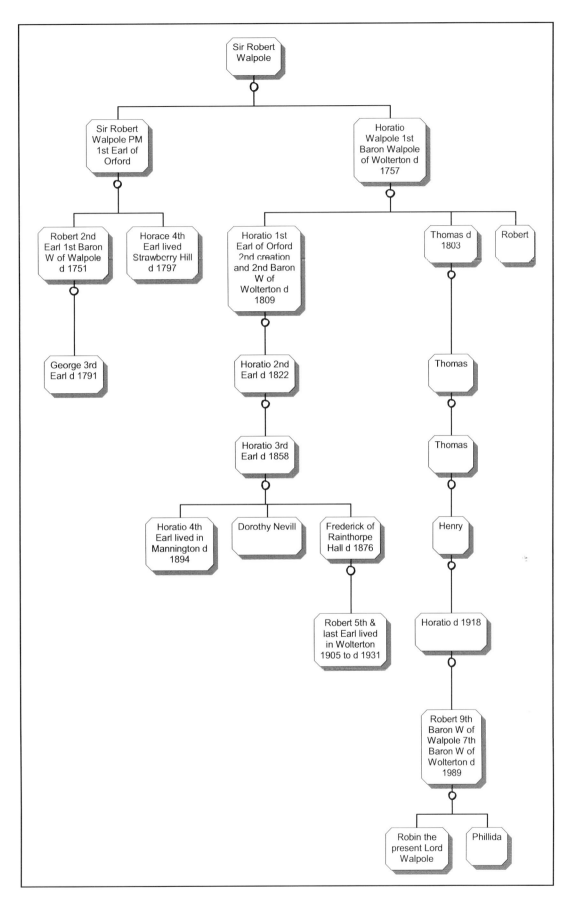

Summary Walpole family tree

By 1725 Walpole employed two bailiffs on the new estate. One was Samuel Newstead, the steward at the Walpole manor of Tivetshall until his death in 1749, when John Jay, previously Wolterton's dairy man, took over. The other, Thomas Bayfield (which he always signed as Bayfeild), became steward and remained at Wolterton until 1738-39.

In time Robert Britiffe, who died in 1749, ceased to play a significant part in local estate matters. It is not clear when Bayfield had been hired but a note in the accounts shows that he was on the payroll by 1722, when he was reimbursed for expenses in London. During the 1730s, Walpole's friend Captain Laurence Charters, had a room in Wolterton and was heavily involved in Walpole's local affairs in 1732 (as described in *See You in Court*). The Scottish Charters (or Charteris as sometimes written) was an unreliable character. The Rector of Aylmerton described him in October 1734 'as mad as any in Bedlam' and reported that he 'came last Sunday into the church of Wolterton, and talk'd so loud to Mrs Gay in the time of prayer, that the Minister was forc't to come down and get him out of Church but he came in again'. He paid bills for food and staff in 1733 for which Bayfield had to reimburse him; he was closely involved with the craftsmen, buying 10 lbs of candles for the joiners 'to work in the mornings in the winter by order'. On 21st June the plasterers must have thought Christmas had come early when Charters gave them 10s 6d to 'drink his and Mr Walpole's health'.

Charters died in 1735 and Bayfield held more sway over the estate. His successor was later critical of the state of affairs that he had inherited from Bayfield. Certainly the accounts by him that survive are fragmentary and brief and relatively few letters from or to him remain. It seems that he lived at Antingham and was not as closely involved in Wolterton affairs as subsequent resident stewards. Nonetheless he was instrumental in helping Walpole with his long-term plan to empark Wolterton village and the green and active in the purchase of the Mannington estate.

For example in January 1737 he wrote to Walpole to say that three leases in the village centre would expire that year. So run down was their house by the church that Thomas Page and his wife Margaret were already living elsewhere. Margaret was the daughter of a local yeoman Matthew Lubbock who died in Wolterton in 1728, having been in the same farm. Across the green Henry Bayfield's house was also in a very poor state of repair. Henry Bayfield was the son of William Bayfield yeoman who died in Wickmere in 1720 but his relationship, if any, to Thomas has not been discovered. Henry had been left property in Kerdiston by his father, but it seems that he took over the Wickmere property left to his elder brother William. In line with Walpole's clearance policy, Thomas Bayfield recommended demolition of both houses. He thought that Page's land should go to Thomas Partridge who held the Wolterton Dairy farm. For some reason Bayfield was particularly vindictive towards Henry Bayfield. He said he should be evicted as a bad tenant who had not paid last year's rent and who, having originally been a weaver, did not really know how to farm. However he warned Walpole that if this happened, 'Mr Robins' would probably write to complain. One of Henry's daughters had married a Robins son: 'one of his daughters which were kept very fine and drank there tea but could give them no money but pleased the young man's eye'. This must have been Ann the wife of Samuel Robins of Itteringham.

While vilifying Henry, Thomas Bayfield sang the praises of his own son-in-law Edmund Greenacre who farmed in marshy land 20 miles away as one of Walpole's tenants at Burnham Overy. He said Greenacre was a good farmer and should be given an enlarged farm based on Henry Bayfield's land, some of Purdy's and Matthew Woolmer's (also due for lease renewal that year). He added that his daughter suffered from the 'bad air' at Burnham.

Although there is no record that Samuel Robins himself wrote to complain, Henry Bayfield wrote at least twice to Walpole to plead his case. In fact each letter was written in a quite different hand, so he had someone write the letters for him – perhaps one was even by Samuel. His letters make one doubt whether he really was the bad tenant that Thomas Bayfield made out. On 22nd January 1737 his son carried a letter personally to Walpole in London:

> To my great surprise I lately heard whisperd amongst my neighbours that Mr Bayfeild intended to turn me out of my farm and on inquiring of him I found the same to be true but without giving any reason for his so doing other than he should lay other land thereto and make it larger; which has made me very uneasy I having been at great pains and a very great expense in improving the land relying wholly that having a person of so much honour for my landlord that I should not have been turned out of my farm so long as I continued to pay my rent, to do which I hant hitherto neglected and as to the making it larger hant any objection thereto in case your honour think proper so to order. I therefore beg you'l consider my condition and the expence I have been at and not suffer me to be turned out without any just cause being willing to comply with any terms your honour shall prescribe being well aprised that you wont put

anything hard on any one and especially on me who have long ye tenancy and always behaved honestly and faithfully. The bearer my son waits on your honour on purpose herewith to implore your favour and I hope you wont suffer me to be driven from my habitation and livelyhood but lett me continue which may prevent the ruin of my self and family. I beg leave to subscribe myself

Your honours most dutifull and faithfull servant

But Henry sent his son to London in vain. Perhaps swayed by Bayfield's assertion that to keep the buildings 'joining to the green by the church' would need more than £100 of repairs, Walpole wrote on 29th January to confirm that his son-in-law could have the farm. Thomas Bayfield had obviously reacted badly to Henry going over his head for, on 11th March, Henry wrote again to Walpole:

> May it please your excellency to give me leave to acquaint you that your farm was in so bad a condition at the time I took it that for the first four years I grew very little corn thereupon but endeavoured to improve it by turniping and mucking, thinking I should have had an opportunity reaping the benefit of that expence which was very great in so much that I have now above one hundred pounds cost in the land which I beseech your honour to take into consideration and also the great inconveniency I lay under in having had so short notice of your honour's intention of turning me out there being no farms now to let but such as would be my ruin to hire. Therefore I humbly beg that tho I can't have the farm of another lease that your honour indulge me so far as to let me continue another year by which means I may have an opportunity of hireing another place and not be quite destitute; Had it been your honour's pleasure to have taken it to your own use I should have endured it patiently but for your honour to take whats mine for the benefit of his son, oh great sir redress the wrong, March 1th being the day appointed for the tenants to pay their rents I sent my son to pay mine. Your steward hissed at him and bid him go to London again, he made no answer, a double suffering to have my own taken from me and be made a jest of who am
>
> Your most obedyent true servant

Henry was evicted – an act which may have underlain Samuel Robins's later animosity towards Walpole.

Was Thomas Bayfield in too much haste to get his son-in-law into a large farm? The changes made after Henry Bayfield's departure can be seen in the estate accounts. In addition to the marsh at Burnham, Edmund Greenacre was indeed given a 260 acre farm which included 80 acres of Bayfield's land, part of Page's farm and Woolmer's 70 acres in Calthorpe. Thomas Partridge roughly doubled his farm to 118 acres with the addition of part of both Page's and Bayfield's. Nicholas Wayt remained in the old Wickmere Hall with a farm of 343 acres. The other large farm, of about 170 acres, was that of the widow Jane Cook still living in the farm across the lane from Wayt. Jeremiah Marshall and Woolmer Cubitt each had about 60 acres and the other tenants were tiny holdings or just cottages. However Thomas Bayfield did not survive to see what happened next. 1738 was his last full year as steward after which he retired to Antingham where he died in 1743. His son-in-law only remained a tenant for 5 years. In 1744 his Wolterton lands were taken in-hand and a large part of his farm became part of the park grazing. A new era had begun.

## Wolterton: Richard Ness

In November 1738, Richard Ness took over as estate steward. Ness was to become a significant local figure, working for 35 years from his own room in Wolterton Hall until his death in 1772. Thomas Ripley, Walpole's architect, was instrumental in getting Ness the job. Both were Yorkshiremen, Ripley having been born in Rillington to the north-east of York in 1682. The Ness families - the surname is rare elsewhere at this time - were clustered in nearby Malton, Foston and Pickering. The name Richard was used in baptisms in all of these families but Richard Ness seems to have been the son of a John Ness baptised in May 1701 or 1702 in Foston-by-Malton. From a letter he wrote in 1739, Ness said he had been living and working in Norfolk for about 16 years. That Thomas Ripley had got him the job at Wolterton and that the two of them came from the same area of Yorkshire suggests that Ness had been working in a bailiff or steward's role at a Norfolk estate with which Ripley was also involved. In Norfolk, Ripley is best known for his work at Houghton and modifications at Raynham Hall. Ness could have worked at either or both in some capacity. However, it is also possible that Richard developed his skills as a steward at Holkham as he bought property in the area around there. Any of these estates would of course have equipped him with the knowledge of farming on Norfolk's lighter soils.

Ness later became, deservedly, hugely trusted by the Walpoles. But in the early years this was not always the case. It is clear from the content and tone of his surviving letters to Ness that the first Horatio was what in today's parlance we would call a 'micro-manager'. Though neither a farmer nor truly knowledgeable about farming matters, his letters to Ness contained extraordinarily precise instructions. As to the house and garden design his detailed instructions were obeyed not just by Ness but also by Ripley. Whether in house, garden, park or estate it is clear that Horatio was constantly questioning the cost of what was being done.

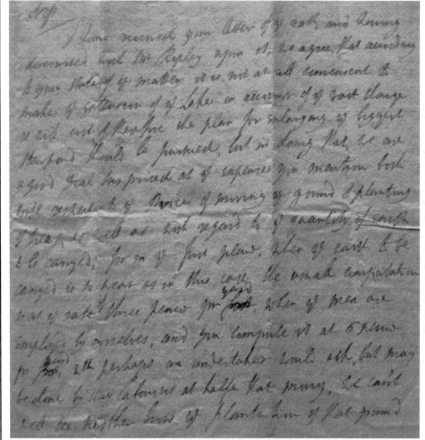

Horatio Walpole wrote from The Cockpit in Whitehall in 1741 to tell Richard Ness that he had agreed with Ripley that Ness should not go ahead with enlarging the lake as the expense was too great. Instead the biggest stewpond should be extended where the earth-moving would cost much less. The undertaker jibe shows that this letter was a rebuke.

An example of Walpole's handwriting

Naturally, the capable Ness resented Horatio's nit-picking. On 16th November 1742 Ness wrote to Ripley, retaining a copy as he so often did with his important letters. He complained to his friend about Walpole's apparent lack of trust over the expenditure necessary to put the estate, park and gardens into good shape.

Honoured Sir,

I observe in yours that what is done at the lower end of the pond here has given satisfaction. I have endeavoured in everything that has come under my care with as much diligence and frugality as I was able in order to procure the same end. But I am sorry to tell you that all I have done or can do I find will not. And if my master continues to be so jealous uneasy and fretful I cannot serve him if he would give me one half of his estate to look after the other. The estates was much out of repair, whereby your recommendation I came first to serve him for which favour I most heartily thank you, and have got them now in pretty good order that the annual expense will be reasonable. The expense has been large tis true but then I have not done anything but what has been really necessary, but as he is no competent judge himself, which is a great nuisance to me, neither will he give himself the trouble to look over what is done, and perhaps may be informed that his repairs are done too well (for that is always his expression) which I must think is a wrong idea in him, and he forgets ye old proverb if a thing be once well done it is twice done. I am sure no man could have his interest more at heart than I have had but where no contentment can be given it makes the spirit languid.

I am Sir your most obliged and obedient humble servant

In 1742 Walpole had clearly conducted a major and unusual review of his accounts and expenditure, with extensive notes and jottings in his own hand showing that he had spent considerable time looking at the books. His audit was probably carried out after the end of September – the farming and accounting year ended at Michaelmas. This was almost certainly what provoked Ness's outburst to Ripley. Perhaps Ripley helped him understand that it was just Walpole's way and not to take it as personal criticism. Ness stayed and although Walpole senior's letters never lost their micro-managing edge, they obviously built up a good working relationship. Despite their earlier frictions and subsequent occasional stiffness, Richard Ness was clearly delighted to be at Wolterton and no doubt counted himself lucky to have the position. Four years later he wrote a delightful letter to Walpole. As if embarrassed at his initial show of emotion he moved on to a much more practical comment – his favoured remedy for gout which he heartily recommended to Walpole.

In May 1746 Richard Ness wrote to Horatio Walpole to sing the praises of how everything looked at Wolterton. An apology shows they had had yet another falling out.

An example of Ness's handwriting

Walpole wrote a few days later thanking Ness for his 'agreeable letter' relating to the beautiful views over the new paddock and explaining why he had been tough on the issue of economy. Confiding his concerns over the future of his son, then 23, he gave Ness his absolute support in an equally emotional reply:

I am extreamly desirous to enjoy them upon ye spot which I shall doe as soon as I possibly can, but I cannot yet fix ye day; as my natural disposition leads me to keep to an old acquaintance both with respect to friends and servants, especially where I have an opinion of their integrity and merit; I can have no thoughts of parting with you; but I must as I have always done desire that fidelity may be accompanyed with a proper economy; for you must see that a young heir that comes to a landed estate in Norfolk considering ye necessary taxes and repairs that attend it lendes other causality; must be a good manager, not to be uneasy in his affairs if he has no other income; and as this is like to be ye case of my son; I would leave behind me for his example in living a precedent of doing what becomes him, but no more than his circumstances may afford; I doe not, I assure you, by way of reproach to you, but as opening my heart to one that I have real confidence in.

Ness carried out Horatio's wishes: his relationship with the 'young heir', Horatio junior was equally warm. A more restrained, urbane character Horatio spent much of his time in London happily leaving Ness whom he had known since he was 14, in charge of affairs. In November 1757 nine months after his father's death and months of correspondence and visits, he gave Ness a present of 26 pint bottles of rum for his help in the transition. The rum would have been a welcome addition to Ness's normal 'old red port' which cost him £8 for half a hogshead from Walpole's wine merchant Benjamin Nuthall.

## Ness: his private life

During his time at Wolterton, Ness managed to build a small estate of his own. He never married nor had children, a situation that may be partly explained by his early upbringing. In February 1739, shortly after arriving at Wolterton Richard Ness wrote to Horatio Walpole explaining the loss of his personal 'estate' in Yorkshire. The precise nature of his property is not known but was probably a middling-sized estate. Only this letter survives, but it tells a plaintive story of bad behaviour within families and the greed of lawyers:

> Honoured Sir,
> This is the true state of my affair to the best of my knowledge. My grandfather had two daughters, the eldest Margery, the other Francis, Margery married Ness my father, Francis married Barns. This Barns displeased my grandfather so that he made a deed of gift of his estate in 1713 to the children of my father. After my grandfather's decease, my father soon after thro' misfortunes, and his own mismanagement was obliged to abscond, and took away with him this deed so that I never since have been able to come at the deed, nor ever heard of my father since, which is about 25 years ago. My attorney Conyers made the deed and has a copy of the instructions by him, but I cannot tell if that will be of any use.
> My grandfather dyed about 16 years ago, my aunt Barns was ever importuning him to make a will which he would not consent to. However when she see that he must die, she goes to an attorney and gets a will made for all he had to her and her children and brought the will home and sent for 3 of her friends and obliged him to sine it. I was then in Norfolk. My grandfather then died. My aunt injoyed the estate about six years and then she died and her three daughters all 4 in about 6 days time. I was informed of it I went over and took possession on the estate about six months after. Mr Grimstone and one Mr Paul (who is since dead) found out this Barns, who is a brother's son to Barns who married Francis. So they served ejectments and I had a triall, which was about the validity of my grandfather's will. One that was witness to the will swore that my grandfather said to my aunt when she would have him sine the will, he would not, however my aunt, and one that was a favourite of hers, raised my grandfather up in bed and put a pen into his hand and oblidge him to sine it. Judge Carter who tried the case exclaimed against the will, and rebuked the attorney for making a will at his own home and being a neighbour and not taking instructions from the testator, and gave a charge to the jury against the will, and such proceedings, and a verdict was given in my favour.
> Notwithstanding I should be very glad to have the affair accomodated without a trial if possible, and am very glad your honour has persuaded Mr Grimstone to stop his proceeding against me. And am in hopes thro' your kind intercession for me, the affair will be made up on reasonable terms. I return your honour many thanks and am your obedient servant.
> Richd Ness
>
> I told Mr Greenacre you expected he should hold the marsh another year I believe he will comply to hold it.

Even such a personal letter as this ends with a practical note on an estate issue.

Richard Ness sold all or most of his restored Yorkshire property and reinvested the proceeds in Norfolk, largely for the benefit of his sisters' children. He seems to have had a number of sisters who had married and produced children – Jackson/Simpson, Temple, and possibly Bowman. It is clear that he had tried to follow his grandfather's desire to leave his property to Ness and all his siblings. Many of the family had followed Ness, now head of the family, to Norfolk and he had built up real estate holdings in Burnham Thorpe and Wells, with more at Thornage and a mortgage in Binham, all lying near the Holkham estate. He was meticulous in ensuring that all his near relations were left legacies. His nephews Simon Simpson (later of Binham) and Robert Temple were the executors of his will. Robert Temple, the son of his sister Mary, was a farmer at Tivetshall, quite possibly a tenant of the Walpole manor there. He was left Ness's property at Thornage, Robert's parish of birth and where his mother and father were still living. His daughter Elizabeth was left the substantial sum of £500 when she became 21. Ness's sister Anne, presumably deceased, had married first Anthony Jackson and then John Simpson in Crambe. Property in Wells was allotted to look after one of her sons, William Jackson, who was given a £30 annuity for life: it seems he needed looking after. Anne's later children Simon, Francis and Hannah were also provided for. Her daughter Rachel left Thornage after marrying Yorkshireman Thomas Cook. Ness was a witness at the marriage and no doubt gave Rachel her legacy as a wedding gift. Her first son, baptised at Kirkby in Cleveland, was called Richard Ness Cook with the 66 year-old Ness standing as his godfather. 'Ness Cook' was left £100 in Richard's will. The Ness name also continued in Simon Simpson's grandson Ness Harvey and Robert Temple's heir Richard Ness Temple.

Ness also left money to his cousins Thomas and John Baker. By 1772 John Baker was in Gayton, but Thomas had gone to Yorkshire to Pickering marshes. Another relation Clemence, possibly another niece, had married Henry Bowman shopkeeper of Wells. Ness was joint executor with her when Henry died in 1769. Their children Henry and Richard were left legacies by Ness.

Ness's generosity was not restricted to his named family. He also left an annuity to Elizabeth Fortescue, someone who clearly mattered to him in his later years. Elizabeth, the daughter of Andrew Fiddyman the thatcher and parish clerk of Wolterton, was probably not much younger than Ness. She had made an unfortunate marriage to a Thomas Fortescue. They had a daughter Elizabeth in December 1732 but she lost her infant daughter Esther who was baptised and buried in Wolterton in 1734. When Walpole bought her father's cottage after his death in 1746, one of the conditions of the deed was that Elizabeth was to have £20 a year for life; another was that her mother Hannah was to be allowed to lease the east end of the rather dilapidated parsonage house as her home. This was to compensate Hannah whose husband's will, made in 1737, had made provision for her to continue to live in part of his own house in Wolterton. At that time Elizabeth Fortescue was living in another part of the family house, her husband having left. Andrew clearly disapproved of 'her husband Foscue', declaring that if she took him back into the house in Wolterton she must move out forever! In the 1746 deed Elizabeth was described as a widow, although Fortescue may have been alive. In 1741 Ness had paid Elizabeth 'Fos'que' for gathering stones on 'the Clover lands'; a back-breaking way of earning a little money. By 1744 she was being paid wages of £2 5s 6d a quarter. Now the organiser of the gangs of women and children who weeded the turnip and wheat fields, she and her 'company' also helped with hay making and gathering in the corn. Had Ness been quietly helping her and her family for some years? The generous annuity may have been his suggestion. Perhaps after her mother died she may have become housekeeper for Ness. Had their relationship been even more than friends – if her husband had disappeared without trace, she may not have felt able to marry and Ness never married. In his will she was left, for life, the interest from a mortgage he held on property in Binham. Or was Ness was simply being generous to the mother of his nephew's wife? For he had witnessed the marriage of his nephew Robert Temple to Mary Fortescue of Wolterton at Thornage in May 1763. Unfortunately the date and circumstances of Mary's birth have not been found. Temple's will showed that he had been married twice. By Mary Fortescue he had son Richard Ness Temple and three daughters: Mary Roberts married to a Norwich bookseller, Anne Colman married to a Norwich linen draper and Bridget married to John Rose a farmer of North Barsham and son of Robert's second wife. In July 1777 he married in Tivetshall to Tabitha Rose a widow of Weston. Their son Thomas Temple was farming in Thornage when he witnessed his father's will. No doubt the Ness family property there had already been settled on Thomas as he did not receive a significant legacy. Robert Temple was obviously worried about grave robbers: he required a stout oak coffin, buried six foot deep with a cartload of stones to be tipped on top of it before the earth replaced.

In a codicil to his will Richard Ness also left £20 to Joseph Carter, his successor as Walpole's steward. The action suggests that Ness had retired from active duty in about 1770. In September 1770 the estate accounts show that Henry Walton - then starting his career as a portraitist - was paid five guineas for drawing Ness's picture. As Ness was clearly well-regarded by the Walpoles, perhaps the drawing was a retirement gift to the trusty retainer. The fact that the drawing did not remain in Wolterton adds to the supposition – was it kept by Elizabeth Fortescue? Ness died on 24th April 1772 aged 71. His devotion to his employer was shown by an extraordinary act. He began his will with a bequest of a cottage and a few acres that he had bought for £80 in Calthorpe in 1751. This he left to his master, Horatio Walpole later the 1st Earl of Orford 'as a small acknowledgement for the humane and kind usage I have received from him and his family'.

Neither Joseph Carter in the 1770s nor his successor Henry Wegg in the 1780s appear to have shared the same closeness with their employer. Richard Ness's trusted stewardship had been pivotal to the Wolterton estate's history and his dedication to the family was unique.

**Sources**

NRO: COL/13/123; WAL 261/3-4, 271x6; MC3/252, 468x4

Wolterton archive: accounts: 3/1/3 & 5 /1/6; 3/7/2; letters: 8/5A, 6, 7, 8, 9, 20, 30, 42, 51

Ness's stone in Wickmere Churchyard.

# Chapter 5

## *Olland and Summerlay*

---

*While Itteringham is in the productive corn-growing area of north-east Norfolk, the parish sits astride two distinct underlying geological formations. The eastern side of the parish and Wolterton are better arable soils. To the west the light sandy loams tend on the upper sections to be acidic, free draining and poor at retaining both nutrients and water. These characteristics, confirmed by modern soil analysis, would have made the arable hard to keep in good heart in an era without modern chemical fertilisers. Upper slope land in these parts of Itteringham and Mannington was used for sheep grazing except when population had grown to a peak requiring more arable. When ploughed as arable they needed significant periods of fallow under grass and nitrogen rich clover, meticulous application of marl to improve soil structure and dung to increase fertility. Turnip crops both helped to fix nitrogen and provided fodder for cattle in the winter thus increasing the amount of muck available to each farm. All the farms in the 18th century would have had a good mix of arable and animal husbandry. Wolterton's home farm with its extensive parkland had an even greater bias to livestock. There were no smallholding farmers and no freehold farm land outside the tenant farms of Mannington, Wolterton, the Robins estates and Hill farm. Farm leases show how the soil fertility problem was managed, with precise requirements for the closing years of each lease showing the crop rotations needed to leave a farm in good shape for the next tenant. This chapter describes some of these arrangements and gives a sense of the look of the landscape and an impression of the hard work that went on every year for the whole community. Before describing later farming practices it is worth noting two documented cases of share farming occurring locally in the 1660s. The practice is rarely found in formal farming records and these provide additional evidence for Dr Elizabeth Griffiths's seminal work on farming to halves.*

### Early evidence of farming to halves

In 1675 the vicar of Heydon and Irmingland sued William Porter, latterly Dame Alice Smith's farmer at Irmingland, for higher tithe payments. Only the depositions made to the Court of Exchequer survive. They show that local opinion was firmly of the view that on this 130-140 acre dairy farm on Irmingland's meadows the custom 'since time out of mind' was only to pay calf tithes in full discharge of all proceeds and profits from the herd. The witnesses gave great detail regarding who had held the farm at various times (including Dame Alice occasionally holding it in-hand) and whether the farmers had paid tithes in kind or compounded with the incumbent for a cash payment. The sums involved were small, but the case was vigorously and convincingly defended. Exactly ten years later another local issue was taken to exchequer. This time it was an inheritance issue relating to the heirs of John Hilton, the farmer of the same farm, who had just died. He had sold his personal estate to one of his sons-in-law Timothy Purvis as trustee rather than convey it to his heirs by will. This was designed to protect a half share in his estate to be paid to his other daughter who had married a man who had languished in gaol for debt for many years. The action produced further depositions which commented on the nature and history of the farm. Notable among them was Richard Sexton, previously a farmer in Mannington and by this time Hilton's neighbour in Elmerdale farm. He said that Hilton was a good farmer and kept a well stocked farm as appropriate for this sort of farm. Both actions included numerous references to farming to halves.

William Porter had leased the farmhouse near Irmingland Hall, its dairy, dairy vessels, meadows and rights to graze cattle on Dame Alice's stubbles for a rent made up solely of an annually negotiated cash payment per cow. In 1672 he had hired 38 cows at 40s each, in 1673 38 cows at 42s 6d, and in 1674 36 at 40s. Porter was liable for tithes and other local charges, but he had all the profits from the calves of Dame Alice's cows and consumed the milk in his own home. These arrangements were very similar to those used for leasing the dairy on the Felbrigg estate at this time. In 1685 witnesses said that Purvis had, for at least the last two years, been farming for his sick father-in-law and had hired 40 cows each year from him. Hilton by this stage was paying rent of £174 to General Charles Fleetwood (who now owned the Irmingland estate) and so he may have acquired the cows at Dame Alice's death in 1678. But since Dame Alice had occasionally held the farm in-hand the inference is that she owned the cows throughout her life and leasing them had been the standard practice for running the dairy farm perhaps for the whole 40 years since her husband Sir Owen's death. Hilton was simply perpetuating the normal system with Purvis. Witnesses also recalled that during the 1660s the farm was held by Thomas Child. For just two years, 1668 and 1669, in addition to the dairy operation he took on Dame Alice's arable lands. These he sowed to halves for just those years. This detail was noted since his arrangement with the vicar was to pay tithes on the corn and hay only in those years he managed to achieve a crop – £14 in 1668 and £18 in 1669. It seems that here the land was so marginal for arable that regular cropping was problematic and farming to halves was a sensible risk-sharing arrangement.

The other recorded occurrence happened on the Mannington estate on an interesting farm first created in the 1660s. Sir John Potts, the first baronet, referred in his will of 1673 to his 'halvinge lands' – lands let on a sharecropping basis to a tenant. For convenience it is described here as a farm, although at the time documents simply listed the tenant's name and the fields included. There were no buildings of any kind with the land and in due course the fields simply became an established part of other tenant farms. The letting to halves indicates that a significant part of this farm was closes that had for a long time been in animal husbandry and which were now being switched to arable. The uncertainty about their productivity was reflected in a risk-sharing approach rather than a fixed rent. The lands were largely on the upper slopes and there would have been doubts about whether the land could be kept in arable use with standard cropping and fallow periods. This farm was created at a time when the Potts family was wrestling with significant debts built up largely from the heavy taxation of the civil war period, coinciding with a decade of low prices for agricultural produce. The earliest family deeds addressing these problems date from 1661 and the halving lands probably emerged from the early 1660s energetic work on the estate by Sir John Potts, his son John and grandson Roger. The farm appeared in mortgage deeds of 1668 and 1693-99. Initially it was described as a 140 acre farm held by Richard Sexton 'to be by him tilled and sowen to halves', but by 1693 the share farming reference was dropped. It is not clear if the whole acreage was shifting from pasture to arable. Since some previously arable land was included it is likely that much but not all was to be farmed to halves. Subsequently the farm was described as the same closes but with the addition of several strips of land in Wolterton open field that had been in the occupation of William Sexton, perhaps Richard's father. It has not yet proved possible to show a link between these Sextons and Thomas Sexton whose family were graziers at the Felbrigg estate and who share-farmed in Reepham in the 1660s and 1670s. In 1668 the halving lands were mortgaged on their own for £200. This rather modest amount relative to the farm's acreage probably reflected a low rental value for land already arable and a conservative estimate of the revenues from the lands sown to halves. The fields let to halves were probably those that previously had been sheep closes. Perhaps initially, from 1661 or 1662, Sexton had a 14 year lease to halves and subsequently took on the farm with further good field lands as a normal tenancy at a fixed rent.

| Close name | Acres |
| --- | --- |
| Wolterton Close | 15 |
| Johnson's Close to the south | 6 |
| Woolgrove Pit Close/ a grove called Wolgrove | 1 |
| Woolgrove New Closes – 5 'lately parted' in 1668, 3 in 1693 | 14 |
| | 13 |
| | 8 |
| 2 closes north of Wolgrove Pit, 'lately parted with a ditch', both called Old Wolgrove | 16 |
| | 18 |
| 2 closes - Maxon's and Great Gravel Pit Close, together | 25 |
| Pound Close 'lately divided' in 1668 – 2 closes in 1693 | 23 |
| 5 acre close north of Pound Close | 5 |
| 9 acre close north of that | 9 |
| Plus in 1693 various pieces of land in the field of Wolterton, acreage unspecified | |
| Total in 1693 in specified closes | 153 |

**Potts's halving lands farm in 1668 and 1693**

The table shows a summary of the fields listed in 1668 and 1693; the names and acreages differ slightly – in 1668 the total was underestimated at 140 acres, with the 1693 description being more accurate. The difference in total acreage may simply reflect a rather inaccurate guess at the total in 1668 (or earlier) before the ditching and partition of the previously larger closes was carried out by Sexton. A similar variation in acreages can be found in Elmerdale farm, where the lands involved were constant even though estimated acreage varied from 290 or less to 310. The closes can be identified precisely from the 1595 and 1742 Mannington estate maps. The closes on either side of the Barningham road in 1595 were shown gated at their junctions with the road – ie used for animal husbandry not arable. Maxon's Close was a swap for the old close of that name in the Wolterton open field area. It seems likely that the Wolterton field lands leased to Sexton were the old strips nearby, consolidated by Potts. Similarly Wolgrove New Closes had been open field, where Mannington controlled a number of specially labelled strips. Even so, to enclose this area would have required purchase or repossession of the other strips held by both smallholders and larger tenants and an exchange of land to move the large allocation of Itteringham glebe land closer in to the village. Wolterton Close was probably earlier a sheep close but Johnson's, before its acquisition by Potts, might have been arable as was the land immediately to the south. The 1660s conversion of this whole area from sheep closes and open field strips to tenant farm closes was later copied by Thomas Robins who consolidated most of the remaining open field strips on either side of the Itteringham to Wolterton/Wickmere road.

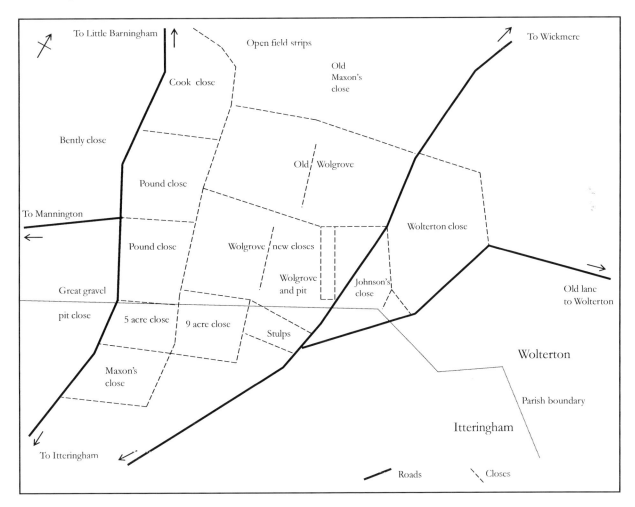

**The halving lands in the seventeenth century**

By 1676 Richard Sexton had graduated to the large Elmerdale farm in Irmingland. He must have proved himself a competent farmer on the halving lands. In 1693, by which time the halving lands unit was one of a number of estate farms listed in a large mortgage arrangement, the halving lands was simply treated as a normal tenancy farmed by Richard Lowe or Love. The Sextons moved on. By 1700 we know from his son Richard's will that Richard Sexton senior had moved to Blickling. The Blickling estate map of 1729 shows Sexton's land as a small parcel of largely pasture fields just past John's Bridge on the lane from Blickling mill to Moorgate, his lands clearly marked near the surviving wooden cart shed. There is, however, no evidence of farming to halves on the Blickling estate.

In early 1697 the 30 acres of Wolterton closes were without a tenant, last having been leased by Daniel Abell a butcher of Itteringham. This probably indicates that he was tenant of the whole farm, but since he was a butcher he may have been most interested in closes best suited to grazing. Daniel seems to have followed Sexton into Elmerdale farm. In February 1697 Sir Roger Potts sold these 'six closes of arable and pasture called Wolterton closes' to James Scamler of Wolterton – the break-up of the farm had begun. Most of this Scamler purchase would in due course find its way into the estate of Thomas Robins of Itteringham as exchanges for land close to Wolterton's lake and gardens. The other fields of the halving lands farm were reallocated to other tenants. Some of those to the southern end were added to the fields that went with Itteringham Old Rectory. The others to the north were added to Mannington Hall farm.

Much later there is fleeting evidence in the Wolterton accounts of another form of share farming – cow leasing. In 1739 Richard West, dairyman, was to pay £40 annual rent to lease 16 cows at 50s each. As an offset he was to be paid £30 for driving a team ploughing and harrowing and he was also allowed £3 to bring up 3 young calves. So he was provided with the capital (cows) to run a small dairy herd, but had to take the risk involved in managing their welfare. If any had died he would have been liable. The cost was further offset by the wages for ploughing. This arrangement was not repeated. It seems likely that this was how Bayfield had run at least part of the home farm (early accounts are negligible and so his arrangements are uncertain). A letter from Bayfield to Walpole of February 1737 shows that Walpole had been uneasy at the practice, but Bayfield defended it:

> Your honour seeme not to be satisfied in that way of letting a dairy on that part of the farm late in Jackson's use and desire to know howe many cows are let there, the number is forteen at £35 per annum and the man which hire them is wholly implied in your honour's services in carting to fetch and carry all materials for the building, coals for the house, lyme kiln furrs for the brick kiln and plowing land and sowing the same etc, for which he have board wages for himself and a fellow to help him and £30 per annum for their board and wages, which I know no cheaper way nor more to be made of the farme. We have this year about 100 combs of barley and about 30 or 40 comb oats and about 50 combs wheat and hay for all the herde, I could let the land but then what will your honour do for hay and horse to cart all materials and it take 2 horse continually for to rowle [rolling the lawns] and cary earth muck etc for the gardens, and horse your honour must keep for to doe the business. We have not bought any hay for several years for no accation. I rearly believ your honour make as much of that farme as any farm you have of the same value.

This must have been a debateable view given that the rent had been twice as much in Jackson's tenure. Ness had the dairyman on annual wages from the outset and in his accounts there are no further examples of farming to halves.

## Crops

Normal crops grown in the area were barley, wheat, rye (sometimes called darnel), buck, oats, clover, turnips and peas, with of course extensive fallow periods under grass. Copious loads of animal muck would have been carted out to be spread on the fields before ploughing, as well as the managed grazing of livestock on the stubbles. Much labour would have gone into ploughing and harrowing with horses. Young lads were employed as bird scarers – Edmund Brown's boy was paid 12s for 6 weeks' work for keeping birds off the wheat in 1739. Turnip fields were weeded – a task for Elizabeth Fortescue's gangs of women and young boys who also helped with harvesting. Hay had to be mown and stacked. Corn crops were harvested by hand – a major undertaking. Where straw could not be stored in a barn it was stacked outside and properly thatched for protection by Andrew Fiddyman or another thatcher. No doubt all deserved their beer at the end of harvesting as supplied by Edward Bateman alehouse keeper at Wolterton in 1744.

Harvests of course were vulnerable to bad weather and the threat of food shortage was never far away in a poor year. For example in early February 1757, just after the first Lord Walpole's death, Ness wrote to the younger Horatio Walpole his new boss:

> ... prices of corn and they rise every week, that I am really afraid if no corn can be imported, nor the distillery put a stop to till next harvest, the prices will be so high, the wages of the labourers and mechanics if they have constant employ will not find them bread that has familys. Wheat is now 24s a comb viz 4 bushels to the comb, barley 14s, oats 9s and pease 17 and god only knows what may be the consequences. Necessity has no law. Your lordship has about 40 comb of wheat when it is thrashed out, [if] I could prevail with your lordship I would all those labourers that works for you have such a quantity weekly as would supply their necessaries weekly at the rate of 5s the bushel they paying for it upon the delivery which would be setting a good example and gaining goodwill amongst the lower people which I think will be prudent as well as charitable proceeding in case any disturbance should happen.

The light soils of the area needed substantial help to maintain long term productivity. Clay was dug and spread as marl on the fields or burnt in the lime kiln to produce lime. Marl helped the soil to become less acid and more moisture and nutrient retentive. This was a heavy task. For example in 1740 the estate paid £1 10s for 100 cartloads of marl. At just over 1s per day standard wages this was more than 20 man days' work. In November 1743 John Barnard and company were paid £6 9s 4d for 97 days work at 16d per day to dig and uncoat marl at Mossymere for use at Mere farm. Ness noted that only 140 loads were dug out. There were also disagreements about where the marl could be dug. Commons were always a prime target, but in 1745 Ness made a note to talk to William Robins about his apparently having allowed an Oulton man to dig marl on Itteringham Common. Where the marl was dug from usable arable land the pits were filled in after the digging. So although many old pits remain in the landscape, particularly in woods, a great many more would once have existed. The aim was to find clay and marl close to the fields to minimise carting. Clay was also used to make barn floors, packed down to a hard surface. The estate ran a brickworks for a number of years and the brick kiln just to the east of Mannington Hall was still going strong in the middle years of the century, when in 1743 William Spink was making bricks there. Earth was burnt at the kilns to spread on the meadows to improve their fertility as well.

Carting was a major activity. When not busy with clay, carts were used to bring coal from the north coast ports for the larger houses and local firings and ling or heather for the rest. The estate landlord supplied large volumes of 'covenant wood' to each farm tenant each year, presumably in part to prevent the tenants from cutting valuable large timber on their farms. Huge quantities of faggots of whin or gorse were cut and tied up in the Mossymere area and carted off for use particularly as firings for the kilns. Edward Edwards who was tenant there supplied 8,000 faggots in 1747 for example. Whin seed was purchased to replant areas cut. This was good cover for game as well as a firings crop. When the estate took the small Mossymere farm in-hand in 1752 it had 14 acres tilled for wheat, but 29 acres mown for grass and 13 loads of hay and 3,000 whin faggots had come off the farm. 260 sheep had also been kept up there for 6 weeks' grazing. Cartloads of ling were cut locally and brought in from Cawston common. In addition of course there was quite a trade in timber carting, bark for the tanner and gravel from Mannington's pit and elsewhere for use on the roads and paths. 'Paving stones' were brought from Sheringham.

## Hops and sunflowers

In addition to the standard crops, it appears that, rather surprisingly, hops were grown locally between 1801 and 1802 at least. The Wolterton estate spent significant sums buying hops from John Oakes and B Carter. At this time Oakes had just become an estate tenant with Walpole's purchase in 1801 (subject to legal action, which was resolved) of the Itteringham Hall estate from the Robins family. The occurrence of hops is odd since Norfolk is not much known for this crop and local light free-draining soils and fairly dry weather do not suit the needs of hop-growing. Having said that, there is a surviving 1554 deed noting a close in Wolterton called 'le hoppyard' on the Calthorpe side of the parish. However, as will be seen later, Oakes had extensive connections to Kent and as part of his major improvements to the farm he obviously tried new crops. It is known that he did extensive drainage works on the 'horse marsh' meadows below the Hall – the ponds and deep ditches are still there to be seen. It is quite possible that he used the better drained meadow land for hops. In support of this it is quite noticeable that on both sides of the river between Blickling mill and John's bridge hops remain prolific, naturalised among the trees and scrub. Perhaps they are the last remnants of his harvests. Hops are not a normal hedgerow plant locally, although there is a stray growing in Itteringham churchyard hedge. Perhaps this came from the large patch at the site of the old ponds near the Manor House in the village, another Robins farm. Maybe Garnham, then the tenant, inspired by John Oakes's efforts, tried hops around the edges of his fish ponds. A couple of plants also survive growing from a deep and damp ditch on the way to Calthorpe from Wolterton's gates – perhaps at or near the fringes of 'le hoppyard'. Otherwise they are hard to find.

Hedgerow hops near Wolterton gates

Sunflowers were not a usual crop in 18th century Norfolk but other countries were beginning to appreciate the benefits of sunflower oil. In early 1775 the Society of Arts in London offered a prize of £20 'for the Culture of that Plant in England, in order to ascertain whether oil could be advantageously obtained from the Seeds in this Climate'. Henry Bryant, rector of Colby, and curate of both Heydon, where he lived, and Itteringham parishes, had taken up botany after his wife died in 1770. He decided to rise to the challenge and planted a large area of sunflowers, presumably at Heydon, no doubt much to the amusement of his neighbours. In November, he harvested 15 bushels of seed which he sent by stage wagon to the Society at the Adelphi in London, hoping they would 'all come safe to hand and in good time'. He suggested they should address themselves to whether the plants would 'yield an oil sweet and well flavoured' and 'in such a quantity as to merit cultivation in this kingdom'. His efforts which he stressed were for the 'public good' won him the £20. North Norfolk was again in the vanguard of agricultural innovation.

## Crop rotations

Richard Ness wrote a small note apparently planning crop rotation on one of the farms for the 1740s (rather than recording past usage). Typically just over 200 acres were in consideration for active farming as opposed to permanent grazing. This looks like Wolterton's home farm – it seems unlikely that he would have planned in detail the rotation for any other farm. On average nearly half the acreage produced a grain crop each year, with a very strong bias on the light soils to barley. Plenty of turnips were to be grown each year for winter feed for cattle. The fallow grass and summerlay ploughed for autumn reflect much the same requirements imposed on tenants. The lack of summerlay in the first 3 years and the rise and fall of the total acreage perhaps indicate grazing was being planned to be converted to one cycle of arable use. This note shows that he instituted the new and more onerous requirements for fallow and turnips from the very earliest stages of his time as steward.

| | Wheat | Barley | Turnips | Barley | Olland | Olland | Summerlay | Total |
|---|---|---|---|---|---|---|---|---|
| 1741 | 69 | 40 | 21 | 28 | 23 | 26 | | 207 |
| 1742 | 19 | 33 | 47 | 21 | 61 | 24 | | 205 |
| 1743 | 16 | 19 | 39 | 47 | 15 | 87 | | 223 |
| 1744 | 24 | 16 | 19 | 39 | 47 | 15 | 87 | 247 |
| 1745 | 63 | 24 | 16 | 19 | 39 | 47 | 15 | 223 |
| 1746 | 15 | 63 | 24 | 16 | 19 | 39 | 47 | 223 |
| 1747 | 47 | 15 | 63 | 24 | 16 | 19 | 39 | 223 |
| 1748 | 39 | 47 | 15 | 40 | 28 | 18 | 26 | 213 |
| 1749 | 26 | 38 | 28 | 21 | 40 | 28 | 18 | 199 |
| 1750 | 18 | 26 | 38 | 28 | 21 | 40 | 28 | 199 |
| Total | 336 | 321 | 310 | 283 | 309 | 343 | 260 | |

Crop Rotation planned by Richard Ness

Another note showed the 1749 and 1750 usage of the 175 acres of Thwaite Hall farm and the 65 acres in Calthorpe Hook Hall farm – in this case by field. At Thwaite about 145 acres were available for arable. An average year would see 51 acres under grass, 74 with a grain crop (wheat more than barley on the good soils here) and 18 acres of turnips.

| Acres | Roods | Perches | 1749 | 1750 |
|---|---|---|---|---|
| 14 | 2 | 7 | Grass | Grass |
| 12 | 1 | 10 | Wheat | Barley |
| 6 | 3 | 3 | Wheat | Barley |
| 9 | 0 | 6 | Grass | Wheat |
| 13 | 1 | 9 | Grass | Wheat |
| 16 | 3 | 0 | Wheat | Turnips |
| 17 | 2 | 36 | Barley | Grass |
| 20 | 2 | 38 | Turnips | Barley |
| 10 | 0 | 10 | Barley | Grass |
| 13 | 3 | 9 | Olland | Wheat |
| 9 | 0 | 31 | Grass | Wheat |
| 11 | 1 | 14 | | |
| 3 | 1 | 9 | | |
| 2 | 2 | 2 | | |
| 3 | 3 | 10 | | |
| 1 | 1 | 27 | | |
| 0 | 2 | 3 | | |
| 7 | 2 | 9 | | |
| 174 | 3 | 16 | | |

Thwaite crop rotation

## Farm leases

Farming practice is indicated by the terms relating to crops given in leases. Unfortunately by their nature leases were considered ephemeral once ended and were routinely destroyed. The Walpole papers, in common with many large estates, do not include many leases for their farms in the 18th century. However, a few examples have survived and the similarities across them show a standard approach was taken locally. From this small sample it is clear that very little changed during the century. The mix of crops and rotation systems was much the same in each example. With a little imagination they tell us much about the landscape of the time as well as the farming activities of tenant farmers and their labourers.

In 1722 William Daniel was a tenant, probably of Mere farm, on the Mannington estate. That year he leased a small tenement of his own in Thurgarton to William Spurrell of the major family in that village. It is likely that Daniel would have used very similar terms to those he had accepted in Mannington. His lease may therefore reflect the standard form for the estate. He did not mandate the maximum number of arable crops directly, but he ensured that in the final years of the lease the majority of the land would have had 1-3 years with clover or grass. This, with the mucking requirements, would have ensured that the land stayed in good condition for the next tenant.

---

Lease of April 1722 to run from Michaelmas for 21 years

William Daniel of Mannington yeoman leased to William Spurrell of Thurgarton yeoman Daniel's house in Thurgarton now/late in occupation of Benjamin England with 17 ½ acres. Timber and underwood excluded. Rent of £16 10s to be paid annually at Daniel's present dwelling house in Mannington.

Tenant to make good mucking on 3 acres every 2 years on some part of the land throughout the term.

The pightle now summerlayed at the end of the term to be so left on the third earth. The marlpit close upon wintercorn stubble. 3 acres of land of 3 years, 3 acres of 2 years and 3 acres of 1 year lying and to be laid down with clover or other small seeds.

In the last 2 years tenant to spend all the stover on the premises.

Landlord to allow so much muck as valued by 2 independent men and 12 pence per coomb for all the stover then left.

Tenant to keep in repair glass windows, gates, styles, posts, pales, rails, hedges, drains and watercourses with landlord providing the rough timber to do so. Landlord will ensure all are in good repair at the start of the tenancy.

Landlord may only repossess during the term if he wants to live there. If so 2 referees to assess the damages he should pay to the tenant.

Glossary:

*Summerlay* – land not cropped that summer, but may, as here, be ploughed.

*Third earth* – 3 ploughings, sometimes with harrowing between each. After the third ploughing the land was ready to be harrowed and drilled with autumn sown wheat, barley, etc. A spring sowing might be done after just 1 or 2 ploughings.

*Stover* – fodder from crop waste, but can also include hay from clover and grasses. Here the fodder is to be consumed by animals whose muck will be spread on the tenancy.

---

## Summary of Lease in Thurgarton

Daniel was a respected yeoman farmer, just under gentlemanly status. After his lease at Mannington ended, he moved with his wife Catherine and their eight children to Matlaske where he died in 1731. He had also provided a mortgage for William Spurrell (then gent) for £300. One of his friends and neighbours Richard Whitaker, the well-connected gentleman of the tanning family of Matlaske, had been High Sheriff in 1725.

Among Walpole's leases is a draft 9 year lease of 1737, at £178 rent, for Nicholas Wayt at Wickmere Hall, together with a farm called Snellings. This large farm then also held the land across the road that was William Symonds's blacksmith shop and cottage and the land earlier occupied by Henry Purdy. Wayt was allowed to take pigeons from the pigeon house when Walpole was not in residence in Wolterton. This lease is interesting as it was drawn up by Thomas Bayfield and had less onerous arable stipulations than those negotiated by Richard Ness after 1738. It was even somewhat less onerous than William Daniel's lease of his own land. Bayfield had also drawn up an outline of the clauses that Samuel Newstead should use in leases on his patch at Tivetshall. This shows the same modest requirement for fallow land in the final years of a lease. Wayt was required to leave 3 parcels each of 25 acres: 1 as 1 year fallow sown with clover and grass, 1 as 2 year olland (grass previously ploughed), 1 as summerlay of the 4th earth mucked and being on 2 year olland or on buck stubble, the buck sown on 3 year olland. Like the Daniel lease, there was no requirement to plant turnips. On this 294 acre farm these acreages were well below the 1/6th shares later to be stipulated for fallow periods. Similarly the lease did not include the specific limitations on numbers of grain crops that Ness was to insist on. If all Bayfield's leases were of this form the estate lands could have been exploited by tenants with a short term desire to take the maximum yield they could.

By November 1749 the new style Ness lease was in operation with a draft made for Robert Woods of Plumstead to take over Mannington Hall and its large home farm from George Copland from Michaelmas 1750. The 14 year lease at £151 called for greater attention to the last few years' crops. Parcels of 30 acres each were to be left in 1 year olland and 2 year olland, with 20 acres to be 3 year olland and 25 acres of turnips. The latter was to be valued independently and paid for by the incoming tenant. A maximum of 3 crops of corn and 1 of turnips was allowed before land had to be put down to grass for 2 years before again being ploughed. Clauses required 2 days carriage work from the farm and the tenant had to provide thatching straw. Walpole however was responsible for building repairs.

In September 1746 Horatio Walpole granted a 14 year lease to Thomas Plaford of Itteringham carpenter of the old Copeman farm which by then Plaford was already using. The lease seems to be of very standard terms despite the small size of the farm. Timber and underwoods were excluded. All the usual clauses were there to ensure the property was kept in good repair. This included Plaford doing 20 rod (1 rod or rood equals 16 ½ feet) of hedge cutting and ditch scouring work every year from which he could keep the proceeds for firings. At the end of the lease significant fallow acreage was required to be left as olland under a sufficient quantity of clover, grass and nonesuch seeds – 4 acres of 3 years laying, 4 ½ of 2 years, 5 ½ of 1 year. In the last year of the lease Plaford was to sow in with the summer corn such quantity of grass seed as Walpole saw fit, with Plaford harrowing it in for free. This was standard practice to ensure productive stubble for grazing after the harvest. During the term Plaford was not to sow more than 3 crops of corn and 1 of turnips without first laying down the land with clover and nonesuch. In the last year he was to leave 5 acres that had been olland for 3 years summer tilled in the third earth (therefore ready for autumn harrowing and drilling). This last year's summerlay acreage was to be mucked ready for planting wheat, the most demanding crop in the cycle. And at that time 5 acres was to be left sown with turnips. Plaford could use the turnips to feed his cattle in the farm's closes up to 15th March after the end of the lease. Plaford's cattle were to consume all the hay, straw, chaff and 'colder' (broken ears of corn and chaff), except that used for thatching, and all the muck was to be disposed of wherever on the premises most needed it. The muck in the last year was to be left in the yard shovelled up in heaps. In the winter after the end of the lease Plaford was to bring the last year's straw to Walpole. Plaford was to find sufficient winter corn straw for thatching at the farm if he could.

In July 1750 a lease was drafted with the intention that Thomas Partridge would take over Hospital farm in Calthorpe from John Cubitt. This farm had its house and yard at the corner of Fring Wood and is now known as Fring Wood farm. It took its name from Doughty's Hospital in Norwich which benefited from the rental stream. Partridge had to comply with the terms of the long lease by which Walpole held it from the Corporation of Norwich. The eight year sub-lease was at £46 per year, to which was added £30 for the meadows and lands of Mrs Hays occupied by Jacob Mountain (the estate's major tenant in Calthorpe) and here Partridge had to comply with the terms of Mountain's lease of 1737 from the late Reverend Mr Lombe. Also packaged into this farm at £17 was to be 20 acres recently bought from John Bell and £12 for 20 acres in Walpole's own use, these elsewhere described as fen lands. At a total of £105 a significant new farm had been created. But in fact that year Partridge added Mannington Hall farm to his old Wolterton acreage when Thomas Oakes moved into Mannington Hall itself. John Cubitt continued in the estate accounts for some years in a large farm presumably including the Fring Wood area.

In September 1751 Walpole made a new 11 year lease at a rent of £119 for John Cook in his existing farm in Wickmere, just across from Wickmere Hall. Three 27 acre parcels were to be left as 1 year olland, 2 year olland, 3 year olland well mucked and ploughed three times. 20 acres of turnips were to be planted. Assuming this was still the 170 acre farm from 1732, these 27 acre parcels roughly match the 1/6th approach – varying proportions of meadow land in the farms make the 1/6th approach only a rough guide. As elsewhere a maximum of 3 corn or grain crops had to be followed by 1 of turnips and then 2 years planted with grass seed.

Correspondence in January 1752 between Richard Ness and Horatio Walpole showed how difficult some of the lease renewals were and the difficulty of agreeing lower terms of years when a tenant negotiated hard. Landlords were keen to keep their farms let and the tenant often got his way. As so often in letters from Ness to Walpole there was an undercurrent that Walpole, even at this late date, did not fully understand all the ins and outs of running a farming estate and dealing with tenants. On 4th January Ness wrote to Walpole about the ongoing negotiation with the Emersons over their farm in Burnham:

I have received yours of December 31ˢᵗ and I told the Emersons that I was certain that your honour would object to the term of 21 years and would gladly have had the term limited to 15 years telling them that you had made it a rule to let none of your estates here for a longer term than 11 years. They said their term would in fact be no more than 19 years as they gave up 2 years in their present lease. I doubt it must be complied with.

With regard to the turnips, what you honour observes that you would rather choose that 50 acres should be left ploughed upon the 2ⁿᵈ earth and the succeeding tenant have the liberty to sow them himself, which might prevent future disputes in the valuation, and I suppose your honour means without any consideration to Emerson, if so, to be sure it is giving the rent of one year of 50 acres of land and 2 earths or ploughings of the said 50 acres, which is computed at 5s an acre, to the incoming tenant which Emerson will not care to comply withall, and whatever tenant shall succeed him will think himself well off to have such a quantity of turnips at a fair price for the support of his stock and flock of sheep. And perhaps it may so happen that the tenant that shall succeed him he may live at a distance and the expense in carrying out the muck and ploughing and sowing them and the damage they may receive before Michaelmas if Emerson does not take good care of them, as there is no good reason to expect he should, I am afraid it will be of small advantage. But there is a possibility of it being a disadvantage to the tenant all things considered, especially should they turn out to be a bad crop. However I will see if he will comply with it.

No doubt Ness did not try too hard to pursue a clause he thought wrong. Later in the month he noted that he had resolved Emerson's lease and on 30ᵗʰ January Walpole wrote:

I have received yours of 27ᵗʰ, Emerson's obstinacy provokes me much and if I had time ... my prejudice I think I would be tempted to part with him altogether, but as I see that cannot be conveniently done we must submit.

When Horatio Walpole junior took over the estate in 1757 after his father's death there was no material change in the nature of leases or the size of farms – agribusiness as usual. In 1762 Thomas Partridge made an agreement to take over the farm at Wickmere Old Hall formerly Mary Wayt's. This was another promotion for a favoured tenant. The farm was large and as required by the lease he would have lived in the fading but grand old Hall. The lease, for the first time among the surviving examples, made explicit that the olland and turnip requirements were each 1/6ᵗʰ of the arable. Perhaps reflecting rather better soils here there was no 3 year olland requirement, but otherwise the fallow, turnip, maximum 3 grain crops and muck clauses were unremarkable. Noticeable too was the clause preventing the tenant from taking game or allowing anyone else to do so.

At Michaelmas 1771 Richard Ness renewed Thomas Oakes's lease of Mannington Hall. The lease was guaranteed for 3 years and after that was to continue without any end date, with either side being able to terminate at will as long as notice was given before 25ᵗʰ March. Leave was granted for Oakes to assign the lease to others, although there is no evidence that he ever did, either in whole or in part. As elsewhere on the estate, Walpole undertook all house and building repairs and Oakes had the use of the barns until the May following the end of the lease to store his crop. However, Oakes had to keep in repair all the glass windows and their lead work – an interesting indication that the Hall still had most or all of its windows in use. Oakes had to deliver 2 loads of repair and thatching materials each year to Walpole and provide free 2 days per year of a man with a wagon and 5 horses to do whatever carrying tasks Walpole specified including fetching coals. Old grass land and field borders could not be ploughed up without penalty.

At the end of the lease there had to be a large acreage in olland – 40 acres of 1 year and 20 acres of 2 years were to be 'fed with cattle in the last year' (ie dunged) and ploughed by 5ᵗʰ July and to be ploughed three times that year. A further 20 acres of olland was to be made summer lay with all the previous year's muck on this parcel, except a reasonable amount for the turnip land. 40 acres of turnips were to be sown either on wheat stubble or after a first crop of barley. The incoming tenant was to be able to sow grass seeds in the summer corn in the last year. Overall he was limited to 2 crops of corn and 1 of turnips after which each field had to be sown with grass seeds in the following crop of corn. This had to be left for 2 years before being ploughed, with a significant penalty for breach of this clause. The farm was thus running a standard cycle with 3 grain crops (wheat and barley), 1 turnip crop, 2 years under clover and grass and a year summer ploughed but not sown until the autumn. The lease, being at will after the first 3 years, effectively mandated this crop rotation on a permanent basis. The farm was about 320 acres, excluding in-hand woodland, and obviously some of that was permanent meadow and grazing (about 18 acres was listed as pasture in 1809).

Ness to the very end of his life stuck to the same approach for all his leases. In August 1771 an agreement was made for Robert Breese to leave his Saxthorpe farm at Michaelmas 1772. He had to leave 14 acres of 1 year olland, 21 acres of 2 years, 5 acres summerlay ploughed 3 times and 10 acres of turnips which the incoming tenant would pay for.

By the end of the century the local leases had altered a little. In October 1802 Walpole leased the Elmerdale farm in Irmingland to William Mack of Tunstead who was already in occupation having taken over from the heirs of Thomas Bulwer. The farm was just over 268 acres of arable and 42 acres of meadow and a covenant allowed Walpole to take up to 10 acres to plant with young trees – to create yet more game cover. The rent for the 11 years was £240 per year. Standard clauses excluded taking timber, required Mack to pay up to £5 worth of materials for repairs each year, to provide straw for thatching and set penalties for ploughing meadow. A new clause required the tenant to level molehills and anthills on the meadow and within the first 5 years he had to gather and spread 1,000 loads of [leaf] mould on the meadows. In parallel there was a requirement to spread 5,000 good cart loads of marl or clay on the arable. While marl spreading had always been a feature of local farms, the new requirement made the volume visible and mandatory. But in other respects the crop rotation requirements and the final year stipulations had not changed much and indeed the early set numbers of ploughings no longer featured. A maximum of 3 grain or pulse crops was allowed before laying over to grass. Every crop of winter corn or pulse was to be sown on land broken up from olland or grass of 2 years' laying. The arable was divided notionally into 44 acre parcels (1/6th of the arable) and was to be left: 1 as olland of 2 years, 1 as clover stubble or olland of 1 year, 1 as stubble of the first crop which shall have been sown on 2 year olland, 1 sown with turnip seed and well mucked and twice hoed and 2 parts to be left as stubble of the 1st and 2nd crop equally. The turnips would be valued independently and the incoming tenant would pay Mack for them. Presumably it would have been acceptable, in place of turnips, to plant 'mangel wurzel or root of scarcity'. The 'new root' was noted by *The Norwich Mercury* in September 1787 as having just been introduced to the country. They described it as a variant of beet and a good substitute for turnips for winter forage being a hardier plant with higher yields.

## Animal husbandry

All the farms would have had livestock. Muck was necessary for soil fertility, livestock were productive in their own right and every farm had a section of meadow grazing beside the Bure or one of its tributary becks. Large numbers of cattle would have been seen in the meadows and sheep on the pasture and fallows on the lighter soil of the higher closes. But the estate accounts also show considerable consumption of pork and bacon and trade in pigs. Most farmyards would probably have had a quantity of chickens, geese, ducks and even turkeys. Horses of course were both tractors and transport and again every farm would have had a stable of beasts of different sorts.

The larger households, particularly when entertaining during game shooting season, consumed prodigious quantities of meat. A typically quiet month in 1758 saw the Wolterton Hall household consume 43 stone (602 pounds) of beef, 16 stone of pork and 188 pounds of mutton. The busier month of August that year saw the following tally in the accounts.

| | £ | s | d |
|---|---|---|---|
| 75 stone 9 pound beef at 3:6 | 13 | 4 | 9 |
| 2 stone 3 pound of mutton at 4:1 | | 9 | 1 |
| 8 stone 2 pound veal at 3:6 | 1 | 8 | 6 |
| 346 pound of mutton at 4d a pound | 5 | 15 | 4 |
| 7 comb 2 bushels wheat | 7 | 10 | 0 |
| 148 pound of butter | 3 | 14 | 0 |
| 84 chickens | 2 | 2 | 0 |
| 220 eggs | | 6 | 0 |
| | 35 | 9 | 8 |

August 1758 Wolterton household accounts

Keeping the animals in good condition required constant attention. The dairyman and his wife looked after the cows and made the butter and cheese. In 1740 William Kendall, of a family that had been a minor tenant on the Mannington estate, was dairyman. By 1743 John Jay had taken over and after his departure in 1749 to Tivetshall a succession of other husbandmen ran the farm and dairy. The estate accounts show all sorts of activities: sheep washing and clipping, drenching the cows and a note in 1743 of the costs for driving 168 sheep down to London.

But, despite all the care and attention of men like Francis Williamson the shepherd in the 1730s, animals still caught diseases – dizzy sheep, sheep with sore heads and horses with the 'mad stagger' were from time to time noted in the accounts. Far more serious was the major outbreak of highly contagious cattle distemper (now known as rinderpest) in 1748. Notices started appearing in the Norfolk newspapers and by late 1749 it was widespread in many parts of Norfolk. In order to contain the disease all markets to the north of Norwich including the major St Faith's horse fair were stopped. The local justices imposed a ban on moving cattle without a licence but this was widely ignored. The orders had to be repeated regularly and people were convicted for contravening them. By 1750 parliament enacted the continuation of the laws to prevent the disease and the St Faith's horse fair was moved to 'Castle-Ditches' where it would be held for the future. This national outbreak lasted from 1745 to 1758. George Copland's herd at Mannington Hall seems to have been particularly badly affected. The estate accounts show Copland allowed £8 10s off his rent for 17 infected cattle that had to be slaughtered. A schedule for April that year showed the value of the 17 cows before they were killed and the total of the 50% allowance from the government. John Fish and John Buck, both servants of Copland (farm workers), testified that they had seen the animals killed, their skins slashed to make them worthless and the cows buried 4 foot deep in the Chapel Grove at Mannington. In September 1748 the accounts noted that Copland had been allowed by the government £28 18s for the loss of his cattle. But despite the precautions the distemper problem was a fairly regular visitor in the middle of the century, even if not actually endemic. In 1749 there was an outbreak in Calthorpe and in 1754 John Thirtle, farming in Itteringham, was allowed £15 5s for distempered cattle. Even when diseases were not a problem, the economics of farming were difficult to predict. In November 1777 the Blickling estate steward Robert Copeman had been embarrassed at how difficult it was to sell the estate's lambs and sheep, so depressed were prices that year. By contrast the barns were full with a huge crop of corn and beans.

## Labour on the farm

What else occupied the farmer and his men? As if all these activities were not enough, there was a heavy load throughout the year of maintenance tasks. Ditches and drains had to be kept clear. River weed was cleared. Hedges had to be cut and laid. Gravel had to be spread on the roads. Grain had to be carted to and fro between farm, mill and market. In those few extra daylight hours, domestic gardens and orchards had to be tended and vegetables dug, apples picked and fences mended. The farmer also had the constant business of hiring (and firing) seasonal and yearly workers. Some would be found at the hiring fairs but others, like Richard Ayton, offered themselves directly to employers. In October 1815 Richard, who had been born in Itteringham in 1792 and had previously worked at Irmingland for Brett Sands, came to Robert Copeman's farm at Itteringham Hall. He was taken on as a yard man for a year at 12 shillings a week, a pint of beer a day and his dinner on every Sunday. He was allowed the same arrangements about the summer as the other men, that, after late July, he would be free to take on other work until the harvest when he would get harvest wages. Copeman re-hired him in September and paid his harvest money in late October 1816. Up to then Richard had been living in Itteringham but before his new contract was made on 5th November, he had married and so had to find his own lodgings. When labourers fell ill wages were deducted or, as Richard found in April 1817, could be discharged whether they agreed or not. The nuances of employment agreements took up many hours on both sides.

Boys were employed to reduce numbers of pests: moles and rats had to be trapped and at Blickling in 1759 eight polecats were caught in one year. The Vermin Acts allowed churchwardens to pay a bounty for hedgehogs - considered one of the greatest threats to birds' eggs - and, at 4d a head, it was easy money. Hedgehogs then were so numerous that hundreds were killed every year in some parts of England. Itteringham's churchwardens paid up for 14 bodies in 1737 but far more were probably destroyed by the estates. Gamekeepers were still controlling their numbers in Norfolk in the 1950s.

## Flies and weather 1782-83

In the summer of 1782 the turnip crop of eastern and central Norfolk was wiped out by 'the black canker caterpillar'; the devastation was recorded by Henry Bryant who spent much of his time observing insect life on his local journeys between his churches. He was a friend and admirer of the Norwich-born James Edward Smith. Smith, later Sir James, bought the collection of Linnaeus, the pioneering Swedish botanist whose principles he and his friends followed, and founded the Linnaean Society.

Bryant wrote to Smith from Heydon on November 11th 1782 asking for his help:

> We have had a very wet, uncomfortable, sickly summer and I have suffered from the epidemic influenza ... Our turnips in Norfolk this season have suffered greatly from a species of black caterpillars; thousands of acres have been destroyed by them and no method could be found so effectually to stop their ravages than employing women and children to pick them off, either by the day or at three halfpence the pint.

He described the yellow and black fly that emerged as having four wings and thought *Tenthredo Rosae*, a sawfly, was the most likely identification but being unsure sent a specimen to Smith. A few months earlier, William Marshall the agent at Gunton for Sir Harbord Harbord, had written similarly to Charles Morton at the Royal Society and sent specimens of both caterpillar and fly, which he also described as mostly yellow and with four wings. Marshall wrote on agricultural conditions and was 'an almost entire stranger to natural history' but he gave a very full description and also tentatively suggested the *Tenthredo* family. He noted that the turnip crop was then the basis of Norfolk husbandry and once lost affected not only the bullocks that depended on the roots but also the future corn crops through lack of manure and trampling.

Marshall added that the same pest had stripped the fields about 20 years before but in other years no attacks occurred. His enquiries had discovered that fishermen had seen 'cloud-like flights' of yellow flies being blown in from the sea onto the east coast. After lying 'so thick and so languid that they might have been collected into heaps' they flew off inland and were seen amongst the plants. Ten days later young caterpillars were first seen on the underside of the turnip leaves and within 7 days the plants were stripped completely. The roads were 'covered with caterpillars travelling in quest of a fresh supply' and the centre of the county had been affected as much as the eastern part.

Bryant was keen to offer advice to farmers to avoid a repeat of the 1782 disaster and in July 1783 *The Norfolk Chronicle* published his letter in full:

> The time is now at hand in which you ought to expect another visit from the turnip fly, the same which committed such devastations in your fields last year, and very probably they will be as numerous in this. You ought, therefore, to watch their approach, and to take the best methods you can to destroy them, which will be easiest done in their caterpillar state. At their first coming the caterpillars will be very small, green, and nearly the colour of the leaves; their bodies will be quite transparent, very tender, and ... therefore the smallest pressure upon them would put an end to their being. In which case I need not suggest to you the use of the roll slowly passing over them; but it is to be feared you will very seldom have an opportunity of putting this method into practice, because the eggs from which they proceed are deposited in parcels, at different periods of time, from the same flies, and, consequently, there will be a succession of broods, so that you will see black and green caterpillars frequently together upon the same plant.
>
> Those which have turned black have gained too great a degree of firmness to be much affected by the roll, and, therefore, your best way then will be to employ children and women to collect them - Ducks cannot always be had, and if they could, they would be of little use to you; for however greedily they might devour them at first, they would soon grow sick of their diet, and would ramble in search of water and a change of food, and while the keeper is engaged in running after one straggler, he may loose two others for it; and, perhaps, at the close of the day, might have done you as much good with his own fingers as they had done with all their mouths put together.
>
> But if it should happen that you cannot, by any means, prevent your turnips from being devoured close to their crowns, never plough them up; for last year's experience is sufficient to convince you that they will throw out fresh leaves again, and become a better crop than any you can get upon a second sowing.

Although the farmers would have smiled at the idea of trying to keep ducks to stay put while eating the intruders, they may have found his closing optimism helpful. Although Henry also applied his energy to the problem of the wheat disease, brand, and even published a shilling pamphlet the same summer against treating the seed before sowing, his ideas on that issue did not meet with general agreement. He did however leave a beautifully vivid description of the strange weather in the last week of June 1783, that Itteringham villagers would have experienced:

> [For seven days] there was an uncommon gloom in the air, with a dead calm - the sun was scarce visible even at mid-day, and then entirely shorn of its beams; so as to be viewed with the naked eye without pain ... on the 29th about seven o'clock in the evening, this gloom began to disperse, by a few bright clouds from the west, and in some places it fell in drops, like a small shower of rain; since which time the sun has assumed in wonted splendour

Little did he realise he had witnessed the worst volcanic eruption for centuries - Laki in Iceland - which changed global weather patterns. New Jersey had the largest snowfall ever known and toxic clouds of debris blotted out the sun over Europe, creating havoc with harvests that year.

1703 June 23 Norwich inundated as River Wensum flooded.

1703 November 26 The Great Storm, the worst ever known, lasted 4 days. People afraid to go to bed; steeples and windmills lost. Afterwards price of tiles trebled.

1704 January 19 Guestwick pastor preached after the most dreadful storm both by sea and land the like not known in the memory of man: A great many killed on land by the fall of houses and chimneys but many more destroyed at sea.

1706 December 7 Bad flood in Norwich.

1708 Very cold winter.

1715 Very cold winter.

1720 'these two last dry summers have impoverished' Southrepps/Blickling.

1732 June 21 Calthorpe had hailstones of about 3 inches; thunder and rain but fine weather then for haymaking.

1734 December 31 The worst flood in Norwich since 1696.

1735 February 15 Cley flooded by storm at high tide destroying 80 acres of wheat in the marshes.

1737 January 17 Very cold.

1737 January terrible storm - Ness writes anxiously in a letter about ships lost at sea.

1737 October 4-10 Rain fell at Norwich almost continually for 6 days causing floods and bridges lost.

1739 December 24 Huge gale; 16 ships lost with all hands.

1739-40 Severe frost from December 25 to February 26. March was cold, April wet, with snow on 20th; combination of all this destroyed the Turnips 'in open parts of Norfolk'. However the Norfolk winter corn was plentiful - that year Norfolk was granary of England when other places suffered, but furze and ling were badly affected. By 1744 there was little to be seen.

1740 January 16 Coldest day ever known (worse than 1708, 1715) followed by major thaw flood.

1741 September 8 Huge storm of wind and rain damaged church spires, chimneys and trees at King's Lynn.

1755 November 1 Lisbon earthquake felt in Norfolk - fish thrown out of ponds and died.

1756 January 10 Earthquake felt in Norwich.

1759 June 21 Violent hail at Norwich 2 inches long.

1762 October 27 Norwich flooded out - 2ft in 24 hours. 8 churches and 300 houses affected.

1763 December 2 High wind at high tide wrecked ships at King's Lynn and drowned marshland sheep - second year running.

1767 May 31 Tremendous storm caused injuries and damage around Norwich.

1768 August 11 Major storm in Norwich a boy killed by lightning.

1770 November 19 Norwich flooded, 4 inches deeper than '62.

1770 December 19-20 Major storm for 2 days; trees blocked roads; windows and lead roofs smashed; mills and ships lost with 32 dead at Happisburgh.

1772 June 2 Huge tempest, lightning strikes killed dog in Norwich pub.

1772 June 21 Storm and lightning at King's Lynn flooded roads and hit church.

1772 July 26 Storms at Norwich, more churches damaged and another dog struck.

1772 October 26 Violent storm at Blakeney; 4 inch hailstones smashed many of the windows.

1773 April 29 Violent hail at Horstead, thunder and snow in Norwich.

1773 August 20 Three-hour storm at Norwich; carrier at Dereham trampled by his startled horses.

1774 June 17 Thunderstorm in Norwich.

1774 November 25 Major storm along coast: most severe wind for 30 years. Many ships lost.

1775 November 13 Huge storm over the county lasted 20 hours; fireball split Happisburgh steeple.

1776 January 13 Norfolk had snowdrifts up to 12ft; worst winter since 1740.

1776 February 26-28 Major storm for two days 30 ships lost off Great Yarmouth.

1779 January 1 Flood at King's Lynn and terrible windstorm blew down 12 buildings at Coltishall.

1780 June 3 Major thunder storm at Norwich shook houses.

1782 September 20 Violent storm off Blakeney coast at night killed many sailors.

1784 July 7 Flooding in Norwich followed tempest of lightning; house at Bramerton hit.

1784 August 24 Strong winds blew down a steeple in Norwich.

1787 August 9 Severe lightning and thunder storm in Norwich lasted for 4 hours at night.

1791 February 2 High tide took part of Great Yarmouth jetty.

1791 December 27 High tide breached sea defences from Winterton to Great Yarmouth.

1794 August 25 Violent thunderstorm at King's Lynn killed an 8 year-old girl.

1794 November 6 Heavy rainfall flooded Wensum at Norwich; rowing boats in the streets.

1795 February 7 Huge flood 6-8 ft deep in Norwich from melting snow.

1795 November 5 High wind across county; several mills lost sails or were quite blown down.

1795 November 18 Wednesday 11 o'clock at night: 3 second earthquake shock felt all over Norfolk.

1796 December Monday 5 afternoon 2 violent flashes of lightning rattling thunder and heavy hail storm. 'Air completely impregnated with the electrical fluid that it appeared on fire' - amazingly no 'mischief' was done.

**As if a farmer's life wasn't hard enough: 18th century weather**

## Sources

NRO: See the 1792 lease renewal for 54 years for £10 rent pa of Doughty's Hospital land in Calthorpe, from the Corporation to Walpole WAL 291, 272x2; WAL 372, 273x2; WAL 622, 276x5; WAL 1166, 287x1; WAL 1442, 290x3; WAL 1443, 290x3; WAL 1444, 290x3; MC 259/37/1-2, 712x3; FX 257/1; NRS 26217A, 143x5; COL 5/20

TNA: E 134/27Chas2/Mich19; E 134/36&37Chas2/Hil23

Wolterton archive: 3/1/1, 2, 3; 3/4/1; 3/5/1, 4; 4/1, 3, 4; 8/8, 9, 20, 24, 40, 42, 45

E Griffiths & M Overton, *Farming to Halves*, 2009; John Broad, 'Cattle Plague in Eighteenth-Century England', *Agricultural History Review*, 1983

NSRI, *Cranfield University* soil reports

Weather table based on Pamela Brooks, *The Norfolk Almanack of Disasters*, 2007, with additional entries from Norfolk newspapers. P*hilosophical.Transactions of The Royal Society London*, 1783 73, p 217-222

# Chapter 6

## *Estate Farms in Itteringham*

---

*Farms were the lifeblood of the parish, providing employment both for villagers and hired labourers. For most of the 18ᵗʰ century, the largest of the farms were owned by the Walpole and Blickling estates.*

## Mannington estate

The estate was wholly in established tenant farms.

### *Mannington Hall, home farm and Hall farm*

As we have seen in Chapter 2, after Walpole's purchase, Mannington Hall itself became a working farmer's home. The farm, Hall, gardens and avenue walks in the parkland carried a small premium on the rent, even though the Hall was not in great condition. The tenants were not at all grand – as the steward had hoped the 'industrious' Coplands did sign up to take on the Hall and extended farm. George Copland played his part as churchwarden and overseer in the village as was expected of most of the working farmers. In the early 1750s the Coplands were briefly succeeded by Robert Woods of Plumstead about whom little is known. Perhaps he had followed Hammond Farrer as the tenant of the old Plumstead Hall. Then in 1754 Thomas Oakes was promoted from Mannington's Hall farm, where he had obviously proved to be a capable farmer and reliable rent payer, to take on Mannington Hall itself and the home farm. The Oakes family had roots in the Cromer and Sheringham area where the family had business as well as farming connections. It seems that they were much more like the ideal tenants that Walpole envisaged for his larger farms and Oakes senior was fairly early on rewarded with more land near Mossymere. He lived in the Hall until his death in 1779, followed by his eldest son, Thomas. After the latter's death in 1809 his widow remained in residence for a few years.

In 1755 the favoured Thomas Partridge from Wolterton took over from Oakes at Mannington Hall farm at the rent of £100. By adding this to his nearby Wolterton land rented at £64 10s, another large farm had been created. The Partridge family were to stay in Mannington Hall farm for many years: William Partridge (b 1733) took over from 1763 after his father was again promoted to the major farm at the old Wickmere Hall and his elder brother Francis Partridge from 1765. Richard Robins 4 of Itteringham Hall leased it briefly from 1780, followed by his brother-in-law John Leeds who farmed there from 1783 until about 1802. Both the latter described themselves as of Wolterton, reflecting the core site of the farm.

### *Mannington Mere farm*

The Mere farm was already a significant tenant farm by 1595, with good arable land as well as access to the Mannington heath sheep walks. William Ryall was tenant here in 1682, presumably until his death in 1687. In his will he made his brother-in-law Robert Jackson senior one of his supervisors; the other was Clement Ives of Little Barningham whose son James Ives 'yeoman of Mannington' probably had Mere farm until his death in 1692. Ryall's will is unremarkable, except that a daughter, Anne, was to have two leather chairs, perhaps an indication of some comfort in the Ryall home at Mere farm. Ives was followed in the farm by John Farmer who was also linked to the Jacksons – his daughter Susan had married Thomas Jackson, another of Robert senior's sons. In his 1708 will John Farmer (possibly the second generation of this family in Mannington) made his son-in-law Matthew Digby his executor (his own son John died the same year). Digby and Anne Farmer had married in Edgefield in 1692. As executor, Digby probably took over the remainder of Farmer's lease until Michaelmas 1710. The next lessee William Daniel was there until at least 1726 and probably until close to his death in 1732 by when he was a yeoman of Matlaske. This would fit well with a 21 year lease from autumn 1710. John Willamott junior was tenant in both 1737 and 1742. Before him a short tenancy was held by Mr James Bartram who appeared in the 1734 poll list as resident in Mannington with property in Southrepps. By 1745 Hammond Farrer was paying the rent of £111 at Mere farm. He held Mere farm until 1758 – presumably on a 14 year lease. In 1759 Thomas Plaford senior, the carpenter from Itteringham, took on the lease which by then was set marginally higher at £117.

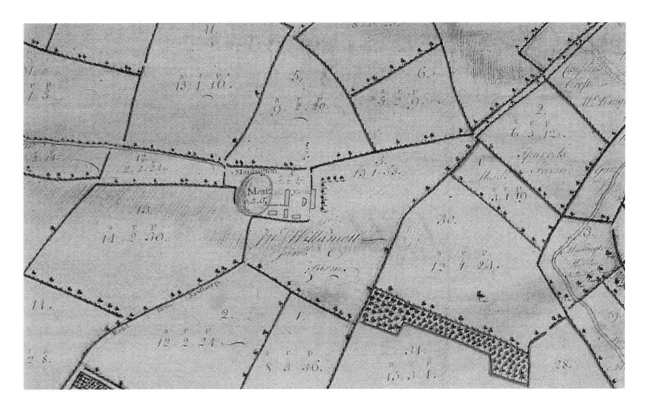

Mannington Mere farm of John Willamott junior in 1742

The Plafords were long-term tenants in Mere farm: Thomas senior died in 1789 followed by John one of his younger sons and his widow Elizabeth was there in 1800. Along the way the family had also leased for another son, Stephen Plaford, a modest acreage of land around Mossymere Wood.

### Mossymere

On the 1595 map a tiny cottage can just be made out at the site of what later became the keeper's cottage, now Mossymere House. Distant from Mannington Hall (actually in Itteringham parish) and out amongst the sheep walks, this was probably originally a shepherd's cottage. It may well have been the home of Henry Kensey of Itteringham who died in 1630 owning a significant flock of his own sheep. He had 125 ewes and hogs, 74 wethers and '10 of the worst sort of sheep', altogether valued at £65. As this was his own flock, it may be assumed that the estate flock was considerably larger. His personal goods in his great chest were only worth about £10, most notable for '7 old knives in their old sleeves and an old rapier' – defence against poachers or sheep stealers perhaps in this lonely spot.

At that time the area was far more open with the woods smaller in extent than they became under the shooting-oriented Horatio Walpole. The 1729 plan of the farm shows that the woodland was still modest and a fair-sized farm had been created out of what had once been Mannington heath and sheep closes. On part of the farm, in 1738, Walpole still paid an old due of 13s 4d for a year's 'herbage' - the right to graze animals - to the vicar of Saxthorpe, Cornelius Harrison. No doubt the land was of poor quality for arable (two marl pits are shown on the plan) and this would never have been a particularly desirable tenancy. In 1729 the tenant was Benjamin Bennington. Even though they were 'of Itteringham', he and his wife Jane baptised their children in Saxthorpe church in the following two years. In 1737 William and Henry Kendall were there. The Kendalls, probably originally of the Edgefield Kendall family, had been in Itteringham for some time – in October 1714 William Kendall of Itteringham married Mary Fish of Briston. She may well have been related to the Fish family later to run the village shop. By 1742 Edward Edwards held the Mossymere farm but as the woodland increased in size and was kept in-hand by Walpole for shooting, so the importance of this farm diminished. By 1751 Edward Edwards had gone and the farm was all in Walpole's use. The following year the expenses allowed against this farm included £2 for William Kendall's rent – presumably the old tenant still lived in a cottage there (perhaps as a gamekeeper's assistant). In 1761 twenty-eight acres of the old Mossymere farm - referred to as 'late Stagg' - were added to Thomas Oakes's holding at the Mannington Hall home farm and his rent was increased by £14. Mossymere now comprised woods held in-hand and a keeper's cottage and barn with about 15 acres on 'keeper's hill'. John Lylestone, Walpole's gamekeeper, and his successor Thomas Nelson and his family of six, may well have lived, rent-free, in the cottage in the 1750s and 1760s. Wood farm and the remaining Mossymere lands were farmed by Robert Breese between 1758 and 1772.

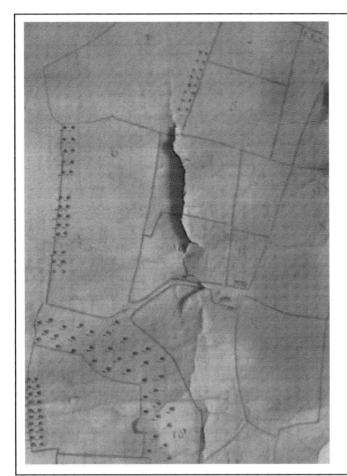

A section of the 1729 map of the Bennington farm at Mossymere, the site of Mossymere House.

The fields were closes created from Mannington heath and the amount of woodland was modest prior to Walpole's plantings.

The barn was taken down in 1776.

## Mossymere farm

In April 1771 Walpole paid over £18 to Edmund Christmas for major tree planting works at Mossymere which included 440 ash trees in the 'seven acres at Mossimer', 147 oak and 535 scotch firs. In neighbouring Fox Borough and Poplar Meadow another 660 oaks, firs and ash were added. As the barn was no longer needed, the steward in 1776 was instructed to 'take down the old barn ... and rebuild [it] at Wolterton'. By 1779 Sebastian Daniel the estate gamekeeper appears in the list of tenants; now paying £6 rent he almost certainly had the cottage here together with the small area of land around it. 'Sib' as he was often called had been living in Itteringham at least from 1771 when he and his wife Elizabeth baptised their baby Elizabeth. As he had been employed as the gamekeeper since 1775 they had probably lived in the cottage for most of the decade. We will meet Sib again in the chapter on poaching.

The year 1779 marked the start of another significant increase in the amount of woodland here reflecting the growing importance of Wolterton as a shooting estate. Oakes lost the extra 28 acres he gained earlier (at least for about ten years) and Mannington's Wood farm, on the Saxthorpe boundary, was also reduced in scale to increase the woodland at Mossymere. Stephen Plaford, who followed Robert Breese as tenant there, saw his rent fall from £40 to £20 in the 1780s. When Stephen died in 1787, the remaining land of Wood farm was taken in to Mere farm by his brother John Plaford the following year.

Sib died in March 1784 and the cottage would have been needed for the next keeper. The following summer his widow Elizabeth Daniel married a Corpusty widower, Minns Stagg, possibly related to the previous tenant of part of Mossymere. The couple stayed in Corpusty where Minns died in 1828. The Keeper's Cottage, on the edge of the woods, remained a working cottage until the 20th century.

Mossymere cottages mid-20th century


## Old Rectory and Larwood's Messuage (1)

The house now known, and described here, as the Old Rectory and the lands around it seems to be a very old homestead. It has even been suggested the village may have originally been based here although there is no good evidence to support the idea. However the site was probably a long-standing part of the Mannington estate and there may have been a small hall here in the medieval period. In 1595 the house, shown as the second largest after Mannington Hall, had been the home of John Potts, the estate's new owner, before he and his wife took over the Hall. In the 17th century it seems to have been let as a high status home without significant farm lands. Alongside the main house in 1595 was Larwood's messuage – a smaller, but potentially equally old, hall house set in the meadow next to the churchyard and not at this time a Mannington property. It is probable that this was the house in the 3-acre meadow named Graver's Close which by 1639 was leased by Thomas Skinner, farmer at Hill farm. John Thorn was the tenant in 1693 and in between it had been occupied for a time by John Bullemur.

In 1639, thirty-three acres in five named fields just to the north of the house were leased to Thomas Jackson the rector. Jackson probably lived for most of his time in Wolterton, of which he was also rector and where there was a good-sized parsonage house. By the 1660s Daniel Muddiclift the long serving steward of Sir John Potts almost certainly lived in the old Potts house. However the Jacksons remained connected to the property. As we have seen, the rector's son and grandson, Robert senior and junior were farming at Hill farm. Robert Jackson junior was also paying £53 rent for Itteringham Old Rectory. If the main house was still let (or sublet) separately Jackson may have lived in the adjoining Larwood's messuage. By 1737 Cornelius Graver had taken over this farm from the widow Jackson. (The Gravers had not remained in the village much after 1600 so the name appears to be co-incidental.)

Widow Jackson was Mary the wife of Robert Jackson junior. He and his father had died within a year of each other in 1716-17 and had been predeceased by Robert senior's wife Mary Ryall, of the Mere farm family, in 1711. Cornelius Graver was still Walpole's tenant of The Old Rectory in 1742. The estate map has his name written around the smaller Larwood's house but the size of the rental confirms that he leased the whole site and its farm lands. Larwood's - which gradually reduced in size - may have continued in occupation throughout the 18th century as a cottage tied to Old Rectory farm. By 1823 the premises were used only as outbuildings.

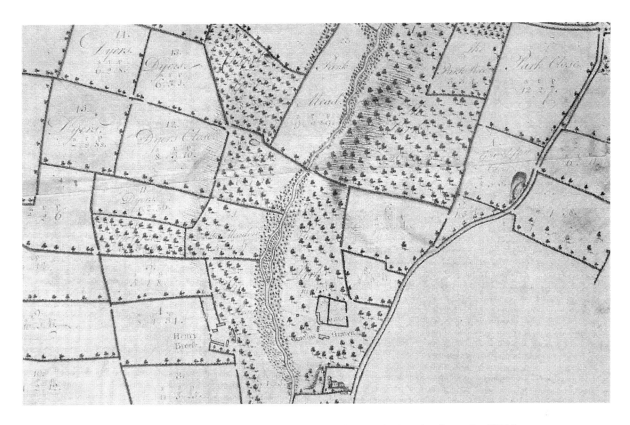

Cornelius Graver & Henry Breese's farms in Itteringham in 1742

In 1742 the site of the Old Rectory and garden was surrounded by tree covered park land, indicating that it probably still had some status. It was however now a farm. To the north and east, the fields that straddled the Barningham Road included Gravel Pit Close – a dip in the field level marks the spot of what was once a substantial pit. Graver's farm also crossed the Cut and included Dier's meadow and a large part of Dier's closes on the site of the old West Field of Itteringham. There is no sign on the 1742 map of the small water mill on the Cut that had been adjacent to this site in 1595. However, the mill dam certainly survived as at very least a decorative feature or fish pond. Remains of the sluices are still there today. Like most of the tenant farmers, Cornelius, although illiterate, seems to have been expected to serve as overseer of the poor. He was elected for 1737 and 1742 and the next tenant John Thirtle was chosen for 1746, 1750 and 1754. Under Thirtle's tenancy this farm and the West Field farm to the south and west were combined. In 1752 the accounts show significant sums spent on improvements to the farm buildings in the Old Rectory yard. He and his son John were there for many years and in 1789 they built, at Walpole's expense, the new south-facing wing of the house, with its view of the church. Yet again this showed that, for no increase in rent, the landlord was prepared to improve the lot of his good tenants to keep them in place.

The Old Rectory – the 1789 wing

Rather surprisingly then, the tenancy changed the very next year to Thomas Dix, who held it until 1798. Dix was a farmer from Oulton and trustee for the meeting house there. He also stood as overseer for Itteringham in 1790 and 1794. In 1798 the Old Rectory was taken for one year only by John Beane, who then moved to a farm in Wickmere. By 1800 John Jarvis was in residence in the Old Rectory and still held the 218 acre farm in 1809. The house and farmyard on its eastern side remained a tenant farm until 1857. The new rector Peter Elwin had complained that there was no suitable house for him, the only property belonging to the living being the small cottage in the centre of the village, Glebe Cottage (now the much larger Glebe House). Walpole's house, being so near the church, was far more suitable (with a little modification) and he and the Church Commissioners exchanged houses and land. Only at this point did the old Potts house become the rectory. No mention was made of where the sitting tenant James Burrell was to go! The house was used as a rectory until 1969 when the new Rectory was built on the south side of the church and the Old Rectory became a private house.

## West Field farm or Dier's (2)

The tenant farm then known as Dier's, just across the Cut opposite Itteringham church, was already well established by 1595. It had been created from what once had been Itteringham's west field – an open field farmed in strips which had been enclosed probably in the 1540s when its tenants were moved to the main field of Itteringham and Wolterton. The name West Field farm has been coined here for convenience. The tenant in 1595 is unknown, but in 1639 this 76 acre farm was held by John Jolly (sometimes Jolle or even Gelley). Jolly was probably followed directly by Robert Jackson senior (who held it in addition to Hill farm) and he, by the mid-1690s, by William Davy.

A fairly small farm with its meadows by the Cut and probably arable in the mid-slope fields towards Mossymere, it lay next to the lands of Bintry farm, which was run in conjunction with the village tannery. In 1710 Robert Rose, the tanner held West Field as well as Bintry's farm land. This arrangement was continued by William Bayly, tanner, in 1721 and 1726. By 1737 however, Henry Breese was tenant of just West Field. Henry was one of the large Breese family originally from the Kerdiston area. (The next year Robert Breese, probably his son, took over at Wood farm on the Saxthorpe boundary.) Henry stayed in the farm for four years until his death in 1741 during which he stood as parish overseer twice. The house is still named for him on the 1742 map. His widow Sarah was buried in Itteringham in 1755. There seems to have been a short period with Thomas Hannant put in as temporary tenant, but he was not given a long-term lease. That was given to John Thirtle in about 1743 who clearly proved to be a good tenant. As we have seen, he soon took over Graver's farm as well and moved into Itteringham Old Rectory. Dier's farmstead continued as cottages and a yard well into the 19th century, but the focus of the farm shifted to the Old Rectory site. It is important not to confuse the old west field farm with the present day Robin farm and the remains of brick farm buildings nearby. The two sites are entirely different and Robin farm was a much later addition to the landscape.

## Elmerdale farm, Irmingland

Although not in Itteringham, this is included here for several reasons. Firstly it was the largest farm on the Mannington estate and had been a favourite holding of the Potts family. Secondly its tenants were deeply intertwined with the Bell family and the Oulton Meeting House. Thirdly early architectural features mirror a cottage in Itteringham.

Most of this large farm - in the past called Elmingdale or Elmendale (for elmen meaning of elms) - on either side of the Holt road in Irmingland had been bought by John Potts from the Bettes family in the 1590s. It had been extended via a small purchase of meadow from the Bells of Oulton. The Potts purchase was sometimes described as 260 acres and later as 290 acres, but close analysis of all the old document references shows that the actual total area was always the 305-310 acres confirmed in later surveys for estate maps in 1729 and 1809. For much of the 17th century it was divided into two farms – one of about 240 acres on the east and north side of the Holt road and the other of about 65 acres on the Oulton side. The smaller farm included a house and dovehouse near the site of the old parish church of Irmingland. This was almost certainly the site of the old manor of Whitefoot's. The church fell into ruin during the 16th century and the farm and dovehouse was demolished in the early 1660s. For many years the lands were leased by the Bell family of Oulton and were probably largely grazing land for cattle of the butcher William Bell who died in 1687.

At some point all the acreage was put into the single farm of Elmerdale which now had the only house at this end of the parish. This farm was of particular importance to Roger Potts, the future baronet; in 1662 his grandfather Sir John had entrusted the young man, then in his early twenties, with it to help him to learn how to manage an estate. Elmerdale is one of the relatively few local houses which can demonstrate its old timber framed construction hidden away behind the brick facade. The fine ceiling beams have been dated tentatively to the first half of the 17th century from the decorative chamfer stops; however similar chamfering has been interpreted elsewhere as more likely to be 1660s-1670s. Interestingly, the main beam in 100 The Street in Itteringham has exactly the same chamfer stops and may well have been crafted by the same carpenter at much the same time. This suggests the village went through a period of general upgrading of old properties in about the 1660s and 1670s.

Elmerdale farm (left) and 100 The Street chamfer stops

Elmerdale tenants in the 17th century included Edmund Bell in 1639, Richard King in the 1660s (he had married a second wife Mary Smith of Itteringham who as 'widow King' leased Love's messuage in Itteringham to Richard Robins) and Richard Sexton in 1676. Both King and Sexton were favoured Potts' tenants for whom Roger might have enhanced the status of the farmhouse. In 1697 Daniel Abell, previously a butcher in Itteringham came into the farm when Sir Roger sold off the Wolterton closes farmland which Daniel had been leasing from him. Abell was buried in Itteringham in 1701 as 'of Irmingland'.

Thomas Dewing maltster of Oulton, who was listed as the tenant between 1710 and 1721, may have taken over after Abell's death. In 1723 his daughter Mary 'Dewen' of Irmingland married John Bell of Green farm Oulton. She baptised her only son John Bell at Elmerdale just after his father's sudden death in 1724. At the end of his life John would live in Itteringham as the tenant of the Thomas Robins manor house (see Chapter 9). In 1729, when Elmerdale was mapped by James Corbridge, the farm's tenant was shown as 'Late Duen'. Thomas Dewing died early in 1734 but the map implies he had relinquished the farm a few years earlier. By this time the farm size was up to 311 acres, then slightly larger than Mannington Hall's home farm. As will be seen a cottage property in Itteringham was bought by his son Thomas Dewing a grocer and merchant of Cawston.

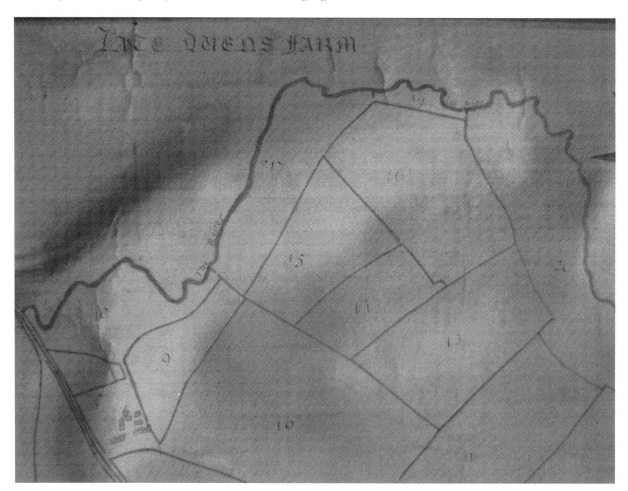

A section of the Elmerdale farm map of 1729 showing the fields near the farmstead

Elmerdale field names in 1729 included: the evocatively named Deadman's Hill - running up the west side of the Holt road; Marlpit 18 acres - showing large pits where St Andrew Spinney is today; Chapel yards - including the site of the ruined church of St Andrew near Spa Lane; Spa meadow - beside Copping's beck running from Oulton spa towards the Bure near the Meeting House; Drum Close - a large meadow and arable close alongside the beck to the north of the Holt road, possibly named for the distinctive drumming sound of mating snipe; Whinn Hill - up behind the farm house and buildings and obviously poor quality upper slope land; Bridge meadow - by the main road; Old Bridge meadow - with the site of the 'old bridge' over the Bure marked at the same spot where there is a crossing today at the northern end of the quarries/fishponds; Sluice Close - the meadow between the 2 bridges, perhaps implying some sort of small scale milling or water meadow management perhaps relating to the now disappeared Lake farm on the north side of the Bure here.

It seems that in about 1729 or 1730 Simon Starling took over the farm. He and his first wife Elizabeth baptised a child in Saxthorpe in 1739 but Elizabeth must have died in or soon after childbirth. He soon married again to Martha who may have pushed for improvements at her new home. The Wolterton accounts show that in October 1740 the 'dairy house and backhouse' were pulled down and in February 1741 plastering work on site indicates that rebuilding or improvements to residential buildings were done for the Starling family. Perhaps this was the point when the house was first connected to the building close to it, as shown in later ground plans of the farm yard and the present shape of the house. Simon died unexpectedly in 1741 and without a will. Administration was granted to Martha his widow and Francis Read a yeoman of Tunstead, perhaps her father or brother. Martha continued to run the farm for some years. In late 1743 and early 1744 major carpentry work was done on two new estate barns, one of which was described as 'the Elmerdale barn'. This seems likely to date the construction of the large single barn as a replacement for the one or two smaller ones on the 1729 plan.

In 1746 Richard Ness witnessed an assignment in trust of Thomas and William Bell of Oulton to Peter Elwin esq of Booton to ensure the education of Simon and Martha's children. Martha's link to the Bell and Elwin families is not clear. By this time she had remarried and her husband Thomas Kyball ran the farm. However, he was replaced in 1747 by William Loads, of an Itteringham family. In 1752 Loads threatened to leave the farm unless his rent, inherited from Kyball, of £140 was reduced. In October 1752 Ness wrote to Walpole regarding Loads the tenant in 'Elmendale' farm. Loads had told Ness he planned to leave at next Michaelmas if he could find a farm he liked better. If he stayed, he expected a rent abatement of £5 and to have one end of the new barn converted into a stable and hay house. He also wanted an allowance for firings. Ness had warned Loads that Walpole would not agree and he now told Walpole that he would soon have to start looking for another tenant. He was obviously reluctant to do so, since although Loads was 'an obstinate man' he was a 'good tenant but a dissatisfied one'. On 19th October Walpole wrote from his house in Putney directly to Mr Loads castigating him for not being decisive with Ness over the lease renewal. He said that he would not be trifled with and would not change the lease terms or rent if Loads did renew. The tactic did the trick; as a result Loads renewed the lease with a reduction in rent to £125! He held it until his burial in Itteringham in July 1768 when, as 'William Loades of Elmendale House yeoman', he left his personal estate to his wife Ann (a local Sendall girl) to bring up their young children. One of his executors and a guardian of his children was Francis Partridge of Wolterton, then the tenant of Mannington Hall farm.

In 1769 Thomas Bulwer, gentleman, took over at much the same rent of £130, showing how important it was to the landlords of these big estates to attract good tenants even if the rent did not increase substantially. In 1790 Thomas Bulwer was still the farmer at Elmerdale, when he was also a trustee of Oulton Meeting House. In 1798 his rent was increased to £145 and two years later it was noted in the accounts that he had gone. He died in 1802. As noted in the previous chapter, William Mack of Tunstead negotiated a new 11 year lease for Elmerdale in 1802. He and his wife baptised several children in Itteringham in the following few years. But by 1809 his brother James held the lease. At the end of the lease John Middleton took over, having been promoted from a smaller farm at Fring Wood. It is possible that the brick facing on the front of Elmerdale house, its distinctively large downstairs front windows and other improvements were made to the property at around this time. Middleton would no doubt have had some ability to secure improvements as a favoured tenant being promoted. Much later the farm would be used to house the bailiff or agent for Irmingland Hall.

## Wolterton estate

The estate had farms across several parishes including its own home farm, the old Wickmere Hall and property in Calthorpe and Thwaite. Coverage is here restricted to Walpole's interests in Itteringham.

### Meadow House (7)

Meadow House now sits in a large garden in the middle of the village but this originally was part of a small farm with a working farmyard that had belonged to the Bell family of Oulton. It was a modest estate constructed in the late 16th and early 17th centuries from the purchases of Jarvis and Langdon properties, with a few additional pieces from the Mannington estate. Identified from the 1595 map, most of the land lay in the fields between the two roads leading out of the village and in the open field. Some was further to the east near the Calthorpe parish boundary. Meadow House itself was the house of William Jarvis gent in 1595 and in 1602 he sold it to Nicholas Bell of Oulton (d 1612). At least as far back as 1696 the land was split into two farms, with both tenants apparently living onsite.

By the 1730s John Bell, the great-nephew of Richard Bell Itteringham's first grocer, was in financial difficulties and he mortgaged the property to Peter Thompson. As we have seen John and his wife Alice did not live locally and the two parts were let to John Dix and John Parker by 1734. In 1744 Bell sold their 96 acres of Itteringham land to Horatio Walpole. The tenants in 1744 were John Copeman in the larger 50 acre farm with the main house and yard, and Thomas Hannant in the 46 acre farm.

It is unclear if Thomas Hannant had his own farm buildings or what mix of lands he had. It seems some of his land near Wolterton lake was quite quickly taken in-hand to be incorporated into Wolterton park, leaving Hannant with a very modest holding. He never appeared as a tenant in the accounts and effectively he was probably simply a lodger in Copeman's farm yard. It is likely that a large proportion of the Bell lands was in the open field area and would have been exchanged to Thomas Robins in his drive to consolidate the open field. In any event this smallholding was absorbed into larger farms and did not survive as a farm entity.

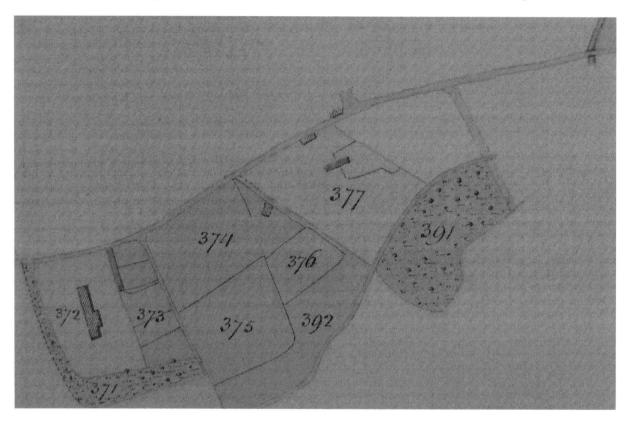

The Church, Church Row, Meadow House (centre) & Glebe Cottage in 1809

Soon after the 1744 purchase, Walpole and Ness ran into trouble with John Copeman, the more significant of the two tenants. A Francis Cobeman or Copeman (the name appears in many guises with variations on the hard syllable, including Cokeman, Coeman and Cobourn) had been tenant of the farm in 1696. In June 1688 he married Margaret Dyball in Norwich and they baptised Stephen in Itteringham in September 1690. In June 1715 Stephen 'Cobeman' baptised a son John, who it seems became the tenant of the farm by 1744. There seems to be no connection between this family and the Mary Copeman who was cook and housekeeper at Wolterton Hall for many years in the 1730s and 1740s. John Copeman, despite also being in business as a small scale local carrier as a young man and continuing this as a sideline, had clearly got into financial difficulties. Before the sale, he had been saved from debtor's prison by William Robins of Itteringham Hall who had bought out his debt from Bell. He was now also in arrears of rent due to Walpole. Richard Ness and Horatio Walpole corresponded about the situation, but were taken by surprise by Robins's rapid action.

Ness wrote to Walpole on 15th January 1746:

> Honoured Sir, yesterday I was informed that William Robins your honour's neighbour had got a bill of sale of John Copeman your tenant's goods and stock and that he had in part put it into execution. I went to Mr Robins to know the truth and he told me that he had a bill of sale which he took of Mr Copeman in July last for John Bell the person your honour bought the estate [from, who] arrested him for rent to £25 which Mr Robins paid for him otherwise he must have gone to jail. Then I told Mr Robins that

I must seize immediately on Copeman to secure your honour if he proceeded to put his bill of sale in force. They both came to me this morning and begged that I would write to you to desire that Copeman may continue until Michaelmas next and Mr Robins will forbear him until then and they both seemed confident that there will be enough to pay both Mr Robins and your honour and he will then sell off his stock and surrender up the farm to your honour. His lease expires at Michaelmas 1749.

Your honour will please to give me orders whether you are willing to forbear him or that I must seize on him now and take the farm into your own hands until Michaelmas next or until I can dispose of it.

This showed at least a brief period of good neighbourly behaviour all round. There was a prospect that the value of Copeman's stock plus his crops in the ground would be sufficient to pay the approximately two years' of rent he owed. Walpole's reply in a letter on 18th January was brief – such were his priorities, he wrote more at length about the work on the park palings that Thomas Plaford (or Playford) the carpenter was doing for him:

I am very unwilling to distress a poor tenant and therefore if Mr Robins will give me a note to be answerable for Copeman's rent I have no objection to his continuing in the farm. This I think Robins can make no difficulty to do if he is of the opinion that Copeman's stock and goods will be sufficient to answer both demands.

However Walpole's next letter shows that Robins and Copeman had done a deal not to Walpole's advantage. Ness obviously felt he needed to talk to Edmund Jewell the Aylsham lawyer often used by the Robins family:

I have received yours of the 22nd relating to the behaviour of Robins and Copeman and after what had passed before between you and them by which I supposed you concluded that matters should have rested as they then were until you should hear from me. And you perceived that Robins proceeded so unfairly in concert with Copeman as to lessen the debt from £25 to £15 by taking I imagine some of the effects of Copeman. I wonder you lost any time in taking the necessary measures for securing my debt by seizing the remainder of Copeman's stock or by other legal measures that might best answer that such. Without knowing the nature of the bill of sale which Robins has obtained against Copeman I can't tell whether Robins has acted legally or not but if judgement has been entered up in consequence of that bill I apprehend that I have for a year's rent the best title to Copeman's stock. You may talk to Mr Jewell in an amicable manner on this affair to know how it stands but if he has acted for Robins I would have you speak to Mr Bennett of Aylsham he is an honest sensible man.

Ness's next letter has not survived, but Robins's and Copeman's behaviour continued to upset him. Walpole's only and wry comment in his letter of 28th January was: 'I find that Robins and Copeman do nothing but amaze you and you suffer yourself to be amazed'. If that sounds like a goad to action, it was unnecessary – Ness certainly was hard at work. On 1st February he wrote:

Honoured Sir, On Wednesday last I went with Copeman ... to see what his brother would do for him, but he had no compassion on him so that on Thursday morning last I seized on him when I found there was no other remedy to secure your honour. The effects will be appraised on Monday, there will be enough and more than will pay your honour a good deal, but what his other creditors will do with him I cannot tell. I must take the land into your own use, and the house I do not know how to get him out of but I think as he desires to live in it until Michaelmas next I must let him live in it until then at a rent to be agreed upon.

On 4th February Walpole wrote positively to Ness:

I approve what you have done relating to Copeman. I have no objection to his living in the house at a certain rent till Michaelmas if you don't want it although I don't see how he will be able to pay me. Does Mr Copeman's farm lie convenient to be added to Partridge's? If Partridge or any other tenant takes it perhaps the house may be suffered to fall down or taken away to use the materials for other purposes.

No doubt there are those today who are grateful that Meadow House was not pulled down! Ness answered on the 8th having taken action to settle the matter:

> As to the disposal of Copeman's farm I have had the same reflections about it as your honour mentions but it lies inconvenient for Partridge and is very dear in comparison with his own that he will not have it. ... I have let Copeman's to Thomas Playford and he is to enter thereon at Lady Day next and to pay £20 for this year and £24 (being the rent now let at) every year he has it afterwards. And Copeman is to let your honour all the muck that is in the yard which was valued at £4 for his living there until Lady Day it being his.

Those were the days when you could quite reasonably deliver a pile of cow manure to your landlord as rent!

As agreed, in September 1746 Horatio Walpole granted a full 14 year lease of the old Copeman farm to Thomas Plaford of Itteringham carpenter. Walpole was to keep all the houses and farm buildings in good repair. At the end of the lease Plaford could use the barn belonging to the premises for storing the last year's crop but Walpole could then specify what hay he wanted to be left in the cart house and hay chamber. This was a proper small farmyard at Meadow House. By 1759 Thomas Plaford senior had been promoted to Mannington Mere farm but he also continued to pay £8 per year rent for his son Thomas Plaford, also a carpenter, for the cottage and 3 acre meadow around it. The rest of the farm land disappears from view in the accounts, so was probably taken in-hand too. The Plafords retained the lease for decades and it seems were now sole occupants. Their 3 acres of meadows later became the recreation ground. The house was called The Long House in the middle of the 20th century but later renamed, very appropriately, Meadow House.

## Blickling estate

Fiddy's farm bordered the Itteringham parish boundary with just a few acres lying in Itteringham parish. His farmhouse and yard is no longer there but was shown at the southern tip of the old area of woods by the track that emerges at wood gate onto the lane to Itteringham Common. A steel cattle pen is all that there is now to mark it, but the lane leading from it in the direction of Oulton can still be made out in crop marks. Edward Vincent, who in 1729 held the fields around Blickling mill, had both Samuel Goldsmith's farm and Thomas Fiddy's few fields in Itteringham in the 1740s. In the Itteringham poor rates, by 1746 John Sendall had 'late Fiddy's' farm while Edward Vincent paid a reduced amount for his farm. William Gedge took over from Vincent and in turn in 1753 gave way to Mr Cornwall.

From Gedge onwards the 'Goldsmith' farm was combined with the old Erasmus Buck farm based at what is now Oulton Lodge on the Blickling to Holt road. In the Blickling estate survey of 1756, the farm of John Rackham, with its reference to a two (threshing) floor barn, can confidently be identified as this farm. Sold to the Earl of Buckinghamshire in the late 1740s when James Dewing was tenant, it was rapidly combined with his lands in Itteringham to create a single good-sized farm, albeit of rather modest land. Rackham 'an industrious young man' had a new lease from Michaelmas 1756 for 21 years at £95 rent. The survey described the farm as in 'Old Town' (Oulton) and Itteringham. This included all the Goldsmith pasture and meadow in Itteringham. The 120 acres in Oulton were described somewhat positively as 'middling turnip land', but the Itteringham 90 acres of arable in ten closes were described as 'a dry burning soil' – a precise description of light sandy acidic ex-heathland pasture which had not yet been properly converted to arable. But the surveyor noted approvingly 'the tenant is trying for marl or clay in Old Town and if he succeeds will make it an extraordinary good farm' – the poor soils would be much improved and for the first time able to sustain regular arable cropping. Rackham also had the 18 acres in two meadows in Itteringham. On these had stood the cottage and barn in Goldsmith's use. They were not now mentioned and must have been pulled down, probably just prior to this new tenancy once the Buck purchase had been completed. Rackham was still in the farm in 1768.

The Sendall 'Fiddy' element of the rates remained separate and in later years was always entered as paid by the Earl of Buckinghamshire not by a tenant – the old farmhouse itself had been pulled down and the land was seen as part of the park and home farm. The Blickling estate did not play a dominant part in the parish until the very close of the 18th century.

## Sources

NRO: Kensey DN/INV 36/46, 1630; WAL 333, 272x6; WAL 346-350, 273x1; WAL 374, 273x7; WAL 1166, 287x1; WAL 1470, 290x5; MC3/252,468x4; PD 434/24; FX 257/1; Wolterton 1809 estate map and survey Acc MJ Sayer 26/2/1970

Wolterton archive: 3/1/1; 3/7/7; 8/4, 53/8

Vaughan-Lewis NAHRG articles; *See You in Court* on John Potts and the 1595 map

# Chapter 7

## *Independent Farms in Itteringham*

*Three farms that sat outside the large estates were held by freeholders who never achieved the scale of their neighbours. Hill farm's acreage was never increased. The two Robins family lines created two substantial farms but the momentum of development was not sustained.*

### Hill farm (24)

Originally a small manor controlled by one of the Wolterton manors, the land to the south of Itteringham parish was once an open field that subsequently became a single tenant farm. In the 16th century it was owned by three generations of the Payne family. The second Thomas Payne, married Elizabeth Boleyn of Blickling where he was estate steward. By the early 1550s Thomas built and lived at Itteringham Hall (23), now White House farm, on a piece of land on the other side of the Bure, surrounded by the lands of Nowers manor which were in different ownership. At this time it is not clear whether there was a farmhouse of any kind on the current Hill farm site itself. The Payne family moved away around the 1590s and sold the Hall and Hill farm to Robert Houghton of Wolterton. In the early 1630s Robert Houghton determined to buy Earlham manor near Norwich which belonged to the Hemmings, a Norwich trade family. Just before the sale to Houghton they had granted a long lease on the property to a cousin Thomas Skinner. Houghton's purchase arrangement to buy Earlham reflected Skinner's interest; a combination of cash and all his lands and houses in Itteringham was handed over to the Hemming and Skinner families.

Hill farm, showing altered windows

It seems that the Hemmings probably lived for a while in Itteringham Hall while Skinner took on the farming – the whole of Hill farm and a number of copyhold strips in the main field of Itteringham. Some farm buildings at least, if not a house, would have been necessary on the site of the current Hill farm farmhouse. In due course the Hemmings moved to Hindringham and Itteringham Hall was sold to the family who owned the surrounding Nowers land (see Itteringham Hall **23**). All the farm land stayed with the Skinners through to the 1660s. If they did not live in a house on the farm, the old Larwood messuage by the Old Rectory might have been their home. Unfortunately we cannot find any firm reference to the arrangements at this period.

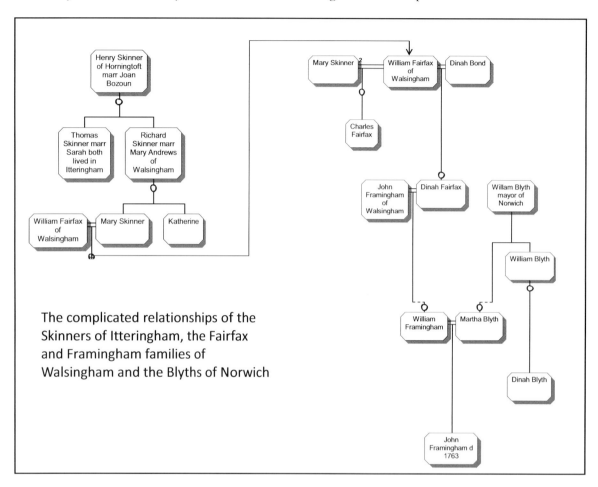

The complicated relationships of the Skinners of Itteringham, the Fairfax and Framingham families of Walsingham and the Blyths of Norwich

**Outline tree for the Skinner, Fairfax and Framingham families**

Thomas Skinner left the property to his brother Richard who in turn divided it between his wife and daughters. Only Mary married and through her the whole of Hill farm came to the Fairfax family of Hindringham and Little Walsingham. Her son Charles Fairfax seems to have conveyed it around 1703, in return for an annuity, to John Framingham. Framingham was also from Little Walsingham and had married Charles's half-sister Dinah Fairfax. The Mannington court roll records Framingham taking over the copyhold strip lands in 1704, at which time Robert Jackson senior occupied the farm as tenant. John Framingham was never resident in Itteringham, having considerable property elsewhere. Why then in 1704, as its gable end proudly states, did he build such a fine farmhouse? At this period, tenants of a mid-sized farm would not expect such a house. Perhaps the Jackson family simply took advantage of a new owner to press for an improvement in their accommodation. Perhaps Mary the wife of Robert Jackson junior was a Framingham or Fairfax? Or perhaps Framingham himself planned to use the house for a family member?

In any event the Jacksons farmed here until the deaths of both the father and son in 1716 and 1717. Whatever his plan, John Framingham the house-builder died only five years after building the house, in 1709. By Dinah Fairfax, he had had a son William. William married Martha Blyth daughter of William Blyth of Norwich, a former sheriff and mayor, in early 1715 at the Cathedral church; within two years he was dead, leaving his infant son John in the guardianship of Martha. John Framingham junior inherited the Itteringham property but remained in Walsingham and rented it out until his death in 1763.

Gable end of Hill farm 1704 John Framingham

Having no children of his own John made various generous bequests to his servants and left his extensive real estate largely to his friend and executor William Churchman of Mangreen Hall in Swardeston. Churchman was responsible for ensuring that his daughter Mary Churchman received in her own right Framingham's property in Itteringham. At the end of his will, John Framingham had a rant about his Blyth relations. His uncle William's wife Ann had obviously come between him and her daughter Dinah Blyth:

> Also my once dear cousin Miss Blyth, whom I had the tenderest affection for as a relative, I have nothing to bestow upon her but my pity, in return for that insolence and distrust her mother instructed her to treat me with. Occasionally thereby contriving a breach between me and the young lady in order that I might take an affront and refuse my friendship to the young lady in the discovery of thousands of pounds which the mother has secreted from the daughter. What an unnatural mother must that be, who not content with pillaging her own offspring herself must throw the rest of her child's fortune into the hands of an ignorant stock jobber; a man with scarce any visible estate and who is constantly spreading his ill laid nets to swallow the rest of the child's fortune.

The tenants immediately after the Jacksons are not known, but subsequently two generations of Elizabeth Blyth's family, from Horsford, rented Hill farm and worked the land. It is tempting to believe that they were related to John Framingham and his Blyth cousins. Unfortunately, despite some earlier Blyth references in Mannington, there is nothing to indicate that the Blyths in Hill farm were related to the Norwich Blyths or the Framinghams. John Blyth, a brewer and maltster, and Elizabeth Kent had several sons including Henry and Robert. When John Blyth died in 1725, for some reason his widow moved to Itteringham and took on Hill farm, either on her own or with one of her sons. She was obviously a woman of some ability as she was elected overseer of the poor three times, first in 1740, then 1745 and lastly in the winter of 1748-49 shortly before her death. Henry Blyth her son (born in Horsford, 1713) set up home in Blickling possibly working as the blacksmith's assistant, but his brother Robert may have come to Hill farm with Elizabeth. After her death (she was buried in Horsford in February

1749), Robert took over the farm. In late 1751 he married Elizabeth Colls the daughter of the miller. Although both of Itteringham the couple had a licence to marry in Edgefield church, the parish where young Benjamin Wrench was curate. Benjamin was the son of the Aylsham rector and was also curate at Itteringham at the time so would have been well-known to them. Robert acted as overseer for Itteringham for two years but in 1754 they moved away and Henry Blyth his brother took over the farm.

Henry's son Samuel was born in Blickling in 1753 immediately before the family moved into Itteringham where more children were baptised. Henry continued working at the blacksmith's forge in Blickling - probably taking over the lease after John Graver died - but obviously settled into Hill farm with his large family. One of his daughters also married in to the Colls family; another, Mary, married Edward Plane who farmed at Salle. In the family tradition Henry was overseer four times before his death in 1796. He had stepped up from being a younger son trained as a blacksmith to become a yeoman farmer renting a fine house. As was often the practice with tenants, the family had some property of their own; Henry had cottages in Blickling, Ingworth and Oulton which he left to Samuel. Samuel stayed on farming in Itteringham until his death in 1827, setting a family record of serving five times in the role of overseer.

One of the Blyth's farm men, was Robert Baxter, who was born about 1777. He was probably the son of Jonathan Baxter the owner of the short-lived Oulton windmill. Questioned when he was 55 and still in Itteringham, Baxter said he had been 'a servant in husbandry' for both Henry and Samuel Blyth and had worked on the farm for 40 years. He had heard it said that 'Squire Framingham gave Miss Churchman the estate for Pin Money'. Baxter regularly went to Mangreen Hall to carry 'game, fish and turkies from the Blyths to Miss Churchman their landlady'. He described Hill farm's fields prior to 1823 as:

Mill Pightle 4a
New 12 acres 12a
Pightle by meadow 1a 2r
Hansey Close 6a
Pithole [Pightle] Close 10a
8 acres between Pithole [Pightle] Close and Well Close 8a
Well Close 9a
Shop Pightle 5a
Barn Close 13a
9 acre close 9a
Rhen [?] Close 10a
6 acre close 6a
Poverty Ten Acres 10a
12 acres close 12a
8 acre close by the house 8a
4 acre piece across the meadow 4a
Plantation 5a
Field lands 22a
Meadow 18a
House stead yard garden 1a

During the Blyths' tenancy of Hill farm, the ownership passed from Mary Churchman at her death in 1803 to her 'old friend' Mrs Mary Moxon widow of Woodford in Essex for life. Baxter remembered he sometimes took turkeys to Mrs Moxon at Christmas when she was staying at Norwich with her mother.

The house then reverted to Mary Long of Dunston Hall, the daughter of Mary Churchman's nephew Robert Churchman Long. When the lease expired and the old tenant Samuel Blyth died in November 1826, Mary's father helped her put it up for sale. £50 an acre was thought a fair price but although Lady Suffield expressed an interest her steward Robert Copeman (the son) had made a lower offer. In December the same terms were offered to Walpole through a letter to the Reverend Robert Walpole. Obviously the Wolterton estate decided not to bid and the opportunity was missed. In 1832 Mary sold the farm house and 177 acres for £7,000 (roughly £39 10s an acre) to the Blickling estate of which it remains a part, farmed by the Fowell family who themselves can show roots in Itteringham back into the late 18th century.

## Robins family estate: Thomas Robins

The growth of the estate of the Thomas Robins line will be described more fully in the section on the blacksmith in Chapter 8. Two farms were owned by this part of the family one of which, an old Potts farm, has long gone; the other still exists although without a house.

### Daniel Robins or Purdy farm (22)

Very often properties that have long since vanished reveal the most interesting stories. This farm, which lay on the east side of the open field and butted up against the Wolterton parish boundary, we have called Purdy farm, later the Daniel Robins house, for convenience. It should not be confused with Purdy House at Wickmere (where Henry the butcher lived) nor the cottage on Wolterton green referred to earlier, although all were probably lived in by members of the same Purdy family.

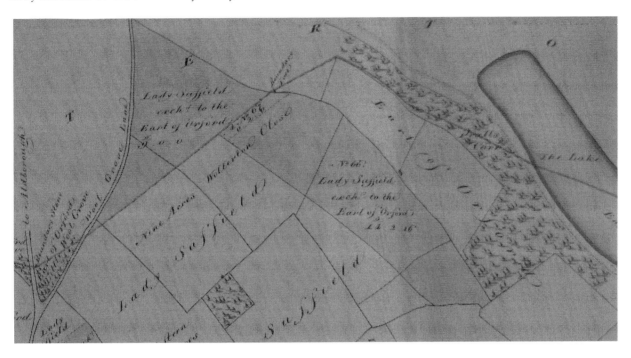

The small shed just to the east of 'No 66 Lady Suffield' on the enclosure map of 1823 marks the location of the former Daniel Robins farm

At the end of March 1696 Thomas Robins worsted weaver of Heydon paid Sir Roger Potts £570 for the farmhouse and approximately 115 acre farm in the occupation of Thomas Purdy. The large closes on which it was based are identifiable on the 1595 map, but no farmhouse was indicated and it may have simply been in-hand sheep grazing land. By 1639 it was an identifiable farm unit, then in the occupation of John Hardiman, who had it on a 7 year lease started in August 1636. By this time it would no doubt have become a mixed farm, paralleling the shift from grazing to arable in the halving lands farm. By 1665 the farm was tenanted by Urith Purdy, the widow of Bartholomew Purdy and mother of Thomas. With Purdy paying £56 rent this appears to have been a very advantageous purchase by Robins and shows how desperate for cash Potts was at this time – 20 not 10 times the rent would have been more usual (unless the land was deemed very poor quality). As Thomas of Heydon was then 82, this may have been a purchase designed to help his Itteringham cousin Thomas Robins 1. The next year, in 1697, Thomas Robins 1 of Itteringham bought a 2 acre piece of the Purdy land from his cousin for £20 to consolidate his holding in Muckle Meadow Hirne. Thomas may well have 'managed' the farm for the Heydon family. Old Thomas died in 1698 and his son William, dying childless in 1727, left it to Thomas Robins 2 of Itteringham.

In May 1726 Richard Robins 2 of Itteringham and William Robins of Heydon had exchanged some of the Purdy farm lands with Horatio Walpole. Walpole was already leasing them and had separated them from the main Robins farm by a ditch or pales; now he was able to begin consolidating his parkland near Wolterton Hall. In return the Robins family received 14 acres in four closes in Wolterton parish in the fork of the then two roads at the Stulps. With Thomas 2 inheriting his cousin's lands and thus the Purdy farm, in June 1728 he bought these 14 acres from his uncle for £250.

At some point, his uncle Daniel Robins, the youngest son of Richard Robins 1 the blacksmith, returned from Norwich with his family and took over the farm. A devout dissenter, his earlier story will be covered in the story of the meeting house; the baptism of his last son Samuel was registered in both Itteringham church and the Norwich meeting house in 1709 suggesting he may have moved at that time. Certainly by 1720 his house in Itteringham - possibly Love's messuage - was licensed for meetings to be held there. Daniel was a trustee for the marriage settlement of Thomas Robins 2 and Mary Jefferies in 1724 by which the younger Thomas gained all his father's Itteringham property. Daniel's son Samuel was the default heir to Purdy farm should Thomas Robins 2 not have children and around this time Daniel and his family moved in to run the farm. When Thomas 2 died unexpectedly in 1732, Samuel became the guardian of the heir Thomas 3.

Daniel lived in the old Purdy farm house for the rest of his long life, in full view of Horatio Walpole's new Wolterton Hall. By the 1740s Walpole had increasingly been turning his attention to the outer landscaping of his new park and Daniel Robins's house was a constant blot on his western view. In 1747 Walpole had given orders to pull out a hedge and stop up the main lane that gave access from the Daniel Robins farmstead to Wolterton. If he thought he would be able to do as he wished, he had reckoned without the Robins spirit. Samuel was running the farm for his father by this date. He had already had a brush with Walpole in 1737 when his father-in-law Henry Bayfield was ousted from his farm in Wolterton to make way for the park.

Walpole had started changing the lanes around his new house by 1741, usually just by negotiation with his neighbours rather than the proper process which entailed having a hearing at which anyone inconvenienced by the change could have their say. In a letter from Walpole to Ness on 27th November 1741 he wrote about a planned change on the Calthorpe side of Wolterton:

> … I have seen Lord Hobart and acquainted him with my design of turning the road in the manner proposed from Abbots Wood, he made no objection to it but hinted in a very friendly manner as if he should be glad that a footpath might be left for the miller, perhaps the miller may have complained of being put by though his Lordship did not say so. I would be glad to know how far it may be convenient or not.

Walpole had now made five changes to the routing of roads around his new house, Wolterton Church and the green immediately to the north of the house. One of these roads had previously provided Daniel Robins and Samuel the most direct route to Wolterton village and onwards to Calthorpe, there being easy access to it through the meadow surrounding their house and lying on the western edge of Walpole's garden. For a while it seemed that he was to go unchallenged but Samuel was preparing to do battle on behalf of his beleaguered family. At the beginning of 1749, he was, at 40, now the head of the Robins clan in the village. His wife Ann had died in 1748 leaving him with two very young children to care for; his mother Mary was elderly and may have been ill as she died in February the following year. His father Daniel was 82 and his cousin William of Itteringham Hall, although only in his late 40s and potentially a steadying influence, was probably ill – he made his will in May 1749 and died later that year. Samuel was still guardian of his 18 year-old cousin Thomas 3 of the Manor House, with whom he probably lived. Richard Robins 3, the 21 year-old son of William, was unlikely to have been one with whom Samuel could share family responsibilities. However alone he felt, Samuel took on the might of Walpole and, of course, of his county friends. The surviving papers explain the old layout of the area. They are also worth quoting from at length, to show the way the legal system was manipulated by the lawyers!

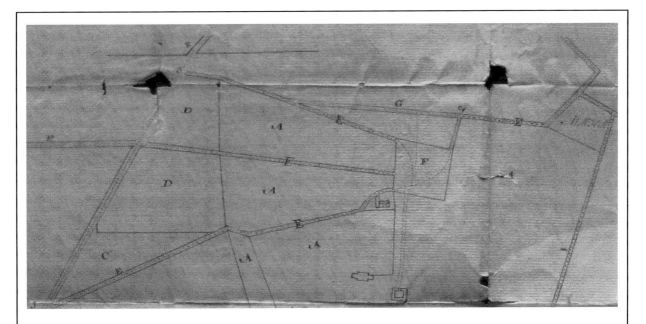

The key:

A  Park gardens and plantations
B  Inclosed land of Mr Walpole's in his own and Mr Cubit's use
C  Lands of Sam & Wm Robins
D  Land of Mr Walpole's in Thos Partridge's use
E  The old roads from Itteringham & Barningham to Woolterton, Calthorp & Wickmere
F  Woolterton Green where the three old roads centered or met
G  And the red pricked lines are the road with the alteration
   The length or distance in the old road from 1 to 2 is 292 rod at 5 yards and ½ to the rod 1606 yards
   The distance from 1 to 3 by 2 is 331 rod at the same proportion 1820 yards - difference 214
H  The road from Itteringham to Blickling to Calthorp
I  Road from Blickling Mill to Wickmere

Point 1 was at the 'stulps' junction on the Itteringham road to Wolterton and Wickmere, point 2 to the north of Wolterton green and point 3 at the junction by the modern Wolterton park farm. This was the origin of the Wolterton/Wickmere parish boundary road now lined with a wall running along the northern edge of the park. This set of road changes of course also marked the end of Wolterton green where by this date the cottages and farm buildings had been acquired by Walpole and taken down. The convenience to Daniel Robins of the old lane from Wolterton church to Itteringham was at the heart of the action.

1749 sketch map of the road changes around Wolterton

## *An unneighbourly proceeding*

Without notice or warning Samuel Robins presented an indictment of Walpole's road closure to the Grand Jury in Thetford:

> … relating to the King's Common Highway from Itteringham leading through the town of Wolterton to the town of Calthorpe … on 1 May 20 George II [1747] Horatio Walpole the elder of Woolterton, Esq. two certain wooden gates and a certain wooden stile and three certain wooden posts within certain rails and pales unlawfully wilfully and injuriously did put in place set up and fix … across a certain part of the said ancient Kings Common Highway … by means whereof … (it) was and still is obstructed and stopt up … to the great damage and common nuisance of all … still obstructed now at 18 March 22 George II [1749] …

> Signed: Samuel Robins prosecutor (no attorney attended on his part)

> Witnesses: Samuel Robins, Robert Thorpe, John Davy

The news rapidly got to Walpole and Ness. Apologising for his scrawl written hurriedly in court in Thetford, Mr Custance wrote to Walpole on 21st March 1749:

> Sir, as a bill of indictment for putting by the highway leading from Itteringham to Wolterton to Calthorpe was this day preferred against you by Samuel Robins of Itteringham I thought an early notice of so extraordinary and unneighbourly a proceeding might not be improper, however disagreeable it may be to you to receive it, and therefore take this liberty of setting pen to paper. The witnesses to prove the obstruction of damage done to the country besides Robins were Robert Thorpe his servant and one John Davy. The prosecution appeared to every gentleman of the Grand Jury to savour greatly of malice, but that could not be a sufficient consideration with them not to find the Bill which was accordingly done …

The road indeed had been closed and the jury legally had no choice but to allow the action to proceed. In a letter to Walpole of 28th March 1749 James Barnham explained the next steps in the process of the indictment and explored the possibility of trying to influence Robins to desist via his friend Edmund Jewell their family lawyer. Barnham referred to Robins's complaint as 'frivolous, vexatious and malicious and must appear in that light to all disinterested persons'. He went on to speculate that Robins might find the process of suing a Member of Parliament difficult and so give up. Walpole was obviously heartened by this idea, but it came to nothing. When preparing their case, Walpole and Ness referred back to an understanding that they believed Daniel had agreed to in 1741 concerning the road diversion:

> It is to be remembered that in 1741 when Daniel Robins was the tenant to the farm now occupied by his son Samuel Robins who lives at the capital house at Itteringham, he the said Daniel Robins several years before the Park was made, or there were any thoughts of making one, came to a verbal agreement with Mr Walpole, as to the convenience of both, to put by the road through his meadow over Woolterton Green to Calthorpe, and Mr Walpole at the same time agreed that the remaining part of the lane from the second post of direction down the old lane leading to Woolterton as far as Mr Robins land goes on each side might be taken into his ground, and belonging to it, and in consequence of this agreement Daniel Robins had begun to pull down the hedges on each side of the old lane to lay it into his grounds, but was diverted from doing it by the advice of his neighbour Thomas Partridge as thinking that it might be more convenient for him Daniel Robins farm to let it remain as it was on account of its being a drift way for his grounds on each side, which made Daniel Robins lay aside his design and repair the hedge again.

But this was their view. Samuel seems to have seen it differently, as recorded in a memorandum by Richard Ness on 29th March 1749:

Samuel Robins told me and I consented to it that the damage should be viewed that was done him by getting of the thorns out of his meadow. And also told me that Mr Walpole had done him and his father £150 [worth of damage] at several times since Mr Walpole came to Woolterton at the same time.

This is the only item in the papers that indicates how Samuel Robins felt about his intrusive neighbour. Perhaps in an attempt to get Robins to withdraw Ness had spoken to him but had no doubt got an angry tirade for his trouble. Samuel and his two witnesses were now up against Walpole, ably supported not only by Richard Ness but also his bevy of lawyers – Messrs Barnham, Nuthall, Fowle, Capper, Ryder and Hooke. Of the lawyers Thomas Nuthall was perhaps the most eminent. Son of Benjamin, the Norwich merchant and Mayor, he gradually rose to prominence, being well connected to the Walpoles and other politicians. He ended his career as Solicitor to the Treasury, although he far from covered himself in glory in that role.

Sitting firmly on the fence was Edmund Jewell of Aylsham, the Robins family lawyer and trustee who also worked for Walpole. Jewell's role in this affair is interesting. Typical of family attorneys of the age he wielded great influence in the Robins family affairs, particularly in looking after the interests of both Thomas and William's son Richard in their minorities. Despite this he did not act for Samuel in this matter and apparently had no success, at least early on, in making him see sense and withdraw the action. Richard Ness related something of this in his letter to Walpole on 29th March 1749:

> ... I went on Monday afternoon to Norwich to Mr Barnham but ... I did not see him until Tuesday at Two a Clock. I shew him all the letters from you to Mr Jewell and Mr Jewell to you and explained the whole case to him ... He said the indictment could not be found until the summer assizes and then perhaps your Honour might have a summons which your Honour might chuse whether you would regard it or no, then at the assizes this time twelve months there would be an attachment if they proceeded in the prosecution issued out against you to appear there to answer the indictment ...
>
> I called at Mr Jewells as I came home last night ... and he asked me if I had heard of Robins proceedings against you. I told him I had that day, he said he was surprised at it, and solemnly declared that he did not know that Robins intended to do it, neither did he advise with him, or any body for him on that account. ... I told him I thought it might not be amiss if I should make your Honour acquainted with what he said. He said he was really ignorant of the affair, and what he said was true, and said he would be obliged to me to mention it, he said he had mentioned it to Mr Earle by Mondays post.
>
> I have herein inclosed a sketch of the park and marked the roads as they formerly lay through it, and the road as it now is, is distinguished by red lines, and dots.

Two weeks later on 15th April Ness wrote to Walpole describing a meeting with Mr Jewell who 'declares he had no hand in drawing up the Robins writ and says he is disappointed not to have been asked to act for Walpole' (rather than Mr Barnham). Ness agreed knowing how close Jewell was to the two younger Robins heirs:

> ... I really wish you had as there is no great necessity to be in haste about it, that your Honour might have had a frequency of conversing more with him and engaging him more in your interest, for you may depend upon it that he has got such hold of young Robins affairs that when they come to their estates, they will be both of them under his direction and influence they being both of them very much young lads.
>
> I have heard it said that young Thomas Robins that Samuel is guardian to, begins to be uneasy about Samuel's proceedings, and that he has some intentions to come up to London along with a brother in law that is lately married his sister, whose name I think is Cressy, and lives in Martham in Fleg Hundred, and is a grocer or shopkeeper and they intend to wait upon your Honour ...

It seems that William Creasey (who married Thomas's sister Mary in March 1749) did not call on Walpole: certainly Samuel did not cave in. After the initial shock and affront the Walpole camp rapidly started to develop a plan to deal with the nuisance. James Barnham wrote to Walpole on 1st April 1749 suggesting that the writ of *ad quod damnum* that should have been taken out before the road was stopped up (a gentle rebuke) should be entered now as a counter writ. As the replacement road was only 400 yards longer and the hearing would be at Wolterton (unlike the Grand Jury at Thetford) the unreasonableness of the action would be clear to all sensible people – ie the Sheriff and jury who would be present. If successful this tactic would give Walpole retrospective approval for his road closures and make it extremely difficult for Robins - the only complainant - to pursue his case. To ensure success, Barnham 'organised' the jury in what is to a modern spectator as close to jury rigging as makes no difference, but which was not that unusual at the time. Barnham referred to not having anyone 'below the degree of esquire' on the jury and in a letter of 18th April he listed proposed members of the jury for the hearing at Wolterton and explained that Walpole should talk to them about 'their disposition on the matter' <u>before</u> telling them of his intention to proceed with the writ.

Ness wrote to Walpole on 19th April 1749:

> … I see Mr Barnham yesterday and I suppose … he has given your Honour … a list of the jury that certified for Sir Jacob Astley, Colonel Townshends and Mr Bristow writs of ad quod damnum, and also a list of what gentlemens names he and I could think of for your Honours appointment …

Samuel Bellard, land surveyor and map maker of Coltishall, who had the previous year produced the estate map for William Robins at Itteringham Hall, was now employed by Walpole to build his case by showing the modest impact on journey distances caused by the road closures. The argument being developed was on 'the state of the question relating to the high road from Itteringham to Calthorpe':

> There were two highroads from Itteringham to Calthorpe. The one leads from the first post of direction by William Robins to Calthorpe and measures upon a survey taken 2 miles 4 furlongs and 16 perches. The other leads from the first post of direction to the second post of direction and then through a lane to Woolterton Church and then over Woolterton Green to Calthorpe and measures 2 miles 2 furlongs and 35 perches.

It was the closure of the second one that Samuel Robins had challenged. The papers go on to say that the new road from Itteringham to Calthorpe, north around Wolterton, was in fact shorter than the route via William Robins's house and while it was a furlong longer than the old road through Wolterton green it was far better in 'goodness and breadth'. Walpole also seems to be making a special provision for Daniel:

> That lane was so bad especially from the Park Gate to Woolterton Church that in some places it was hardly practicable in winter and so narrow that it would be dangerous for a horseman to attempt to pass if met by a wheel carriage in many parts of it. But that part of the road from the second post of direction to Calthorpe, that is made new, is from 20 to 30 foot wide, and an extream good road in all respects ... But it is indeed true that Daniel Robins who lives next to the west side of Mr Walpole's garden could through a meadow belonging to him on the backside of his house and near where Mr Walpole's park pale is at present, goe immediately into the lane leading to Woolterton Church and over that Green to Calthorpe ... And this road from Daniel Robins house through his meadow over Woolterton Green has been put by ever since and so continued without any complaint made by Daniel Robins or anybody else and even by Samuel Robins, that now occupies the same farm to which his father was tenant, but lives at the capital house in Itteringham, never made the least complaint of putting by this road [or] other high roads until the year before the last when the Park was finished, and then he complained that the Park pale being carried directly cross that lane where Mr Walpole had land on one side and he a meadow on the other which included the half of the lane that lay to his meadow, upon which Mr Walpole caused the pales to be removed, and carried zigzag leaving that half of the new lane lying to Robins lands out of the Park ...
>
> So that the objection made ... is intirely new, and not of longer date than two years, although the road through the old lane to Woolterton Church and so over Woolterton Green had been put by four or five years before without the least complaint.
>
> But although the commodiousness of the new road ... is visibly much preferable to the old road over Woolterton Green yet Mr Walpole to obviate the least colour of objection has caused a road to be carried from Daniel Robins meadow directly through the lane and the close over against it through or near Partridges Yard into the new road which besides being every way broader and better ... exceeds in length the old road no more than 1 furlong and 24 perches and is done for the sake only of that house where Daniel Robins lives because it can be of no other use to any other person whatsoever and is much more convenient than the former road ...

The idea of undermining Samuel's case by making a new road just for Daniel had been devised by his lawyers closetted together one summer evening. The element of surprise would be vital. Thomas Nuthall wrote to Walpole on 13th June 1749 at 8 o'clock at night:

> I write this from Mr Capper's chambers where we are all met to consider the affair you sent Mr Ness to town upon. Mr Fowle Mr Capper Mr Barnham and myself are jointly and unanimously of the opinion that the opening of the way and making a new road in a direct line, as it were from Daniel Robins's house by the side or near the park pales into the new road will be a prudent and effective measure to take away all cause of complaint ... and therefore we advise it to be done, but ... to keep from Robins if possible the knowledge of your design; The stakes may be put down at any time without suspicion and the hedges need not be levelled till the morning the jury meet ... I will venture to say that there never was a writ of this sort executed where there was so little cause for opposition

Despite the strength of his case, Walpole was worried about the outcome. A letter from Fowle on 15th June 1749 tried to put Walpole's mind at rest and stated that Robins was unlikely to get any support to mount a subsequent appeal if he lost the hearing. Walpole was quick to act at the slightest hint of any other neighbours joining Robins. A draft letter of 21st June 1749 to Mr Framingham of Little Walsingham (the owner of the Hill farm estate in Itteringham) reassured him that the writ to stop up the road 'in that angle of the country' where Framingham had land would not affect any roads leading to his lands in Itteringham.

As the hearing at Wolterton approached, Samuel Robins at last sought legal representation but found it hard to find a lawyer not already engaged. Edmund Hooke in Norwich to Walpole on 23rd June 1749:

> ... now I take occasion to acquaint you that Mr Robins of Itteringham this day came to retain me and mentioned Mr Bare's compliments. Upon this I immediately answered that I was retained for you and then he left me with asking only when I received the retainer, but which question wanted not, nor had a particular answer from me. I had a mind to give you a line of the industry of the man upon the occasion

It seems Samuel Robins had no idea of the concerted action being taken to face him with a jury already in support of Walpole. Correspondence on 24th June 1749 from both Nuthall and Ryder related to one of the potential jurors for the hearing at Wolterton. Nuthall argued that one of the jurors could probably sit at both the hearing and any subsequent appeal at sessions. The inference was that Walpole was trying to use Sir Jacob Astley of Melton Constable, his most powerful local ally, as visibly as possible. However, a note from Ryder said that in his opinion this would not be proper and would probably be illegal. But this was only a minor setback. In the few days before the hearing Walpole received several short personal letters from jurors saying that they would be very pleased to wait upon him on 3rd July, the date set for the hearing at Wolterton. The letters were addressed to Walpole, note, not to the Sheriff.

The hearing took place, at Wolterton before Thomas Sotherton Sheriff of Norfolk. Sir Jacob Astley sat with 11 other local landowners of substance. Short and to the point, they determined that 'it is not to the damage of the King to enclose the 5 parcels of Highway ... because Mr Walpole has set out other roads'. So the day had gone exactly as Walpole's lawyers had said it would: a local walk about and a walk over for Walpole.

James Barnham noted that Robins and his attorney were present who 'after making some trifling objections declared themselves well satisfied and promised not to appeal to sessions or to give you any further trouble'. He told Walpole 'Robins cannot appeal after this publick declaration of his to the contrary, but I will be watchful'. Despite the aggressive nature of the response from Walpole's lawyers, it is hard to feel sorry for Samuel Robins. In the context of the times he picked an un-winnable fight, but he had acquired a new access lane for his father and made Walpole realise his actions could be challenged.

As far as we know Samuel Robins and Walpole subsequently co-existed peacefully, but no doubt with at best rather frosty relations between them at first. But Walpole still hankered after the Robins farm and when the young Thomas 3 inherited, he made a move again.

## *Walpole and Thomas Robins 3*

By 1754 Horatio Walpole was actively trying to persuade the young 'Tom' Robins to exchange lands to give Walpole the meadow along the west side of his gardens. His aim was to secure the house and farmyard occupied by Daniel Robins. He was determined to deal with the family by careful negotiation and even viewed 'Sam' Robins, his earlier opponent, as a potential ally. Ness as ever was the key to the business and was using his knowledge of Thomas's personality and relationships to assist Horatio.

On 7th December 1754 Walpole wrote:

> Ness, ... I like the step you are taking to come to an agreement with the Robins [over] the two pieces of land next Partridges ... I would be glad to have them. And I think you should in talking on the heads endeavour to put the value upon them according to the rent that Partridge payd for them when I parted with them. As to the years purchase that will be another question upon which you will hear what they demand upon the foot of that rent. Your notion of getting as much as you can from him nearer time is extremely right if he will not take money and preferable to giving him money. I much approve of Mr Town and Mr Barton dining with you.

On the 14th Walpole wrote with news designed to flatter Thomas Robins's desire to be accredited with the status of esquire rather than gentleman: 'I have caused young Mr Robins to be added to the commissioners of the land tax by the title of Thomas Robins Esq, if he does not care to act there is no harm done'. On 19th December 1754 Walpole, anxious about such an important deal, wrote to Ness a classic letter leaving no room for initiative. He felt strongly that the young man should be allowed to make up his own mind and that lining up mutual friends, such as Michael Towne the tanner, to persuade him to agree might be counter-productive. He was keen that Thomas should be on good terms with himself and his son in future:

> I have received yours of the 14th giving an account of your conversation with young Mr Robins by which I understand what passed on the subject of exchange was between you two only without the presence or intercourse of any other person, from whence and from other observations I find that he is desirous of doing his own business himself and therefore you must not be too hasty in calling in other persons to your aid, nor perhaps in communicating to others what passes between you two alone unless he does it himself, taking only opportunity to engage Sam Robins Town and Barton to be favourable to me in case the young man should speak to them or any of them on the subject. And you should by no means press Sam to interfere for it is plain to me that unless Tom himself should advise with Sam the efficiousness of Sam to meddle on my behalf will do more harm than good and create jealousy and suspicion in the other. However you will continue to live in a friendly manner with Sam and as to Town who I look upon to be the more sensible person I think he should act no other part but that in case this matter should fall accidentally in discourse between him and Tom he should take an occasion to represent to Tom how much may be in his convenience to establish a good neighbourhood with me, not only on my account but also for the sake of an intimacy with my son who is to succeed me of whom everybody speaks very well. And you will therefore continue your conferences with Tom alone putting things in the best light for his advantage and flattering him in the best manner you can.
> And I think the fewer this transaction is known to the better for should it get out there may be those who will by some means or other seek to prevent an agreement between us.
> I like the manner you have hitherto used in talking with the young man which you will continue and as your knowledge in things of this nature is superior to his you will manage it accordingly taking care not to give him an occasion to his thinking that you would impose upon him. You will give me a minute account of all that passes between you from time to time but come to no agreement without acquainting me with it first.

The patient negotiating strategy ultimately paid off. In September 1755 an agreement to exchange lands between Thomas Robins and Walpole was made and signed in December. Thomas Robins's house, barn, stables and yards lay in Itteringham and Wolterton and totalled 41 acres. Daniel had died in January 1755 and the house and its acre orchard and gardens was now occupied by Richard Robins and Samuel Robins. The central part of the farmlands comprised 25 acres in 6 closes around it in the occupation of Thomas and Samuel, and 15 acres in 2 closes nearby in the occupation of Richard and Samuel. These were swapped with Walpole's 28 acres occupied by Thomas Plaford also in Itteringham and Wolterton – in various parcels intermingled with Thomas Robins's in the old open field area. All were close to the Itteringham to Wolterton road and on both sides of it. As a result they extended Thomas Robins's consolidation in the area. Field names included Schoolhouse pightle, South pightle, Barton's pightle, Johnson's pightle, gravel pit close and an adjacency to glebe land known as Thoroughfare Close. Thoroughfare Close was in the heart of Itteringham between the two roads, with Thomas Bond's pightle behind 98-100 The Street a field away to the south.

Robins had negotiated skilfully; initially only 17 acres nearer to Wolterton had been offered, but Thomas pressed for the extra 11 acres which were those closest to the centre of Itteringham. In addition Walpole had agreed that a barn with 'convenient leantooes' was to be built for him in Itteringham at a place of his choosing to the same dimensions as the barn he was losing to Walpole. Ness argued that the barn would cost about £250 to build. Walpole was also prepared to offer £100 for the house that would subsequently be demolished. Notes written by Richard Ness show that he and Walpole tried to negotiate hard on the multiples of rent that should be used to value each others' land. They tried to argue that both were worth 30 times the rent, even though Ness's private notes showed Walpole's at a 'common value' of 24x. Ness also pointed out that Robins would avoid perhaps £150 of repairs to the barn and outhouses by getting a new one. They ended up at an extra £437 10s paid to Thomas Robins to reflect the differential value.

Michael Towne, Thomas Robins's tenant in Bintry, wrote to Walpole on 7th September showing that he had been instrumental in getting young Thomas to the negotiating table. His handwriting was very good, his spelling less so but his Norfolk voice comes through. Thomas spent much of his time hunting but also travelled with Towne on his business trips:

> Worthy Sir, According to your desire I have don all in my pour to complete this affair, I have applied my self to Mr Robins and have argued and reasoned with him, he seems to put of treating with you at present, but at last did condesend to cum if you should send for him, and will argu with you on the particulars drawn up by Mr Ness, so I have given him a coppy in righting of it, so if you should ask him for the particulars I due judge that he will give you them although they may be of my righting but he will have the 11 acres and £500 besides which your honour was willing with all, tomorrow he go a shooting with Mr Elwin of Oulton, so I suppose Tuesday morning to be the properest time, for we go to Lynn together on Wednesday morning. This from your most obedient and humble servant

On 6th December Walpole wrote to Ness to say that 'the matter is happily concluded'. However Thomas had asked a further favour:

> Mr Robins desired that I would procure some place for his cousin Samuel Robins. I told him in general terms that upon his account I should be willing to [pro]cure any body. But he and Mr Jewell let fall some words as if Samuel was in a very bad situation ...

Whether Walpole helped Samuel or what his circumstances were we do not know. His parents, wife and sister-in-law, Mary Bayfield, were all dead and his two children do not appear to have survived to adulthood. The house and farm were now Walpole's and his guardianship of Thomas was over. Samuel died in 1764 aged 55 and was buried with his wife Ann in the floor of the church, under a large black memorial stone. Despite his weaving background and his being a founder trustee of the Oulton Meeting House, he was the only one of the Robinses to be so honoured. Presumably this was arranged and paid for by Thomas 3, his former ward. His stone includes a device which, although not strictly heraldic, reflects the arms of his mother's family, the Stewards. This was the closest the Robins family came to bearing arms.

Steward family arms on Samuel Robins's gravestone in Itteringham Church

The old house was removed leaving only a small farm building. In 1779, years after the 1755 exchange, the 'shed in Robins' meadow' was taken down and rebuilt and close-boarded. This last remnant of the Daniel Robins farm had become just a quaint feature in the landscape (still visible on the 1823 enclosure map). There is no trace of it today. To this day the present Lord Walpole remembers 'that man Robins' as he walks over his stone on Sunday mornings.

## Dairy farm, Itteringham (21)

The land of Dairy farm, the core farm of Thomas Robins, had been farmed by a tenant farmer from the Manor House during the minority of Thomas Robins 3. As he approached his 21st birthday in March 1752 he appears to have set about building a house for Dairy farm to enable his tenant, Thomas Barton, to vacate his Manor House. In 1752 he bought 15,000 bricks from the Wolterton estate which might well have been for this purpose. The 1755 exchange with Walpole resulted in a fine new barn being built which still stands in the yard at Dairy farm. The dimensions were given in a note in the accounts and the brickwork was done by Robert Ward: 53 yards of foundations, 24 ½ rod of brickwork, 166 foot of French eves and 6,233 pantiles. Other entries showed a further 2,400 pantiles and 150 roof ridge tiles.

Richard Garnham, the tenant of the Manor House at the end of the century, also held the farm house or cottage at Dairy farm, noted on the 1778 plan:

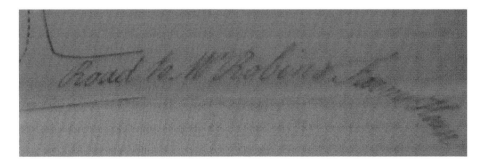

Much later this would become two semi-detached cottages before becoming derelict. They were eventually demolished to make way for the building of a 20th century barn.

## Robins family estate: Richard Robins of Itteringham Hall (23)

Richard Robins 2 was the third son of Richard 1 the blacksmith of Itteringham. Richard 2 was born in Itteringham in 1658 and left Cawston property and rents by his father in 1689. It is not clear what he did in his early adulthood: was he too a blacksmith or, like so many of his cousins, was he a weaver? By October 1690 he was a 'yeoman of Itteringham' when he granted to Erasmus Earle esq of Heydon a right of way across 2 acres of his land which sat between Cawston heath and Beer House farm.

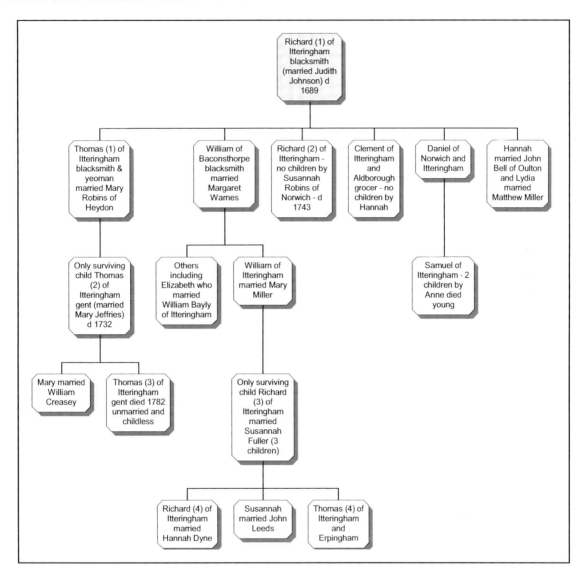

Summary family tree for Richard Robins

In September 1696 in Norwich, Richard Robins 'gent of Itteringham' married his young cousin Susannah, the orphaned daughter of Daniel Robins and Susannah. As residual legatee of a dornix weaver (her father was of the family of John Robins the Norwich weaver originally from Heydon) Susannah may have brought some money to the marriage, but her parent's wills do not suggest that she and her brother John were left much. In a deed of 1712 he was still a yeoman so it remains somewhat of a mystery how Richard Robins came to elevate himself from younger son status to yeoman and then to 'gentleman' of Itteringham, owning Itteringham Hall and a good-sized farm around it. His estate lay on the eastern part of Itteringham parish and covered premises in Ingworth and Erpingham as well. Itteringham Hall had a fine setting facing down the slope to the Bure. It was set in gardens and orchards; its dovehouse has since gone but the fishponds remain below the present White House farm.

As we have seen when discussing Hill farm, Itteringham Hall had been built by Thomas Payne junior of Itteringham in the middle of the 16th century. He had not owned extensive lands but, as steward for all the Boleyn manors and lands in Norfolk, he was an important local figure and his fine 'mansion' house befitted his status. The Hall had been built on land granted - at a small fixed rent - from the manor of Nowers whose lands surrounded the small plot. At some point, probably in the 1620s, the Godfrey family had acquired the manor from the Howard family, Dukes of Norfolk and Earls of Arundel, who had held it for about a century. In April 1641 a marriage settlement conveyed all the Godfrey family lands in Hindringham and Itteringham to Richard Godfrey the eldest son of Richard Godfrey esq on his marriage to Anne the daughter of Sir John Tracy of Stiffkey. Coincidentally but confusingly they also held a manor called Nowers in Hindringham. The Itteringham property was only sketchily described as the manor of Nowers and a messuage called Andrew Thomas, both in Itteringham.

It is not clear at this point if the Godfreys now also held Itteringham Hall. The Payne family had moved away from Itteringham by the early 17th century and Itteringham Hall had become the home for a succession of tenants. At one point the Houghton family, who owned the old Wolterton Hall in 1595, also purchased Itteringham Hall. Robert Houghton lived there and baptised many of his children in the village in the 1620s. After Robert built himself a new house at Earlham in 1642-43, his eldest son Richard moved into Wolterton with his new wife. Sometime in the 1640s Itteringham Hall was sold to the Godfrey family, probably to fund Richard Houghton's improvements to Wolterton. Godfrey was now able to position Itteringham Hall as the 'manor house' of Nowers.

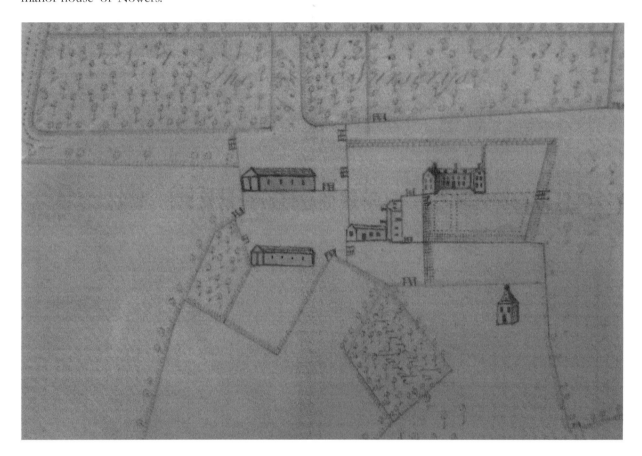

Itteringham Hall, dovehouse and farm in 1748

In April 1664 Richard and Anne Godfrey conveyed the whole of the manor of Nowers in Itteringham, with other property in Hindringham, to their eldest son John and his heirs. It was probably this generation who sold Nowers and Itteringham Hall to their Hindringham neighbours, James Ward and his wife Ursula Nabbs. Ursula's father was John Nabbs who had Hastings manor in Hindringham; her grandfather Edward had been very friendly with Sir John Potts's family and she may have been named after his daughter Ursula. As James and Ursula lived in her father's fine house in Hindringham after 1666, the Itteringham lands and Hall were leased to various tenants. Their son Hamond married John Godfrey's sister Anne, further cementing the links.

The Nowers land was still owned in 1697 by James Ward - not Hamond his son - but by January 1712 the estate had been bought by Richard Robins of Itteringham. That year Richard and his brother Clement the grocer sold to their brother Thomas 1 for £290 a parcel of fields totalling 44 acres and including the old site of the manor of Nowers at St Nicholas green, sections of the old Barkers farmstead and the lands and meadows comprising the village end of the manor. They had purchased the property from Hamond Ward of Hindringham and Anne his wife, Ursula Ward his widowed mother, and his sister Katherine and her husband Augustine Holl gent. This deed is important as it showed that the Nowers/Itteringham Hall deal was completed by Richard and Clement without any Heydon cousins' funding. While it seems likely that Clement made profits as a merchant and retailer in both Aldborough and Itteringham, it is not clear where or how Richard made sufficient money to afford the purchase, particularly as Clement, while involved in the purchase, does not seem subsequently to have enjoyed any ownership rights. Clement had no surviving children, so he may have been quite happy to use his wealth to help his brothers and their families. Certainly when he died in 1737 his will favoured very strongly his brothers Richard and Daniel in Itteringham. He may have provided the immediate purchase money with Richard repaying him from farming profits (and of course from the partial sale to Thomas). The £290 paid by Thomas for his acreage looks very low and cannot be used to estimate the overall price, but even if the estate had been bought at a modest multiple of the rent it is hard to see it going for less than £2-3,000. Had Richard Robins become tenant of both the Nowers manor and Itteringham Hall and seen an opportunity to buy?

One explanation of how he might have afforded this comes from an earlier gamble. In 1709 Richard and his brother Thomas 1 appear to have had £1,000 available to invest although how they generated this surplus is not clear, particularly coming so soon after Thomas's expense in building his manor house. In July that year they were assigned a £1,000 debt of Edward Paston, the beleaguered Earl of Yarmouth, who was then living in Barningham, his family's last major house. The debt's previous owner, John Gascoyne of London, had as security a Queen's Bench judgement of 1702 which was enrolled in chancery in 1709, enabling Yarmouth's trustees to sell real estate if necessary to honour this debt. But it was not without risk; described the year before 'as low as you can imagine ... scarce a servant to attend him ... or a horse to ride', Yarmouth was so deeply indebted that the loan was not at all safe. Perhaps it carried a very high annual interest rate that made it an unmissable investment. Whether repayment was made (from his £2,000 annual government pension) or the debt sold on, the high risk loan no doubt helped to fund both Thomas and Richard Robins's property purchases in Itteringham in 1711 and 1712.

Itteringham Hall now became the permanent home of Richard Robins and his wife Susannah, devout members of the Irmingland meeting house congregation. After the separation of the western fields to Thomas Robins, a small number of adjustments were made to the Itteringham Hall estate. These were neighbourly sales and exchanges of small parcels of land around Wolterton lake to enable Horatio Walpole to progress his design for his gardens and park (see Chapter 15). Richard and Sir John Hobart of Blickling exchanged tiny parcels of land and meadow between Itteringham Hall and Blickling mill to rationalise their holdings in March 1722. The larger meadow then still held by Hobart - Hubbards Herne - and Clement Johnson's meadow, beside the track leading from Itteringham Hall to John's Water, were both acquired before 1748.

Although the couple had a long married life, they had no children. Richard had made his will in 1741 to make provision for his wife Susannah who was 15 years his junior. He left her his carriage ('chariot') and pair of horses, the pigeons in the dovehouse, and a substantial £40 annuity. He also provided for Susannah to stay in part of Itteringham Hall for as long as she wished. She was also guaranteed the use of the back house, brew house and wash house and all the utensils for brewing baking and washing. Sadly Susannah died before him, aged 71 in 1742. Richard survived her by a year, dying when he was 86.

Richard, despite his dissenting beliefs and his generous legacy to the Oulton meeting house, expected a traditional gentleman's funeral. His maidservants' suits were of 'black and white stuff' and his menservants were dressed in suits of grey cloth trimmed with black with hats. His body was taken across from the Hall by four of his workmen, similarly attired, to be laid under a ledger stone in the churchyard.

His heir was his great-nephew Richard Robins 3 who at this time was only 13. He had started life in Briston near the village of Baconsthorpe where his grandfather William Robins senior had been the blacksmith and where, in 1722, his father William junior had married his cousin Mary Miller (the daughter of the Hunworth tanner). Richard 3 was baptised by the dissenting minister at Irmingland in 1728. However by 1733, William was given as of Itteringham and may have already been running the Itteringham Hall estate for his uncle Richard 2, who was by then 76. William and his wife Mary were probably living in one of the houses Richard had bought in Erpingham as, when Mary died in 1732, her body was brought from Erpingham to be buried in Itteringham. By Richard 2's will, William inherited all the Itteringham and Wolterton manors, houses and lands, of which the largest part was the Itteringham Hall estate, until his son Richard 3 reached the age of 25.

William himself inherited Richard's lands and houses in Erpingham and Ingworth which he had bought from John Warner and Robert Woodrow (and another probably smaller purchase in Erpingham from William Picton and Anne his wife). From a later sale to the Woolsey family of Ingworth and the enclosure map, the Robins property in Ingworth and Erpingham can be identified as the main farm based at what is now Ash Hill farm house on Priory Lane running from Ingworth to Scarrow Beck ford, with the majority of its lands running down the slope to the river. This site was close to Itteringham Hall, in full view from it across the water meadows. There were also cottages, all now gone, in that farmyard, opposite West End farm down the track by the main farm, and two on the east of the lane just before reaching the ford. After William's death these too were to pass to Richard 3.

William and his teenage son moved into the Hall and when Richard was about 20, in 1748, his father proudly commissioned a fine estate map from the local cartographer Samuel Bellard. All the estate fields in Itteringham were shown and named and their acreages given.

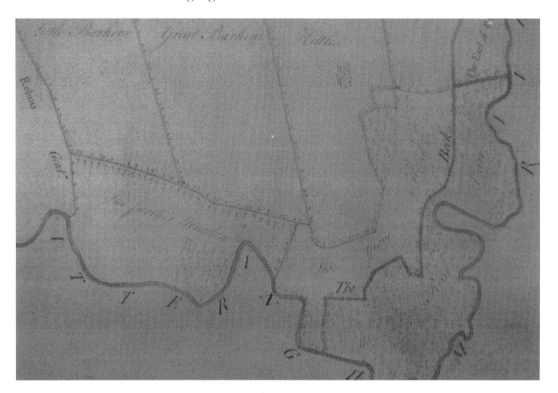

Old tenement names Barker's and Kettle's and meadows of the Hall farm

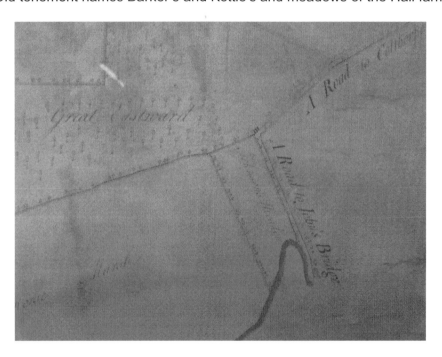

At the big bend in the river Bure now known as John's Water, the bridge was then much nearer the present lane rather than at its present location

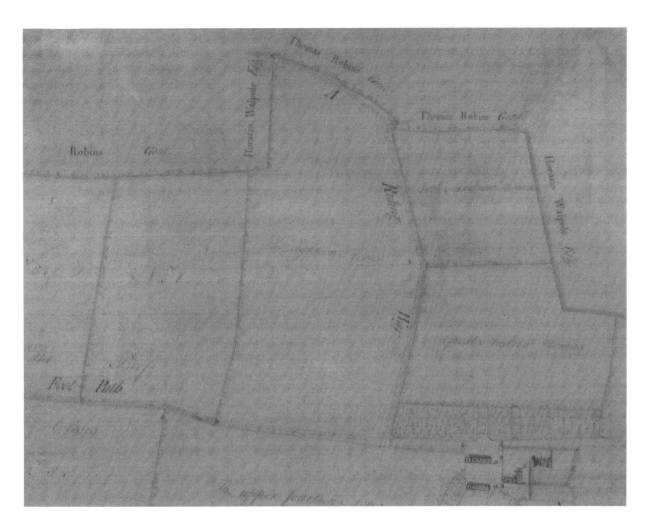

The old Riding Way and footpath to the village past the Andrew Thomas fields

When William died the following year, Edmund Jewell the family lawyer and trustee was left to see Richard 3 through the last four years before he inherited the estate. At 21, he married Susannah Fuller of Wickmere in North Barningham in 1749. As soon as he was 24, the Erpingham lands were mortgaged to raise cash to pay for their lifestyle. Their son and heir, Richard 4, was born in Itteringham in October 1754, followed by Susannah in 1756 and Thomas in 1757. The loan was increased in 1766, again in 1771 and again in 1786 by which time the main Itteringham Hall estate was also mortgaged. At no time did Richard reinvest in the estate and his management of the farming business seems lacklustre. He lived as a country gentleman, most noted for his love of hunting, a right he claimed from his manor of Nowers. His behaviour in the 1750s was a thorn not only in Walpole's side but also threatened to upset the neighbourly balance that his cousins had achieved with Horatio (see Chapter 16).

Susannah his daughter had married John Leeds in July 1784. Rather belatedly the 70 acres and 4 cottages in Ingworth and Erpingham were settled in 1792 on Leeds, albeit with a mortgage for more than half the value still in place. £1,200 was to be paid off and Susannah was to receive £900 from William Clayton Leeds, dyer of Norwich in trust for John Leeds then described as a Wolterton farmer. William was John's brother, who had been witness at the marriage. John and Susannah Leeds took over the lease of Walpole's Mannington Hall farm after Susannah's brother Richard (4) left the area. Although the farm lay at the Mannington end of Wolterton parish, the old church was now defunct and most of their children, including son and heir John Leeds, were baptised in Itteringham. In 1809 when the whole Erpingham property was sold to the Woolsey family, John and William Leeds surrendered a small piece of copyhold land near Oak hill (now Ash hill) in Erpingham and a cottage and 9 acres. By this time John Leeds had moved away to another Walpole tenancy in Burnham Thorpe.

A family settlement of 1783 had settled Richard 3's lands on Richard junior and his heirs so Richard 3's simple will left all his personal estate to his wife Susannah. He died in 1787 and his widow moved out of the Hall with her comfortable £80 annuity from the estate. When she died in 1793 she was buried in Erpingham where it was noted that she was then from Ingworth where she may have been living with her son Thomas 4. Her will, made that year, seemed to hint at some unease in the family. She made no mention of Hannah the widow of her son Richard and only mentioned one of Hannah's children, Rebecca, to whom she left a £40 legacy. In fact as we shall see, both Hannah and her son Richard Story Robins were very much alive. Susannah made a good provision from her personal resources for her own son Thomas – £700 to be invested for life to provide him and any children with an income. Her daughter Susannah Leeds was the residual legatee.

Itteringham Hall and its farm was now run by John Oakes, a younger son of Thomas Oakes senior of Mannington Hall. Oakes, as we will see, had married Hannah the young widow of Richard Robins 4. By this time the estate was suffering from years of neglect and lack of investment by Richard 3. Oakes was an ambitious modern farmer and rapidly took the property in-hand. It was in such poor condition that the rental value was deemed to be only £160 per year. It was described as: 'the lands poor and full of beggary and much run out' (beggary, common fumitory or *fumaria officinalis*, being a climbing weed of arable land). Oakes spent time and money repairing the house, rebuilding barns in brick and tile where they had only been wattle and thatch, improving the soil and drainage and planting osier carr on the 14 acres of 'morassy ground' or very marshy water meadows. The drainage ditches all around the water meadows in the vicinity of White House farm still bear witness to the scale of his work.

Some timber, mostly oak with some beech and ash, had to be felled to pay for improvements to the house and buildings and for use in their repair, together with reinstating fences, gates and styles. The house was in a ruinous state, being neither wind nor water tight since the window casements had rotted. The house was patched up. At one point workmen repairing the roof feared it would give way and in time a chimney and part of the building did indeed collapse. In 1796 the building was therefore partly dismantled and rebuilt, which explains why the old Tudor hall house has not survived. The form of the present house dates from this time. A new backhouse with a dairy and cheese chamber was built, together with a new bullock shed. Proceeds from timber sales - about £700 in total - had also been used to pay the £500 of legacies in 1794 rather than extend the mortgage on the property. Oakes and Hannah were only guardians of the estate, for her young son Richard Story Robins. They felt justified in using the balance of the proceeds from the mature timber to reinvest in the estate on his behalf. The full story of Richard Story will be told at the end of the book. The Oakes were later offered a larger Walpole farm - over 500 acres at Burnham Norton - and when Walpole finally completed the purchase of the Itteringham Hall estate in 1805 the house and 252 acres were then occupied by Richard Pratt.

Remains of Itteringham Hall now White House farm

## Sources

NRO: NRS 13234, 28A1; NRS 15049, 29F1; NRS 20995, 69x3; NRS 20998, 69x3; NRS 21002, NRS 21006, NRS 21017, 73x4, NRS 21026, 21027, 21032, 73x4; NRS 22884/1, NRS 22289; PD 434/24; MC 310/6; MC 2555/1, 980x8; MS 12609, 30D7; MS 17962, 39B6; WAL 336, 272x6; WAL 342, 272x6; WAL 1148, 286x4; WAL 1441/7, 290x3; WAL 1552, 291x5; BRA 2373/1/1-12, 822x1

TNA: Chancery papers listed in Chapter 19

Wolterton archive: 3/7/8; 8/40, 60, 61, 68, 75; 20/4/9A

Norfolk Genealogy, vol 6, 1974
RW Ketton-Cremer, *Norfolk Portraits*, 1944
Norfolk E-Map Explorer website
*ODNB*
For more details of the Long family see *See You in Court*.

# Part 3

## THE HEART, SOUL AND LIFE-BLOOD OF THE VILLAGE

*He earns whate'er he can,*
*And looks the whole world in the face,*
*For he owes not any man.*

W Wordsworth, *The Village Blacksmith*

The tradesmen and their premises; the clergy, the church and the meeting house; the cottages and their occupants

# Chapter 8

## *Trading Places*

---

*The range and viability of trades in Itteringham at any time depended on several factors including the size of the village population, the early prevalence of travelling salesmen and the growth of permanent shops in Aylsham. Perhaps most important of all was the presence and patronage of wealthy customers. The mid-1660s services described in Chapter 1 benefited from the long-term residence of the Potts in Mannington. In the 18th century, Horatio Walpole's acquisition of both Wolterton and Mannington gave an impetus to many craftsmen and suppliers. Occasionally the Blickling estate may have created some demand but Aylsham would have satisfied most of their local needs. Of course, most of the finer goods, where fashion and choice prevailed, were purchased in Norwich or London and the seasonal nature of the families' residence must have created some problems. However it is clear from the Wolterton accounts that Walpole did his best to support local suppliers of all kinds; the downside was that, like most customers at that time, settlement might only be made once a year! Many tradesmen, especially the better-off, held land or other businesses in other Norfolk parishes – vital if trading was uneven and if their working premises were rented from one of the estates. Rice Wickes, Blickling's tanner, owned a house and lands in Guist and the Robins family increasingly became substantial landowners. In this way, trade families created networks across larger areas, added more lines of income and ensured their children had opportunities in the future. Usually only smaller craftsmen, outside of these groups, with no reserves or flexibility, fell on hard times; in old age many became reliant on the parish. Here we look at the main trades and premises they occupied. With the blacksmith, the full story of the Thomas Robins estate in Itteringham also begins.*

### The Blacksmith and his forge: the creation of the Manor House

The blacksmith's forge was a central feature of most rural villages from medieval times to recent memory. The sounds and smells of horse-shoeing and smithy work, hot and physically demanding, were familiar to all. As we have seen in Chapter 1, Richard Robins 1 was the first blacksmith recorded in Itteringham. His father William of Heydon had been both a wool chapman and yeoman in the 1590s; clearly an entrepreneur, William built a new blacksmith's shop in Heydon, with a shoeing house adjoining and a parcel of land to the south, which he left to 28 year-old Richard in his will of December 1647. William and his two wives had baptised sixteen children; only Richard, one of the younger sons, had been apprenticed as a blacksmith. Perhaps he was tall and strong and a relative had offered to take him on as an apprentice. As he would have finished his training by about 1640, his father may have built the forge for him. However, as after Richard's death the property was to revert to his elder brother Thomas of Heydon, Richard had no long term interest in it as an estate that he could pass on to his own family. This might have motivated him at the earliest opportunity, and certainly when he married, to set up in business elsewhere while placing a tenant to run the smithy at Heydon. William Hall was 'blacksmith of Heydon' when making his will in 1653, a will to which Richard was witness. The Halls had been active as blacksmiths from the late 16th century in Horstead and Hevingham where they owned their own premises. In 1655 Richard also witnessed Peter Hall's will in Hevingham.

Richard married around the time of his father's death, in or after 1649; Judith was the daughter of Thomas and Judith Johnson of Gresham although her father had died a few months before she was born at the end of 1631. Her mother had married again to Roger Neale of Gresham and later wed Robert Page of Baconsthorpe. Richard and Judith chose to live in Itteringham where the 21 year-old gave birth to their first child in the summer of 1653. She would have ten children of whom seven survived to marry.

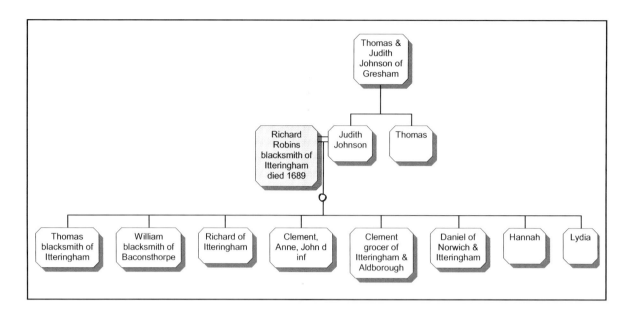

## Richard Robins blacksmith of Itteringham and his family

Why Itteringham? As we have seen the village had grown in the 1630s and was ripe for trade development. Whether Richard happened to seize a first chance to lease land or whether Judith had a relative in the village, we do not know. Richard started to operate as a tenant from a cottage and yard in the centre of the village which had recently become free following the death of Widow Grand in 1650. Helen Trew, from a Wolterton family, had married Thomas Grand in 1623 and raised three children in Itteringham. Thomas, who died in 1641, was a husbandman and nothing from the deeds suggests there was a smithy on the site at this time (**16**). It seems likely that Richard leased the cottage from Grand's son who had moved to Aylsham; following his father's example Richard then built a forge with yards and outhouses. The cottage was the western end of two adjoining cottages (the other being owned by William Bateley's widow) which are today incorporated at the back of the Manor House. The forge appears to have been where the present kitchen now stands. Inside the kitchen chimney stack, chains and wheels were found by a modern blacksmith which might well date back to the old smithy. By 1660 Richard was assessed on £100 of stock and he paid tax on 3 hearths in 1664. By this time he and his family were living nearby in an old small hall house, owned by the Mannington estate, called Love's (**14**). Long demolished, it stood nearer to the road, in the present Manor House farmyard. It is not clear whether the 3 hearths covered both Love's and the forge but later evidence suggest he may only have been assessed on his house. In 1672 he managed to persuade Francis Bacon JP that smiths' forges were not liable for hearth tax and Bacon ordered William Beaumont, one of the Collectors, to reimburse Richard the 3 shillings levied on his forge. His argument was that forges were not firehearths but should be treated like braziers' furnaces which were specifically exempted in the act. The Lords of the Treasury however were sure that smiths' forges (defined as 'houses wherein the mineral ore is smelted down into metal') were included and sent Bacon a firm rebuke for interpreting the wording wrongly.

Richard Robins was obviously not one to let any opportunity pass – a trait inherited by the next generation. A shrewd business man, Richard not only had use of the Heydon and Itteringham forges but by leasing Love's from Roger Potts (later the 3rd baronet) he held 50 acres of land, much of it strips in the old open field. He also leased 3 closes nearby: Shop (sometimes sheep) Close, Broom hill Close and the long meadow. With these lands and others he was leasing from his brother-in-law Robert Eston in Cawston, he was able to diversify to support his business income stream by farming. Next he had the chance to buy the cottage next door; the widow Bateley died in 1663 and by January 1673 Richard was described as the owner. That month, having been Roger Potts's reliable tenant for over 10 years, he was in prime position to capitalise on the growing debt problems facing the Potts family. For £340 Richard bought Love's and its 9 acres of meadow and arable land rising up onto Broom hill and the other lands he had previously leased. In September 1682, William Grand finally sold to him for £12 the little cottage where the forge began. Two smaller pieces of land in Itteringham had also been acquired: some meadow purchased from John Bell of Oulton and a parcel of land from John Hobart esq of Blickling. Richard now owned the freehold of a significant part of the centre of the village and of the old open field. More importantly, in the year before his death he was able to lend Richard Gay £380 secured as a mortgage on the old manorial site of Bintry where the tannery operated. By his careful acquisition of lands and by making his ready cash work as loans, he ensured the platform for the success of his heirs as landowners.

When Richard died in 1689, a 60 year-old widower, he was sufficiently wealthy to provide for the seven children. His will - which he signed with a clear, confident hand - was witnessed and written by the family friend Thomas Newman, the ousted Heydon preacher who had become a lawyer. Richard's eldest son Thomas 1 inherited all the Itteringham property and continued, at first, as the blacksmith. His second son William had also been trained as a smith and was left property in Baconsthorpe where he was working. Presumably his father had purchased sufficient lands and buildings there to set his son up in business – in the same way his own father had helped him. Richard 2, his third son, was given the Cawston estate. Out of these estates, Richard's other children Daniel, Clement, Lydia and Hannah were to be paid a total of £760, a substantial sum. Lydia married into the tanning trade; in 1695 she and Matthew Miller of Hunworth wed in Norwich. The year before, Hannah married John 'Jack' Bell of Wood farm, Oulton at the Bishop's Chapel.

### Thomas 1 and the Manor House

At his father's death Thomas 1 was probably living in the Grand/Bateley's house. Having seen his father's rise in society, he, like his brothers, aspired to be a gentleman. By 1690 Thomas had his house and 9 acres around it - mostly on Broom hill - and about another 34 acres in 15 pieces in and around the open field of Itteringham. In 1696, a month after he purchased Purdy farm (**22**) from Sir Roger Potts, he also bought the cottage, buildings and 1 acre of yards and land on the east side of the Wolterton road (**6**). As with other purchases from Roger Potts, the Robins family cleverly went for those marginal parts of the Mannington estate which could easily be sold off with good title. In the same £250 deal, Thomas acquired a long list of pieces of arable and meadow. Included were Harts Yard - the 5 acre field across the road from the pub - 3 acres of land and meadow to the west of the Cut adjacent to Bintry Close and 18 acres of open field arable strips in 15 pieces. This significant piece of open field consolidation was followed the next year by his purchase from John Bell jnr of Oulton gent (of the Middle farm line, d 1704) of just under 5 acres of land in 4 pieces in Itteringham's open field. These were in Muckle Meadow Hirne, still a furlong of strips in multiple occupation, and in unnamed furlongs just to the east of the Itteringham to Wolterton road – another step in Thomas's consolidation of open field furlongs.

He further benefited from his marriage to his first cousin Mary Robins of Heydon. Her father was Thomas Robins, the Heydon worsted weaver discussed in Chapter 3. Their forthcoming marriage was referred to in Mary's father's will in 1691 and a long deed of January 1691 in which, before the wedding, Thomas conveyed all his real estate in trust to Mary's brother, William Robins of Heydon, and his own brother William Robins of Baconsthorpe. The property was then to be for the couple's use and subsequently their heirs. Thomas received £200 on his wedding day in June from Mary's father. The marriage and his acquisition of the manor of Bintry the same year (see below) quickly achieved his goal to improve himself. Owning the tannery was a useful addition to his holdings but the real stepping stone was gaining manorial status. In 1707 Thomas Robins clearly felt secure enough to build the fine Manor House on the ground in front of the smithy. Attractively proportioned and of reasonable size for a gentleman and lord of the manor, it must be assumed that this was a considerably better house than whatever stood at Bintry and certainly much finer than the now very old-fashioned Love's messuage.

Perhaps Thomas Robins had acted compulsively in building the house. In 1704 John Framingham had built a not dissimilar house at Hill farm. The Robins house with its rear range made up of the old cottages was of course a little finer and certainly larger.

Unfortunately the house was not to be filled with a large family. Unlike most of the Robins lines which were very fecund, the Itteringham branch was to be less fortunate. The cousins were relatively late in marrying - Thomas was 38 and Mary 29 - which may partly explain why Mary only bore three children, two of whom died as infants. Their son Thomas 2 was born in August 1698 and survived to inherit his father's fine house. In January 1724, Thomas Robins 1 settled all his properties in Itteringham on his son Thomas 2 and bride-to-be Mary the daughter of Dr John and Jane Jefferies of Smallburgh. For a few years Thomas 2 enjoyed life as a property-owning gentleman; his wife had given birth to a healthy girl, Mary, at the end of their first year together who was baptised at Bradfield meeting house. All should have been well. However, of their six children four were to die young and Thomas himself, as we shall see later, died unexpectedly young in 1732. Until his son Thomas 3 grew up, the fine house was let to tenant farmers.

Detailing above the front door

The 1707 new front of the Manor House

The side elevation showing four sections: the new front, the kitchen/forge, two cottages refaced in brick as one and the small lean-to at the back

The mystery initials R[P?]TM 1750 on the poor quality lean-to at the eastern end

Later a small lean-to, with a tiny upstairs space, was added to the rear wing in 1750 as a date stone shows. This was just before the young Thomas Robins reached full age and so was probably put up by the then tenant Thomas Barton. However, the initials RTM or PTM have not been identified to any person in Itteringham - a mystery yet to be solved.

Thomas Robins 3 lived in his Manor House but never married. Thomas Robins 'esquire' died on 10th June 1782 without making a will, his passing noted briefly in the Norwich newspaper 'after a short illness in the 53rd year of his age'. He had made little mark on local life and had not added materially to the family property. Thomas's whole estate went to his only surviving sibling, his elder sister Mary. Mary had married well in 1749; William Creasey was a grocer and merchant of Martham, where his family had been for many generations, latterly involved as modest land owners, farmers, tailors and schoolmasters. They moved to Great Yarmouth where they lived off the income from their lands. Of their tenants, John Bell of Oulton - as we will see in the next chapter - lived at the Manor House until his death in 1789. After Bell's death, William Creasey put in Richard Garnham, who ran Creasey's manorial holding in Martham Henegraves and Knightleys. Now as tenant farmer of the 239 acres of the Manor House and Dairy farm, Garnham also had a little under 17 acres described as lands woods and canals. This would have been the meadow in front of the Manor House and the 'park' on Broom hill. The Garnhams were to stay in Itteringham for many years as gentlemen farmers at the manor house after 1799 when the property was sold to the Blickling estate. The house remained let as a farmhouse until the mid-20th century.

### The smithy moves

In order to create the new Manor House, the smithy was moved - one of several moves in its history - and the old site was enlarged and re-fronted. By 1691 the smith's shop and shoeing house, with quarter of an acre of land was described as being on the Wolterton road, abutted by the houses of Charles Jackson and Thomas Rogers (**11**). The site, west of the shop, is now covered by the drive at the side of Wingfield House.

Site of the old smithy opposite the Manor House

Although the very fine ironwork which still survives on the Manor House windows and doors may well have been crafted by Thomas himself, from 1707 onwards Thomas Robins 1 ceased to be a blacksmith. The work of the smithy at some point was managed by a tenant and no later generations of Robins would work a forge again. Nothing more is known of the Heydon smithy which should have passed back to the line of Richard's brother Thomas of Heydon, a weaver; however as Thomas's daughter Mary was the cousin who married Thomas the blacksmith, the ownership could have reverted to them! The Baconsthorpe smithy was left without a smith when William died unexpectedly young in 1705. It appears that another cousin, Jacob Robins then a blacksmith of Buxton, who may have been apprenticed to William, took over. He and his wife subsequently lived in Baconsthorpe and joined with other dissenting members of the family in building the Oulton Meeting House.

**Iron work by Thomas Robins in the Manor House**

The Itteringham forge was run for most of the century by the Jeckyll family, another blacksmithing family with branches in Great Snoring, East Barsham and Thursford. (William Robins the blacksmith in Baconsthorpe had connections by marriage to the Warnes and Favors families, both of which were very visible in the Thursford area.) Edmund Jeckyll had taken up the tenancy and was in the village with his wife Agnes by 1722; he was regularly appearing in the Walpole accounts as smith by 1737. Edmund ran the forge by hiring other smiths on one year contracts. As the men received board and lodging, only bachelors were hired. William Jarvis of Corpusty, who had trained at Saxthorpe, worked for Edmund around 1746 but the young man married towards the end of his term and so, as was the custom, had to leave.

Agnes had only one surviving child, a daughter Mary who married Francis Jeckyll of Letheringsett, probably her cousin. Francis and his brother Robert Jeckyll both worked at the Itteringham smithy in the 1760s and brought up their children there. Widowed in 1764, Francis married Lucy Nelson, the daughter of Walpole's gamekeeper, in 1768. Robert later took over alone as blacksmith and was making metal traps for Wolterton by 1775. Like many tenants who lived and worked in the village, he owned some freehold land elsewhere - his was at his original parish of Letheringsett. He had married Sarah Bird, an Itteringham girl, in 1763 (two years after she had been pregnant by him) and they baptised seven children, at least three of whom married in Itteringham church. Robert Jeckyll still occupied the cottage and smithy in 1799, when the Robins's property was bought by the Blickling estate, and he died at the grand old age of 92 in 1819! He was immediately followed by Henry Hall – quite possibly a descendant of the same family as William Hall of Heydon.

Between 1799 and 1816 Lord Suffield built new cottages on the small strip of land next door to the old smithy and now partly called Wingfield House (the latter being extended later in the century and dated on its gable 1872). According to local tradition, the smithy later burnt down - an occupational hazard - and was moved to a new site opposite the church. With Peter, the last of the Hall line of blacksmiths remaining active into the 1930s, the village has had just three blacksmith families in nearly 300 years.

## The tanner and the tan-house

Tanning was an ancient and noxious trade, where hides were soaked between layers of oak bark in great pits; the tan-house was usually placed slightly away from the village centre but had to be close to a river to provide sufficient water supply. The work was dangerous not only for the tanners' men but also, with regard to anthrax spores, for surrounding areas where animals grazed on the local watermeadows. Wool and animal skins often harbored anthrax spores, which, before modern disinfectants, were hard to kill. As the hide or hair was handled they became airborne and could be inhaled into the lungs with deadly results. Simply handling the spores could give a skin infection which, although not fatal, created a boil-like skin lesion that eventually formed a nasty black ulcer. The raw hides and skins could carry other moulds, yeasts and bacteria leading to tetanus, brucellosis and other pulmonary diseases. Carrying heavy bundles of hides, with hands calloused from scraping, tanners breathed poisonous gases from the tanning processes; many accidents were caused falling into tanning vats and lime pits. Kilns for drying hides were liable to catch fire if not well tiled. Perhaps not surprisingly some tanners died quite young.

---

### Early Medieval tanning

There were two methods of preparing leather:
1. Strip off fatty layer beneath the skin. Remove hair either by scraping, or soak the skin in urine to start decay of hair. Remaining leather will stiffen and may rot unless treated further. A temporary stability can be obtained by smoking over a slow fire and rubbing in an oil dressing of egg yolk, tallow or cattle brains. However decay will set in especially if leather becomes wet.
2. Tanning gives a more permanent result. Pelt should be swollen; partial rotting is encouraged by bacteria from dung or dog excrement. Hides are then soaked in a tan bath, with tannins obtained from oak and larch. The exact type used affects the colour of the leather. After tanning, oil dressings applied to keep leather supple.

See H Hodges, *Artefacts: Introduction to Early Mediaeval Technology*, 1976

---

The rewards, on the other hand, could be substantial as everyone needed leather goods; hides were used for clothing, saddlery, and boots; finer leathers, such as calfskin, went for gloves, shoes, even for bookbinding. In the rural areas, tanning families often acted as local trade networks, protecting themselves against outside competition. Sons followed fathers into the business; daughters were married to other tanners or allied trades such as glovers, cordwainers (shoemakers) or curriers (one who curries or dresses the tanned leather). Fellmongers, graziers and butchers were also useful men to have in the family. The buildings and tools were passed on only to other tanners and families may have run up to four or five tanneries, some owned, others leased. Tanners were often among the most successful businessmen in a village. Rice Wickes (or Wix) of Blickling, who had what a surveyor described as 'the compleatest tan yard I ever saw' also ran three consolidated estate farms of over 198 acres. He left over £1,500 in cash in 1769 to his family. Even a jobbing tanner - not the owner - could aspire to a reasonable standard of living; Roger Selth of Great Ellingham was worth £261 at his death in 1709. Apart from his parlour clock and two looking-glasses his belongings were modest but his leather tools were valued at £149. Tanners were also very heavily regulated, with scores of acts of parliament being passed from the 16th century up to the present day. Hides, like spirits, were subject to government duty, and tanners were regularly inspected by the Excise.

In Itteringham the Bintry Hall site (17) had been in operation as a tannery since at least the mid 17th century and may date back much earlier. Edmund Chapman taxed here in 1660 and 1663 was probably the Edmund who died a tanner at Hanworth in 1671. In the 16th century this small manor had passed from the Lumners of Mannington and was held for many years by the Larwoods. In 1600 it was sold to the Gay family, active in the area as farmers and tanners in the 17th century. There is no indication of a tannery here before their arrival and it is possible that Bintry farm house was not on the site of the original manorial hall. Over the 17th century it passed through different generations of the family and at various times was mortgaged. The mortgage that Richard Robins had provided in 1688 passed to Thomas 1 on his father's death and the property was then fully conveyed to him by Richard Gay in 1691. Thomas now had the house and farm buildings, the tannery and the 70 acre Bintry Close in addition to his other lands. In 1700 a deed committed Thomas and his heirs to pay his wife Mary £30 per year for life from this property after his death. She was also allowed if she did not remarry to live in Bintry and enjoy the parlour chamber and buttery and the garden beside the parlour, together with use of the yard and outhouses.

From this it seems at least possible that Thomas and Mary had chosen to live in Bintry house in the 1690s, leasing the farm and tannery to separate tenants.

At that time Matthew Mason was the first of a series of recorded tenants working the tannery and the 70 acre farm there. Matthew had lived in Itteringham with his first wife Elizabeth since at least 1680, the year they buried their son Robert. He also owned his own tan-house at Lamas and a house in Norwich by the time he died in 1709. The next recorded of Robins's tenants are the Bayly (Baly) family. When William Bayly senior married Elizabeth, a Robins girl from Plumstead, in 1714 at Cromer, he was of Itteringham and probably was running the tannery there for Thomas Robins. In the 1720s he held from the Mannington estate the small farm on the West Field site (**2**) which was adjacent to the Bintry land. Bayly also ran a tannery of his own in Heigham, then a village near Norwich, probably taking over from Thomas Rose who died in 1728. Rose's father Robert had been a friend of Clement Robins who witnessed his will in 1715 along with Samuel Burrows, possibly a currier. Robert Rose may well have run the Itteringham tannery for a while after Mason, as the West Field farm was tenanted by a Robert Rose in 1710. When he married Mary Gay of Wood Dalling in the 1680s, he was living in Hunworth and may have learnt his trade there at Matthew Miller's tannery. Mary's sister Jane Gay was married to William Bell of Oulton, a butcher – a useful brother-in-law for a tanner.

Elizabeth Bayly, buried in Itteringham in 1727, may have been one of William and Elizabeth's children. Their two sons survived, William and Thomas, the first of whom took up his father's trade. William junior married Lydia Bell, daughter of Hannah Robins and John Bell of Oulton (a cousin of the tanning family there) and took on the Itteringham tannery around 1739. Lydia was named after her aunt Lydia Robins, who was married to the Hunworth tanner, Matthew Miller. In 1742 William Bayly senior died leaving his Heigham tanning offices and all stock in trade to his son and was wealthy enough to leave his other, younger, son Thomas £700.

Sadly within six months of his father's death, William Bayly junior also died. As Lydia died the following week, they may have been victims of smallpox rather than a tanning disease; both were buried in January 1743 in Itteringham churchyard where their gravestones still stand. (The date stone is given in the old calendar style as 1742.) William was only 26, his wife 33. With the support of the Oulton dissenting minister, Abraham Coveney and his wife Mary, Lydia quickly made her will the day after being widowed and was able to bequeath over £400 to her Bell and Robins relations, before she too succumbed. William's mother Elizabeth was buried near the young couple four years later. After the sudden death of William and Lydia, one of her relatives, John Bell of the Oulton tanners, kept the tannery going for a year or so but a permanent tenant was needed.

### Towne takes over

In 1744, a young tanner, Michael Towne, took the opportunity. Michael was the third generation of Towne tanners of Gunthorpe, following his father Edward and grandfather Michael. Newly-married, he and his wife Ann Blyth of Colby, settled at the Bintry house and Michael soon became well-established in the village. He was appointed as overseer after two years and held this office again another four times over the next 13 years. Soon after his arrival, he arranged to purchase a supply of bark, vital for his work, from the Wolterton estate; in April 1745 he paid '4s 6d a tun ... for all the bark taken down in Fring Wood' and another three guineas for 70 pollarded trees. The agreement continued as his business prospered and he bought bark from 91 'tops' for £2 15s 6d in 1748.

For the first few years, he only employed three full-time men and bought in the larger and heavier hides ready tanned. For these 'sole' hides he had several regular customers - John Fidgett, Edward Gresham, William Sly, John Narborough, William Walker - who were curriers and shoemakers from Fakenham, Binham, Hindringham and Briston. As these were all in an area encircling Gunthorpe, Michael had inherited their custom along with his father's tannery there in 1734. He let out the house and malthouse but stopped tanning there, preferring the better site in Itteringham. Locally he supplied the village cordwainer, Ark Hurrell, another tenant of Thomas Robins. By 1757 he had five menservants and a bark maker and was processing larger raw hides as well. Of these, he later claimed one was an apprentice, Sam Bircham, and two were old men not capable of doing much work. In 1764 when he wrote his will, eight men and a boy and several maidservants were mentioned, many living-in. As he had land to farm as well, no doubt there was always a variety of work to do. One of the opportunities of being involved with the poor relief system was acquiring the annual contract for supplying firings for the poor's fuel; this could be tan turves (made of bark) or smallwood from his own meadows. All the by-products of his trade were saleable; the hair from the skins, whether normal or 'white' made a shilling a bushel. Walpole bought a large quantity of hair in 1760, for £1 16s, presumably for plastering work. Most tanners, including Towne, also dealt in timber sales. Thomas Bell the Oulton tanner in 1707 bought quantities of bark from the Blickling estate;

at the same time he was paid a salary for organising timber for repairs on the estate and supplied 'covenanted' firewood for the tenants, as promised under their leases.

Towne's business involved trading and travelling far afield. His grandfather had sold his leathers at the great annual three-week Sturbridge Fair, near Cambridge, described by Defoe as better than any of the great European trading fairs; Michael may well have continued this late summer tradition. On Saturdays Towne would visit both Holt and Norwich markets (in one day) to negotiate with suppliers – Norwich for the heavy sole hides and Holt for whatever the butchers were offering that week. His brother John was a wealthy master mariner at Kings Lynn and Wednesdays often saw business transacted there. Small dressing hides (ready tanned) were obtained from Mr Claybourn at Great Yarmouth. Add in trips to North Walsham to the currier Edmund Angel and to Heigham to see Tobias Crowfoot and the picture emerges of Towne constantly on horseback, working his contacts all over north Norfolk.

## *No hiding place – Towne and the taxman*

As we have seen earlier, Towne's steady influence with his young landlord and neighbour, Thomas Robins 3, was much appreciated by Lord Walpole in 1754-55. He was a friend and dinner companion of Walpole's steward Ness. However, despite his apparently good character and reputation, Towne was to fall foul of the dreaded excise officers. The inspectors constantly watched tanners for signs of the many malpractices that were commonly undertaken: selling old as new, not tanning the leather fully, selling hides without their being registered and sealed and adding water to make up false weight. Towne's regular officer was James Griggs in whose patch Itteringham fell and who had been visiting him since at least 1753. One of the Commissioners of Excise for England and Wales in the 1750s, was Augustine Earle esq of Heydon Hall. A few of his papers survive relating to his examination of some of the witnesses in the Court of Exchequer case in 1758 and 1761, shortly before he died in 1762. Some of the exchequer case documents themselves also survive so most of the story is discoverable.

It seems that a Mr James Skoulding of Aldborough, the excise officer who covered the neighbouring area had been hearing rumours from 'his' tanners about Towne. They were upset that although Towne was buying the same average weights of hides in Holt and Norwich markets as they were, he seemed to be paying far less duty than was demanded of them – little more than half as much. In the summer of 1757 Skoulding, who had known Towne for a couple of years, became deeply suspicious of both the tanner and James Griggs who, the rumour-mongers claimed, was colluding with Towne in undercharging by recording lower weights. He asked his superior, John Repton of Norwich, the district collector of excise (and Humphrey Repton's father) to show him Towne and Griggs's accounts for the last year. On seeing these Skoulding was convinced something was going on and on 28th November while meeting at Foulsham he pressed Repton to let him take the matter further. The next day, the 29th, a trap would be laid.

At 7 o'clock in the morning James Griggs turned up as usual to weigh hides in Bintry's yard which was 'kept well-filled and stacked with hides'. Ten hides were registered as weighing 259 lbs. Off went Griggs, presumably not suspecting anything was afoot. Did Towne have a tip-off? Later that day between 1 and 3 o'clock, another officer, Aylsham supervisor James Dewhurst of Coltishall was sent to re-weigh the same hides as a double-check. Against regulations, which required weighed hides to remain on site for 48 hours, the ten had been 'spirited away'. Dewhurst was not very surprised; on two occasions in 1754 and 1756 when he had been on duty, hides had rapidly left Towne's premises after weighing. The hunt was on!

Five of the hides were tracked down by Dewhurst fairly quickly. Two were at Mr Gresham's, a cordwainer at Briston who apparently had been waiting for them at the tanyard that day; they were re-weighed on his premises. The three found on the premises of Ark Hurrell, just up the road in Itteringham, were returned to the yard to be checked.

Dewhurst later reported that Towne, 'on finding himself detected in ... fraudulent practices, made use of fair words to influence the supervisor and pretended to have sent 5 hides to customers 12 miles away'. Towne claimed he had sent the other five hides to John Narborough another shoemaker who had been promised some hides at the end of November. Skoulding, who had stayed the night at the Half Moon pub in Briston, met up with Dewhurst as he knew the way to Narborough's place in Hindringham. Their visit was to no avail as no hides had been delivered. They returned to Briston where another night was spent, with a third excise man, 45 year-old supervisor John Wood. Very early on the 30th when it was still dark, the three set off for Blickling where they settled at the inn there; Skoulding was sent into Aylsham to get Mr Repton and all four went off to search Towne's yard, arriving there at 7 am and spending 2 hours searching the Bintry site. The villagers must have been watching all this activity with great interest. Towne refused to show the officers his books saying he did not have to and insisted the hides had been sent away. Again Dewhurst and Skoulding went to Hindringham but again found nothing.

However the re-weighing of the rediscovered five hides at 180 lbs showed that, to match Griggs's recorded amount, the missing five hides would have to weigh only 79 lbs in total, far too little for large sole hides which often weighed 40 lbs each. This evidence, along with the illegal early removal of the hides, was enough for the excise to initiate proceedings against Michael Towne. It was also clear that Griggs had been deliberately under-recording the hides' weights; he immediately lost his job and was replaced on 13th December by Skoulding. A letter written to Augustine Earle by John Repton in February 1758 gives the local view.

Repton reported that when he was at the Aylsham Assembly, he spoke to Lord Walpole who said he 'had some favourable impressions of Town's case as told by himself'. Repton told Walpole that the officer was sacked in consequence of the report and a great fraud had been carried on but could not say more but he advised 'his lordship to suspend his impression of Mr Town's honesty till more was known'. Griggs had been sacked for allegedly taking 'hush money', a practice that was widespread. He then added that in Norwich any tanner who was apprenticed in that part said it was common practice to give a shilling to the supervisor per hide. 'Weeks [Rice Wickes] of Blickling was as honest as most of them but he was forced to silence the supervisor now and then with side of a Good Fat Hogg'. A shilling must have been much easier to pocket discreetly in Norwich than trying to slip away with a side of pork from Blickling. Despite Towne's denial of giving the supervisor bribes, the Attorney-General had brought charges of malpractice against him. Towne had obviously told Lord Walpole his side of the story and been believed but Repton - who by now had seen the disgraced Griggs' own notebooks - was less convinced of his innocence.

Towne hired Edmund Jewell, the 'eminent attorney of Aylsham' and lawyer to the Robins family, to help him through the case. Jewell left incredibly detailed accounts covering the five years over which the matter ran. The interminable slow processes of the exchequer can be seen from his entries; every fee paid, brief drawn, hearing attended and case paper copied was listed. Unlike criminal courts where trials were often over in minutes, equity cases consisted of a series of hearings of counsel's papers. Suits dragged on while information was given, answers were then presented and responses to those answers then requested. The legal terms were sometimes quite short and papers filed might not be heard for months. In early 1759 Jewell and Towne read the information (the allegations) and prepared their answer, 'making schedules from long and intricate accounts which took up much time.' An amended allegation was sent to them in 1760 which they pored over and Jewell asked for more time to answer in early 1761! Then the accounts read like a diary: while they were working on the latest papers 'a Discovery was made of Mistakes made as to some facts in [Towne's] answer to Original Information':

> For the settling which and rectifying said Mistakes in said former Answer it was thought necessary for me to take a Journey to Town to converse personally with Counsel it being a matter of the greatest Consequence to Deft who thereof insisted on my taking that Journey On which I set out from home that day and returned on the 2nd April for which I charge as follows (to wit) that I paid for Post Chaise & Boys & for Expenses on the Road and in Town £10 12s 0d.

Then came Towne's turn to be examined. Under questioning by the two commissioners, including Earle, in April 1761 at Norwich, Towne denied all the charges that the Attorney-General had brought. The first and second charges estimated very high (and improbable) quantities of hides; the third was based on the evidence. In fact only 1,489 soles were noted as weighed between 1753-1757.

**Firstly** that Michael Towne owes HM Revenue **£2454 13s 6d** for single duties owed on skins and hides by him tanned from 29th December 1749 to 29th December 1757 amounting to 14000 and upwards:
7000 Sole hides at weight 40 lbs, duty on which - £1750
3000 Dressing hides weight 32 lbs 1 qtr, duty - £604 13s 6d
4000 Calve skins weight 4 lbs, duty - £200

**Secondly** that Michael Towne owes HM Revenue a further **£1575** on hides and skins tanned from 19th December 1753 to 29th November 1757 which were omitted or were fraudulently and collusively charged by James Griggs the Excise officer who then surveyed him at the following defective and unjust weights:
8000 Sole hides at 26 lbs, each one in fact on average weighed 40 lbs, so he owes £700
8000 Dressing hides at 18 ¾ lb, which in fact weighed 32 ½ lbs, so owes £675

8000 Calve skins at 2 ¾ lbs, which in realty weighed 4 lbs, so deficient by £200

Because of fraudulent and deficient charges or weighing Revenue sustained loss of £1575

**Thirdly** that Towne moreover owes 12s 7 ½ for duties on 10 sole hides which on 29th November 1757 were fraudulently weighed by the said officer (and afterwards removed by Towne contrary to law) as 259 lbs when they in fact weighed 360 lbs, so short 12s 7 ½ d (101 lbs)

The excise witnesses, interviewed at The Maid's Head in September that year, included Towne's former apprentice Sam Bircham, now aged 22 and living as a tanner in Hindolveston. Sam had been with Towne for six years from 1754 during which he made most of his deliveries. He had left but interestingly he did not appear in his master's defence. Perhaps the presence of other excise officers and the formality of the examination - the consequences of perjury would have been spelt out to him - made him give Towne away. Towne, in his statement, had said that after he was charged 'he had talked to Sam Bircham who had been his apprentice at the time'. Sam had said 'he took the 5 hides not to Narborow but to the house of Robert Porter, a tenant of Towne's and neighbour of Narborow and brought back a comb of malt for Towne'. Towne was suggesting a reason why the officers had not found the hides at Hindringham and also implied Sam had not carried out his instructions. Sam however told the commissioners that Towne had told him to take the hides to Holt keeping out of the way of the excise. Sam had said that was risky being too public a place. In the dusk of the evening on the 29th, he had set off with the cart of hides, through 'places out of the direct road' to Holt, aiming for the public house at Hindringham. They knew the Half Moon at Briston - on the obvious route - was a regular hangout for the excise men and must be avoided. About 9 o'clock Sam said Towne caught up with him between Holt and Sharrington, asked if he had seen any officers and on hearing not, diverted him to Porter's house at Gunthorpe, Towne's old home ground. Towne told Sam he would arrange for Narborough to collect the leather from there later. Skoulding added he believed Towne had told Sam to say his horse was sick so he must leave the hides there. Sam said he stayed at Porter's that night and carried back some malt that Towne had asked for from Porter – no doubt to make the cart trip look justified. Robert Porter, of course, was leasing Towne's old family house and running the malthouse; his loyalty to his landlord would keep him silent.

The case papers, of course, are not that succinct. Many other potential offences were investigated at great length and provide masses of details about skins and practices. Much hung on the average weights of the hides Towne dealt in – both before processing and after. An accusation that may have been too hard to prove was that Towne had wetted the hides to increase the weight, so able to ask a higher price from his customers. Towne said that moistening or sprinkling was both commonplace and legal; his customers knew it added weight but not as much as was being claimed by the official. Some witnesses agreed that this was normal although tanners John Curteis of Hunworth (who had been Wickes's apprentice at Blickling) and Richard Woods of Stody claimed they had no experience of it. (These two were probably the ones who dropped the original hints to Skoulding.) Despite this, Curteis was still able to explain that hides would only be able to hold up to a maximum 2 lbs of water; any more than this, according to Robert Emerson, and the skin was not a 'marketable commodity'. That is the customer wouldn't buy it! Sam Bircham described it as 'a light sprinkle' to hold their weight if being delivered 10 or 12 miles so the hides would not start to dry out. The 67 year-old Lamas tanner Francis Hammond agreed that a little wetting might be needed to smooth over-dry skin before sale but added, very carefully, that of course it was then re-dried so as not to overcharge the customer. Towne also denied the suggestion that he bought ready-tanned hides and sold them 'promiscuously with his own'.

And who stood up for him? Towne only had four witnesses, two of whom were also examined for the other side. Francis Hammond said very little to help or hinder and Tobias Crowfoot currier of Norwich just said he had bought tanned hides 'of the heaviest and best sort' from Towne. His two employees did their best: young Thomas King, now a tanner at Great Ellingham had lived and worked with Towne from 1755 to April 1761. He and Emerson had been present at the November 1757 weighing with Griggs (Towne was not there) and thought everything seemed fair. He agreed with Emerson that Michael Towne 'bears a very good character in his neighbourhood and is believed to be a fair and honest man in all his dealings'. Robert Emerson was Towne's 48 year-old friend of twenty years; since 1755 he had lived at Bintry with him running the tannery as his head man. His answers suggested all was fair and above board, even saying the other 5 hides had remained in the weighing room. Nothing had been done to the hides to change the weight. In addition to the good character statement he added that he did not believe Michael 'would defraud His Majesty of any duty due'. No more evidence was offered and the law term finished for the winter.

In January 1762 Towne was served with a subpoena to hear the judgement. Jewell was quickly summoned:

'Jan 15 Attending Deft on his being served with Subpoena to hear Judgement on the 28th inst when he desired me to go to Town to retain and fee Counsel and prepare matters and attend the hearing. 22nd Set out for London and arrived there next day and pd Mr Peachey with his Brief etc [three others named]. Feb 4 The Hearing put off until that day but did not come on by reason of the Attorney-General could not attend; paid agent to attend. Feb 19 For their attending again at the Sittings in Chancery Lane when nothing done 13s 4d.' The hearing did come on the next day.

'Pd expenses of coach hire etc to & from London and during my stay there on which I was necessarily 12 days from home £5 18s 6d.' Another 12 guineas for his time talking to counsel.

He came back with a copy of the final judgement, the decree, which unfortunately has not survived. There seems little doubt that the excise had won. What was the truth? Was James Griggs the chap of that name from Briston who married a girl in Towne's home parish of Gunthorpe? On the main charges of bribery and evasion there was no doubt that they were acting together and recording lower weights for at least four years as Griggs's notebook showed. Nothing heavier than 29 lbs had been listed where hides of between 30 and 40 lbs would be expected. The removal of the hides off-site earlier than allowed was self-evident and Sam had admitted that this did happen. If moistening was legal, then Towne might have innocently supplied his customers as he claimed. On the other hand, Ark Hurrell's house in The Street was conveniently very close to the tanyard.

But Towne's troubles were not over; he was then indicted to appear at the assizes at Thetford to stand trial for perjury. Again Jewell advised him and helped him get bail at £300. Towne had to find £200 as security; his brother-in-law Samuel Scott glover of Norwich stood for £100 and Thomas Robins of Itteringham, his landlord, showed his support by being bound for the other £100. On 2nd April 1762, Jewell went with the three of them to Justice Thomas Vere's house at Thorpe. This time Jewell spent 14 days in London preparing for the trial and then six days attending the Assizes itself.

Whatever the truth, Towne had been supported by the Robins family. To them he was a good business man, their reliable tannery tenant who played his part in parish affairs. They may have helped others in his family too. Mary Blyth, presumably his wife's sister, had married Elias Drury of Aldborough in 1739. As Elias later set up as a grocer at Southrepps - with Towne lending him £600 secured on his property - he may well have learned his trade as a boy under Clement Robins. Towne's standing in the village had not been damaged; he was elected overseer again in 1763.

Michael Towne died two years after the case ended; he was only 46. Falling sick unexpectedly in March 1764, he made his will eight days before his death. His widow erected a fine brick chest tomb for her husband and their only child, little John who had died early in their marriage, in 1749. Ann was left well off; she had her jointure property, the Towne's malthouse, tanhouse and 18 acres in Gunthorpe, and £24 a year. Two years later she re-married, to Richard Newman the miller of Great Walsingham. Despite the heavy fines Michael must have paid to the excise, he was able to leave around £2,800 in cash bequests. His sister Sarah, the wife of his other security Samuel Scott, received £1,000, half for herself and half for her daughter. Mary his other sister also enjoyed £1,000; two years later she became the wife of Norwich merchant Thomas Emerson. Elias Drury and his children shared £630. Towne's men were not forgotten: his loyal main 'servant' Robert Emerson had £20. (Samuel Bircham, Towne's earlier apprentice, went on to be tanner at Hackford near Reepham. On his death in 1779, Robert Emerson took over that tannery until 1785.) Thomas Page, Andrew Stokely, Robert Breese and Richard Tubby, who all lived on the site, had 2 guineas each and three more live-in chaps, John 'Riseborow', William Reynolds and Thomas Wick received 1 guinea each. His 'boy' Robert Drake and the maidservants, again all resident, might have drunk the health of their master with their 10s 6d. The poor of both Gunthorpe and Itteringham were remembered with bequests of £10 for each parish. Business must have been good but whatever tax-evasion practices may have gone on he seems to have treated his customers well. On his death, amongst the debts due to him was a bill dating from 1748, some 16 years earlier. William Sadler had paid off all but 11 shillings of £22 but Towne had lent him a guinea. Another 10 year-old bill was for £10 in payment for 31 ash timbers. Jeremiah Leveritt had owed nearly £10 for six years for six oak timbers; Joseph Sand owed over £10 for seven oak timbers which he bought in July 1758. He was supposed to have paid it in November that year. Not only did Towne allow generous credit to his friends but he was apparently concerned for their health. In April 1757 he had sold Thomas Roberts of Wickmere a bottle of 'Daffice' for 1s, which he added to his debt of 4 guineas. Daffy's elixir was a traditional cure-all laxative, a health cordial made from a number of strange ingredients and alcohol. It might have here been used to treat a colicky horse, a practice later deplored by early vets.

The tanner John Read, who followed Towne at the Itteringham tannery, had better luck than his predecessors; there is no suggestion of any problems with the law and he lived to the age of 80. He copied the same style of Towne's brick tomb for his wife and himself, as statement of his solidity and duration. He was a 'good tenant' of the house and 65 acre farm in 1799 when Blickling bought the property and he remained their tenant until his death. Read stood by one of his tanners, John Morrice, when he left Elizabeth Bird with a daughter in 1775 by indemnifying the parish. In 1796 Read himself ended up being bound to the parish officers, for two illegitimate sons - one named Trivett Read - who had been born in 1793 and 1794. At the age of 60 in 1800, he married their mother, 38 year-old Sarah Knights an Itteringham widow. In Sarah's death notice four years later, *The Norwich Mercury* described John as 'farmer of Itteringham'.

The tannery offices at Bintry stood until 1858 when a plan to convert them into additional farm buildings was rejected as their being too weak. Presumably at that point some of the old structures were demolished and the small barn (which still shows the date 1859) was built. The site continued as a farm for the Blickling estate.

## The miller and the mill

The other vital large-scale industry traditionally found in a village was that of flour milling; water mills were established on rivers well before Domesday, owned by the lords of the manor who tightly controlled the local trade. From medieval times, the millers have often had a bad press; there were numerous poems and songs about the dishonest miller who short-changed his customers or stole their grain and malt. One suggests that 'a miller who does not steal' is as rare as a 'lawyer who is legal'. Chaucer gives his miller 'a gold thumb' referring to the practice of pressing on the grain scales to increase the weight – and therefore the price. Not keen to operate under the gaze of the customer (or officer), the miller's full phrase was 'keep your nose to the grindstone and keep your eye to the road'. However there is no evidence that our local men were rogues.

Smaller mills sited on less efficient flows of water, such as the one on the Cut noted in 1595, often disappeared fairly early. Itteringham's large mill - Mickle or Muckle mill - was an established part of the Mannington estate for centuries (adjoining **19**). In 1595 the mill house was shown as Bircham's, no doubt the name of the miller at or around that time. With the mill was a small farm of about 15-20 acres, most of which was meadow immediately around the mill; the composition varied over time but sometimes included Harts Yard - the arable field between the pub and the meadows to the west of the bridge - and a number of open field strips. In the 1630s the miller was Thomas Leaman – in 1639 it was noted that he had taken a 10 year lease of the mill and about 25 acres in September 1634. His immediate successor, and still there in 1668, was John Brown. In 1673 the mill was held by William Lee and in 1693 by Stephen Buston. By 1701 Richard Lound (Lounds, Lown) was miller, when the smallholding was up to 30 acres; his first wife Susan died in Itteringham in 1699 and Richard and his second wife Hannah moved away after 1708. By 1710 John Leak (also spelt Leake or Leek) had taken over the mill. Like the other tenant business men of the village, he also owned property outright elsewhere. He was still there in 1726 but made his will as miller of Corpusty in September 1729, where he was buried soon afterwards. While he left his mill and house at Corpusty were left to his son John, a good part of his will involved arrangements for his only daughter Mary, the wife of Robert Bird of Itteringham, to inherit his houses and lands in Cawston.

The Robins family who owned the tannery and the forge were of course not able to acquire the freehold of the mill and were not interested in merely being tenants. Through Jacob Robins, the Baconsthorpe blacksmith who rose to yeoman, the family built up their own baking and milling interests in Cawston and Aylsham.

The other local mill was the estate mill of Blickling, just the other end of the lane from Itteringham mill. In 1756 a detailed survey by Londoner Thomas Browne described it in error as Itteringham mill which has confused some later writers. At Blickling mill the tenant James Smith paid £40 rent for the mill, mill farm and a small white wall and tiled house, together with an 'indifferent boarded and thatched barn stable and carthouse, the whole wants repairing' with 60 acres of land. Browne continued: 'These buildings are but in indifferent repair, there is no French stones only a pair of peak and a pair of cullins. Tenant does all the repairs to the mill, being found rough timber. The arable is dry light land and the meadow very coarse'. But he thought Smith was a good tenant and the rent was sustainable at that level. James Smith had married Sarah the sister of his once neighbouring tenant William Gedge, who by the time Smith made his will in 1763 had moved on to Oulton. At his death Smith was also renting a farm and farm house from his neighbour across the Bure, Richard Robins. It is most likely that this was the Robins farm at Oak Hill, now Ash Hill, in Ingworth and Erpingham. This farm of course was no distance away from Blickling mill, across the river at John's Bridge or via the bridge further downstream opposite Blickling's tannery.

Leak was followed as Itteringham's miller by Robert Colls, who with his wife Hannah Lound baptised six children in the village from 1731. Hannah was probably a daughter of Richard, the earlier miller and Hannah, his second wife. The Colls family had a wide impact on milling in north-east Norfolk; Robert's grand-father, William a husbandman of North Elmham, seems to have had links with Itteringham - his first wife Elizabeth died there in 1668 - but there is no evidence that he was a miller there. Perhaps Elizabeth had been an Itteringham girl. Robert's father was William Colls junior. He became a miller at Burgh next Aylsham, where his sons were born, later moving to Aldborough. After William died in 1740, Robert's brother, also called William, continued milling in Burgh; in 1756 he bought Letheringsett mill from the bankrupt owner John Priest where his son and grandson continued as millers until 1783. Like the Robins's and Bells, his family were also dissenters, in this case Quakers.

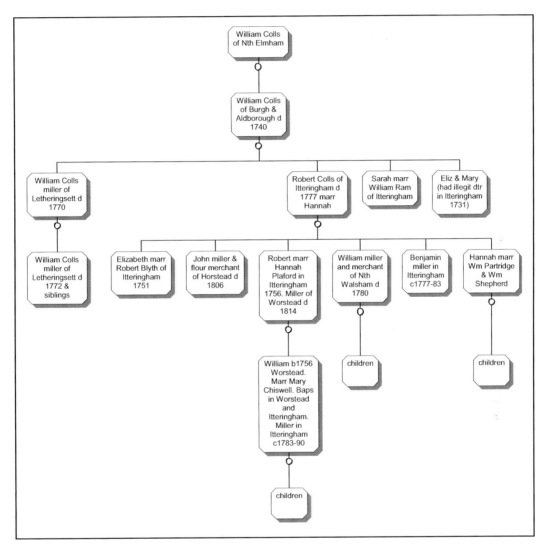

Simplified Colls family tree

As the mill was firmly in the hands of the estate, the conditions of each lease were very detailed. With constant wear and tear - not to mention the threat of fire from sparks - the responsibility for repairs had to be precisely expressed. At the beginning of 1737, almost immediately after Horatio Walpole took over the estate, Robert Colls had various repairs undertaken and new stones installed at Walpole's expense. A French mill stone costing 11 guineas was acquired from Robert Cook and another stone was bought from William Colls costing £2 15s. The repairs had involved blacksmith work by both Edward Carr and Edmund Jeckyll, millwright work by Jonathan Ulphes, bricklaying by Valentine Hardy and a small input from Mr Tomling the brazier. Again in 1740 Robert Colls got allowances for repairs by Jeckyll and Richard Jackson the millwright, ditching by Thomas King (probably in the water system since normally field ditches were the tenant's responsibility) and for Tomling's brass work. In 1743 Colls yet again charged Walpole for a new millstone and other work – this time £9 for a millstone called a peak and £4 4s for a set of cogs for the cullins and a set of cogs for the great wheel.

In 1742 the farm was back to the more traditional 17 acres. In November 1745 Walpole and his steward Richard Ness renegotiated the Colls lease of Itteringham mill and lands, as described in a couple of surviving letters. The renewal seemed as if it should be a straightforward matter of continuing the lease at £27 per year. However, Robert Colls felt that he was not being treated properly regarding the repairs to the 'mansion house and barn', which in common with the mill buildings he was asked to pay for himself. He believed this was unfair since these buildings went with the farm land and under a normal farm lease the landlord would be responsible. He claimed that Walpole had always done all the repairs. In reply, Walpole said he would do the repairs if the rent was raised by £1 and if Colls found the materials himself – an agreement Walpole thought Colls had made when the three men met in Ness's room at Wolterton. Colls said that this was not his understanding but that he would advance his rent to £32 if Walpole did all the repairs. This would seem to indicate that the house and barn was at the time in need of major repair and that Colls was trying to avoid a significant bill for materials. In the event it is not known exactly what deal was struck, but Colls continued as tenant at £27 per year. It may well be that he secured a one-off arrangement for the materials to be paid for, or that he simply had to back down and accept Walpole's terms. It appears to have taken them some time to resolve the lease dispute, continuing on the old terms for 6 years. In September 1751 Walpole made a new long lease to Robert, probably for 50 years. This suggests Colls was a reliable tenant; certainly he was a good citizen standing for the office of overseer for the parish three times between 1744 and 1752. As he grew older, he may well have engaged a miller to carry on the daily business. In 1776 *The Norfolk Chronicle* reported the marriage in April of 'Mr Jonathan Baxter of Itteringham miller' at Drayton. His bride Miss Sarah Frost was described as 'an agreeable young lady with a genteel fortune'; her money may not have been put to the best use. Within four years, Jonathan Baxter was the proud owner of a 'new built' post mill and horse mill with corn chambers in Oulton. Erected on Oulton common, one of the highest parts of the parish, Baxter may have thought he was on to a winner especially with his former employer fading fast.

Robert Colls died at Itteringham on 6th September 1777 and was buried five days later in the churchyard under a large flat ledger stone. On the 13th *The Norfolk Chronicle* recorded his passing 'in his 68th year much lamented by family and all who knew him'. By now three of his sons were well-established millers and merchants in their own right: John a miller and flour merchant in Horstead, William of North Walsham and Robert junior of Worstead. Robert junior's first wife was Hannah Plaford of Itteringham, whose father Thomas Plaford became the new tenant of Mannington's Mere farm shortly after their marriage. Busy with their own businesses, the Colls left it to another brother, Benjamin to look after Itteringham. Little is known about him; born in Itteringham in 1740, he was 37 when he was named as tenant in late 1777. He might already have been working at the mill but no marriage or burial has been found for him. Whether he was not a miller and continued his own life elsewhere or whether he died in the early 1780s is not clear.

What is known is that a new broom appeared by 1783. William Colls, the eldest son of Benjamin's brother Robert of Worstead, moved into Itteringham with his wife Mary Chiswell at the end of 1782. The baptism of their first child Robert was recorded in both churches on 11th December. Over the next 7 years they would baptise six more children in the village including twin sons who did not survive.

In December 1783 Walpole granted a new 50 year lease to William Colls for Itteringham mill and its small area of farm land, explicitly on the surrender (presumably early) of the September 1751 lease to Robert Colls. In this lease the dwelling house, stables and outhouses, like the mill itself and all its waterworks, were in future to be repaired by Colls. In part the new lease was to reflect new terms after Colls had recently rebuilt the mill. 'RW 1783' remains carved in plaster under the first floor near the fireplace – the work of Robert Ward the local bricklayer at the time. The rent rose steeply from the old £27 to £40. Walpole also had a formal arrangement for Colls to leave the 2 pairs of stones at the end of the lease and for Colls to pay for the number of inches lost in grinding over the years: 'the upper and lower stones called the pair of Cullins now standing in the wheat mill 9 inches thick and the upper stone called the Peake now standing in the rye mill 7 inches thick ... Colls to pay to Walpole 10s for every inch of these Cullins and Peake as they shall want of that thickness. And also the lower stone in the rye mill called the French stone of 3 ½ inches to pay 20s per inch used'. The German cullins were for milling wheat to flour while the other pair consisted of a Derby peak runnerstone over a French burr bedstone for milling rye. French burrstones were expensive and were almost exclusively used for flour milling, thus the above arrangement might have come about if the mill had been converted to rye milling by buying a cheap Peak runnerstone.

Robert Ward's initials at the mill

Most of the smallholding was in meadow, so the farming aspects of the lease were much briefer. Colls could not plough any land that had been untilled for the past 7 years unless he paid an additional £5 per year rent per acre. Where he had arable he was only to take 2 crops of grain or corn before summer tilling for turnips and then laying down the same field with good clover and grass seeds for 2 years before ploughing again. Throughout he was able to use the hay and dung, although Walpole would have them in the last year of the lease. Over the next eight years William successfully ran the mill and fulfilled his parish duty as overseer three times. It is likely that he also looked after his widowed grandmother Hannah who was still living in Itteringham, where she would die at the age of 87 in 1800. By 1791 however William had to return to Worstead to help his father Robert, who was in his mid-60s, with the family business there; in fact Robert who had married again after Hannah's death in 1787 lived to the age of 78 dying in 1814. However the business was indeed in trouble; in July 1793 Robert Colls merchant of Worstead was gazetted as a bankrupt. Mary and William remained there working and raising two more sons, William and John. In Itteringham Grandma Colls was buried alongside her husband by Martha Colls, probably one of her daughters, who had married William Bell son of the park-keeper at Blickling in 1778. In keeping with family tradition, William was also a miller – at Blickling mill a little further down the Bure. Their son Thomas followed his father there. William and Martha Bell were buried under the big ledger stone alongside her parents in Itteringham.

The effect of both Itteringham and Blickling's large estate-run mills undergoing complete refurbishment between 1779 and 1783 was to put paid to any hope of success for Baxter's new windmill at Oulton. He immediately offered it for sale in September 1780. In November 1784 it was advertised for sale again at which time William Bell of Blickling mill was the tenant. Whether or not the Blickling estate purchased it for extra capacity - Bell's successor James Savory may have worked it later - the mill was not maintained. Although shown clearly on Faden's map published in 1797, no mill remained twenty-six years later when the common was enclosed and the precise site is not known.

The Itteringham mill was next tenanted by John Skelton who took over as Walpole's flour supplier in November 1790. He paid the village poor rate for the property until 1800 but may have sublet the mill from William Pinkard who appears as tenant in the Wolterton accounts in 1794-95. The Pinkards were also a north Norfolk milling family. By 1809 both the mill and the small farm were in the hands of Thomas Roberts, who was to remain in the village for some years. He and his wife Martha buried two children in 1810: their 18 year-old daughter and three months later son Robert only 20 weeks old. The couple remained in the village until their deaths in the 1830s. The mill was extensively repaired in 1838 and converted into a dwelling in 1938.

## The publican, butcher and market gardener: the Artichoke Inn

And so to the pub, for centuries the meeting place for the village men. In 1595 the site where The Walpole Arms now stands was in two tenements or cottages owned by the Mannington estate (**18**). Its subsequent ownership and role in the community is difficult to follow with certainty. It is clear from inventories before 1650 that most farms and larger houses had brewing equipment and for many years home brew continued to be the wives' responsibility. In towns, on the coast and on major routes, inns became common but in smaller rural areas they were slower to arrive.

In April 1696 Sir Roger Potts, still short of cash, sold to Richard Thompson (or Tompson) the messuage, now a single cottage, with a small parcel of lands attached. Thompson, who paid £110, was then given as a gardener of Matlaske. However, he had married Jane Bird, a widow, in Itteringham in 1685 and five of their children were baptised in the village between 1686 and 1700; other deeds also make it look likely he was more usually of Itteringham. Whether he was an estate gardener or market gardener is not clear. He may have worked for the Potts; certainly he had the ability to buy the property from Sir Roger and later to provide a mortgage on a house in Blickling for Timothy Bullemur, the shoemaker there. The Potts's cottage was then in the use of John Thorne the elder, with a barn and other buildings with rights of pasture on the common grazing. John may have been a long-term tenant since a John Thorne was in the list of Mannington estate tenants in 1668. At the time of the sale in 1696 the close of just under 2 acres next to the house was in use as an orchard. In addition Richard also acquired 5 ½ acres in two closes on the east side of the Barningham road to the north of the village. As one of these was named Maxon's Wood Close the site can be identified from the small wood shown edging the road on the 1595 map. He also rented two strips of glebe land in the close next door to Maxon's, adding another 6 roods. The combination of these lands suggests that Thompson was growing fruit for sale, grazing animals and probably running a smallholding on the 5-6 acres. Although not described as such, was the house an alehouse at this time? Itteringham, vibrant by the 1660s, would have had one such establishment and the site, adjoining two roads leading into the village, was ideal. As in later centuries rural innkeepers ran several income streams: butchery and food retailing being frequent sidelines. However, there is no evidence that John Thorne had been selling beer from his cottage.

Jane Thompson was buried in Itteringham in 1732 and at some time before 1745 Richard moved to Gimingham where, although now elderly, he was still described as in the gardening business. In December 1745, three years before he too was buried in Itteringham, Richard conveyed the property and its fruit orchard to his grandchild Samuel Saul. The property was charged with an annuity to be paid to himself of £6 a year and another of £2 12s to Anne Saul of Mundesley. Anne was the widow of John Saul cordwainer of Roughton, Samuel's brother. Unfortunately it has not proved possible to reconstruct the Saul and Thompson family relationships. We do not know which of Richard's surviving daughters married a Mr Saul. The relationship with Mundesley is interesting as a Samuel Saul was baptised there in June 1724, the son of Samuel and his wife Mary. Richard and Jane's daughter Mary had been buried in 1691 as in infant but they might have had a second of the same name. If the families were closely linked to the late 17th century alehouse keeper Gabriel Saul of Mundesley, Itteringham's alehouse might have emerged as a result of this family connection.

As Samuel was given as 'gardener of Itteringham' he may well have been working there for some time. He had been paying the poor rate assessment 'for Mr Tompsons' since 1740 and in January 1741 he sold 11,750 whitethorn to Walpole. These tiny hawthorn shoots - for hedging a substantial area - would have been grown in nursery beds on the Barningham road land. He ran the business until his own early death in February 1749, only a year after his grandfather died. Samuel's will showed him still as a gardener of Itteringham but earlier that year he was reimbursed 1s 6d from the poor rates for the beer allowance for the workmen mending the poor house, suggesting he supplied the drink. He left his houses in Itteringham and Trimingham to his wife Rebecca for the rest of her life. As the couple were childless, the premises were to be divided up amongst his nieces and nephews at Rebecca's death: the three children of his brother John Saul of Roughton and the two of his wife's sister Hannah Farr, widow of Hugh Farr (of Aldborough). Widow Saul paid the poor rate in Itteringham until she died three years later. She may have been assisted by her nephew Hugh Farr, an Aylsham tailor, who had come to the village by December 1749. 'Rebekah Sall' of Itteringham left a short will in 1751 leaving Hannah her household goods for life and then to Hannah's sons Hugh and Edward Farr and to a kinswoman Hannah White. Mrs Farr then continued to pay the rates for three years.

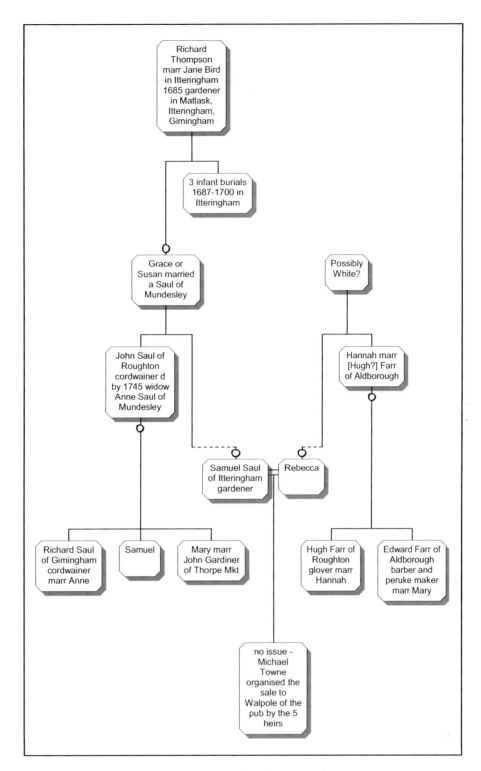

**Thompson and Saul connections**

At this point Abraham Leman was the occupier of the site. Probably a grandson of Robert Leman the dissenting preacher and Bridget Bell of Oulton, by 1756 he had a lease of what by now was definitely an alehouse and the seven acres. The animal pound which went with the pub, lay on the side towards the village. As Barnabas Leman was later a butcher in Oulton, it is possible that Abraham had also dealt in beef. The freehold lay in the hands of the five Saul heirs and it fell to the village tanner, Michael Towne, to orchestrate its return to single ownership. Was he covertly buying it for Walpole or was he interested in the site himself? The deal coincided with the beginnings of his investigation by the excise men so he may have decided not to pursue the purchase. Alternatively his assistance to Walpole would have been helpful to his reputation at a tricky time. First, in October 1756, John's son Richard Saul of Gimingham a cordwainer and Anne his wife sold his one-fifth share to Towne. The following October 1757 Edward Farr of Aldborough, barber and peruke maker, and Mary his wife also sold their one-fifth share to Towne. In February 1760 Michael and Anne Towne, Hannah Farr widow of Aldborough, Hugh Farr glover of Roughton and Hannah his wife and John Gardiner husbandman of Thorpe Market and Mary his wife sold the whole property to Horatio Walpole. An undated note in the Wolterton archive in Horatio Walpole's hand reads 'purchased alehouse at Itteringham with orchard and 5 acres of land £400'. He had to pay £100 to Towne, £40 each to Hugh and John and a yearly £16 for life to Hannah Farr. The estate accounts for October 1760 and September 1762 show other payments – half a year's annuity to Anne Saul (the result of her earlier interest being preserved) and half a year's interest to John Gardiner her son-in-law. In 1762 he was still paying an instalment of £5 as part of the purchase money due to the younger Samuel Saul. Walpole had returned the site to the estate where it would remain for the next 200 years.

During the 1760s Abraham Leman probably remained the tenant but around 1768, the year his 45 year-old wife Thomasine died, he relinquished the lease to widow Smith. Perhaps none of his children, all of whom had been baptised at the Oulton Meeting House, wished to take over running a public house. More likely, it had been Thomasine who looked after the alehouse work while Abraham ran the orchard and smallholding. Within a year Mrs Smith passed the lease on to John Smith, presumably her son. The inventory of October 1769 was signed by John Smith as incoming tenant and for many years after this he was the tenant of the pub and its small parcel of lands:

> An inventory of the several fixtures etc belonging to the Right Hon Lord Walpole upon his messuage in Itteringham taken this 10th day of October 1769
>
> In the garden next the road to Blickling
> 11 apple trees 13 plumb trees 40 nut bushes
>
> In the garden next Mr Blyth's [Hill farm]
> 22 apple trees 2 pear trees 2 plumb trees
> 54 philberd and nutt bushes 28 gooseberry and currant bushes
>
> On the bowling green
> an old table or stand and three seats within an arbour
> 1 apple tree and 1 Bullace tree
>
> And in the back yard 1 apple tree 2 walnut trees
> and a pound for cattle
>
> We the undermentioned having examined the above particulars do hereby certify the same to be just as witness our hands the day and year above written
>
> Joseph Rumball [Walpole's estate steward] and John Smith

Even in 1832 the tenant of the pub and by then 11 acres at a still modest £23 rent was a John Smith, although it is not clear if this was by then a very old man or his son.

### The name: The Artichoke

The use of the name, as an inn sign, is said to date from the time of John Evelyn when the globe artichoke was introduced from Italy to be more widely grown: it was used for an inn at Whitechapel around 1670. However artichokes were being given as expensive gifts in the 1640s and Henry the eighth had had them growing at his palace at Newhall in Essex, brought over by the Dutch. Examples of pubs of this name are found at West Peckham in Kent, Reigate in Surrey and at Broome in Norfolk. Prize examples of the vegetable were stolen in 1716 in Northumberland. Evidence for the link with public houses is also found in Hampshire. A recipe for a decoction of artichoke and other herbs to cure the dropsy was created by an innkeeper at Andover in 1806.

On the reverse of Smith's 1769 inventory is written 'Inventory of fixtures at the Artichoke at Itteringham': the first instance yet found of the name being used here. Given that Walpole purchased the place in 1760, there is a tantalising entry in his accounts for 1758. His housekeeper Mary Copeman was instructed to 'dry the Artichokes': could it be that Horatio 2 had a fondness for the vegetable and gave the little alehouse the name?

Or were they grown by the market gardeners at the pub itself?

At the time of Walpole's acquisition the pub roof was still thatched. The account entry in March 1771 to pay Benjamin Comer £3 6s 1d for thatching 'at the Artichoke in Itteringham' provides a second early use of the name. The small alehouse had chairs and a table under an arbour where men rested between turns on the bowling green. The fruit of the bullace tree might have been white or black; between a damson and a sloe, they might have been picked to eat or in a good year, to make a 'gin'. On the north side the blossom of about 50 fruit trees and 100 nut bushes would have added to the pleasure in the spring. On the other side of the pub stood the pound, with the gentle lowing of cattle. The pub garden is still tranquil today.

Seven years later it underwent a significant set of repairs, quite possibly even extending the premises. In August 1778 bricklayer Robert Ward put in his bill for £18 14s 8d for work at 'Itteringham Pub House' and Thomas Plaford was paid £16 3s 6d for carpentry work at Itteringham 'Public'. Brickwork being in demand, Robert Ward was also to be found doing repairs to Mannington's dovehouse in 1771 (the only known reference to its survival into the late 18th century) and in 1783 he undertook the major refurbishment at the mill.

It is clear from the documents that the Artichoke was the forerunner of the Walpole Arms. (Suggestions that it was elsewhere in the village may be confused with a later 19th century beer-house run by Robert Lee of Wolterton Road.) When did the name change? Once owned by the Walpole estate the name could have been changed at any time. However it was still known as the 'Sign of the Artichoak' in January 1778 when justices Horatio Walpole and William Wiggett Bulwer held a session there to consider local road alterations. A property auction, advertised in the paper of 3rd October 1820, was held at the 'Artichoke Inn' in Itteringham although in 1818 Lord Orford's solicitor already considered the property to be the Walpole Arms. The name was probably settled as the Walpole Arms from the parliamentary enclosure documentation of 1823. However locals retained the memory long after the new name was officially adopted. As late as the beginning of the 20th century, Mrs Ruth Harrison's father always called it the Artichoke, never 'the Walpole'. The children were rather disappointed when they found out it was just a vegetable!

## Other locals

There were of course plenty of other local alehouses. The nearest three were in Wolterton, Blickling and Oulton. The present Saracen's Head is a later addition but Wolterton had an old alehouse fronting the lane (now the back entrance to Wolterton Hall) which then led to the village green. In October 1742 Horatio Walpole purchased the house and its pightle for £85 10s from Thomas Burton who had lived there from before 1732. Horatio allowed the next tenant Edward Bateman a discount in his cottage rent for supplying his workmen with beer. In the other direction there had been an alehouse at Blickling, owned by the estate, since the early 17th century. The current Buckinghamshire Arms building dates from about 1700 but was often referred to as the Blickling Arms. From a few clues it would seem to have had female tenants for at least some part of the premises, part of the time. When Elizabeth Sampson widow of Blickling died on 22nd April 1724 her inventory totalled £115 14s. Her book debts and bond (£90) were not unusual for a widow but when her linen and furniture are added, she appears to have been running some form of hostelry. One can imagine the very full kitchen with its table laid with boardcloths for up to 16 visitors, each with a napkin and pewter plate, sitting on the long form, five chairs and two joined stools. Lit by some of her seven candlesticks, the room was finished with curtains at the windows. At the fire were 4 spits and other cooking tools. In the cellar along with her meat-safe, Elizabeth had 24 bottles, two alestools and 2 'standalls' – everything except the beer! Of course she may just have been a good housewife with a busy kitchen.

John Townsend, when he was buried in Blickling in April 1728 was described as 'alehouse keeper' as was Thomas Bunn who died the following May. Maybe Thomas Archer whose Blickling inventory was taken in June 1734 with cash and debts of £35 and whose will was witnessed by a Richard Sampson, was also involved with a pub or at least with beer. His rooms included 'The Best Room' and his pantry contained 2 dozen bottles and 1 ½ stone of bacon. In the backhouse and larder he had a large number of bushels of barley. He could of course have been a grocer and dealer: his other witness was Clement Robins, Itteringham's grocer. It is of course possible that there was another small alehouse elsewhere in Blickling, perhaps at Silvergate, to which these related. By 1756 Samuel Mills had the main public house and certainly in May 1811 a Miss Bell was of the Blickling Arms inn when she married Lord Suffield's training groom, Mr Alfred Algernon Bloss. They settled down to raise a family and he was given as alehouse keeper by 1826.

In the other direction another alehouse was in business in Oulton. Known as The Sign of The Spa or The Spa House, it may well have been one of the cottages near the Spa Lane junction or a precursor on the site. In the latter years of the 17th century it was run by Thomas Jessopp and then by his widow Frances. Named presumably to attract customers taking the chalybeate spring waters - spas were very popular in the 18th century - this one was a rather minor draw compared to Bath or even Aylsham! More often it was just the 'local'; here witness statements were taken down from residents in one of the many legal disputes between the Bells and the vicar Thomas Curson. The property was bought by Thomas Tanner Bell (d 1721) and was combined with a small amount of land in Saxthorpe acquired from the Potts estate and others. He set up his eldest son Edmund with his wife and children, farming on a very small scale and running the ale house. That he was the eldest is certain from his father's will, yet he did not inherit the main estate and explicitly only had a life interest in his land, which then would revert to his brother. It is hard not to conclude that he was a few pints short of a firkin. At the same time his cousin Nicholas Bell in Malthouse farm Oulton Street had become 'a lunatic' (as his wife put it in her will of 1720) many years before his death in 1734. Perhaps all the marriages to close cousins were taking their toll. Edmund died in 1728 and an inventory of his modest possessions was carried out by his nephew Thomas Bell junior and Stephen Ellison of Oulton. There were a few household and farming items and little to indicate an alehouse. However, 'a bed in the bedhouse' implied a room for overnight stays, and plenty of chairs and a beer vessel suggest the commercial nature of the house. But more importantly Edmund had £33 of ready money to hand and was owed £194 in debts due – in those days customers expected to run up a slate!

## Grocers and shopkeepers: The shop, the house and cottage behind (12) (13)

Grocery goods were available to buy in Itteringham from at least October 1637 and it appears that a shop has been continuously on the present site since that time – over 370 years (**12**). The Mannington map of 1595 shows a house there known as 'Atwood's house'; Edward Atwood, the rector had died in 1585. It was then owned by the Langdons of Wolterton whose Itteringham lands were later acquired by the Bells.

1637 sees the first mention of a grocer of Itteringham – Richard Bell. Richard was by that time a family man, he and his wife Anne Hardwin having wed in Itteringham in October 1633. He had just been given the site of the shop by his father John Bell of Oulton gentleman, on condition that he re-paid the mortgage of £100 from his aunt Elizabeth Baxter who was living in Northrepps. The money may have been intended to fund working capital. Earlier in 1637 Richard was described as 'of Cromer' where he might have been living and working. Richard stayed at the Itteringham shop for several years. His baby daughter Anne was born and buried in the village in January 1639 and his wife died the following March. He and his second wife Elizabeth Risborough married in 1641 at Wolterton. In September he secured another £100 on 10 acres of land in the village from Elizabeth Tubbing. Richard and Elizabeth's four sons and one daughter were baptised in Itteringham between 1644 and 1652 with son William dying in 1651. The following year he seems to have sold his Itteringham property to his brother John (having in 1646 already mortgaged it to him) and moved to Aldborough, where Elizabeth may have come from (Risborough also being an Aldborough name). Three more of their children were baptised there. It is even possible that the later 18th century linkage between the Itteringham and Aldborough shops may have originated with Richard Bell. There is no indication that brother John was a grocer. His son and grandson, both also John, were yeomen the latter being the John Bell who sold the 96 acre farm to Walpole in 1744.

No deed survives for the Bells' sale of the shop to Thomas Jackson the rector of Itteringham and Wolterton but he must have owned the site well before his death in 1674. By October 1667 William Jackson, one of the rector's sons, was certainly a grocer of Itteringham when he witnessed the grant of administration of Robert Empson's affairs to his widow Margaret. As we have seen in Chapter 1, Empson was taxed on stock in 1660 (when Jackson was not) which probably implies William may have followed Empson in the shop. William had baptised several children in Itteringham in the early 1660s, so it is reasonable to assume that the Jackson family may have owned the shop site by about 1660 and possibly since soon after Richard Bell's departure. Subsequent references show that John Bardwell was Itteringham's grocer in the late 1670s and early 1680s. In 1683, then aged 40, he gave evidence that he had known the Potts family for 18 years, implying that he came into the village in about 1665. He may have served as an apprentice of William Jackson and later become his successor.

By the time the rector died there were two houses on the site, both of which he left to his wife Amy for life. That on the shop site was then occupied by John Overton, presumably just living in the house not operating as a grocer since his stay in the village overlapped John Bardwell's. There was no mention of Bardwell in the 1674 will. John Overton was buried in Itteringham in 1701, his wife Joyce having been buried in 1692.

The second house - the cottage set back behind the shop - had been built by Jackson and had a barn, stable, other buildings and small pightle. This had been a small triangular Mannington field in 1595 with no dwelling on it and presumably Jackson had bought it from Roger Potts when Potts started to sell village property to Richard

Robins. In the 1670s and 1680s it was lived in by John Trappitt or Trappett, the brother of William Trappett the Blickling estate gardener who may also have worked at Mannington. The 1678 inventory of Sir John Potts showed dairy equipment - 9 cow racks, four 'killers' (keelers, large wooden milk bowls) and a kettle - held at John Trappett's; might he have been repairing the wooden items in his workshop? John's widow Catherine Trappett remained in the village, dying in 1689. The interests of her only daughter Elizabeth were to be watched over by her brother-in-law William in Blickling or Robert Jackson senior of Itteringham if William died. She may have stayed in the cottage and lived by spinning or tailoring: Christopher Parkins, Itteringham's main weaver, witnessed her will and was to be involved in the valuation of her goods.

After Amy Jackson's death in Wolterton in 1681 both properties went to her grandson Charles Jackson. Charles's father, Richard, had been a cleric like his father and was rector of Little Barningham until his early death in 1670. Charles senior became the grocer in Itteringham and in July 1686 married Susanna the widow of Michael Breese, the tailor of Itteringham. It seems that the Breeses might have been his neighbours in the cottage behind, a suitable size for a tailor's workshop. Charles was buried in Itteringham in 1695 leaving a will (proved in 1698) witnessed by John Osborne his neighbour in the cottage. In December 1695 Susan married Osborne and presumably moved back into the cottage where she died in 1702. Both properties were then left to Charles's son Charles junior, a butcher of Halvergate, who would have reached 21 between 1707 and 1710.

Although no deed survives Charles must have soon sold the rear cottage to Thomas Robins 1 who owned it by 1711. By this time Robins had completed his Manor House on the other side of the road and moved the smithy. The following year between January and March 1712 he acquired the village shop, barn, buildings and yard and the two-acre field behind it from a combination of Charles Jackson junior and Aaron Heath, also a butcher of Halvergate. Charles Jackson had mortgaged the shop property to Aaron, so the conveyance was a rather complicated one, in which for good measure Thomas Robins also paid £30 to Charles's unmarried sister Mary to satisfy her entitlement under her father's will. In total it cost Thomas about £170. From this period the shop and Osborne cottage sites tended to be treated as a single entity.

Apart from it being close to his house, Thomas had another reason for wanting to buy the site. His brother Clement was by that time a grocer and he may well have been leasing the shop since 1698. The present house on the south-west side of the shop bears the initials of Thomas Robins on both its gable ends and it seems Thomas built this as a decent house for his brother Clement soon after the purchase of the site.

'TR' on the gable end of the shop house

The shop house built by Thomas Robins for Clement the grocer

Clement was a good business man running businesses in Itteringham and Aldborough. As we will see when he appears later in the story of the dissenters, he can only have spent a small part of his time at the house. He was in great demand elsewhere. The tiny cottage tucked into the rear of the house and shop may have housed his shop manager or assistant.

The tiny cottage built into the back of the shop

After Clement died in 1737, the shop continued to be run by dissenters: Richard Green had married into the Quaker Wright family. When he died in 1751 he left all his stock in trade to his wife Mary and their son Richard. Mary and her brother Richard Wright took the 'solemn affirmation' in place of the usual probate oath.

## *What kind of shop?*

Of butchers, bakers and candlestick makers there is very little early sign. There is no evidence for a village bakery in the 18th century when many country people would still have made bread at home. At Wolterton Hall, loaves, made from flour bought from Walpole's tenant at Itteringham mill, were baked by his in-house baker. Henry Bayfield 'baker to Lord Walpole' had worked at the house for at least three years when he married Anne Brison 'teacher of French to the young ladies' at Wolterton in July 1763. This arrangement must have already been in place when Ness suggested baking loaves at the Hall for the poor during the corn crisis of the spring of 1757. In 1697 Daniel Abell was a butcher of Itteringham. He rented 30 acres of Wolterton land and would have done his own butchering. The Jackson family were then also butchers. There is no evidence of how the meat was sold in Itteringham, probably still direct to the customer from the farm or possibly through the Artichoke. Later in the century, Walpole was buying meat from Henry Purdy who had a shop at Wickmere. Sunday lunch was very tempting to thieves as Henry discovered one weekend in 1766:

> 1766 May 12 Information of Henry Purdy of Wickmere butcher, That on Saturday night last or on Sunday morning his shop at Wickmere was burglariously broken open and one rump and one marrow bone of beef, value 8s, one loin and one breast of veal value 3s 6d, were stolen and carried away, and he suspects John Wagstaff and Jonathan Burton, both of Wickmere.
> Signed Henry Purdy

By 1782 Samuel Amis, butcher, had moved to Itteringham with his wife Elizabeth and baby Hannah. Until he was married, he had worked on yearly contracts for butchers in Mattishall. Having no legal settlement in Itteringham, he may have moved on if work was scarce.

As for candlesticks, no doubt the blacksmith could make a very serviceable pair in wrought iron if pewter, silver and gold were too expensive.

Our best evidence of what kind of goods were sold in the village shop comes from probate inventories and crime reports. Most seem to deal in a combination of what we would consider grocery items, haberdashery and hardware. In addition Clement Robins was dealing in grains and seeds.

The inventory of John Townsend alehouse and shopkeeper in Blickling gives a picture of a little rural store in 1728. His total worth was £12 15s and in the 'shop' he had scales, soap, candles, blue, 1000 pins, a quart of vinegar, and a meat pickle (meat cupboard). Apart from some pewter quarts and pints for measuring, he had little else except his two pigs in the yard. In 1761 Robert Purdy's shop in Oulton was burgled by Hannah Robertson. She stole 'striped flannel (made into petticoat), parcel of sugar, quantity of sewing silk & laces, parcel of Tea, 4 Handkerchiefs, One knife, a pair of scissors, a Strainer, A Piece of Everlasting, a Parcel of Lawn, a Piece of Holland and 1s 6d in money'. 1772 William Ransome of Aldborough and John Coman of Wickmere, were committed by their own admissions of burgling the shop of Augustine Aldhouse in Aldborough. They helped themselves to sugar and halfpences which were kept in a drawer. The Ransome family did not reform: in 1800 17 year-old Mary Ransome confessed to Justice of the Peace John Gay to stealing a piece of hempen cloth 15s from the Aldborough shop of Thomas Summers.

Town shops were better-stocked and sometimes more specialist: haberdashers in particular seemed to attract female thieves:

> Norwich Assizes 1731 May 14th: Maria Lound late of Aylsham singlewoman charged that at Aylsham she did steal 3 dozen yards of edging (lacin) value 50s 7 yards of Lais (lacin) value 10s and 4 pieces of linen called Cambrick value 10s belonging to James Drake in his shop.

> Information of Elizabeth wife of James Drake grocer of Aylsham before Francis Scott JP 14 May 1731. On 13th in the afternoon she and her servants having been shewing lace and other goods of her husbands for sale in the shop adjoining his dwellinghouse in Aylsham, missed some part thereof and husband asked her to search Mary Lound as she had been in the shop. Found upon her 3 pieces of Mackling lace value 50s and then went with Richard Lound, her father, to Mary's dwelling house or lodging in Aylsham and found

in two of the boxes the remnant of lace and four Remnants of Camrick value 15s which she knew to be her husbands  Signed Elizabeth Drake

James Drake was the Aylsham grocer and draper who supplied Wolterton Hall with goods in 1741-42. His bill listed: salt, candles, starch, vinegar, pearl ash, spanish brown, spanish white, corks, sugar, quires of kitchen paper, pints of lamp oil and a 'pint of neats oyle'. He announced to his clients that he was handing over his trade to his sons John and Thomas Drake in July 1757, reminding customers of their fine teas. John continued to supply Horatio Walpole junior providing grocery and haberdashery between 1763 and 1767 but by 1768 the bill was mostly for kitchen hardware. It seems likely that one of their apprentices was John Fish, the youngest son of James Fish of Aylsham, a glover and fellmonger, who on learning his trade moved to Itteringham to set up there. In 1741 Fish sold a firkin of butter to Wolterton but by November 1767 he put in a proper shop bill for £7 17s 7 ½ d. His bill forms are very like Drake's. At first the supplies were non-food items: '2 pr blankets, 1 set bedcurtains, 1 yd scotch tape & curtain things, thread, silk ... 1 pt oil turpentine, sulphur etc'. The following year, although Ness called him a grocer, the items were still haberdashery but plus gunpowder and shot! The next annual bill, 1769 - cash flow must have been a permanent problem - showed Fish had delivered 'silks, pea-green ribald, Huckaback, thread, buttons, yellow cloth, Buckram & 15 coombe oats' all worth £20. The cash was received by his wife Mary Gunton, the daughter of Dennis Gunton of Aylsham. By 1775 his grocery and drapery bills to Walpole totalled £35 13s 2d. The Fishes had four children who each received £100 in 1786 on the death of their wealthy grandfather Dennis Gunton, by then a gentleman of Matlaske. Mary inherited some of her father's lands in Bodham and Beckham. John continued as the shopkeeper at least until 1790 but, after his mother died, John inherited a house in Aylsham Market Place. Despite the family's comfortable circumstances John may have retained the shop house in the village; he was buried as a gentleman in the churchyard under a fine chest tomb in 1808 at the age of 72.

### *The cottage behind the shop*

After Thomas Robins 1 bought the cottage behind the shop, it was let to fellow dissenting tenants often connected to Clement and the shop. In the 1720s Robert Howard, schoolmaster and possibly tailor and his wife Mary were there. In 1727 they helped with the probate inventory of Clement's shop assistant, Mehetebel Leman who may have lived with them or in the shop rear (see Chapter 11). Robert Howard died in 1732 the same year as Thomas Robins 2. Mary, Thomas's widow, may well have then moved into the cottage behind Itteringham's shop to vacate the manor house for a tenant for the estate. It seems likely that Jane Jefferies came to live there with her daughter as she was buried in Itteringham in 1737. When Mary remarried to John Fletcher in 1738 they lived most of the time in North Walsham but she seemed to have kept the cottage on. William Ram paid the poor rates for Mr or Madam Fletcher from 1740 until 1745. Ram must have left the area or died as the Fletchers paid the rent themselves in 1746 and 1747. Mary died the following year. Ram had a smaller freehold cottage of his own in the village and may have rented their cottage for more spacious quarters. Ram's own cottage was sold to Richard Shilleta, then the tailor, by Henry Purdy in 1749. The Fletcher cottage was next briefly occupied by Robert Breese and his young family before he moved out to Mossymere and Wood farm. Part of the building may have been used for a schoolroom for much of the century but the main cottage was probably still used by one craftsman and family. In 1750-51 Thomas Robins 3 paid the 1s rate 'for the scoolhouse'; now of age Thomas may have been using the house while he was building the house at Dairy farm to free up the Manor House for himself.

By 1774 the cottage was occupied by a tailor again, John Howard, probably Robert's son. As John had been working up at Wolterton since 1760 he may well have lived here for many years. Apart from making clothes for Lord Walpole and his gamekeeper, he was trusted with 'sewing lace and setting loops on to the Tapistry' in 1760 and 'lining the Tapistry' the following year. When he died in 1775 he was unmarried and left his household stuff to his nephew and niece William and Mary Howard. He asked his executor, his neighbour John Fish, to pay a shilling each to the children of Barnabas and Martha Leman, his Oulton relations. John may have been involved in teaching as well, as two of his witnesses were the father and son Russell Alger (see below and Chapter 13).

William Howard, who was probably also a tailor, took over the cottage where he died in 1784. His widow Ann stayed on and married another tailor the following year. The bachelor Benjamin Cousins had come to Itteringham from North Walsham in September 1784, losing no time to fill the vacancy. He took over the Wolterton work, putting in yearly bills between 1787 and 1791 when he died, owed £6 9s. Ann also died in 1791 and by 1799 the tenant of this cottage was John Kidd. Later it was shown as a sub-tenancy of the shop but at this date it seems still to be in single occupancy. Kidd and his wife Mary had three children baptised in the village between 1794 and 1798. He may have used the premises for storage of goods as he appears to be the unfortunate carrier killed in a cart accident in 1802 (see Chapter 12). By 1816, the sole tenant was Thomas Robins, a schoolmaster; his rent of over £6 was about three times a basic cottage rental.

Along with William and Mary Creasey's other property the shop, house and cottage were bought in 1799 by the Blickling estate. In February 1816 Horatio Walpole purchased the shop, its house, the cottage behind it and the two acres of land from the Blickling estate. Quite why he spent £660 doing so is not clear, perhaps a desire to control the shop and ensure it supplied what he and his family wanted. By then the shop was run by Edmund Sims who had taken over about 1806 when John Fish retired to Aylsham just 2 years before his death. The cottage became home to the local police constable by 1900. The shop properties remained in the Wolterton estate until 1985.

## Shoemakers, carpenters and tailors

Many of the cottages in the centre of the village were rented or owned by the skilled craftsmen who worked from home. We have looked at the cottage behind the shop where tailoring tenants and others may have had links to the shop-owner. The other cottages, not having a shop outlet, were often longer or lighter than normal or with an extra yard; in the previous century weavers' houses might have accommodated a number of day workers. By the 18th century, there is little evidence for weavers left in Itteringham although many of the families were still linked to worsted weavers in Heydon, Blickling and Aylsham. The sequence of shoemakers, carpenters and tailors, often in the same premises - particularly 98-100 The Street - suggests that there was only sufficient demand for one of each skill at any one time. In good years, an apprentice or even a contract journeyman, a newly qualified young man, might be taken on.

### Shoemakers

Boot and shoemakers ranged from shoe-menders (John Bird in the 1770s) to cordwainers, originally workers in the superior leathers from Cordoba in Spain. John Gay was briefly a cordwainer in the village and had an apprentice John Chapman from Blickling in 1740. Ark Hurrell, as we have seen in the tanner's story, was cordwainer from the 1750s onwards; he was the youngest son of Thomas Hurrell, a yeoman of Wickmere. He and his two brothers were brought up and educated by his widowed mother Ann who made sure he had a trade. Ark made one foray into property ownership but in his old age, having not benefited from his mortgaged cottages, he and his wife were reliant on the parish for weekly collections until he died in 1802. Ark had taken on John Pearson, as a parish apprentice in 1760 for two years, perhaps to keep him out of mischief and help pay towards the child Pearson had fathered in December 1759 with Mary Hooke, a village girl. The plan failed and by 1763 the constables were after John. Mary, however, picked up with Richard Needham of Wolterton by whom she had at least one daughter.

Thomas Hurrell followed his father's work and was able to make enough to build a pair of little cottages, encroaching on the Common (now Bure Cottage). Another cordwainer, Edmund Fowle and his wife Ursula moved in to Itteringham from Hempstead in 1795, starting the long association of that family with the village.

### Carpenters and tailors

The term carpenter covered a range of skills from craftsmen cabinet makers to suppliers of coffins. As the old village of Wolterton was gradually removed, so some trades went too. The Fiddy family had been the Wolterton carpenters for many years in the late 17th and early 18th centuries. By 1732 Walpole was employing James English to do work in the yard and dairy. By the 1740s Thomas Plaford was turning his hand to whatever was in demand, with building and fencing (paling) work for Walpole bringing in the most regular money. His gang of men included variously Robert Rayner, William Moon, Thomas Burton, Thomas Nunn, James Tompson, John Wright, John Groom, Thomas Neal, William Gill, Richard Lincoln, John Sewell, John Everitt, William Christian, Clement Johnson and George Green. In May 1740 he had completed Ness's room and the butler's pantry in the Hall. The same year he pulled down and rebuilt the dairy at Mannington. By 1743 he was building two barns, one up at North Barsham, the other at Elmerdale farm. In 1745 he was even sent to Burnham 'to break up the wreck' which Walpole had bought a few days earlier for £8.

In Itteringham, carpenter Thomas Purdy had died in 1738 and in 1740 the next village carpenter Edmund

Proudfoot had died aged only 47, at Swannington. Plaford moved his family and workshop to Itteringham, living at Meadow House from 1746. That year he took on a journeyman carpenter, Jeffrey Cremer (or Cramer) from Fring. Cremer stayed with him, renting one of Plaford's small cottages at £2 a year. He married Mary Stavers in 1749 and they had four children. In 1759 Thomas senior went to Mere farm but his son Thomas, now trained and with a family of his own, remained there as the village carpenter. Thomas junior served the Wolterton estate for sixty years as his 1814 gravestone proudly proclaimed.

Like other trades, carpenters intermarried and created small networks covering a local area. Given the low incomes of many, they were only able to move around by producing their settlement certificates, guarantees that they would not become a burden on the parish. Thomas Plaford junior married the daughter of Charles and Susannah Fitt of Wendling near Dereham. Charles and his wife were uneducated small farmers. Their son James Fitt was a carpenter and had married the daughter of the Oulton carpenter John Baldwin (quite possibly his master). James and his wife, although legally settled in Wendling, lived in Oulton where their son Peter was born in 1771. Charles had at some point acquired a cottage in Wickmere which he was intending to give to his daughter. However James decided to take advantage of his father's illiteracy and the resulting scam was reported in *The Norfolk Chronicle* in February 1776. James had craftily drawn up an assignment of all his father's estate and effects to come to him.

There was some conspiracy between Thomas Plaford, Fitt and Russell Alger of Barningham, the schoolmaster. Plaford was an accessory - although his wife would have lost the cottage - but 'on his discovery of the fraud' he gave evidence against the other two who were committed to the Castle to await trial at the next assizes at Thetford. Just before Christmas the unsuspecting father had readily signed what he thought was a document only relating to his cottage at Wickmere and his daughter, Plaford's wife. The moment he got the signature, James rode off to Swaffham to the attorney Mr Whiting to execute the deed. However, Whiting was suspicious and wrote to the father. The parties involved in the scam were charged with intention to take immediate possession of all Fitt's property and rather bizarrely, 'to force the father to live by labour in another county'. In March it was reported that Fitt and Alger were sentenced to two months' imprisonment. How James behaved after that is unknown but when his father died in 1782 he was granted administration with his mother. Whatever he gained he did not have long to enjoy as he died in 1783.

The story of his 12 year-old son Peter adds some light on how a young carpenter managed. After his father's death he was brought up by his mother's father John Baldwin in Oulton (originally from Wood Dalling) who gave him board, lodging and pocket money. He went to school until 1786 when he was taught the carpentry business by his grandfather. At the age of 20 he was given a weekly wage of 3s 6d. He also started to do harvest work for farmers to add to his income - Thomas Cook of Oulton 1788, Coulson Bell esq 1789 and Mr Joseph Robins then of Irmingland Hall 1790 - returning to his grandfather after the season was over. In December 1793 he married Jane Cubitt at Swannington where, armed with his settlement paper from Oulton, the couple settled down. In Itteringham, a second family of carpenters and coffin-makers, the Bretts who had arrived in the village from Reepham in 1752, flourished during the last third of the century.

Tailors, whose skills were more specialised, were particularly affected by the intermittent residence of the wealthier customers: seasons at Bath or in London could leave them with only the overseers of the poor and a few locals as regular customers. Itteringham's early tailors are best introduced by describing the ownership of the row of cottages, now 98-100 The Street.

## 98-100 The Street

The 1595 Mannington map shows two tiny cottages, perhaps only single storey, on the site where 99 and 100 stand today – the northern end of the row. They are set in a slightly curving field stretching between the Wolterton road and the Street. The field was marked as owned by the Langdons of Wolterton. Their ownership in the 17th century is unknown but it seems likely they belonged to a succession of tradesmen in the village. Number 100 retains a feature - a chamfer stop - that suggests it was improved or rebuilt in the second half of the 17th century. A small section of the eastern end of the field was sold into different ownership with a cottage built there by the 18th century.

Following the rebuild of the two cottages, 98 was added around the middle of the 18th century. At the peak there were eight separate tenements or dwellings (separate rent paying tenants) crammed into the three cottages now 98-100 The Street. During the century all the cottages were sometimes in single ownership and sometimes divided. The one acre pightle behind the cottages was later conveyed with number 100. Eventually they all came into the Thomas Robins estate.

## Richard Flaxman and 99-100

At some point between 1675 and the early years of the 18th century, an Itteringham tailor Richard Flaxman came into the two attached properties. By the time he died in 1721 he lived in one of the two cottages and owned both. The witnesses to his will were Robert Howard, the schoolteacher and probably a fellow tailor, William Bayly, the tanner, and Clement Robins, the shopkeeper. Flaxman had probably acquired at least one of the cottages by the 1670s and brought up his four children in Itteringham. The first cottage may even have come to him by marriage from his wife's family but his and Mary's marriage has not been found. His will left his wife a life interest in his houses in Itteringham and Edgefield and then the property was to be split between his son William and daughter Mary. His son Dennis of Blickling and daughter Elizabeth Frost of Great Witchingham were left small sums of money – no doubt they had already been provided for at marriage.

It is probable that his original home was number 99 (now in the middle of the block). His will described his other property as the cottage bought from Sewell Burton and Robert 'Sluis' which had a piece of land separated by pales on its northern side and which probably at one time included the pightle at the rear. This describes number 100 at the northern end and a small piece of ground fronting onto the road and giving access to the field behind. Later the small section on the road was to become part of the site of what is now number 11 The Street, but there was still no building here even in 1839. Sewell (or Sawell) Burton, Itteringham's carpenter, was an exact contemporary of Richard Flaxman; next-door neighbours and friends, both baptised and indeed buried a number of children in Itteringham between 1675 and 1700. Flaxman stayed in Itteringham and about 1700 bought Burton's cottage. Sewell Burton moved out to Sustead to join his son Thomas and his family, where he was buried in 1728.

The other part-owner of 100, Robert 'Sluis', seems likely to have been Robert Sly – Norwich probate scribes struggled with this surname although it is not unusual in our area. He may have been a cordwainer; the earliest reference found to a named shoemaker in the village is not until 1740. No link has been made but he may have been related to the William Sly cordwainer of Briston who was a regular customer for hides from Michael Towne's Itteringham tannery. Perhaps Robert and Sewell had once worked in Itteringham sharing the premises. William's father Robert Sly who died in 1755, was also a cordwainer. William's will, of 1789, is interesting as he describes how, at his modest property in Briston, his son should turn one of his outbuildings into a lean-to single story building capable of being occupied and with a slice of garden given over to it. This shows how local tradesmen increased the living capacity of their small cottages by adding even smaller sections. Even if the Sly family did not do this at 98-100 The Street, there is a good example in Itteringham of exactly this practice at the back of the Manor House. The garden walls here enclose a narrow strip of land just as Sly described in his will. These sloping roofed extensions were often called penthouses (not the American usage we have today).

The typical, poor quality lean-to or 'penthouse' at the eastern end of the Manor House

The northern gable end of number 100 still bears Richard Flaxman's initials 'RF' in iron work which is very like Thomas Robins's handiwork on the gable end of Clement's house in front of the shop. It seems likely that Flaxman had done a major refurbishment of 99 and 100 - they share matching size and brickwork - perhaps soon after acquiring the second cottage in the very early years of the century. Flaxman left 100, at the northern end, jointly to his children William and Mary in 1721. William Flaxman also had number 99, so for a period the two cottages were in different ownership. Neither of them lived here; William and his wife Martha lived in Heigham. They sold 100 to Thomas Dewing grocer of Cawston – William's half in 1736 and Mary's in 1739. Mary Flaxman had married Adam Sewell of Cawston in 1722 and in the early 1730s had baptised a daughter in Saxthorpe. By the time of the sale her husband was schoolmaster at Hevingham. The Dewing clan in Cawston and surrounding villages was a very large one and it is hard to be certain about their interrelationships, but Thomas the grocer would seem to have been a son of Thomas the maltster in Oulton and once tenant of Elmerdale farm. In the 1730s, the tenant of 100 was Robert Bird the village tailor who died in 1736. He and his wife Mary Leak may have lived there since their marriage in Baconsthorpe in 1726. Mary was the daughter of John Leak the miller of Corpusty and inherited the use of his property in Cawston, when he died in 1730, for her and Robert's lifetimes. John's friends who witnessed his 1729 will were Augustine and William Dewing, and Adam Sewell, his son-in-law's landlord.

After Robert died Mary Bird remarried to another tailor, Richard Shilleta at Edgefield in 1738 and they remained tenants in 100. Shilleta was living in Itteringham when they married so perhaps he had been an apprentice or assistant to Robert Bird. Richard was elected overseer in 1739; obviously well-educated his accounts are beautifully written. The cottage, still in one unit, was of sufficient value to pay rates which at this time the tenant is named as paying. At some point before 1744 the Shilletas moved out of 100 to another cottage in the village. John 'Sewel', presumably Adam's relation, appears in the rates for 1741 and 1742 but Mr Dewing himself paid in 1743. From 1744 onwards it was occupied again, this time by Thomas Lound.

## Thomas Plaford and 98

Thomas Dewing in turn sold the cottage 100 to Thomas Plaford senior in 1744. As we have seen Plaford had been Walpole's carpenter living in Wolterton. Two years after buying this cottage he stepped in to take the lease of the little Copeman farm across the road which Walpole was thinking of breaking up. Thomas Plaford also acquired the other cottage, 99 with its smaller area of gardens and yards, at some point probably direct from William Flaxman. He then added a new cottage at the southern end - ie number 98.

At this stage the whole of 98-100 and the pightle behind was again for a while in single ownership. However, in 1753 Plaford sold the northern end (100) and the 1 acre pightle to Thomas Bond a yeoman of Wolterton, although Plaford specifically kept two yards around the northern end to himself. The reason for this is not clear, but it is quite possible that he arranged to lease the pightle from Bond and wanted to guarantee access to it from the Barningham road. He was still farming across the road at this point. Between 1753 and 1763 - perhaps after the death of his wife Lucy in 1756 - Thomas Bond turned the single cottage at the northern end of the row into three units, one of which he occupied. In 1763 Bond sold 100 to Thomas Robins 3, together with the 1 acre pightle at the back. The present occupiers were Bond himself, Thomas Lound and Mary Thompson (probably one of the Thompsons formerly of the pub). It seems quite likely that Robins would have left the cottage in multiple occupation. His interest would have been providing simple accommodation for farm workers. By this time there is no sign of Plaford holding on to the strip to the north, so presumably Bond or Robins bought out this piece. Plaford by now also had added three cottages on the common to his holdings.

Also in 1763 Plaford senior who was now farming at Mere farm (leaving his carpenter son in the cottage and meadow opposite) sold both 99 and the new 98 to Ark Hurrell, cordwainer. The tenants of these two cottages (without the land) were John Reynolds, Charles Brett (the carpenter and wheelwright) and Thomas Page. Hurrell had bought the cottages by mortgaging them immediately to James Thirtle of Trimingham. Hurrell seems to have crammed in a few more tenants, the two cottages becoming five tenements. By 1785 Ark occupied one himself and another for his son Thomas; James Brett (now the carpenter, or at least the coffin-maker), Sarah Sendall, and ' _ Rannells' (widow Reynolds, John died in 1783) were in the rest of the accommodation. Hurrell sold 98 and 99 to William Creasey of Martham in 1785 (by then, through his wife Mary Robins, the owner of 100) who paid off the mortgage to Martha Thirtle.

Fourteen years later the 98-99 tenants were much the same: 'James Brett, Thomas Harrold [Hurrell], Ark Hurrell, Dorothy Bird, Sarah Sandale [Sendall]'. According to the rents, the carpenter had the most space, Thomas and Ark had the next best two areas for their shoemaking and the two women had probably one room each. Sarah

Sendall was able to pay her rent because of the special legacy she received. In William Creasey's will he says that 'by his own generosity' he had paid Sarah a £20 annuity and directed his wife that she should do the same. Mary instructed her executors to continue paying the annuity out of the proceeds of her late brother's estate. As Sarah was of Itteringham it is likely that she had done some service to Thomas Robins and Creasey was carrying out a personal favour. She died in the village in 1803. Charles Brett, presumably now retired, was one of the three tenants in the other end, number 100. The other two may have been John Hannant and Thomas Greenacre with his wife Ann Newell. Twelve years after his disabling accident (see Chapter 12), Hannant died in December 1798; he had been supported by Thomas Robins, the overseers and Walpole during that time.

The whole row of 98-100 and pightle behind was now reunited and were sold in 1799 by Mary Creasey's executors to the Blickling estate.

## Apothecaries and surgeons

Professional men were rarely found in small villages; even the clergy, as we will see, were often not resident. Lawyers and medical men had offices and clerks in Aylsham and Holt; a visible presence with good access to communications was vital. Many had either arisen from village families or had strong links in the countryside. The apothecary of Aylsham named Erasmus Ellis, with whom the Walpole's regularly did business in the 1730s, had close ties to Itteringham. In 1747 in Thornage, already a widower, he married Susannah Robins the daughter of William Robins of Itteringham Hall and his wife Mary Miller (daughter of Matthew Miller and Lydia Robins daughter of Richard the blacksmith). It is clear that over the years Susannah retained her ties to her Itteringham family. She outlived both her husband (who died in 1771) and their eldest son John Ellis who continued in Aylsham until his death in 1800. However John may already have handed over the running of the business, perhaps to a brother, since in the 1793 directory Ross Ellis was Aylsham's 'druggist'. His will refers to Thomas Clover, an Aylsham shopkeeper who may have been his wife's father. Susannah Ellis died in 1809 making her niece's husband John Leeds executor of her will. Leeds was to make sure the real estate went to the next generation, Erasmus Ellis. Erasmus had been under age at his father's death and the terms of John's will allowed for the sale of the shop. Presumably around the turn of the century the long-established Aylsham practice passed into other hands.

## And others ...

By 1751 Itteringham had its own 'barber and peruke maker', Daniel Bell, so that local gentlemen could follow the fashion for wigs. Daniel was a younger son of the family of Wood farm in Oulton; his mother was Hannah Robins and his brother was John Bell an Oulton weaver. John's widow Elizabeth Balderston, married William Robins of Oulton and Irmingland. Daniel was a witness to the will of Rebecca Saul, widow of the gardener at the Artichoke; as her sister's son Edward Farr also became a peruke maker, it is very likely he had been his apprentice. Daniel died in the village about 1776.

At the other end of the scale were the men who dug the materials from the lime and clay pits and kept the lime and brick kilns burning. Both industries were vital to large estates with constant building and maintenance programmes and poorer acidic soils. The lime was also used as a disinfectant for houses and a foot-wash for livestock. The local tanner needed regular supplies as well. In an area where limestone and chalk were not in great supply and coal (the most effective fuel) was expensive to bring in, the activity could hardly have been very economic.

In 1739 three hundred 'whin' or gorse faggots were carted to the kiln in one batch. By the 1740s Mossymere was planted with furze grown primarily for firing the lime kilns and in 1751, 3,000 faggots of whins were made up there and sold to the brick kiln. The production of one batch of quicklime took a week: a day to load, three to fire, two to cool and another to unload. The Wolterton estate ran the lime kilns with 60 acres of land from a farmhouse in Little Barningham. Edward Plane was the tenant between 1701 and 1708 and in the 1710 listing was shown with the lime kiln. By 1720 this farm was held by Thomas his son, who was still there in 1737 although some accounts show, probably in error, Edward Plane throughout. In 1742 when the estate was mapped, the new tenant of the lime kilns and 71 acres was William Riches. The diggings at the old large lime kiln works to the east of the Barningham Road were clearly shown, as were at least two circular kilns in Lime Kiln Yard. The work was hard with carbonic gas giving off unpleasant smells and smoke so kilns were always placed away from houses.

## The lime kilns of William Riches to the north-east of Mannington Hall farm in 1742

In 1749 Walpole acquired an adjacent farm and combined it with the William Riches farm and lime kilns. Riches was succeeded by John Miller, who in 1759 increased his rent from £88 to £124 taking on a much larger farm in Barningham and Wickmere which John Barnes took over in 1769. By 1809 he still had this 248 acre farm, based at Church farm in Little Barningham which included the by then redundant lime kilns.

The brick kiln, for which Brick Kiln Close was named, was located probably near to what is now the south-western end of Wolterton's lake beside the boundary with Itteringham. Which house had the bricks been used for? The old Wolterton Hall and Itteringham Hall were both nearby. Had the brick kiln still been working during the building of the new Wolterton Hall? Certainly Walpole paid William Spink 'brickmaker' at Wolterton in the 1740s and he was buying several 'chalders' of coal for both his lime and brick kilns in 1755. However he paid William Hoddy (well-named for a bricklayer) to make a brick kiln at Mannington in 1741 where Spink also worked. Between 1749 and 1752 the estate sold over 20,000 bricks to local freeholders, the bulk of them to Thomas Robins.

## Sources

NRO: Richard Robins ANW will proved 1689 was mistakenly registered as 'of Hevingham'. His original will clearly says 'of Iteringham'; WAL 30, 268x5, WAL 36A, 268x5; WAL 335, WAL 339-340, 272x6; WAL 345, 272x6; WAL 348-50; WAL 354, 273x1; WAL 355-358A, 273x1; WAL 359-60, 273x1; WAL 362, 273x1, WAL 363, WAL 365-366, 273x1; WAL 367, 273x1; WAL 1127, 286x2; WAL 1129- 1131, 286x2; WAL 1148, 286x4; WAL 1444, 290x3; WAL 1470; WAL 1508, 291x2 and various other WAL deeds; NRS 20970; NRS 21018, 21019, NRS 21021, 73x4, NRS 21023; Full abstract of title in NRS 20982 and deed in NRS 21003; NRS 25641A, 140x4; NRS 15953, 31F7, NRS 20983, 20986, 20988, 70x6; Sly's surname not being clearly written in the original Flaxman will and later deed meant lawyers' clerks had a problem, just as they obviously did with Sewell Burton's odd name. Their solution was to interpret this as 3 people named Sewall, Burton and Robins – a complete mess!
NCC inventory 1728, DN/INV 77B/11; 1731-33, ANW 23/20/11; BUL 4/97 (re Purdy)

TNA: E 134/2W&M/Trin4 and Trin6; E 134/7Wm3/Mich18 and Mich46; Assi 94/964

Wolterton archive: 1/3/5 -6; 3/1/5 -6; 3/7/16/1-8; 8/7, 24, 42; 15/31

P Seaman, *Norfolk Hearth Tax*, British Record Society Hearth Tax Series, Vol III p xxxv 2001. For more on the blacksmiths and Hall family and on the Mill see website www.Itteringham.com and www.Norfolkmills.co.uk. *Norfolk Chronicle* 4th May 1811. Website of Penn State University: Medieval Technology and American History. *Norfolk Genealogy* vol 22, 1990

# Chapter 9

## *Church and Meeting House*

---

*To understand life in Itteringham in the 18th century, the part played by religion must be examined. Yet again, our family the Robins were central to the story. For centuries religious affairs were pivotal to the community; weekly church attendance was expected and the church and clergy played a vital role in the lives of the villagers from the cradle to the grave. The tumultuous changes of the middle of the 17th century led to a diversification of beliefs and practices. Following the execution of Charles I in 1649, the complex swings of royal, political and local policies over the established church, the Catholic church and protestant dissension constantly moved the goal-posts for villagers and clerics alike for the next fifty years. New sects developed; new voices were heard and old traditions had to be reformed in order to compete.*

### The role of the parish church

Norfolk has had a long history of non-conformity. In north-east Norfolk, where Catholicism was never strong after the reformation, the independent-minded yeoman farmers, craftsmen and tradesmen enjoyed the direct and passionate services of the often zealous protestant preachers both in the parish church and outside.

In the 17th century, the moderate presbyterianism of Sir John Potts of Mannington and Sir John Hobart of Blickling had influenced the choice of clergy selected for the local church livings until Potts's death in 1673. Politics and religion were always closely entwined and after the restoration some higher church clergy were quick to pick up and report 'seditious' conversation, especially if the speaker was a low church tradesman. In February 1662 the local justices Sir John Palgrave and Robert Doughty were presented with allegations against Richard Robins the blacksmith of Itteringham. He and some others had been enjoying a pipe and a chinwag on Plough Monday at the Gresham home of his brother-in-law Thomas Johnson. Two witnesses reported what happened next. First the protagonist the Reverend William Harley of Gresham:

> who says on Plow Monday last past at the house of Thomas Johnson in Gresham there being a tobacco box in or on which was the Picture of Oliver late the Usurper, This informant taking occasion first to speake somewhat against his usurpation and thence falling to the due commendation of His Most excellent Majesty's goodness and clemency, One Richard Robins of Itteringham, blacksmith, replied "we read in Scripture of evill Kings as well as of good". Whereupon the informant said "Then you mean our Kings or do you mean our King" and the said Robins therto replied Noe or words to those purposes or effects.

The local tailor William Ellis clearly showed that Robins denied the suggestion politely but firmly:

> On Plow Monday last past at house of Thomas Johnson in Gresham, ther being a tobacco box on or in which was a picture of Oliver Cromwell late the usurper. William Harley clerk took occasion from thence to say he was a tyrant whereunto Richard Robins of Iteringham, blacksmith replies "Let him alone, he is judged already". After which William Harley commending and extolling the goodness and clemency of our now sovereign Lord King Charles II to his subjects, Richard Robins replied "but in Scriptur we may read there hafe been wicked kings too" To which Wm Harley said "then you will say our king is a wicked king" and Robins replied no good Sir I said not so, neither doe I thinke any such things hought you to apply the same, or to the same effects

All over a souvenir picture of Oliver Cromwell! Doughty adds in his note that Harley when questioned agreed that Robins spoke 'no worse words' at the time. The matter was dropped.

During the upheavals of the 1688-89 Glorious Revolution, William III's politically-motivated attempts to improve standards in the Church of England while passing Toleration Acts to allow the non-conformist to worship, created anxieties in the aristocracy and confusion in the working man. In 1693 George Morland, a labourer of Wickmere, was arrested and sent to the Assizes for speaking 'scandilous & reprooveful words against Sir Henry Hobart' and the Government. He was shopped by Amy Lubbock, to whom he was talking, for saying 'Sir Henry Hubbard asked me if I would take the oaths [Act of Parliament called Abrogation of Supremacy and Allegiance]. I told him it was not in his power to give them me, neither would I take them for there are too many forsworne clergymen already, for wee ought to owne our King [King James II lately King of England] be he Papist Atheist Turke or Jew'. The authorities reckoned him to be a bad example in a time of potential political unrest and he was sent to trial.

## Richard Burrell

Gradually, after presbyterianism ceased to be the state form of the church, many livings lost their preaching ministers and some landowners presented more conservative incumbents. Sir John Potts, the 2nd baronet may not have held his father's strongly puritan beliefs and his character was weak and compliant. At some point he had become friends with the young Richard Burrell, a graduate of Caius College. Richard was from a Suffolk family but he may have been related to the Burrells living in Itteringham. His father, Christopher, was famous for being one of the first clergy to be suspended by the anti-puritan Bishop Wren in 1636 and his maternal grandfather was ejected from Feltwell on grounds of his non-conformity. The young man's acceptable pedigree therefore would have been known to Sir John Potts senior. Immediately on Richard's ordination in 1670, John junior presented him to Mannington and he lived at Mannington Hall as his chaplain. Three years later John, at the age of 55, inherited the baronetcy and the estate; now he was in charge, he could ensure his friend was rewarded. The old rector, Thomas Jackson, who had served Itteringham faithfully for 56 years and Wolterton for 17, died in October 1674. In January 1675 Burrell was given the main parish of Itteringham, by Sir John's childhood friend, Richard Houghton, and Wolterton, by James Scamler, Potts's brother-in-law.

When Sir John died, only three years later in 1678, Burrell resigned Mannington – probably under pressure from the 3rd baronet who had little time for his father and his friends. The little church was hardly used for the next 30 years as Sir Roger lived at Ellingham and the small living was held by non-resident clergy. Although Burrell held Wolterton and Itteringham for nearly 50 years, there is little record of his activities and he may not have had his father's zeal. In this period parishioners may well have become dissatisfied with the church. Certainly Burrell's attempt to squeeze more tithes from his small Wolterton flock in 1702 did not help. When not in the parsonage house on Wolterton green, he may have spent time in the small parish of Hepworth, in his home county of Suffolk, which his elder brother had purchased for him in 1672 but it seems that this parish too was neglected. The clergy held their living as a freehold life interest and did not have to retire; they could not be removed unless convicted of misconduct. The 80 year-old Burrell died in June 1721, leaving his nephew Nathaniel Burrell, rector of Letheringsett to sort out his affairs. With the decline of the Potts family and before Horatio Walpole established himself at Wolterton, there was now an opportunity for change.

## Itteringham's advowson

Norfolk, as ever, did things differently; here only 40% of the 396 livings were in the hands of peers, baronets or knights. The lesser gentry had far more potential for influencing local provision of worship, at least in theory. In 1715, perhaps as Burrell grew ill, it was proposed by Richard Robins that a more acceptable style of incumbent should have Itteringham. The living was complicated, the advowson or presentation having historically been divided into three from medieval times. One turn had devolved with the manor of Nowers, one with the manor of Bintry Hall and a third, at least to the 16th century, with Wolterton. Each owner took turns to present the next incumbent, a system inherently doomed to confusion given the longevity of the clergy and the complexity of sales of manors and lands over time.

When Burrell had been presented by Houghton, the turn was that of the Gay family of Bintry; Houghton had the grant assigned to him for that occasion. Richard Robins, as owner of the manor of Nowers, now believed that he had the next turn and promised Timothy Bullemur the next Itteringham nomination. The Bullemurs were a local family of Itteringham and Blickling, and the childless Richard Robins had taken an interest in his young neighbour's career. Young Timothy, the son of shoemaker Timothy and his wife Margaret, had just finished his studies at Pembroke College, Cambridge and been ordained in Norwich in 1712, aged 20. University could cost £10-20 a year, a significant sum especially as he would not have benefited from the generous Norfolk scholarships available from Corpus Christi and Caius colleges. However as a sizar at Pembroke, he would have received free education in return for menial tasks, allowing him to pay for his degree. On leaving college, he sold his leather-bound 1632 Greek version of the New Testament for 7s 6d. While in his first job as curate at Cromer he met Elizabeth Ellis, daughter of William Ellis of Northrepps; she was a good match and they married at Aldborough in April 1715.

Unfortunately his hopes and Robins's plan for Itteringham were dashed; when Burrell finally died, Sir Charles Potts believed the living to be in his gift only. Ignoring the tradition of turns, he presented John Rush to Itteringham in June 1721. Rush was married to a daughter of well-off worsted weaver of Edgefield, William Barker, one of Charles's mortgage lenders. Bullemur was advised by Robert Britiffe to hold his peace despite having the grant papers in his hand. This loss was only a minor financial problem for Bullemur. Timothy had been made vicar of Oulton in early 1715 by the gift of Elizabeth Bell, who had taken over the affairs of her lunatic husband Nicholas. Owners of the advowson but not Oulton Hall, these members of the Bell family were cousins to the main dissenting line which married into the Robins. Another living, Plumstead, in the gift of the Duchy of Lancaster, came his way at the end of 1715 and Timothy was certainly present there in 1723. He was later appointed a Diocesan official, a surrogate, acting as a deputy for the archdeacon or others. By 1729 Elizabeth and he were living on the Blickling estate, rent-free in a house at Silvergate, not far from his Oulton church; his wife acted as one of the witnesses between 1723 and 1731 when he took the oaths for probate administration bonds for local families at Blickling and Oulton. In 1737 he was elected Master of the prestigious Norwich Grammar School - a post which came with a house in the Cathedral precinct - where he educated many craftsmen's sons, like himself. Timothy then spent much of his time in Norwich but with regular visits to his parish and his elderly mother still living in Blickling.

## Mannington church

Sir Charles Potts had however been happy to present another local man, Richard Sibbs, to Mannington parish. From the family of the renowned 17th century puritan preacher Richard Sibbs, he was son of Robert Sibbs, rector of Alby. Richard had held North Barningham from 1721; in 1730 he gained Mannington which he held until his death in 1761. It was not much (he received £5 guineas a year from Walpole in lieu of all tithes) but he had the family living of Sustead as well, where he lived and raised a family. Richard was cousin to Rice Wickes the tanner at Blickling and was held in some contempt by at least one other higher church clergyman who described him as a 'farmer'. Despite relying on their extra income from land, under the Statute of Farming, clergy were forbidden to farm more than a certain acreage of land or to buy or sell in the open market. The Reverend Patrick St Clair, who had for many years lived at Felbrigg Hall with the Windhams, was then living in Sustead, Richard Sibbs's parish. St Clair did not care for Sibbs, perhaps feeling himself far superior in learning, worldly experience and society. In 1738 he complained that 'Sibbs occupies his own glebes at Sustead and Barningham, 18 acres of his land at Thurgarton in his own hand, hires £12 or £14 pa of Mr Doughty at Sustead, 40s or more of Windham, grazing land in Bessingham from Mr Doughty; fats cattle for the butcher, keeps 40 or 50 sheep besides his dairy cows, and gathers all his tithes at Barningham. If that is not farming I do not know what is and yet I dare say nobody will trouble him!' St Clair also commented disparagingly on Richard Sibbs's first marriage: Abigail Sibbs was described in October 1734 as taking 'little care of her children' and said to be going 'to leave her husband for good and all'. The couple were legally separated at her request the following year and Sibbs remarried in 1737. After Sibbs's death in 1761, the Reverend John Dowsing received the small annual payment of 5 guineas for Mannington for sixteen years. At the same time, Horatio Walpole also gave Dowsing the rectory of North Barsham, worth another £6. The little church at Mannington had not been maintained since Sir Algernon Potts had restored it for service in 1714; it was now ruinous once more.

## Dissenting meeting houses

Even where individual clergy were doing their best for their parishioners, this part of the county (more than in other rural areas) continued to give the strongest support for dissenting congregations. Among those most committed were branches of both the Robins family and their relations the Bells of Oulton.

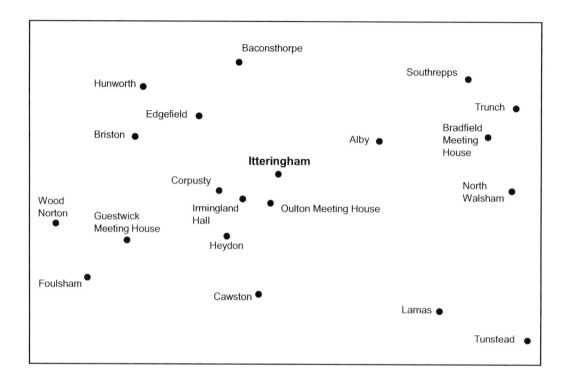

Early network of protestant dissenters in north-east Norfolk

The contemporary term for what later are commonly known as chapels was the meeting house. Meetings are suggestive of the Quaker system but also described the Presbyterians, Independents and those that would evolve into the Congregational church. Many congregations held their meetings first in houses – such as in the chapel at Irmingland Hall. Others used converted barns often with the blessing of the lord of the manor; Edmund Britiffe gave 54 ft of his manor's common land to allow a porch to be built at the Dissenter's Barn at Hunworth in 1706.

### Early dissent and the ejection of puritan rectors

In north-east Norfolk, Presbyterianism, the Independents, Anabaptists and Quakers, filled a vacuum where the local church was failing parishioners. Early Independent meetings were at Guestwick from 1652, Trunch 1651, Southrepps 1650s, Tunstead/North Walsham 1652, Bradfield 1660, all being linked with Norwich and Yarmouth Old Meetings, which split into separate churches in 1644. However, after the Restoration, the Act of Uniformity in 1662 forbade any services other than those of the Church of England and compelled all clergy to be ordained by the bishops – thereby excluding those ordained by the presbyterian method.

Ejected ministers often remained in their old parishes and became sectarian preachers, with a loyal following of parishioners used to their services. In Norwich, the now separate sect of Presbyterians was led by a vicar ejected from his parish in 1662, Dr John Collinges. Their services had to be held in secret until 1672 when Charles II briefly allowed non-conformists to be licensed. In Guestwick a former rector, Richard Worts (having spent seven years in prison for his activities) was licensed to preach in the house of Mrs Mary Hastings and stayed in the area until his death in 1686. His brother Thomas, also suffered ejection and arrest; he preached at Cawston as did Thomas Newman who had been ousted from Heydon parish church after 1662. Born in Hunworth, Newman had resided in Heydon for 12 years since leaving university. For some of the 1660s he lived in Edgefield. He was befriended by Richard Robins, the Heydon worsted weaver; at Robins's death in 1674 Newman was living in Richard's former home. As sole executor, Newman was entrusted with the funds for raising Ann Robins, Richard's only child. An educated cleric, Newman had obviously become Richard's clerk; for the 'many writings' and journeys he had made for him - without payment - he was left £10. Newman later became a successful lawyer and died a wealthy gentleman of Baconsthorpe manor. His son William served as High Sheriff and his daughter was the first wife of Charles Potts, before he became the 5th Baronet of Mannington.

John Lougher, whose father had married one of Sir John Potts's daughters, was ejected from Baconsthorpe and Alby; the new meeting at Alby and Southrepps invited him to be their pastor at Alby where he stayed until his death in 1686. It was not until 1689 when the Toleration Acts came into force, that congregations felt confident to create permanent licensed buildings. These plain, but often striking chapels, were usually found on poor ground, in discreet locations and were still very few in number. Even as late as 1800 only one-third of Norfolk parishes had a place licensed for dissenters' worship.

Several hundred people belonged to this tightly interwoven network which covered an area of about ten miles around Itteringham. Initially mostly women, the members came from local parishes where non-conformity had remained strong throughout the 17th century. There was a noticeable cluster of the dissenters around Saxthorpe and Corpusty. Mary Fisher, wife of George, registered their house in the latter as a meeting house in May 1720; Barnabas Leman arranged for a place in Saxthorpe to be used in August the same year.

Guestwick, sited in the middle of a field, was rebuilt in 1695 as a timber-framed house, when their new minister George Mills arrived from London. One of their 106 members at this date was Ann Robins, the matriarch of the Heydon Robins line. She attended regularly until she died the day after Christmas 1706, one month short of her 91st birthday, 'of sensible and savory spirit to the last'. The Guestwick records show that many people travelled substantial distances to attend the services, having no meeting-place near home. To alleviate the problem, the owner of Irmingland Hall, Smith Fleetwood senior had opened the chapel in his house for use by neighbouring dissenters, several of whom were members of the Guestwick group. Fleetwood had grown up used to the idea of having a conventicle in the house: his mother's house, Winston Hall, at Gillingham held up to 100 members in 1669 and his father, Charles, one of Cromwell's major-generals and a devout puritan, belonged to the London group of Dr John Owen. Smith maintained a chaplain at Irmingland to serve the group, the first of whom was John Asty. The son of Robert Asty, the teaching elder at Norwich, John was a protégé of Dr Collinges, chaplain to Lord Hobart of Blickling and the controversial leader of the Presbyterians in Norwich. Asty stayed from 1695 until 1710, two years after his master died.

## Abraham Coveney

In March that year, the Irmingland group sent a request to Bury St Edmunds for Mr Abraham Coveney, a newly admitted minister who had been trained by Dr Isaac Chauncey, the Independent minister at London. Asty was then working in London with a great friend Isaac Watts who was Chauncey's assistant. Coveney, the son of John and Abigail of Colchester, was then 25 and living in Bury.

Abraham soon settled into life at Irmingland and within a few years married one of Smith Fleetwood junior's sisters, Mary. Mary died, childless, in 1720 and was buried in Wood Dalling. Ten years later Abraham Coveney was given as of Itteringham, widower, when he married Mary Athill, a Heydon girl, in April 1730. Mary was the sister of Fleetwood Smith junior's wife Elizabeth.

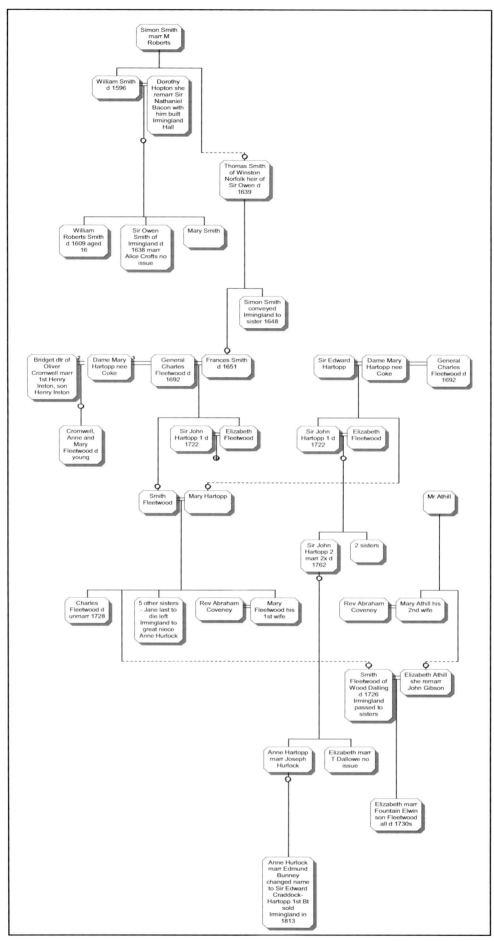

The Smiths and Fleetwoods of Irmingland

The new pastor at Guestwick had taken his post on the condition that a house would be supplied. He seems to have arranged to buy a house and four acres in Guestwick in 1702 for £40 which was later assigned to trustees in return for £100. In May 1720 the list of trustees for the Guestwick manse house demonstrated that the meeting was supported by the closely-related families of wealthy weavers and blacksmiths. Headed by Thomas Bell snr of Guestwick, the deacon, the group included his son Thomas Bell jnr of Oulton, William Bell of Guestwick, Joshua Gay of Wood Dalling, Ebenezer and Joshua Springall of Wood Norton and Simon Peartree of Foxley, blacksmith. Two names lower down the list will soon reappear: Daniel Abell of Edgefield, worsted weaver and Thomas Robins jnr of Itteringham gent. Abell's stepmother was a Peartree girl.

The Bell family had been dissenters for at least half a century; in 1669 William Sheldrake, the Yarmouth pastor, formerly rector of Reepham, had preached at the Oulton homes of William Bell senior and junior. William junior was a butcher and grandfather of John the weaver. Sheldrake's brother John, organised the licences for William Bell jnr and John Bell (probably his cousin of the Green farm line) to have Robert Leman preach in their houses in 1672. Leman married Bridget Bell, the daughter of the tanner Edmund Bell, another cousin in Oulton. The preacher became a 'doctor of physic' and died in Oulton in 1697. As we have seen, yet another branch of the Bells were also regulars at the Guestwick Meeting House where Thomas 'Bradfield' Bell junior had been admitted in 1696 and was made a deacon in 1703. The death of his father, Thomas 'Bradfield' senior - who was very active in the Bradfield meeting - was noted there in 1698. John Bell of the Wood farm line, had his children baptised at Guestwick, including John junior, his second son by Hannah Robins, in 1706. In the winter of 1716-1717 Barnabas Leman, the son of the late Robert Leman, had two other houses in Oulton licensed for religious worship, those of John Archer and Thomas Bell jnr (his cousin, the tanner).

Abraham Coveney had looked after the local Irmingland followers for thirteen years when the minister at Guestwick, Mr George Mills, died in 1724. Much to their dismay, the Guestwick congregation did not appoint Coveney to replace him but the following year appointed Mr Nathaniel Holmes, a widower with 'an unhappy natural temper'. After some debate, eight of the Irmingland and local worshippers formally incorporated themselves into a 'church state' on 4th March 1725 and invited Abraham to be their pastor. He took 'oversight of this little flock' on 30th June and remained in that post until his death in his late 80s in 1772. Amongst this band were John Bell, a worsted weaver and second son of the Bell family of Wood farm, Oulton and his uncle Richard Robins of Itteringham Hall.

The register of Abraham's baptisms, which began in August 1725, gives a good picture of which families were travelling to Irmingland Hall: Jacksons of Blickling, Purdy, Doughty, Elmer and Tompson of Oulton, Brett of Corpusty, Witton of Edgefield. Others came from Hanworth, Briston and Wolterton. East Dereham, Yaxham, Southrepps and Blakeney are also represented. Itteringham families, many in trade, came in great numbers; children of Woodrow, Coborn, Fish, King, Bayly as well as two Robins couples, were christened in the first two years. The popularity of the new congregation (no doubt numbers were swelled by the complaints about the bad-tempered Mr Holmes at Guestwick) led to the decision to build their own meeting house. In August 1728 John Bell, the worsted weaver, made over some of his poorer Oulton land in trust 'to erect a meeting house or place for the exercise of religious worship by protestant subjects of this nation ... by those who then had liberty to meet at Irmingland Hall'. It was 'forever to be used for religious worship by dissenting protestants' and the rents from the house and 3 acres of land were to go to Coveney and his successors as their salary for preaching. This was very timely for Abraham; his former patrons, the Smith Fleetwood family, were suffering a disastrous decline in the male line at this time. His two brothers-in-law had recently died, Charles leaving him a very generous £200; the baby heir, Fleetwood Elwin whom Abraham baptised in 1729, died shortly afterwards and in a few years, the Hall would descend to non-resident London relations and, later, become a tenant farm.

## The new Oulton Meeting House: a family affair

About a mile away, the new building was built on a dug-out and levelled pightle - probably the site of an old gravel-pit - under a steep incline by the road from Oulton church to Itteringham. The land had been left to John Bell by his father's will and included a small double cottage at the front of the site. The two tenants were Richard Thorn and Joshua Leman, one of the younger sons of the 17th century preacher. The other larger piece of land, again of no great value, was called Brown's Yards running between the Spa beck and the road by the common, on the boundary with Itteringham.

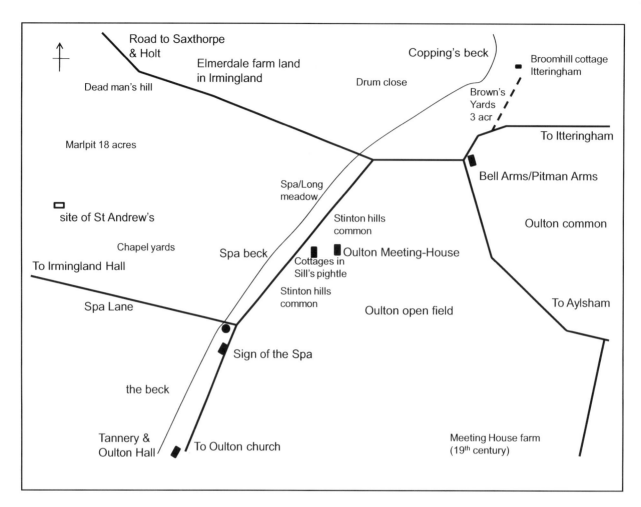

Oulton Meeting House area

Oulton Meeting House

The interior of Oulton Meeting House

The brick-built building has been variously known as the Dutch Church, The Old Meeting, The Great Meeting House and, on the plate dated 1863, the Independent Chapel Oulton. The ironwork date '1728' which is now on the front is a recent addition and reflects the decision to build rather than the date of its opening. The style of architecture was typical of the dissenters' preferred design, deliberately unlike a parish church. The oblong shape allowed for two doors on the long side so that on entering one faced the pulpit, originally tall and imposing. From here Abraham's voice would have rung out, aided by a large sounding board under the canopy. It was not without decoration: the two gable ends were Dutch style, the roof was supported by two fine pillars and an inlaid hexagonal panel would have been visible at the base of the sounding board. Children and visitors would have sat in the elegant three-sided gallery and the whole was well-lit by two storeys of windows. Solid wood pews on the ground floor housed the elders and senior members. Often, as at Guestwick, a burial ground would adjoin the meeting house but this was not the case at Oulton, although funeral sermons were considered an important pastoral offering. (A few, much later, family gravestones are visible today.)

### The trustees (1): the Robins

There were twelve trustees, five of whom were Itteringham Robins: Richard, the gentleman of Itteringham Hall who had failed to gain Bullemur for his parish church, Clement, his brother the grocer, their nephew Thomas Robins 2, gentleman, son of Thomas 1, who had built the fine house in the centre of the village, a third brother Daniel Robins yeoman and his son Samuel. Other members of the wider family made up a further three trustees: another nephew, William Robins, yeoman of Briston whose daughter Susanna was one of the first babies Abraham baptised, Jacob Robins of Aylsham yeoman and his son William. For their Bell relations – Thomas Bell gentleman of Oulton, his son Thomas and William Bell of Wood Farm represented their interests. The twelfth trustee was worsted weaver Daniel Abell of Edgefield, son of the Itteringham butcher and farmer of the same name.

Richard, Daniel and Thomas Robins 2 we have met in Itteringham earlier. Richard's commitment as trustee continued through his life and when he died in 1743, he directed that the interest from £200 should be paid to the trustees to support the preacher in the meeting house. Thomas left £2 a year for 20 years to support the minister when he died young, only four years after the building was opened. Daniel, the youngest son of Richard the Itteringham blacksmith, had lived his early life in Norwich and may well have worked for his relation Daniel Robins, a Freeman and dornix weaver before the latter's death in 1693. Indeed he may have been named after him as the name was not used in the Heydon and Itteringham lines. Dornix or a coarse damask was the material that was used for making bed coverlets, curtains or wall hangings. Daniel jnr and his wife Mary were strong dissenters, despite having been married in a chapel in the Cathedral (which acted as the 'parish church' for St Mary in the Marsh). Mary was of the Norwich and Guestwick family of Steward; Susannah Steward, who had married Daniel senior, was a member of the Norwich congregation when she died in 1695. Her nephew 'Mr Steward the minister', was most probably Thomas Steward another of John Collinges's students. Although he was later pastor in Bury St Edmunds, he was probably the Mr Steward who preached at Bradfield in March 1730. Between 1695 and 1709, while Daniel worked as a weaver in Colegate and St Augustine, they had their seven children baptised at the newly built Old Meeting House in Colegate. They then came home to farm in Itteringham. Barnabas Leman had helped Daniel register his house and outhouses in Itteringham as a place of religious worship in November 1720 so Daniel's role as trustee is not surprising. He was still described as a dissenter in 1737 and his son Samuel Robins, another of the original Oulton trustees, continued in the Independent tradition, baptising two of his children at the Oulton Meeting House in the 1740s.

Trustee William Robins of Briston, son of the Baconsthorpe blacksmith was 27 and had married an Itteringham girl, Mary Miller in 1722. William himself had been baptised by a dissenting minister and despite the distance, they had their first son Richard baptised at Bradfield Independent meeting in 1724. When Abraham became Irmingland's pastor, the next five children could be christened closer to home. By 1730 William had moved to Itteringham and later would take over Itteringham Hall, inherited from his brother Richard. Trustees Jacob Robins, another blacksmith, and his son William passed on their responsibilities later in the century to William's nephew Brettingham Robins, baker of Cawston and a later trustee. Their kinsman, William Robins of Heydon would certainly have been a founder trustee had he lived. This William had joined Guestwick in 1703 and when he died in 1727, he bequeathed £2 10s a year (at first he left £5 but changed his mind) for 50 years to the Minister preaching at Guestwick and 10s a year for the same period to the poor of the meeting. The Minister at Irmingland - now Coveney - received £2 a year for 40 years. Clement Robins was to help with all these arrangements.

## Clement Robins and Bradfield

Trustee Clement Robins, who had grocery businesses in Itteringham and Aldborough, was the financier of the family. In the trust deed, he paid £100 to John Bell for the chapel lands. He was already the deacon and mainstay of the Bradfield meeting, several miles away to the north-east, which he had joined in February 1700 during Mr John Green's time. His business acumen was ideally suited for the role of deacon who was responsible for the temporal duties of the meeting such as distributing money to the poor. There were normally two but suitable men were hard to find. Green was another vicar ejected in 1660 who had remained in his parish, licensed to preach in his own house at Tunstead. When Southrepps meeting dissolved itself in 1697 its southerly members joined Tunstead, swelling its numbers. Bradfield had been run jointly with Tunstead - despite lying on opposite sides of North Walsham - under Green and a co-pastor. Green spent his last two years, very ill, living with Thomas Jeffery, the sympathetic vicar of North Walsham. On Green's death in February 1710, the two meetings then decided to appoint their own ministers. Clement wrote from Bradfield in January 1711 to set up the separation. Despite the distances, the preachers and elders from all the meetings regularly travelled to join in celebrations and to support other events with each other. On this occasion they all met at Tunstead, with Mr Scott of Norwich and George Mills of Guestwick to witness the agreement. Once the congregations were separated, George spent a day with each of them in April and agreed to preach at Bradfield on the appointment of Thomas Jolly a Yorkshireman, in June. In 1707 George had gone with 'brother Thomas Bell' - that is Bradfield Bell jnr - and Ebenezer Springall, a Wood Norton tanner, from Guestwick to celebrate Mr Wills joining Tunstead. The same year Thomas Bell and William Robins (of Heydon) were specially chosen to represent Guestwick at the appointment of the new pastor of Great Yarmouth.

Abraham Coveney, along with others, had preached at the installation of another Yorkshireman, John Fletcher of Hull, in August 1729 as the pastor at Bradfield. Clement Robins, his right-hand man, introduced young John to his nephew and fellow trustee, the 31 year-old Thomas Robins from Itteringham and his wife Mary, the daughter of Dr John Jefferies of Neatishead. Mary was widowed unexpectedly in December 1732, four months after her last child was born. Seven years later, Fletcher became her husband and step-father to Mary and Thomas. The Fletchers lived in North Walsham and Trunch but on her death in 1748, at 45, Mary asked to be buried in Itteringham, between her first husband and her mother Jane. Just over a year later, at Westwick, Fletcher married a 42 year-old widow of Hanworth, Deborah Lightfoot. He was now step-father to John and Deborah Lightfoot and, perhaps unexpectedly, became a father himself a year later. Mary Robins, by now 24, had married well in Norwich Cathedral a year after her mother's death. Thomas, the heir, was about 17 and may already have been living with his guardian Samuel Robins in Itteringham, keeping an eye on his inheritance. Fletcher made no mention of any Robins family in his will thirteen years later. Perhaps relations with his former step-children were not good or maybe they had all just moved on.

When Clement Robins died in 1737, Fletcher wrote 'not only we that are present but the neighbouring congregations sustain a loss that deserves to be lamented ... He attended the affairs of this church, of which he was several years an officer, with a most exact care, and was ever forward in any service in which the welfare of it was concerned; ... and you know how much it was owing to his care that you have an opportunity of attending on religious ordinances with so great a conveniency at all season. What a wide gap has his death made!'. This could suggest he played a major part in building their meeting house - a converted barn - too. Certainly the stables there bore his initials C.R. 1736. Clement's wife, Hanna Breviter, was the daughter of Richard Breviter the former vicar of North Walsham, who had resigned to become the founder of the congregationalists there. They had married at Alby in 1690 when she was 37 and she had died some time before him leaving no children. His wedding ring, inscribed 'As god decreed, we agreed', he gave to Mrs Elizabeth Lightfoot, a recently widowed lady of Alby, who may have been Hanna's sister and possibly Deborah Lightfoot's mother-in-law. His heart and soul were committed to his family and brethren at Bradfield and Oulton. Fletcher, his 'highly esteemed friend', was left £100 and £4 a year towards his salary for 25 years, with £5 straight away for the previous year. Abraham Coveney also had £4 a year for 25 years. Unfortunately the law, under the 1735 Statute of Mortmain, prevented Bradfield from benefiting from the £100 he left them to buy more land for their uses. Clement left the most needy poor of the two meetings (one of whom was to be his neighbour 'Urslay' [Ursula?]) £10 for clothing; he was remembered by two silver communion cups bearing his name and the year 1737. Fletcher preached at Bradfield until his death in 1773 but this seems unconnected to the fact that his £100 legacy would have to have been returned if he 'left his people belonging to Bradfield meeting'.

## The new meeting house and its neighbours

There was no bad feeling about the breakaway Oulton meeting: in October 1729 Abraham Coveney was asked to preach at Guestwick for Joseph Astley's ordination there, the fiery Mr Holmes having resigned. Mr Astley repaid the compliment when he preached at the opening of the new Oulton meeting house on Wednesday 7th April 1731; also speaking were the new pastor of Tunstead, John Fletcher, Mr Scott and Mr Brooke from Norwich, Mr Saunders of Denton and of course Abraham. The covenant that Abraham and the members signed up to was a code of daily prayer, bible study and good behaviour, including the promises 'We will be strictly honest in our dealings; We will show Patience, Meekness and Peaceableness towards all men'. They certainly expected their pastors to be good role models. Unfortunately Mr Astley was stretching the patience of the Guestwick meeting; within 18 months of arriving the complaints about him had started. He was living extravagantly and owed £100. Two months after the Oulton opening, he was publicly admonished – the deacons' private warnings having had no effect. The final straw was his attempt to seduce a chamber maid at the Bull Inn in Norwich. A meeting was held in Mr Scott's study and the girl was called to attend. When asked about the gentleman who had offered her 'lewdness' at the Bull, she singled Astley out from about 20 men in the room, saying, 'that's him'. The girl's evidence, taken earlier, was reported verbatim in Astley's presence – including his offer of a reward if she had sex with him. Did he resign in shame? On the contrary, quite unrepentant, he offered to go only if paid for a full year and allowed to stay in his dwelling. Finally he was removed the following March – 'cast out ... for his immorality'. All this of course swelled the numbers at Oulton until a new pastor was found a year later.

Members still used their parish churches for marriage and burial and were happy to hold parish offices; the Robinses were overseers of Itteringham 12 times between 1706 and 1787. Thomas Dix, the grandson of Thomas Bradfield Bell jnr was baptised at the chapel in 1735 and later became a chapel trustee; he stood as Itteringham overseer 3 times from 1790 after moving into the village. It was quite usual for the preachers to time their Sunday services so as not to compete with the parish church attendance. For many, there was little tension between the two.

Certainly, on John Fletcher's death, Henry Headley the vicar of North Walsham parish wrote an extraordinarily warm entry over 200 words long in the burial register. He and Fletcher - the Great Good Man - had been 'firm' friends for many years:

> 1773 June 6th The Revd Mr John Fletcher, Aged 68. He was upwards of 45 years Minister of a small congregation of Protestant Dissenters at Bradfield; in which humble sphere, were circumscribed such talents and virtues, as would have acquired Dignity and Respect, in a far more Exalted Station: He was a good classical scholar and was versed in several other branches of polite literature; He had a sound

judgement, a refined taste, a lively and persuasive manner of delivery, and possessed the most engaging and instructive powers of conversation: But his ambition was confined to the acquisition of useful knowledge, and an unremitting exertion to render himself serviceable in the small circle in which he moved, as a minister, a neighbour and a friend. Very few men lived under a more constant and devout sense of the Divine Omnipresence; and perhaps no man expressed a more habitual cheerfulness, and polite complacency to mankind in general; He was sincerely candid in his sentiments to those who differed from him; it being as much his endeavour to make Religion appear amiable, by expressing his good will towards men, as it was upon all occasions that offered to give Glory to God - In grateful remembrance of the firm friendship between us, I have inserted the above faithful character of the Great Good Man.  H Headley, Vicar.

In Itteringham too there seems to have been no problem financially supporting both church and chapel; in Oulton however the Bells, who were lay impropriators of the great tithes, had long-standing rows with the vicar Thomas Curson and appeared in chancery at least twice in the 1690s.

A 19th century print of Oulton Meeting House

### The trustees (2): The Bells and Abell

Of the original 1728 trustees, Thomas Bell gent was of the tanning branch of the family who owned the site of the present Oulton Hall. His house had been licensed as a meeting-place in 1717. His son Thomas Bell junior would become sheriff in 1738 aged 32. William Bell, the elder brother of John Bell the land donor, was the first son of John and Hannah Bell and was living with his mother in a new house in Oulton Street, now Wood farm, which his late father had built in 1698. As Hannah was a Robins girl, William was nephew to Clement, Daniel and Richard Robins. Of all the trustees, only Daniel Abell was not, as far as we can tell, family. The Abell family had early connections with Wolterton, and farmed in Mannington. Daniel senior, his father, worked as a butcher there and lived in Itteringham. He was described as a widower of 'Armingland' at the time of his second marriage to Mary Peartree of Edgefield in 1698 in Wolterton church. He died in 1701 in Irmingland. Trustee Daniel, a worsted weaver of Edgefield by 1728, was his son from his first marriage. Might his mother have been a Bell girl? As well as helping Oulton, he also attended the Guestwick meeting. It was he who took time to travel to Norwich to see Mrs Wingfield, the innkeeper at The Bull and interview the poor chambermaid before adding his signature to the complaint against Mr Astley's scandalous behaviour in 1731. He was later described as of Hempstead in the members' list.

So the meeting house at Oulton was built by a very small, tightly-knit clique of substantial men, yeomen, blacksmiths and weavers who had long-standing dissenting connections; and it was they, through their generosity, who would maintain the chapel and its ministers. The Robins's legacies were matched by others. When trustee Thomas Bell senior of Oulton made his will in 1736, it was his lands at Broom hill cottage in Itteringham, immediately adjacent to Brown's Yards, that he left charged with the payment of '£5 a year to the elders or trustees of the congregation of dissenting protestants ... for the support and maintenance of a preacher or teacher of God's holy words in their meeting house lately erected in Oulton'. With the uncertainty of religious toleration on his mind, he added that the payments would cease should such dissent be made illegal. Abraham Coveney was one of the witnesses to his will. His income, from these various payments and the rents of the trust land, would have been modest but comfortable. Unlike Guestwick where the congregation had provided a manse for George Mills, Abraham had to find his own accommodation. As both his wives were from families with property, this would not have been a problem.

## The parish church mid-century

Despite the success of the meeting house, it was felt by the dissenters that it remained important for the parish church to be served by a minister who would benefit all the inhabitants. The Robins family now tried again to influence the Itteringham living.

For 26 years, the 'learned and gentle-mannered' John Rush had spent much of his time at his main living, Baconsthorpe, where he died in 1747. So much time in fact, that between 1722 and 1744 twenty-eight Itteringham parishioners who wanted to get married had to go to Baconsthorpe, despite any inconvenience and the cost of licences which some had to obtain. As there is no evidence of Itteringham church being unusable, Rush was not behaving properly and no note of the marriages was made in the register to explain the gap. In his will, he did remember the poor of Itteringham, leaving them £5 as he did Baconsthorpe.

He also held Hunworth, from the gift of Robert Britiffe, in 1719. Perhaps the Britiffe family's bias towards Rush explained the dismissive handling of Bullemur's nomination in 1715. Britiffe had told Timothy to wait for the next presentation, suggesting misleadingly that Richard Robins had two turns and would be next in the sequence. The matter had rumbled on for some years and Horatio Walpole of Wolterton, as the new owner of Mannington from 1737, was keen to claim full ownership of the advowson. Like Sir Charles Potts he conveniently ignored the rights to the Bintry turn which should have come to Thomas Robins on his buying the manor from the Gays. However he asked his steward Thomas Bayfield to sound out Richard Robins on the matter of the Nowers turn, so that they would not fall out over it. Dr Thomas Fowle, the suggested intermediary, was Commissary to the Archdeacon of Norwich; he may not have been completely neutral as he was also Walpole's great-nephew. His clerk's letter to Robins, while very polite, left little room for debate:

> Mr Robins is desired to let Dr Fowle know what his pretensions are with respect to any turn he may pretend to, as to the presentation to the living of Itteringham, and how matters stand with Mr Bullymere on that account, but as Mr Walpole insists as the family of the Potts's did before him on the sole rights of being patron of the said living but is desirous, as Dr Fowle is fully persuaded, of living well with the familys of the Robins's the said Dr Fowle, in order to prevent any dispute that may arise between them is ready, as a common friend, to use his endeavours to remove that which may possibly arise relating to the said living, if Mr Robins will let him know what he is disposed to do relating to that affair.

Robins must have proved to Fowle's satisfaction that he did legally hold part of the advowson as in May 1738 he wrote to Britiffe to instruct him to draw up deeds relating to his sale of the Nowers manor right to present every third rector to Itteringham. He did not forget his promise to Bullemur and insisted that the sale was conditional on the same arrangement.

> Sir, I have agreed to sell to Mr Walpole my right of presentation to the Rectory of Itteringham for 50 guineas. You are sensible I made a deed of trust in order to convey the next turn to Mr Bullimere or his son upon condition they were capable of holding it in their own persons. I desire therefore that you

would make a proper conveyance to the use of Mr Walpole and his heirs for ever of my whole right and claim to any parts of the advowson of Itteringham upon the condition that Mr Bullimere or his son may have the same benefit from Mr Walpole's deed of trust (or any other instrument you think proper) as they have had from mine.

I am Sir your humble servant

While it is perhaps too simplistic to equate Tory politics with high Church and Whigs with low church, Horatio Walpole senior did seem to be quite content to assist the locally-born clergy in line with the villagers' preferences and he was content to agree to Robins's condition. The next month, he as 'undoubted patron of the advowson' granted the next turn in trust to Britiffe who at the next vacancy was to appoint one of the Bullemurs. On July 24th 1747, four days after John Rush died, Timothy Bullemur's only surviving child, Ellis, was presented to Itteringham. Timothy, perhaps to reassure Walpole about his position, had researched the turns in the Bishop's books. He wrote in August that 'the advowson is wholly your own in one or other of your rights ... Twice you have presented and the third turn backwards has all the probability in the world of being likewise filled up by your estate; so that were the living resigned by the present incumbent any clerk would thankfully take it in the same right and make no scruple of defending his own title'. No-one would again challenge the patron.

## Ellis Bullemur

Ellis had followed his father to Pembroke College in 1733 when he was just fourteen, no doubt well educated by his father. He was licensed as a schoolmaster in the summer of 1740 and at 24, in November 1743, he was ordained a priest. He was appointed Usher at Norwich School where his father was the Master, with the annual salary of £30. Ellis seems to have been able to tread the path between being the popular choice as his father's son and being acceptable to higher society as a gentleman and landowner. He looked after his Itteringham glebe property as the dilapidation report on the old parsonage house, taken on John Rush's death, shows (see page 150). A week after Ellis was instituted the survey was made on 31st July 1747 by Mr Gallant and two others. 'Mr Wrinch' was probably Jonathan Wrench jnr, the vicar of Aylsham although his son Benjamin, fresh from Corpus Christi College with his BA but not yet a curate, may have been given the job. Although the cottage was also freshened up it was very small and it is unlikely that Ellis intended to live there. Either his curate Mathews or a tenant would have used Glebe Cottage as it was later known. Ellis himself may have lived with his father Timothy in Norwich at this stage, or at the house his parents now had in Stalham. After his parents' deaths in 1750 and 1753, he inherited the manor house of Lidfords and Wilds in Stalham and lived there for the rest of his life.

Despite having nominated Ellis under his agreement with Robins, Walpole obviously thought highly of him. Ellis had excellent fish ponds at his estate and in 1756 and 1757, ever willing to please, he kept dozens of pike and tench there which he obtained for both Horatio, by then the 1st Baron Walpole of Wolterton and then his son, Horatio the 2nd Baron. His letters to Richard Ness show how carefully he had them transported to Wolterton. In 1760 he not only sold over £4 worth of fish to the estate but also a colt. At the time of the earlier fish negotiations, Walpole senior wrote from the Cockpit in Whitehall, his London house: 'May 8 1756 Mr Bullemur dined here last night for my intent to get him two livings in the gift of the Chancellor of the Duchy [of Lancaster] but I was engaged before for Dr Offleys son altho I don't know whether I shall succeed in favour of him'. The Duchy Chancellor at the time was Lord Edgcumbe, a great supporter of Sir Robert Walpole. The Norwich physician Dr William Offley was married to Mary Nuthall, the daughter of the City's mayor Benjamin Nuthall. Walpole frequently relied on the services of two of Mary's brothers – Thomas the London lawyer and Benjamin junior, mayor of Lynn, who was his wine merchant! John Offley the son mentioned here was rewarded with the living of Burnham Overy in 1758 but his mother's will made 15 years later suggests no further promotions were forthcoming.

As so many livings were of low value, it was standard practice for clergymen to hold multiple livings and in 1762 Philip Yonge, the new Bishop of Norwich commented on 'the amazing non-residency of the Clergy' in one Deanery covering the Broads. This was common to many rural parts of Norfolk (and was a bit rich from a Bishop who spent much of his time in London). It was partly due to the Bishop's ancient right to allow clergy to hold two parishes by 'personal union' which were supposed to be adjoining. Everything depended on the patron, the owner of the advowson. The parishioners usually had no choice in most appointments and livings often were passed around as favours or thanks for favours done. Local magnates, such as Walpole, could easily influence even those nominations that were in the hands of the Crown or colleges. As we shall see, curates, on even lower incomes and dismissible at will, were the mainstay of most parishes.

When first ordained, Ellis had been supported by Ashe Windham of Felbrigg who gave him Runton on the coast, next to Cromer, and by the Duchy of Lancaster from whom he received Beeston Regis. Perhaps in order to accept the Itteringham living in 1747, which Robins had made conditional on being run personally by the rector, Ellis had resigned both Runton and Beeston in August 1746. On his father's death in 1750, Ellis also held Oulton vicarage, to which he was presented by Nicholas Bell jnr. Perhaps with the influence of Horatio, the 2nd Baron, he was re-instituted to Beeston Regis in 1762 at which time he resigned Oulton. Walpole was still enjoying his fish; in January 1762 he paid Ellis more for those than for his tithes. Ellis died in November 1764 at Stalham and was buried at his mother's parish of Northrepps alongside his parents and his three siblings. Into the Oulton vacancy, at Bell Cook's presentation, stepped 39 year-old Benjamin Wrench, the long-standing curate of Edgefield, who sadly only lived to enjoy his new living for a year. Wrench had been one of several young university-educated clergymen Ellis had as his curate at Itteringham to ensure the parish was well served. Nicholas Mathews (later Vicar of Runham and Rector of Hainford and Hoveton) was his first in 1747; Benjamin had been in Itteringham 1749-53; and John Sibbs joined Ellis as his last curate, 1761-64.

## William Barker Rush

It is not surprising that the Church of England was often unpopular with the working people – the philosophy of equality and inclusiveness of dissenters, particularly Independents and Quakers, differed so radically from the formal hierarchy of the church. After Ellis, Itteringham returned to a more conservative cleric, William Barker Rush, the earlier rector's son, who had been born at Baconsthorpe. Privately tutored at home, he also studied under John Holmes at Holt prior to university. A senior fellow of Caius College and Greek lecturer, William Barker (he always used both first names) became a freeman of Norwich in 1750. In 1749 Augustine Earle had granted him the next nomination of Heydon, which occurred in 1757. Earle's steward at Heydon was Edmund Jewell, the Aylsham lawyer; he acquired the grant of the turn of Itteringham from Horatio Walpole junior and presented William Barker. From his institution to Itteringham in 1764, Rush was the archetypal non-resident rector, living at Catton certainly from 1766 to his death eleven years later. William Barker was typical of the class-conscious clergy, despite his grandfather having worked in the corn trade in Norwich. In 1747 his cousin, John Plumstead, a surgeon at Edgefield, where Rush held some land, told him that a local tenant farmer had sat in Rush's pew in the parish church; Rush extracted a most grovelling written apology from the unfortunate man:

> 1747 [1748] January 22 Whereas I Richd Girdlestone, occupier of the Estate in Edgefield belonging to my Brother Mr Jn Girdlestone, have set in a Seat in the Parish Church of Edgefield of and belonging to William Barker Rush Clerk, Now I the said Richd Girdlestone do hereby own & acknowledge that I had no Right so to do and do further request of the said Mr Rush to give me leave to set there for the time to come (during his Pleasure)
> witness my hand
>
> Richd Girdlestone
>
> Witnessed by John Plumstead

Girdlestone was of a good family. Zurishaddai Girdlestone had become the new Rector of Baconsthorpe in July 1747 on the death of John Rush; no doubt William Barker, who had been his father's curate there from 1743, felt he should have followed his father at that church. Otherwise his reaction seems over the top for a pew he could hardly ever have needed! There is no evidence as to his reaction when the Baconsthorpe parsonage burnt down on 1st April 1754; however after Girdlestone's death in 1767, he made a point of contributing handsomely to the church restoration fund set up by the next rector, a man of great generosity. William Barker may simply have wanted to keep up appearances in Edgefield. From 1729 to 1747 the living had been held by Dr William Herring and his son Dr William junior, close relations of Archbishop Herring. The new incumbent Thomas Bott was a personal friend of Sir Benjamin Wrench, the Norwich physician whose daughter Rebecca had married Col Harbord Harbord of Gunton. In addition, the Rush family had married into the Barkers of Edgefield; William Barker's aunt Mary Barker was a wealthy woman there after the family mortgage to Sir Charles Potts on Mannington had been repaid at Walpole's purchase in 1737.

Rush's attitude was also somewhat dismissive to his own curate at Itteringham. John Sibbs, the only son of Richard and his second wife Sarah, having grown up in Sustead and studied (like all the Sibbs) at St Katherine's

College, was ordained in 1761. On his becoming Ellis Bullemur's curate at Itteringham, he had been given 10 guineas as a 'present' by Lord Walpole in October 1761. After Ellis's death in 1764 the incoming William Barker Rush, living away, seemed to ignore the young man. John found he was working for nothing and eventually in 1766, Rush asked his friend Edmund Jewell to rectify the matter, suggesting that Walpole had not paid his dues:

> I have still to request and that most earnestly, that you would, before we meet again, adjust the Itteringham affair with Lord Walpole. Two years were due at Old Michaelmas last & I shall take it very kindly if you will be pleased to pay that poor wretch Sibbs five pounds for the Quarters services there ended at Mich: last, taking from him a Receipt in full.

Rush's use of the word wretch may have been deliberately derogatory if he felt Sibbs was low church. Fortunately John Sibbs now 23 had just inherited his family's own perpetual curacy, that of Sustead, and some property. Unfortunately the young man had only eight years to enjoy his new position before his death.

As William Barker had had a very experienced older clergyman, Henry Bryant, working for him as curate at Heydon and Irmingland since 1767, he now added Itteringham to Henry's workload. Forty-seven year-old Henry, the son of a Norwich weaver, lived with his wife Sybilla in Heydon. Very often an incumbent would be happy to perform neighbouring minor posts in addition to their own living so for Rush's last eight years, 1769-77, Itteringham parishioners enjoyed the services of a former minister of St Stephen's in Norwich, and current vicar of Langham near Holt. For all practical purposes Bryant was their minister. He also acted as surrogate, proving local wills in Oulton in 1769. Perhaps not surprisingly, despite WB Rush's status as a Norwich freeman and his self-importance, his passing in September 1777 was noted without comment in *The Norwich Chronicle*.

## Wolterton clergy

Wolterton parish, with ever fewer souls to care for, was often held with Wickmere and Alby. In 1733, Horatio Walpole presented George England, the Vicar of Hanworth, and Lord Hobart's chaplain, to the living – an unusual choice, considering his father George had been the long-standing MP for Great Yarmouth for the Tories. George senior had been sufficiently wealthy in 1714 to buy the Clippesby estate from Sir Algernon Potts of Mannington for £3,500 as well as acquiring the Stokesby estate from the Windhams. Had there been some form of promise of a turn made by the Potts? Although they did not own the advowson of Wolterton, after Burrell's death in 1721, Sir Charles (Algernon's brother) had presented the next incumbent, Benn Harvey, presumably on behalf of the Greys. Perhaps Walpole, who by 1733 was pushing to buy Mannington from Charles's widow Dame Mary, thought it tactical to offer the parish to England. George, the asthmatic son, whose claim to fame was the publication in 1735 of his work *An Enquiry into The Morals of the Ancients* (translated into German in 1775), lived quietly with his wife at Alby, his main parish. By this time the family's money had dwindled, his mother, Alice Jermy of Bayfield, and his wastrel brother Tommy being dependant on her family connections. When George England died in October 1740 after some years of ill-health, Horatio Walpole had a plan to offer the parish to his nephew, Horace Hamond. As Horace was not yet of age, Walpole did not want to block the position with a young incumbent – Alderman Custance of Norwich was keen to have it for his son John. So he suggested to Ashe Windham that his great friend and travelling companion, Patrick St Clair, who was at that time holding Thurgarton and Aylmerton should move to Wolterton. The Bishop was to offer Thurgarton to Custance and Walpole wanted Windham to do the same for Aylmerton. The old Scotsman was approaching 80 so Walpole could be sure Wolterton would become vacant again within a few years. St Clair agreed - the livings were more valuable than his former ones - as did the Bishop but Ashe refused and bestowed Aylmerton on another.

Surrendering his former two parishes, St Clair was instituted to Wolterton, Wickmere and Alby in October 1740. However he remained in his comfortable house at Sustead Old Hall - later the home of Humphrey Repton - leaving his new parishioners to be served by a curate whom he could now well afford. In the end Walpole's manipulations failed. He had not insisted on a resignation bond - a rather unfair, but legal, device whereby the new incumbent agrees to give up his freehold on request - and Patrick lived another 15 years, dying at the grand age of 96. Horace Hamond never took up the living at Wolterton. The old round-towered church of St Margaret's gradually fell into decline as the community shifted its centre and the Walpoles patronised Wickmere church for their family services. Just a few late 18th century entries were made in the register – those of the family of Richard Robins 4 living at nearby Mannington Hall farm.

## *Mordaunt Leathes: the disappearing rector*

The last 18th century Itteringham rector, presented by Horatio Walpole junior, was Mordaunt Leathes, who came from a Westmoreland family. After obtaining his BA at Corpus Christi in 1768, Mordaunt joined his father, Stanley Leathes, who had held Matlaske parish from 1741, and Plumstead from 1750 after Timothy Bullemur died. While curate at Matlaske and Erpingham, Mordaunt finished his MA before taking up the rectory of Itteringham in 1777 (a week after Rush died) and Mannington in 1779. Despite his 30 year stint, Leathes also left very little mark in Itteringham. His tithes, which were a third more than in Bullemur's day, were paid to Mr Adey (of Aylsham) who presumably handled his affairs. During his time, in 1780, Mannington and Itteringham were permanently united but the living still would not have provided much income. Itteringham was given as not worth more than £130 a year and Mannington not more than £12, together a 'moderate provision for a minister'. His other living was Sheppey in Kent – an even smaller, very remote parish which was busy only with the funerals of those drowned at sea.

Good old Henry Bryant had remained curate after Rush died, despite being given the rectory of Colby by Sir Harbord Harbord that year. Henry continued to live and act as curate in Heydon until 1784 when he moved to his Colby house. At Itteringham, he stayed as curate for Leathes until his son, Henry Bryant junior, was ordained in September 1788. In a churchyard case against John Bell, Bryant senior had to do all the work, admitting to the church court that in June 1788 Leathes 'had absented himself and could not be found'. Where was he? By 1784 it was so common for Norfolk rural clergy to live in towns - where life was more stimulating - the Bishop spoke out against the practice. However Aylsham was not far away and Leathes would have been easily found. Although his parents were still in the area, Mordaunt was probably in Kent or even London. His father was buried at Erpingham in 1793 and his widowed mother Alice lived in Aylsham. Leathes's absence however was not acted on by the Bishop; he is not among those appearing for non-residency before the Court of Audience at this time.

How Henry managed to keep everyone at Colby, Itteringham and Langham happy is made more mysterious by his fame as an amateur botanist. He had taken up this absorbing hobby after his beloved wife died in 1770. His friend Sir James Smith, founder of the Linnaean Society and Deacon of the Norwich Octagon described Bryant as being 'sufficiently master of his own time to devote a considerable time to his new pursuit'. The outcome of his efforts has been seen in Chapter 5. After Bryant senior's death in July 1799, Henry junior and his wife Ann Aldhouse left Itteringham. Benjamin Suckling finished the century with a three year stint as curate (1799-1802). Benjamin was the young Rector of Matlaske and Plumstead which he had held since 1793 after the death of Mordaunt's father and was no doubt happy to help him out. Benjamin had started his career as curate at Burnham Thorpe in 1792, working for his uncle the Reverend Edward Nelson, Admiral Horatio Nelson's father. Not only was he Horatio's first cousin but he also shared the same link with the Walpole family. His grandmother was niece to Horatio Walpole, 1st Baron Walpole of Wolterton and another uncle, Maurice Suckling had married Mary Walpole the daughter of Horatio, the 2nd Baron, Nelson's godfather. Benjamin would have been a regular visitor at Wolterton, so assisting at Itteringham would not have been inconvenient.

## Later dissenters

In the last third of the 18th century, the 'Old Dissent' was still flourishing locally and occasionally the old families railed against the Church. After 60 years of ministering the Gospel at Oulton, Abraham Coveney had died in 1772 and was much missed as an excellent 'minister, husband, father and friend'. He was buried at Heydon church with his second wife Mary and her sister Sarah Athill who had died a few years earlier. The next pastor, a Scotsman, Ames Kirkpatrick ran Oulton and Guestwick together for three years; Guestwick was then looked after on its own by John Sykes who stayed 48 years. Oulton was not so quickly settled and it was three years before Reynold Hogg came from Yorkshire in 1779. In July 1780, Joseph Robins, then a farming tenant of part of Irmingland Hall, found it necessary to register the kitchen chamber (not the kitchen as has been stated elsewhere) as a meeting house. Had he applied, fearing Oulton would never find a suitable candidate, or was it at the request of people from Guestwick who missed the laying-on of hands, no longer provided by their new man? Interestingly Jacob also registered the barn of The Feathers at Holt at the same time. Mr Hogg left Oulton in 1785 and matters improved.

More moving though, was the tale of Miss Bell. Elizabeth Bell was the only daughter of John Bell, gentleman. His father, also John, had died in 1724, the year John was born and his widowed mother, Mary Bell (née Dewing) of Irmingland, had married Thomas Scott, a dissenting minister later of Ipswich and Hapton, famous for his hymn and poem writing. Scott's father, brother and uncles were all Independent ministers (his father, pastor of the Old Meeting in Norwich, regularly preached locally) so John would have been brought up in a strongly non-conformist family. Around 1774, John and his wife Mary Baldwin moved out of Green farm Oulton into Itteringham. Shortly after the death of the unmarried Thomas Robins 3 in 1782, they went to live in Thomas's Manor House in Itteringham. John doted on Elizabeth, his only child, and was broken-hearted when she died aged only 27 in the early summer of 1786. He arranged and paid for a brick grave, arched over with a brick tomb, covered with a black marble stone 8' 6" by 5' 8" and inclosed by iron palisades in the churchyard about eighteen feet from the north-east corner of Itteringham church. To his great fury, the church authorities ordered that it should be taken down. A cause in the church court was a slow and laborious process with archaic language and delays. With several no shows on both sides and repeated petitions being entered, the case dragged on. In his anguish John Bell penned the following inscription intending it to be placed on public view – probably on his gate in the heart of the village:

*A few yards from hence in the adjoining Church yard over the remains of Elizabeth Bell an only child a tomb was erected by the most affectionate of fathers. That monument of paternal fondness was not suffered to wait the all destroying hand of time but by the rapacity & malice of a spiritual court was decreed to be demolished at a time when the wounds of grief were still fresh in the afflicted father's breast. Impelled by such oppressive consequences of ecclesiastical power thus to commemorate the virtues of his daughter; let those (who feel his wrongs) pity rather than condemn the bitterness of sorrow and resentment which dictated these lines.*

> Shall not the ashes of the dead remain
> untouch'd by impious hands? - To thee in vain
> Eliza! did I rear [in holy ground]
> The Tomb - and fenc'd the sad remembrance round,
> inscribing it with Virtues add thy name,
> On which e'en Slander's self cou'd fix no blame:
> a name - which consecrates this sacred spot
> Far more than that, in which thy bones <u>must</u> rot
> Tho' hallowed by a Bishop - while thy mind
> Enjoys that Peace, the Good are sure to find,
> where haughty Churchman can no more perplex,
> And rav'nous Proctors lose their powers to vex.
> Did the Sharp Sting we feel for friends deceased
> Unabated last we must with anguish die
> But nature bids its rigour should be eased
> By lenient time - and strong necessity
> These calm the passions and subdue the mind
> To bear the appointed Lot of human kind

What was behind such passion? It seems that John had built the monument without requesting the licence to do so. This was not particularly unusual; the next year John Peterson did exactly the same in Aylsham churchyard for his parents and asked for permission afterwards. Although Bell later did apply, having failed to appear at court three times, in November 1787 he was declared 'contumacious' and bound over to come next time. On 11th December John's proxy applied for a licence to continue the monument and the judge agreed unless the rector and churchwardens could show any cause why it should not be granted. On Sunday 16th December the congregation listened to the petition. All should have been well but the draft contained the phrase 'to be granted to him and his heirs exclusive of all others'. Quickly the parishioners were up in arms and two counter-petitions (the first dated 20th January 1788 was deemed inadmissible and they returned with another, better written, of 11th February 1788) were signed by over 17 inhabitants and presented to court. They asked for the faculty to be refused on the grounds that 'the churchyard was for the use of everyone' so granting sole use to Bell and his heirs as freehold was a violation of their property. They added that 'his heirs might not always live in Itteringham'. It was of course true that the Bell family was from the neighbouring parish of Oulton. John himself had been baptised at 'Elmindale' and lived in Oulton for many years before selling his farm to the Earl of Buckinghamshire and coming to Itteringham. On 12th February 1788 the order or monition of the Proctor was recorded that Bell should 'erase and pull down the Tomb ... to level the churchyard and put it into the same order it was before the tomb was erected'. This was to be certified by the rector and churchwardens. In the summer of 1788, two years after the young woman's death, Henry Bryant, as curate, certified that Bell had erased the tomb and levelled the ground. Bryant presented for the rector; on the back, churchwardens John Oakes and William Colls the miller said what Henry had certified about the tomb was true and 'that Mr Leethes the Rector is not to be found'. In July, Bell undertook to pay costs of £5 10s.

What happened next? A third petition signed by the same people on 17th July was entered in the court on 30th September 1788 but this time agreeing to the erection of the tomb. The faculty dated 5th August was read out by Bryant on Sunday 31st August 1788 'with the greater part of the congregation present' and sealed by the court on 30th September. Curiously it still included the words appropriating the area to the Bells and their heirs 'exclusive of all others'. Within five months of finally winning the battle, John himself had died. His will made no reference to the church or his funeral but he was buried in the churchyard on 22nd February 1789. The brick-built chest tomb containing Elizabeth and her father and mother still stands and the remains of the railings can still be seen. Presumably Mary Bell had it re-erected for her husband and daughter before she went to live in Norwich. The simple line for Elizabeth 'who never grieved her parents till she died' was perhaps a more eloquent memorial than her father's outpourings. Mary asked to be buried with her husband when she died in 1808.

The Oulton chapel and its ministers were still reliant on bequests such as that of John Bell's relation Martha Scott of Aylsham, the elderly widow of Dr Joseph Nicolls Scott, Thomas Scott's brother. Martha had grown up in Oulton as Martha Bell, daughter of Thomas Bell senior (original trustee) and sister of Coulson Bell senior. There, in 1729, she married Dr Scott then a young widower and himself a dissenting minister who became famous for his sermons printed in 1743 – he believed the wicked were doomed, not to eternal punishment but complete destruction. In 1744 he qualified in medicine in Edinburgh, practising in Enfield, Middlesex where he spent his time revising a 60,000 word dictionary which was successfully published the same year as that of Dr Johnson. Having inherited an estate in Felsham, Suffolk, he and his wife were living there when he died in 1769, following a premonition of his own death. He was buried in the Old Meeting in Norwich and Martha returned to Norfolk, a wealthy woman. Dying in Aylsham in 1799, the 87 year-old left £100 invested at 3 ½ % 'for the benefit of the Minister of the Dissenting Meeting House at Oulton' and 10 guineas to 'Mr Cowen' a former Oulton dissenting minister who had gone to Stowmarket. Thomas Colborne had been at Oulton from 1785 to 1791 before going to Stowmarket for four years. When Martha died, he had in fact already returned and remained in charge of the Oulton flock until he died in 1822. He was buried in front of the pulpit. The trustees were still mainly locals like Samuel Blyth of Itteringham although by 1807 they included Joseph Hooker senior of Norwich and his sons, Joseph junior and William Jackson Hooker, then 22 and gentleman of Norwich. The boys had been baptised, not in their parish church but at the Tabernacle in Norwich, not long after it was sold to the Evangelical peer the Countess of Huntingdon. Joseph junior died in 1815 but in 1854 his brother Sir William J Hooker, by then famously of Kew Gardens, was still named as a trustee. In 1854 a bible, believed to be the bible from the dedication of the chapel in 1728, was found discarded. What remained was re-bound. The missing end pages were thought to have been used for toilet paper!

By the end of the 18th century the Baptists, who tended to attract the less well-off workers, were also growing in strength locally. The very radical Anabaptists of the 16th and 17th centuries had flourished at Great Yarmouth and there was a meeting house at Ingham in 1764. Around 1713, Thomas and Ann Mack, later described as Anabaptists, decided not to baptise their baby son Daniel. At the age of 18, when a young apprentice in Blickling, he desired to be baptised into the church and the rector there gave him 'instruction'. Although the Baptists of the later 18th century were more moderate, they were still not tolerated. Joseph Kinghorn, the Baptist pastor of Norwich, wisely chose 4 am as the time to baptise his first five adults by total immersion in the River Bure, at Aylsham on 22nd April 1791. Locals later rioted against his followers. No Quaker meetings were held very close to Itteringham. Mary Green, wife of Itteringham's grocer in the middle of the century, and her family, the Wrights, could have attended Norwich, North Walsham or Holt Friends' Meetings. The Norwich group benefited from a bequest by Samuel Robins in his will of 1711; for once not one of our local family!

One of the effects of the local strength of the Independent congregations was to delay the arrival of the Methodists who were already filling the vacuum in other parishes especially where agricultural and social unrest was increasing. Itteringham's first Methodist chapel was not built until the mid-19th century. The parishioners remained both fiercely independent - sometimes attending both chapel and church - and supportive of their parish church.

## Glebe land and Itteringham parsonage house

In 1595 the estate map showed a 'messuage' on the site of the old parsonage house, now Glebe House next to Big Yard. It was almost certainly even then a parsonage house for the rectory but it was never a very substantial property. As we have seen there followed a long tradition of rectors living elsewhere. In the 1580s Edward Atwood the rector had lived in a house near the shop site; the 1595 map still showed this as 'Atwoods House' even some years after his death. In the 17th century the long-serving Thomas Jackson was also rector of Wolterton and lived in the more substantial parsonage house there. After moving out of Mannington Hall Richard Burrell also went to Wolterton. Later rectors were completely non-resident. In the church terrier of 1706 the property was a 'dwelling house with a barn stable and other edifices to the same belonging and land containing 2 acres adjoining between the street of Itteringham towards the east, and a comon stream towards the west and the houses and grounds of John Bell towards the north, and of a small cottage and yard toward the south'. Unfortunately the terriers do not mention the cottage again after 1709 until 1827.

Each new rector was keen to ensure any repairs needed to glebe property fell to the estate of the outgoing rector and could sue for the work to be done. A good example of carpentry-based building repair work comes in the 1747 schedule of work to be done at the parsonage house. Incidentally it gives some idea of the buildings on site, including the 'head hous' – the outside loo. No doubt Thomas Plaford got the job as he was the new next-door neighbour at the old Bell's farm, now Meadow House:

| A copy of the delapidations taken at the parsonage at Itteringham with Mr Gallant and Mr Wrinch and George Church July 31 1747 for Mr Bullamore and Mr Rush | £ | s | d |
|---|---|---|---|
| 1 stout iron anker over the parlour chamber | 0 | 4 | 0 |
| To thatching the barn and hous | 3 | 15 | 0 |
| To a new barn door and mending the other | 0 | 17 | 0 |
| To a spurntree and putting down | 0 | 6 | 0 |
| To a stable door | 0 | 4 | 0 |
| For repering the fenc between the estate of late Bells and the parsnage | 1 | 0 | 0 |
| To 3 rod of 3 foot paling at 10s 6d | 1 | 11 | 6 |
| To underpining the barn and plastering the head hous bricks and lime and bricklayers work | 1 | 10 | 0 |
| 3 rod of 3 foot paling before the front of the house | 1 | 11 | 6 |
| To carpenters work of putting down the pals and mending the doors and floors | 0 | 15 | 0 |
| For nails for the paling and other jobs | 0 | 8 | 0 |
| For 2 squar and ½ of flooring | 2 | 2 | 0 |
| | 14 | 4 | 0 |

The long-suffering curates were usually left to find lodgings in the village and some of these may have had a room in the cottage although probably not all of it. The rest of the glebe land, some 28 acres, was in eleven pieces around the village. In the 18th century and into the 19th there is evidence of the rector's glebe land being farmed by others: Richard Shilleta clearly rented the glebe farm land and possibly lived in the parsonage house for a time. William and Rachael Bayfield rented the glebe lands (and the gravel pit field) and lived in the parsonage house by the end of the century; Rachel, then a widow, was still there in 1823. In 1827 it was described as 'brick-built & tiled' but it was too small to be suitable for a 19th century clergyman. It ceased to have any link to the church after 1857 when the incoming rector Peter Elwin refused to consider it as a residence. An exchange of lands between the Church Commissioners and Walpole created the rectory at the old Potts house just to the north of the church. The present Rectory was built in 1970. Glebe Cottage was substantially extended in the late 20th century and is now Glebe House.

**Sources**

NRO: DN/CON/117; DN/REG/23; DN/DIS 1 and 2; FC 58/8; FC 112/1; BUL 4/300/3, 614x4; BUL 11/79, 615x7 for print of meeting house; MC 2577/4/1-3; MS 21630/161, 502x2; WAL 344, 272x6; WAL 1453, 290x4

TNA:  Assi 94/62 Sedition

Wolterton archive: 8/8, 63A

BL: Add 27967 Robins sedition

Clergy of the Church of England Database (online)
Venn, *G & C*
R W Ketton-Cremer, *Country Neighbourhood,* 1950
W M Jacob, *The Clerical Profession in the Long Eighteenth Century,* 2007
W M Jacob, *Clergy and Society in Norfolk 1707-1806,* 1982, Thesis (PhD) Exeter
N Virgoe and Tom Williamson and others, *Religious Dissent in East Anglia,* 1993
J Browne, *History of Congregationalism and Memorials of the Churches in Norfolk and Suffolk,* 1877
C Jewson, 'Return of Conventicles in Norwich Diocese 1669', in NA 33.1, 1962 pp.6-34
G L Turner, *Original Records of Early Nonconformity Under Persecution and Indulgence* v 1-3, 1911-1914
Aylsham Local History Society Vol 2 No 9, 1990

# Part 4

## DAILY LIVES OF THE RICH AND POOR

*The murmuring poor, who will not fast in peace*

George Crabbe, *The Newspaper,* 1785

At home; care of the poor; disease and death; education; gardens; hunting and poaching; entertainment

# Chapter 10

## *One Up One Down*

---

*Tied cottages were often available for working men and their families whose lives revolved around the agricultural calendar. Their histories ebb and flow with economic changes. Some were always estate cottages, others went in and out of freehold ownership. The very earliest were rebuilt or vanished completely; others were added and altered many times with ever increasing numbers of villagers squeezed inside. Those which were carved out of other properties were not associated with any land-holding in the open field and were homes and work places of tradesmen or labourers. As we have seen with 98-100 The Street, the larger freehold cottages housed better-off tradesmen throughout.*

## Wolterton Road west (5)

On the 1595 map there was no dwelling house on the west side of Wolterton Road. The site was simply part of a field owned by Langdon (with part of 98-100 The Street at its other end). Since by the first half of the 18th century the field behind 98-100 had to ensure an access route off the Barningham road, the Wolterton Road site must by then have been built on – most likely in the mid-1600s well after the Bell family had acquired Langdon's land.

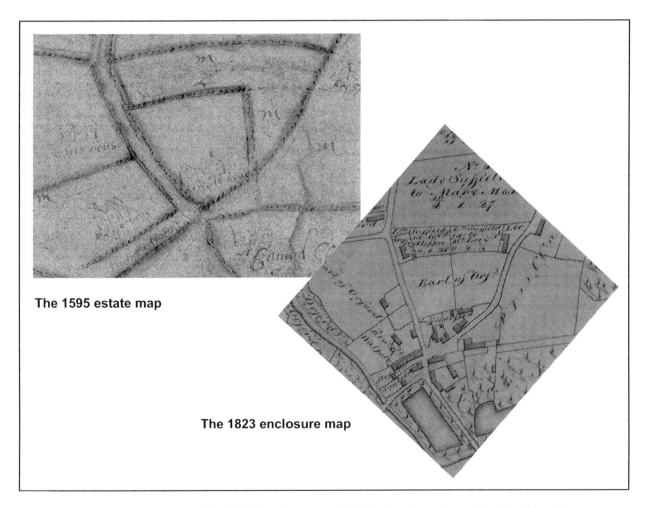

**The 1595 estate map**

**The 1823 enclosure map**

Field strips connecting 98-100 The Street and Wolterton Road west in 1595 and 1823

This house was shown on the road order plan of 1778 which is the earliest known reference to it. The distinctive shape of the field and its protuberance can be seen on the 1823 enclosure map when it was split in two with half allocated to the Slipper family of Big Yard and the other half to the Lee family of Wolterton Road. For the freehold cottages where title deeds have not been found, there can be very little certainty about their 18th century occupants and owners.

One of the village freeholds can be tracked in the middle years. Prior to 1740 a cottage was owned by William Ram. Thomas Ram and Mary baptised a son Matthew in the village in 1710 and in 1730 William and Sarah Ram (a Colls girl from the village milling family) baptised a son John. The property may have been in the Ram family for two generations. The Rams disappear from the poor rate list in 1748 when the family seem to move out of the village, perhaps to Colby where a later John Ram lived. In 1749 Henry Purdy sold the house and premises late William Ram's to Richard Shilleta, the tailor, for £21. Presumably Purdy had bought the house only to sell straight away. As Shilleta was to receive the rents from Michaelmas 1749 he did not move in, at least at that time. He bought 2,000 bricks from the Wolterton estate which was sufficient to build a small single storey extension but not enough to build a complete new cottage. After this the trail goes cold. Shilleta died in 1772 and his will does not indicate any freehold property. (The 1773 poor rate shows an unexplained Mr Dennis. Had he purchased Shilleta's property?)

It seems likely on balance that this cottage was the one on Wolterton Road west. In 1823 it was still a single building whereas Big Yard, the other candidate, was clearly by then two separate dwellings with significant outhouses. Shilleta was not a wealthy man and it seems unlikely that he owned the larger site. By 1816 the Lee family had the freehold cottage Wolterton Road west and a deed of that date, concerning the shop's field, shows Robert Lee had the property to the north. In 1823, at the time of enclosure, because the property was freehold and outside the main estates, the owner was allocated land in lieu of common rights. Robert Lee was still the owner, officially describing himself as a warrener but variously later described as rat catcher and beer-house keeper. He shared his one cottage with two other tenants, James Forrow and John Allen. The Lee family had been in Itteringham during the second half of the 18th century - James Lee was Walpole's rabbit killer in 1787 - and may have held the Wolterton Road site for a considerable period. As with Big Yard there appears to be no deed survival and nothing in the documentary record to identify previous owners for certain.

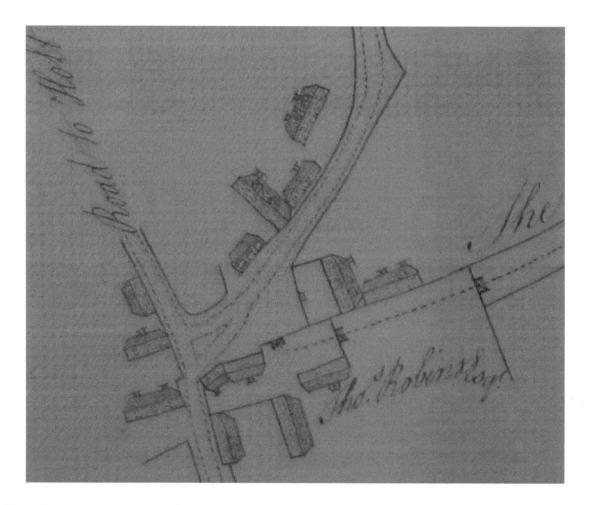

The village centre in 1778: the smithy next to the shop house; the first Big Yard cottage; three houses in the manor farmyard and Richardson's house opposite were still standing.

## Big Yard and Richardson's house (9) (10)

On the 1595 map no dwelling is shown on the site of the modern Big Yard cottages. A modest cottage called 'Richardson's house' lay next to the Barningham Road (The Street), alongside the track to the site of Bintry farm. It had the whole piece of land between the track, the Cut at the rear and the Glebe cottage to the north. A barn lay behind the house. In 1649 Thomas Richardson noted that he had bought a cottage in Itteringham from his brother Samuel. The Richardson family continued in Itteringham at least into the 1670s and Thomas's will was proved by his widow Margaret in 1672. At some point after 1672 the cottage and its 1-2 acre meadow came into the ownership of the Johnson family. By 1724 the house and all the land except the northern strip had been acquired by Thomas Robins 1. The cottage is shown on the 1778 road order drawing as a decent-sized house with 2 chimneys. At the time of the sale to Blickling in 1799, this house, with the meadow and its large pond, would appear to have been home to five tenants (plus their families). The property (apparently numbered 1 Big Yard) remained a dwelling in Suffield ownership until after 1823 but no trace remains today except the small cottages at the rear which were later conversions of the original barn.

The main row of Big Yard as it is now, seems to have been carved out of the northern piece of Richardson's land and was never part of the Robins estate. The ownership and occupancy are therefore very hard to discover. It is possible that Big Yard was the long-term home of the Lound family. They were present in the village from the last quarter of the 17th century right through to the end of the 18th. They appeared regularly as rate payers in the poor accounts, even after the dates when one or other of the family was the miller. That implies they owned or leased some land or were engaged in trade to a significant extent, but it is not possible to be certain this was at Big Yard. Henry Lound also had a cottage on Itteringham Common by 1754 – another indication that they were of some modest economic standing in the village. Perhaps they, like the Plafords, were carpenters and able to act as builders. In the 19th century there is evidence of the Brett family of carpenters living in Big Yard. Had this always been the site of a carpentry business? Unfortunately there are few Lound wills and nothing that indicates their occupation apart from their early mill leases.

At least one cottage is shown on the 1778 road plan and by 1823 there were two. Each had an outhouse or barn attached so the two cottages were divided. At some time, probably in the 1860s or 1870s, the row was converted into several cottages and later extended further towards the Cut. The property being freehold, it has not proved possible to identify the owners in the second half of the 18th century, nor how the houses came into the Slipper family. In 1823, at the time of enclosure, Big Yard was owned by James Slipper. James and his wife Mary Worme baptised children in Itteringham from the late 1790s when he arrived in the village from Crostwick, where he had, like his father, become a carpenter and wheelwright. It is not clear from whom he bought the cottages or when but in 1810 the parish paid for the rent of Robert Pratt, one of his tenants, when Pratt was sick. The two cottages, in three tenancies, housed Pratt and his wife Elizabeth, James Ayton and the Slippers. The Pratts had lost their son Robert to smallpox in 1783 and lived on the poverty line. They probably stayed in Big Yard until their own deaths, Elizabeth in 1815 aged 62 and Robert in 1821 at 84.

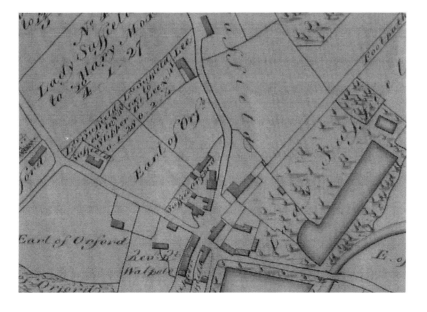

The village centre in 1823: Richardson's house stands in Big Yard

The main row of Big Yard (numbers 4-8) and the two cottages (2 & 3) that had been in Blickling ownership came into the Wolterton estate. As none of the property was shown on the 1859 estate plan, it seems that Horatio Walpole, the 4th Earl of Orford, bought them some time between then and the early 1880s by which date they appear on the estate rent roll. Numbers 2-8 Big Yard were sold by the Walpole estate in 1989.

## Wolterton Road east (6)

This long-standing dwelling site was a freehold owned by the Breese family in 1595. By the 1630s the Mannington estate had bought it from John Crome. In 1639 Edmund Clarke was tenant. In 1696 Sir Roger Potts sold the cottage, buildings and 1 acre of yards and land stretching northwards along the east side of the Wolterton road to Thomas Robins 1. The cottage was then lived in by Edmund Proudfoot; when Edmund died in 1709, Thomas Robins helped his illiterate widow Elizabeth with his administration. The 1724 marriage settlement of Thomas Robins 2 included a dwelling with half an acre paying a rent of £3 10s. Occupied by Henry Bird, this is likely to have been the old Proudfoot cottage on Wolterton Road east.

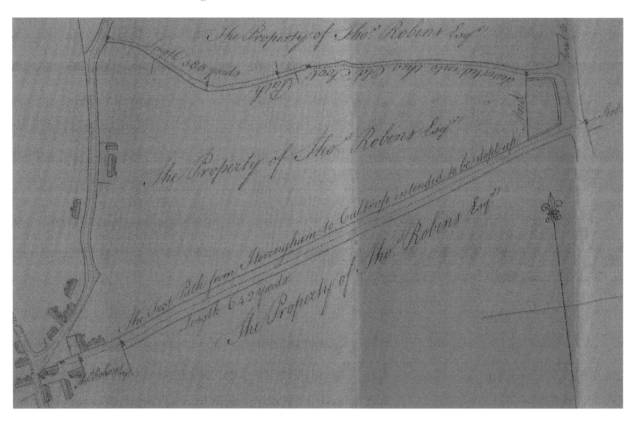

1778 plan showing houses on Wolterton Road west and east

In 1778 the Wolterton Road east cottage was drawn with only one chimney, implying limited size and small potential for multi-occupancy. Perhaps it had become two units by 1799, when sold to the Blickling estate, but is unlikely then to have been bigger than that. The Wolterton Road east house has been rebuilt and extended since Thomas Robins's day and is now owned by the National Trust.

## Manor House farmyard (14) (15)

The 1724 Robins marriage settlement described another cottage then in the occupation of widow Bird and her sons John and Robert. The rent here was £4 10s with no land attached, so it could be one of the cottages in the Manor House farmyard, possibly the old Love's messuage. Robert Bird was the village tailor who later lived in 100 The Street. The old farmyard across from the Manor House had three distinct cottages on two sites in 1778. By 1823 the single one had gone, but not the row immediately behind the site of the modern telephone box and bus stop. It seems likely that the old single cottage was converted into farm buildings before 1799, leaving simply one double cottage facing onto the road. This site certainly had high occupancy in the 19th century and it seems possible it had as many as five tenants in the 18th. Most of these cottages, like others that were in the Robins's possession housed a mixture of working labourers and poor people. At the time of the Creasey sale to Blickling these included Stephen Bunn, Martha Bell and Matthew Mitchell. There is no way of telling which of the two buildings had been the original Love's messuage. Only the barns now survive.

## Broom hill cottage near Oulton (25)

Another Itteringham smallholding was the small cottage and about 18 acres of land near the parish boundary with Irmingland, at the other Broom hill in the parish. The land, once common heathland, had been acquired by the Blickling estate in the 16th century. A contemporary reference to a cottage near Copping's beck (the stream from Oulton spa to the Bure) indicates it was a very old dwelling site. By the 18th century the land and cottage was owned by Thomas Bell tanner of Oulton. Thomas had bought the property from Sir John Hobart of Blickling and when he died in 1736 he left it to a younger son John Bell, for the support of Oulton's meeting house. In the 1740s and 1750s the tenant was Edward Smith who paid poor rates in Itteringham. It is possible that in the 1750s Abraham Leman may have lived here before taking over the site of the pub.

Later tenants are not known but the site remained in the ownership of the Bells until the Reverend Samuel Pitman married Barbara Bell and inherited the main Bell estate. The house on the corner of the main road there (The Old Forge) was The Bell Inn in the 18th century and The Pitman Arms in the 19th. The Broom hill property stayed in the Pitman family's ownership until 1867 when Samuel Pitman junior sold the cottage and 18 acres (together with Irmingland Hall which they had acquired in 1813) to the 4th Earl of Orford. The cottage remained in the Wolterton estate until 1989.

## The Common (26) (28) (29)

Although a large area of common heathland had been sold to Blickling in the 16th century, an area of common remained which stretched from the lane to Blickling up the hill to the main road out of Itteringham. Freeholders in the village had rights to use the common for grazing and taking other resources such as marl and heather or ling for firings. The residual common survived the 18th century intact. Where many other parishes were enclosing their commons, Itteringham's land was of fairly poor quality and there was no local drive to extend arable farming beyond the existing farms – arguably an opportunity missed by the two Robins families. This only changed in the final national round of parliamentary enclosure, in our case in 1823. At this point the common land was divided up amongst all freeholders in proportion to their land holding. At the same time a complex sequence of property swaps enabled allocations to be converted into gardens for small freeholders and into consolidated larger fields among the bigger owners.

As a result, the cottages on Itteringham Common, which had formerly been tiny encroachments on the common with very little land around them, gained gardens. Enclosure also enshrined their status as freehold, title before this point sometimes being questionable. Despite the potential legal uncertainties, there had been half a dozen early encroachments clustered around the town houses for the poor.

The first were probably those built by the Lound and Thorn families – two tiny cottages side by side on the site that is now the extension of the chapel. The existing building is probably a complete rebuild of what originally would have been very modest shelters right on the road with no garden or yard. Francis Thorn in his will of 1749 left to his wife and children 'my little house standing on the lord's waste'. In a much later abstract of title, a deed of November 1754 was recited which showed that 'John Thorn labourer of Little Barningham, Thomas Thorn labourer of Cawston and Francis Thorn labourer of Sculthorpe sold to Thomas Plaford carpenter of Itteringham a messuage or tenement with the little house adjoining standing in the lord's waste abutting on the highway from Itteringham to Blickling, with the town house behind and a cottage of Henry Lound's to the south' (ie away from the river). There is no further clue as to how long these cottages had been there. Both the families had been in Itteringham for many years and could have put up cottages for workers at any time from about the 1690s onwards.

Around the 1750s Thomas Plaford built further cottages on the common across the road from these two. Both were probably originally single cottages but are now doubles – on the sites now C and E on the sketch plan in Chapter 1. Plaford's three tenants (these two plus the Thorn cottage), all poor people, were listed in Thomas Plaford junior's will of 1814 indicating very small dwellings still at that time. He left all his cottages as security for his wife and her children. At enclosure, widow Sarah was living in one of the cottages with John Peart and Sarah Bacon as her tenants; she was allotted a piece of land down the lane towards Blickling woods on which other cottages were later built. Her daughters married the Blyth and Blomefield owners shown on the enclosure map, identifying which cottages Plaford had owned and built.

At some time in the middle of the 18th century the Blickling estate appears to have abandoned its earlier cottage and barn (Goldsmiths) down the lane and built a replacement cottage adjacent to the town house on the common. In 1756 the Blickling surveyor described a different estate cottage on the lane between the mill and Moorgate at what in 1729 was described as Mackerel's land. The description would probably also portray the cottage and barn near Itteringham common: the tenant John Amyas paid £10 rent for a small white wall and thatched house, a small mud wall and thatched barn and stable and 21 acres of land, mostly meadow – 'the buildings bad and will be scarcely ever repaired'. The replacement for Goldsmith's, if the enclosure mapping was precise, would have been on the front lawn of the modern Orchard farm. However, apart from its appearance on the 1823 map, no details about it survive.

The next buildings erected on the Common and the last before enclosure were those now the authors' home known as Bure Cottage. Thomas Hurrell the village shoemaker, emulating Plaford's successful encroachments, built his first cottage in 1792, a one-up one-down cottage set back from the lane. Four years later he added another in front, squeezed onto the plot right beside the lane. His original date stones survive for both. Like the Plafords, the Hurrell family did not live in the cottages but used them for renting out. The whole of Itteringham Common appears to have evolved as a village self-help dormitory for poor labourers and their widows. The remaining current cottages were not built until later; by 1839 there were another five cottages, mostly in double occupation, on the Common.

## Sources

NRO: NRS 21001, 73x3; NRS 20999-21000, 69x3; NRS 22810, Z72; C/Sce 2/1/24

T Williamson & S Wade Martins, *Roots of Change*, wrongly identified the cottage near Blickling mill as an Itteringham cottage

# Chapter 11

## *Lumber and Things Forgotten*

---

*Our 21st century comforts and consumerism make it increasingly hard to appreciate how different households were in the past. The few 18th century inventories that survive for Itteringham and the immediate area, with extracts from local wills, help to give an impression of the interiors of houses ranging from the Hall to the smallest cottage.*

## Mannington Hall

An inventory was made of Mannington Hall by Horatio Walpole's steward Thomas Bayfield in late March 1737 when Walpole had almost completed the purchase of the hall and estate from Sir Charles and Dame Mary Potts's heirs. These were Sir Charles's nephew Isaac Long and Dame Mary's niece Katherine and husband John Turner. Bayfield sent the inventory to Walpole on 25th March with a letter describing the overall state of the tenant list and highlighting the financial problems of a tenant William King who still owed arrears to John Turner. From this letter and other passing references it seems that the Turners may have been living for at least some of the time in Mannington with Dame Mary. Bayfield's letter was scathing about the poor quality of the goods in the Hall:

> I have also enclosed a particular of Mr Turner's goods in the house which are so ordinary in the general as I never see in a gentleman's house there being not one bed in the house except a bed in the parlour chamber that is good enough (hardly) for a servant to lay on, the bed on the said chamber is a wrought bed by some of the familly the hangings all over the house if baten down [auctioned] would not I think fetch 40s. There is aboot a little cart and a pair of small wheels (new) which are usefull for the garden at Wolterton and carrying earth etc. There is allso tyle brick etc may be usefull to Your Honr, some boord and spares [spars] in the barne which are new and good.

Now of course they might be seen as fascinating antiques dating back to the early-middle of the 17th century, the peak period for the Potts family. The inventory is reproduced here in full to enable comparison with the inventory made at the death of the second Sir John Potts in 1678 (published in *See You in Court*). No values were ascribed to any items or total given, this was simply Bayfield's notification of what was in the house.

A schedule of the household goods in Mannington Hall 23rd March 1737

In the hall a large oval table, one small ditto, a tea table and old tapistry chairs two old arm'd chairs, scrutoir [writing desk], 50 pictures, a glass lanthorn, a pair of hand irons, three tapestry fotclothes

In the great parlour six coverd chairs, three cane chairs, 7 sconces [candlesticks], 2 card tables, a fire harth with brass embellishment and brass accutrements, ie fire shovel, tongs and fender, a fire piece and 15 family pictures and a tea table

In the little summer parlour a squob [thick cushion], an arm chair and 4 small ditto cane, part of a fire harth, fire shovel and tongs, 2 earth sconces and old window curtins

In the little parlour an oval table and a small mahogany table, 5 cane chairs and cushions, a lather screene, a stove, fender, fire shovel, tongs, poker and bellows, 2 sconces, three family pictures, a fire piece and three other pictures, a looking-glass, old window curtains and a teabel

In ditto a large quantity of china, dishes, plates, tea china etc

On the staircase 35 pictures besides a great many small ones, a strong chest, a corner cupboard, 5 old cushions and a large old screene

In the kitchen a quantity of pewter, three coffey potts, three copper potts, an old range, two spit-irons, jack and weights, 2 boilers and 2 fish kettles, two old tables, part of an old knapkin prese, a small boyler, two small belmettal morters, a freestone-morter, 2 small gridg-irons, beef forks and a driping pan

In dry larder two meat vickles [meat safe]

In best chamber a wrought bed as it stand, 6 wrought chairs, a fire glass and looking glass, fire shovel tongs hand irons and bellows, a small table and dressing box, old window curtins and hangings

In little parlour chamber one bed as it stand, tapstry hangings, 6 chairs, a sconce, a table, a looking-glass, fire harth, fender, handirons, fire shovel, tongs and brush

In servants room adjoining a bed as it stand

In dining room 5 cane chairs, 7 cushions, fire shovel, tongs and hand-irons, a spinet, a little table, a picture called chivy-chase [a hunting scene]

Midle chamber part hung with old tapestry

In dressing room a toylet, a cabinet, a repeating cloth, an old spinet, old window curtins, 5 old cane-chairs, some old tapestry hangings, a range, fire shovel, tongs, poker, fender, bellows and brush

In lodging room adjoining one bed as it stand, 5 old cane chairs, a cabinet, a pair of hand-irons, an old tea table and some old tapstry hangings

In servants room adjoining one bed

In steward's lodging room one bed as it stand, one table, three old chairs, a squob and an old cole grate

In garret over the stody an old bed an old table and two old chairs

In garret adjoining an old bed as it stand and an old bedstead

In garret over dining room one bed as it stand, 5 old chairs, a table and an old cubbard

In long gallery a large Cyprian chest, a slide great table, old chests and old boxes

In room adjoining two beds

In the pantry a table, a bulting trough [flour sifter], a small lead cistern

In the laudry a piece of a Limbeck [alembic – distilling apparatus], three stills, two free-stone morters and two tables

In the brewhouse a large copper and irons, a mash tun, under beck and two coolers, two lead pumps, one to the copper and one to the under beck

In the barne a small new tumbrel cart and two pair of wheels for ditto, a parcel of spair pieces and some board, a hogshead of tarrass and part of another, a new pair of hinder coach wheels and some old ditto

In coach house a coach and chariot pretty good

In store house some Holland pan tile and roof ditto, a parcel of English square tile, a quantity of ½ rounds for toping walls, and some white bricks

At brick-kiln about 18 or 20000 red brick

In the garden 3 rolls and some garden tools and potts

A large quantity of glass bottles, square with arms of family

In the pond a boat

The Bayfield letters make clear that these goods were still in Turner's ownership. In July the major sale of Mannington's contents was advertised and most of the sale lots match the items in this list. The library and musical instruments (over and above the two spinets) were sold separately the day before. These last were presumably in the study - in the inventory noted only by the garret above it - which was presumably locked to protect the more valuable items. The overall structure of the main part of the house does not look significantly different from the 1678 layout; the following sketch plan shows the best assessment possible from what is known about the structure of the building and the room sequence in both inventories. However, by this stage there were only 14 upstairs rooms compared with 21 in 1678. It is clear that the rear range had been much reduced, or at least part of it was not used. Almost certainly Sir Algernon Potts and Frances had modified the house to reflect their circumstances. The large number of rooms for chaplain, elderly relative, husbandman, nurserymaids and boys were not required. The rear wing had been reduced to just a kitchen and its services. The estate accounts show some of these rooms were in poor repair – the building over the old cellar was to be knocked down a few years after Walpole's purchase. The rear range was now probably just on the ground floor although still, as the 1742 map shows, stretching to the moat. The 1830s water colours of the Hall show that most of the service rooms were demolished leaving just the kitchen and perhaps a larder and scullery.

The kitchen hearth and oven, throughout this time, would probably have used the house's northern-east corner chimney stack. The stairs close by were built into the massive rear wall and protruded slightly, encased in a brick tower as the 1830s paintings show. Fireplaces were along the back wall and on the lines of the two main east-west dividing walls. Those near the front west face may have been blocked up by the time of the 1830s sketches and thus were not visible – some of the larger rooms had blocked up windows and some of the chimneys may have been capped. Or perhaps they had small flues with very low chimneys not visible above the parapet.

Within the main body of the house, the rooms were being used in much the same way as in 1678 but with some exceptions. The ground floor was unchanged. The emphasis on tea things in the small parlour reflected the early 18th century emergence of tea drinking as a polite ritual in better homes. The naming of the summer parlour reflected how difficult it was to keep rooms warm in winter if they did not adjoin the rear wall and major internal walls containing built-in flues for fires or stoves. On the middle floor the little parlour chamber was now separated from the study, where in 1678 it seems Sir John had this whole space as his chamber. The great parlour chamber seems to have been divided to create a dressing room as a day room at the front of the building. As the room had windows, furniture, a spinet and a fireplace, it is hard to place it anywhere else but here. With the addition of the large turret space, it would have been most attractive.

The upstairs dining room, using the cosy space with the two small low-set windows in the middle of the west face, was a new feature. No doubt the downstairs hall could still be used for larger gatherings, bringing the big table down from the long gallery. The unfurnished middle chamber was probably just a wide passage, but capable of taking a bed if necessary. The lodging room adjoining the dressing room looks and sounds oddly placed, but given the sequence that the rooms were listed in this would be a reasonable descriptor for the next room after the dressing room. Again, it is hard to place this minor bedroom anywhere else. On the top floor the best explanation is for the long gallery to run all the way along the back wall, providing servant access to the rooms below via the small south-east turret stairs. At the north end the old nursery had been divided, creating a good room for the steward or senior servant. The garrets would have provided basic accommodation for other servants. The large room at the south end that had once been part of the family rooms was now a rarely used under-furnished bedroom.

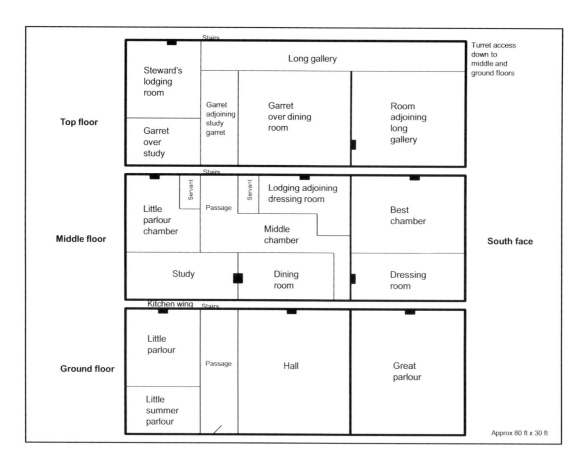

| | | |
|---|---|---|
| **Top floor** | Steward's lodging room / Garret over study | Stairs / Long gallery / Garret adjoining study garret / Garret over dining room | Turret access down to middle and ground floors / Room adjoining long gallery |
| **Middle floor** | Little parlour chamber / Study | Stairs / Servant / Passage / Servant / Lodging adjoining dressing room / Middle chamber / Dining room | Best chamber / Dressing room / **South face** |
| **Ground floor** | Kitchen wing / Little parlour / Little summer parlour | Stairs / Passage / Hall | Great parlour / Approx 80 ft x 30 ft |

Probable layout of Mannington Hall in 1737

Water colours of Mannington Hall with blocked up windows and reduced rear ranges

## Robins family homes

While the Robins occupants of the Manor House and Itteringham Hall did not leave surviving inventories some details can be gleaned from their wills. Richard Robins blacksmith had from his father William a posted bedstead, mattress, cord and curtains in his parlour chamber, with his feather bed, best bolster, pair of blankets and best coverlet lying on it. No doubt this remained part of his household stuff that he later left to his son Thomas 1 (together with his best coverlet) and which later furnished the Manor House bedroom. Richard and his brothers shared a number of household items, most of which no doubt stayed in Itteringham for many years.

In 1727, when Thomas 2 inherited the real estate of his uncle William Robins of Heydon, he was also promised William's prize clock, his coach, harness and coach horses after William's sister died. Although Thomas 2 did not live long enough to enjoy them, his son would have claimed these trappings of luxury. Thomas 3 also inherited his mother's best crimson bed with all its furniture which presumably came back to the Manor House in Itteringham. Richard Robins 2 of Itteringham Hall left a lengthy will in 1743 which gives some idea of the rooms in the Hall and some of his best possessions. His widow Susan was to have, for as long as she wanted, the use of the parlour, parlour chamber, the chamber next to that, the garret over it and the pantry. This was probably effectively one complete wing of the house. As well as the backhouse, brew house and wash house she could also use all the facilities in the yards and take pigeons from the dove house. She was to have two horses, his carriage and the two pairs of harness belonging to it. All the cheese and butter in the dairy, all the fowl in the yards, all the plate and linen and her choice of other household goods were to be hers as well. The couple were active members of the Oulton Meeting House and it is likely that the books he also left to Susan were worthy works. Perhaps they had read them together in the long evenings of their 47-year marriage.

## A farmer's life

For smaller houses, attempts to match inventories with specific buildings are fraught with problems as the next two examples show. Both of the possible candidates have long disappeared leaving little to help with identification. Small tenant farmers, in the early 18th century, often lived in relatively simple farmhouses which may have once been small hall houses - good structures of some status in their day - but which had not been enlarged or improved. The tenants also held different leases over time, sometimes holding more than one farm holding in a family and living in the most suitable accommodation available. Sons with children would be given the larger space and widows might be allowed to remain in one section of a farmhouse for the rest of the lease. Estate accounts show that it often took some time to get a permanent tenant in place and over time it was accepted practice when necessary and practical to let a tenant's widow live at a farm even when a new tenant was installed.

The inventories themselves related only to the farmers' goods and the naming of rooms was purely a practical device. Unlike in the grander houses, the goods, being fewer in number, may have been moved into one or two rooms; the widow's clothes and any items of furniture she might have inherited from her mother would not be included so a small bed chamber of her things might be omitted. Where the farmer, if older and not active, had been living with his wife only in part of a larger house, most of the rooms would not be mentioned at all.

The Jackson and Breese examples highlight these problems. In June 1716 Robert Jackson junior, grandson of Thomas the rector, died unexpectedly, leaving no will; he may have contracted the smallpox that was rife at the time. His father Robert senior died the following year at Wolterton where he was probably living with his daughter Mary Bond. Robert junior's possessions were valued by Thomas Robins, Thomas Fulcher and William Daniel. Because both Roberts were active at the same time it is not certain which farm Robert junior had at his death. However Robert senior had been the leaseholder of the larger Hill farm with which the modest 32 acres of planted crops listed here would not be consistent. The likelihood is that Robert junior, married and with a young family, was leasing the small farm at the Old Rectory (see Chapter 6), as indicated in the Mannington estate accounts from 1710.

Jackson had at least two possible places to live: the Old Rectory itself and Larwood's, the old small hall house in the meadow nearby. The inventory seems far too small for the Old Rectory unless they only had part of the building. As the house had been let separately from the farm land in the past, it would seem more likely that the family lived in Larwood's. This was shown on the 1595 estate map and by 1716 was still very simple. The old central hall may now have been used as the large kitchen, with a parlour and dairy on either side. Two rooms had a chamber above. There may have been only one fireplace - the kitchen hearth - although a fire in the parlour would seem a possibility, even though no fire goods were noted. Jackson had few possessions of any note and no special pieces such as a clock or picture. This was home for a working farmer with a typical small arable farm and good mix of livestock. The 'lodging room' was not described as a chamber and was probably on the ground floor at the back of the service area. Of the two beds there, one was a flight bed - stuffed with the husks of oats - suitable for a hired husbandman or servant. If we assume the goods had not been moved around, the old hall kitchen was the hub of activity with the long table and seating for at least ten people (more depending on the length of the forms). The 12 pewter plates would have been for the family; the 12 wooden trenchers in the dairy for the farm servants.

| Goods cattle and chattles of Robert Jackson of Itteringham | £ | s | d |
|---|---|---|---|
| His wearing apparel linning and woolling | 3 | 0 | 0 |
| In the paller | | | |
| 1 bed and bedstead as it stand | 4 | 0 | 0 |
| 1 ovell table, 1 old cubbert, 1 neast of drawers, 1 pair of small drawers, 6 cheaires | 1 | 10 | 0 |
| 3 paire of course sheets, 3 table cloathes, 12 napkins | 1 | 12 | 0 |
| In the kitchen chamber | | | |
| 1 bed as it now stand | 3 | 0 | 0 |
| 1 chest, 2 cheares, 1 stand | 0 | 5 | 0 |
| In the dyery chamber | | | |
| 1 old bed as it stand, 1 stand, 1 old cubbert, 1 settle, 1 coffer | 1 | 10 | 0 |
| In a lodging roome | | | |
| 1 bed as it stand, 1 table, 1 stand, 1 stoole | 1 | 12 | 0 |
| 1 flight bed, 1 cheaire, 1 table frame, 1 foarme | 0 | 7 | 0 |
| In the kitchen | | | |
| 1 long table, 1 small table, 6 chaires, 2 foarmes, 3 gint [possibly jointed] stooles, 6 peuter dishes, 12 peuter pleats | 1 | 13 | 0 |
| 1 warming pan, 2 iron pottage potts, 3 kittles, 3 skillets | 2 | 10 | 0 |
| 1 jack, 3 speets, 3 hakes, 1 rost iron, 1 cliver, 1 paire of tongues, 1 friring pan, 1 fire pan, 4 iron scuers, 1 smothing iron and hets [heats – heated lumps of metal placed inside a box iron], 1 choping knife, 2 candlesticks, 1 driping pan | 1 | 5 | 0 |
| In the dyery | | | |
| 1 mash fatt, 4 stands, 2 cillers, 3 beare feirkings, 3 small beare vessells | 1 | 6 | 0 |
| 1 churne, 3 pailes, 7 boules, 1 cheese press, 5 chees fats, 2 cheeses breads, 1 milch sive, 1 paire of tongues | 1 | 2 | 0 |
| 1 duzen glass and stone bottles, 12 trenchers, 6 wooden dishes | 0 | 3 | 0 |
| 1 minging trough, 2 sives, one tunnel [funnel] | 0 | 2 | 0 |
| In the bearne and chamber | | | |
| 30 coomb wheat threshed and to thresh | 16 | 0 | 0 |
| 2 fanns, 2 redles, 1 bushell, 1 casting shovel, 1 wide redle [riddle] | 0 | 15 | 0 |
| 12 sackes, 5 rakes, 5 forckes | 0 | 14 | 0 |
| 7 horse and mare cattle | 18 | 0 | 0 |
| 4 paire of cart traice, 4 helters, 4 plough helters [halters], 2 cart sedles [saddles], 2 slips, 1 saddle and bridle, 1 pannell [wicker baskets slung on either side of a horse] and strops | 2 | 10 | 0 |
| 1 spade, 2 shovells, 2 muck forks, 1 madock, 2 hoocks, 1 hatchit, 2 paire of cheanes | 0 | 12 | 0 |
| 1 plough, 1 paire of harrows | 1 | 0 | 0 |
| 2 carts | 8 | 0 | 0 |
| 10 cowes, 1 bull, 6 calves | 25 | 10 | 0 |
| 12 twoo yearleing and yearleing cattle | 12 | 0 | 0 |
| 3 sowes, 2 brannes and 7 shotts | 4 | 0 | 0 |
| 7 acres of wheat and rye | 12 | 0 | 0 |
| 20 acres of barley at | 24 | 0 | 0 |
| 5 acres of oats at | 2 | 0 | 0 |

| | £ | s | d |
|---|---|---|---|
| 23 stone of cheese at | 1 | 14 | 6 |
| 15 geece, 1 percell of hay | 2 | 10 | 0 |
| 10 hens, 1 duck, 1 cock | 0 | 4 | 0 |
| 8 cowes racks, 3 hogs troughes | 0 | 10 | 0 |
| 1 paire of scales, 3 stone 7 pounds of waights | 0 | 5 | 0 |
| 1 cart roap and for lumber and things forgotten | 0 | 5 | 0 |
| | 92 | 18 | 6 |

Robert junior's yeoman brother Richard died in Wolterton in 1728 and again an inventory was made. Richard leased the 120 acre farm just to the east of Wolterton lake, later keeper's cottage. Its larger size is evident in the somewhat greater number of cattle. His house also had 6 rooms, but the parlour obviously had its own fireplace and the house drawing on the 1732 map shows 2 chimneys. His belongings were not materially different from his brother's – no significant items, although he did have a handful of silver spoons valued at £1. Surprisingly he had £480 of ready money – a large sum which would seem to be about 7-8 times his annual rent. While this may have been savings over many years, a reference to colts perhaps indicates that he had a profitable horse breeding business.

The inventory of Henry Breese should be similar to that of Robert Jackson. Breese was the tenant of West Field farm (**2**), a small farm with a small farmhouse, across the Cut from the church. This was also shown on the estate map of 1595 again suggesting an old hall house. Henry died in early December 1741. His widow Sarah took possession of his goods and that month they were inventoried by George Copland (of Mannington Hall) and Cornelius Graver (of Itteringham Old Rectory and its farm). From the estate accounts it is clear that Breese died owing fairly substantial rent arrears. The estate, which paid for the inventory-taking, must have taken all his farming stock in lieu of rent as it was not included. In 1746 Michael Towne, the tanner, bought from Walpole, for £18 10s, three horses and one mare 'that had been Henry Breese's'. However the inventory mentioned no upstairs chambers, just a small parlour, kitchen, pantry, backhouse and dairy. Had Henry's goods been gathered downstairs or were Henry and Sarah living in only part of the house? The only bed listed was in the parlour. A third possibility exists: the 1595 map suggests there had originally been two dwellings at this site. Perhaps Sarah had already been moved into a smaller cottage in the farmyard while the next tenant took over the farmhouse.

| Inventory of Henry Breese  December 1741 | £ | s | d |
|---|---|---|---|
| His wearing apparel | 1 | 0 | 0 |
| Cash in the home | 11 | 5 | 3 |
| *In the kitchen* | | | |
| 5 tables and 11 chairs | 1 | 6 | 0 |
| One dresser and one jack | 0 | 6 | 6 |
| Two pair of tongs, 2 spits, one fire iron, two dog irons, one grid iron, one fire pan, one gim [or ginn: gin - a hoist in the fireplace seems possible?], one cliver, two hakes | 0 | 10 | 0 |
| Four candlesticks, one brasse ladle, one pair of meat forks, one pair of bellows | 0 | 2 | 6 |
| One metal pott, one bushel of meal | 0 | 7 | 6 |
| Six pewter dishes, ten plates, one bason | 0 | 17 | 0 |
| Two spades, one shovel | 0 | 5 | 0 |
| *In the little parlour* | | | |
| One bed as it stand | 1 | 10 | 0 |
| One chest, one stool, 5 chairs, one table | 0 | 8 | 6 |
| One mortar, one pestle | 0 | 2 | 6 |
| *In the pantry* | | | |
| Two beer tubs | 0 | 1 | 6 |
| *In the backhouse* | | | |
| Three kettles, two skillets, one saucepan | 0 | 1 | 0 |
| The brewing utensills | 0 | 10 | 0 |
| One beer tub, six pails | 0 | 7 | 0 |

<u>In the dayry</u>
One lead, one butter keeler, three bowls                                      1    8    0
                                                                          _____
                                                                            23    9    9

## Cottage industry: weavers and carpenters

Richard Robins the son of William of Heydon (one of the elder half-brothers of Richard Robins blacksmith of Itteringham) made his will in 1674 and after his death that year a full inventory was made of his household and trade goods. As a worsted weaver his inventory might be taken as a reasonable stand-in for a tradesman living in Itteringham in the late 17th century, such as the weaver Christopher Parkins. The volume and standard of household goods is probably a good indication of any senior tradesman's house through much of the 18th century – such as Itteringham's tailors, barber and shopkeepers. Equally the small amount of livestock and a little leased or freehold land (often brought by the wife at marriage) were again typical of many such households.

His daughter Anne was to have her deceased mother's gold ring and the trunks containing her clothes. Thomas Newman (clerk of Heydon who turned lawyer) was executor and was then living in one of Richard's houses. The bedstead, curtains and valance that used to stand in the parlour chamber of that house were also to go to Anne when she reached 18. He hoped that Lucy Jay of Cringleford would remain a friend to his daughter and left her a silver salt, with a small legacy to Lucy Barber who usually lived with her. A silver cup was left to his kinsman Richard Fulcher his godson. His inventory was taken on 28th November, two days after his death, by Thomas Robins and Thomas Hall who failed to total the sums correctly.

| Inventory of Richard Robins of Heydon | £ | s | d |
|---|---|---|---|
| His wearing apparel with some few things that have been his wives | 2 | 10 | 0 |
| In ready money by him | 1 | 14 | 6 |
| In debts due and to growe due to him most sperate [hopeful/good] part desperate | 87 | 19 | 0 |
| His bibles and a few other small books | 0 | 10 | 0 |
| <u>In the kitchen</u> | | | |
| One posted bedstead with the beds and bedding thereon as it stand, a pewter cold [cowl – cupboard], two tables, one cupboord, one chest, a little trunk, one forme, seven chayres and ten stooles | 6 | 7 | 0 |
| Pewter dishes and other pewter with brasse in the kitchen | 3 | 10 | 0 |
| Two payre of dogirons, fire pan, gridiron, bellows, tongs, iron bair [bar], andirons, spits, hakes [hooks], a tosting iron, a chopping knife, three wedges, two smoothing irons, halfe a bend [band] of leather, ten old cushings, a little box, Holland dyshes, earthen pots, dishes, tranches and other things of small value | 1 | 13 | 0 |
| <u>In the dayry</u> | | | |
| Bolls [bowls?], cheesefats[cheese-vat - the mould], one cheesebreed [cheese-bread - the cover], all the cheese and butter with other lumber | 0 | 10 | 0 |
| <u>In the bedchamber by it</u> | | | |
| A bedstead with the bed and bedding therewith as it standeth, an old carpet, a looking glass, a wicker chayre and some other things of small value | 2 | 10 | 0 |
| <u>In the chamber over the kitchen</u> | | | |
| One chest, three broken boxes, cheese, a pot with about a pint of honey in it, nigh three pecks of wheate and mixtling [maslin – mixed rye and wheat] and lumber | 2 | 0 | 0 |
| <u>In the chamber over the chamber and dayry</u> | | | |
| One boorded bedstead with old bedding thereon, old chests and lumber | 1 | 0 | 0 |
| <u>In the shop and chamber over it</u> | | | |
| Divers tubs, a chirne, pavements, firing and lumber | 1 | 10 | 0 |
| <u>In the cupboard and chest in the kitchen and Anns trunks</u> | | | |
| A silver porringer [small dish], a little silver lace and linen with a small silver spoon | 2 | 12 | 0 |
| A bushel, an old fann and three sacks | 0 | 8 | 0 |

| | | | |
|---|---|---|---|
| Hay in the hay house and barne | 1 | 15 | 0 |

At the house where hee did live where Mr Newman doth live

| | | | |
|---|---|---|---|
| Two tables, an old carpet, an old jack, an old counter, a broken chest with some leades and old iron in it, a little colfer, an harrow, a tub, a minging trough[mixing], a coverlet, a blanket and some painted papers | 1 | 10 | 0 |

At Francis Messenger's a bombe [leather jug?] and a trundle [trendle? – bedstead]

| | | | |
|---|---|---|---|
| | 1 | 0 | 0 |

In the yards

| | | | |
|---|---|---|---|
| Two old cowes, one heffer, two calves, one hogg, one shot [young pig] and neare three bushels of buck [buckwheat, here for fodder] in the shop | 8 | 17 | 0 |
| Fyring and spars newly hewne | 1 | 15 | 0 |
| Two neates racks, a swines trough, pultry and other things that may unwillingly bee omitted | 0 | 7 | 0 |
| And he hath a lease of certaine lands let at thirteen pounds per annum under a small rent for a terme not yet expired | | | |

Goods given to be preserved for Ann his daughter

| | | | |
|---|---|---|---|
| A bedstead with curtaines valons mat and cord | 2 | 0 | 0 |
| Two trunks in one of which the bible that was her mothers, a gowne and two petticoats. In the other of them bee three silver spoones and seven napkins, two boor clothes [table cloths], a payre of fine sheetes, two pillow beires [pillow cases], four little boxes in one of which is a silver whistle, in an other of them a gold ring that was her mothers, silver lace, ribbonds, a white silke whood, two blacke whoodes, a black whiske [collar], scarfe and wearing linen that were her mothers | 8 | 0 | 0 |

Goods given to be delivered to other persons

| | | | |
|---|---|---|---|
| To Mrs Luce Jay one silver salt | 0 | 12 | 0 |
| To Mrs Luce Barber one piece of gold | 0 | 8 | 0 |
| To Mr Richard Fulcher one silver cup | 2 | 8 | 0 |
| To Ann Robins his aunt one cheese press | 0 | 10 | 0 |
| | | | |
| To of what the executors may be chargeable with besides the lease as above | 130 | 9 | 6 |
| To of the goods given to bee preserved for the daughter as above is | 10 | 0 | 0 |
| To of the goods given as legacyes is | 3 | 12 | 0 |
| The totall summe of the inventory beside the lease is | 144 | 1 | 6 |

[signed] Thomas Robins Thomas Hall

As we have seen Thomas Plaford, father and son, were carpenters in Itteringham. Neither left an inventory but the goods of Edmund Fiddy (Feddee) a Wolterton carpenter were inventoried in 1699 and no doubt the Plaford home, now Meadow House, would have been much the same, including small scale farming as well as carpentry. Fiddy's cottage, however, was very basic, with no rooms above the parlour or kitchen which may even have still been open to the roof. Often a small storage space was created above the parlour. Fiddy's will showed that he and his wife Elizabeth Cooke had three daughters, who were provided for from property in Sustead and Swanton Novers. The feather beds in the room over the dairy may have been the children's. His brother Thomas Fiddy farmed in Blickling.

| Goods and chattels of Edmond Feddee of Woolterton 4th September 1699 | £ | s | d |
|---|---|---|---|
| | | | |
| His wearing apparell | 3 | 0 | 0 |
| In ready money in the house | 5 | 0 | 0 |

In the parlour

| | | | |
|---|---|---|---|
| One feather bed, two bolsters, two pillows, two blankets, one rug with bedstead curtains and vallens | 3 | 0 | 0 |
| One table, ten chaires, two chests, one livery cupboard and three boxes | 2 | 0 | 0 |
| Fifteen pair of sheetes, four table cloaths, two dozen napkins and eighteene pillow beeres | 5 | 0 | 0 |

<u>In the kitching</u>

| | £ | s | d |
|---|---|---|---|
| One feather bed, one bolster, two pillows, rugg, blankets, curtaines, vallens and one bedstead | 2 | 0 | 0 |
| Ten pewter dishes, eleaven plates, one small kettle, one brasse porridge pot and two iron potts | 2 | 0 | 0 |
| One jack, three spits, two hakes, one coalecradle, one iron burr, one paire of tonges, two dogg irons, five candlesticks, two smoothing irons, four heates, eight skures and one warmeing pan | 1 | 2 | 0 |
| Two tables and six chaires | 0 | 5 | 0 |

<u>In the brewhouse</u>

| | | | |
|---|---|---|---|
| One brasse copper, one small washing copper, one guyle tubb [for fermenting the wort], one mash tubb, nine beer tubs and four standles | 4 | 0 | 0 |

<u>In the diary</u>

| | | | |
|---|---|---|---|
| Tenn milk bowles, one milk lead, one cherne and one meat fickle [meat safe] | 1 | 0 | 0 |

<u>In the diary chamber</u>

| | | | |
|---|---|---|---|
| Four feather bedds with four coverlids and four bolsters | 6 | 0 | 0 |

<u>In the yards</u>

| | | | |
|---|---|---|---|
| Four old horses | 8 | 0 | 0 |
| Two other horses | 8 | 0 | 0 |
| Two carts, one plow, one paire of harrowes | 5 | 0 | 0 |
| One sett of iron trace, plow trace and other implyments of husbandry | 3 | 0 | 0 |
| One fann, one bushell, six sacks, three ridles, one wire seive, five forks, two dragg rakes, five hand rakes, one shovell and one muck forke | 0 | 10 | 0 |
| Six old cowes, two heifers and four calves | 15 | 10 | 0 |
| Tenn acres of wheate | 14 | 0 | 0 |
| Nine acres and an halfe of barley | 9 | 0 | 0 |
| Two acres of oates | 1 | 0 | 0 |
| Seaven roodes of vetches | 1 | 5 | 0 |
| One acre of buck | 0 | 12 | 0 |
| Four old swine and nine shotts | 4 | 0 | 0 |
| Poultry in the yards | 0 | 5 | 0 |
| Fireing in the yards | 1 | 0 | 0 |
| Hay over the stable and hay house | 4 | 0 | 0 |

<u>Timber in the yards</u>

| | | | |
|---|---|---|---|
| Seaven peices of oakk timber | 3 | 0 | 0 |
| Seaven peices of ash and one of elme | 3 | 0 | 0 |
| Three loads of willow and ebell | 2 | 7 | 0 |
| 99 foote of ashen timber | 4 | 19 | 0 |
| Three pair of skrewes | 1 | 0 | 0 |
| One pair of tackle roapes and chaine | 1 | 10 | 0 |
| Six long sawes | 0 | 10 | 0 |
| A jack | 1 | 15 | 0 |
| One grindstone and three workeing benches | 0 | 15 | 0 |
| Five oaken trees at Alburrow | 3 | 0 | 0 |
| His working tooles | 1 | 15 | 0 |
| Booke debts good and bad | 88 | 3 | 0 |
| For lumber and things forgotten | 1 | 0 | 0 |
| | 212 | 3 | 0 |

## A spinster dressmaker

Mehetebel Leman was the unmarried daughter of Robert Leman, sometime dissenting preacher and practitioner of physic of Oulton (d 1697) and his wife Bridget Bell. Mehetebel died in Itteringham in 1727 and four inventories were needed over the next six months to list her goods some of which had already been dispersed to various people. The initial arrangements by her brother Barnabas were obviously challenged at some point. At his main valuation in November 1727, her clothes and ready money were worth just over £10. She also had £31 in bonds due to her and in total her inventory showed assets of £42, the balance of about £1 made up of a trunk, a coffer, a box, a pewter dish, a silver bodkin, a silver spoon, an earthen melter, a mustard pot, a basin, a brass candlestick and a brass basting spoon. Jane Dyball of Loddon separately listed a callamacoe [glossy woollen cloth] gown, a gold ring, a fan and a small book that she had received. Elizabeth Varden (who worked for Clement Robins, the shopkeeper) reported another set of items, which in part imply Mehetebel was working as a dressmaker, perhaps with Mrs Howard the schoolmaster's wife. The Howards lived in the cottage set back behind the shop and Mehetebel may have lived with them or in the tiny cottage attached to the back of the shop. Mehetebel it seems had some trade goods on credit from Clement which one of her brothers as administrator was sending back to the shop.

> One gown delivered by the administrator to Jane Dybell as also one gold ring
> A black damask petticoat desired to be given to Mary Bird by the administrator
> Her best riding hood, her best stays and green purse with the money in it desired to be given to Mary Leman and taken away from Mr Robbins' by the administrator
> Some linen found about the house and put into her drawers and delivered to the appraisers
> Delivered to Mr Robbins my master by his order four shifts, two dimity waistcoats, a linen waistcoat, six laced forehead cloths, nine white handkerchiefs, a mental apron [possibly mantle or cover, more likely a long apron up to the chin - mental meaning pertaining to the chin], 2 large pin cushions, 2 ditto small, a small hussy [*housewife* – pocket sewing kit], a pair of scissors with a chain, a fan, 5 white hoods, one wrist banded sleeve white, two linen socks, two small caps, one ounce of white thread, a yard and a half of stuff, a yard and better than a quarter of broad black ribbon, all taken out of her boxes or drawers in the presence of the administrator and his brothers and sisters and delivered to Mr Robbins by their consent
> Found since a pair of old patterns and some odd things valued sixpence all in the custody of Mrs Howard of Itteringham

In April 1728 Clement Robins made another list of Mehetebel's goods, obviously having been called on to comment on the first inventory by Mehetebel's brother Barnabas. The first part repeated the items delivered to him in the previous list. He added a number of names and showed that Mehetebel also worked for him in the shop. Perhaps she ran the haberdashery side of the business. Jane Dyball, wife of James, was Clement's niece, a daughter of his sister Hannah who had married John Bell of Oulton.

> A bible and a hymn book, a large book containing an exposition on part of the book of Job
> A pewter pan
> An old pair of patterns and as many other small things I ordered to be carried in at Mrs Howard's of Itteringham and I hear are appraised by her at sixpence, but I know not their particulars
> A coat gown and a pair of bodies sold by her to her kinswoman Sarah Thorne of Oulton on or about the 14th April 1725 at seven shillings and two pence
> Part of a screen, a callemancoe gown and a gold ring I hear Barnabas Leman administrator delivered to my kinswoman Jane Dybell
> A black damis [damask?] petticoat I hear he also carried to his kinswoman at Itteringham Mary Bird
> A riding hood and a pair of stays I have heard he carried from my house which the deceased desired his daughter Mary Leman might have with a green silk purse with money in it, but I never saw the purse nor money in it since her death, neither do I know that any of the above goods in the inventory Barnabas Leman had
> I also know of two bonds she kept of £15 each principal in his inventory with interest due, but I remember not the interest due
> There is also in his inventory 12 shillings, a debt due from the administrator to the deceased before her death
> I also paid him her Michaelmas quarter's wages being 12s 6d
> As to her ready money and the other particulars in the administrator's inventory I cannot remember, as witness my hand 2nd April 1728, Clement Robins

## Pauper homes: Blickling and Itteringham

No inventories for the poorest villagers survive for Itteringham but in August 1723 Thomas Purdy (the carpenter) and Richard Thompson (the gardener) made a short inventory of all the goods and personal estate of David Cook of Itteringham. There is no clue to his occupation, although he may have assisted Thompson or Purdy. Totalling just £12 8s 6d, his assets included £7 of debts due to him although he also owed money to Mary Daniel. His clothes, old sheets, table linen, drawers and an old table, pewter dishes and plates and a few other bits and pieces made up the rest. Two examples of pauper inventories taken by the Blickling overseers give some impression of the simple belongings of the poor:

Thomas Buck, undated but late 18<sup>th</sup> century:

Household furniture: 1 Brown table, 1 Brown Cubbord, 1 clock, Chest Draws, White table, White Stool, 5 Chears, 1 Great chear, 3 Bear Tubs, 1 Bear Stool, 7 Blew & white pleats [plates], 1 Spond [spoon?] Chamber: Brown Ches with Rabittskins, Small box with Flax, An Iron Bond Tub, 1 Beed and Beding, 1 Brass Kittle, 1 Pair of sheets, 1 Stool, Handsaw

James Smith, November 1791:

1 Bed, 1 Chest Drawers, 3 Tables, 1 Cubbard, spice drawers, 4 chairs, 1 chest 1 pot 1 camp oven 1 pail 1 spit & Dog irons 1 Tea Kittle and Saucepan 1 Jug & Earthing wear pewter Dish & plate, 1 Candlestick 1 Lamp and tinware, 1 Skillett, 1 Hank 2 pot Irons 1 Cullender, Beam and Scales, 1 Waterpot, 1 Basket & Skepp, 1 small box, 3 Tubbs, 1 half peck 1 funel, 1 handle cup, 1 Ironbox and heater, 1 paire Tongs and sinderpan
£3 4s 6d

The very poorest would have had far less, just a few clothes, bed coverings and a chair.

### Sources

NRO: ANW inventory 1716 DN/INV 73/11 (2); ANW 1728-29, 23/18/17; ANW 1741, 23/24/15; ANW inventory 1674-75, 23/3/206; 1699-1700, DN/INV 68A/52; Leman INV 77A/58, INV 77B/93, INV 78A/149-150; Cook NCC 1723-24 DN/INV 75B/65; Buck & Smith, Blickling PD 434/42

Wolterton archive: 3/1/3; 8/20

More details on the purchase of Mannington in *See You in Court*

# Chapter 12

## 'Dis Burst in all'

*[1753 clerk's attempt at 'Total Disbursements']*

---

*Itteringham, like many rural parishes in the 18th century, had to be self-reliant in looking after its poor. Although some parts of East Anglia were experimenting with group-run Houses of Industry, the centralised union workhouses would not emerge until the 19th century. Here, though, responsibility for implementing the system which had evolved and grown over the previous 100 years fell firmly on the senior inhabitants of the parish.*

## The overseers of the poor

Two overseers were elected by the principal men (and women, as they too could be overseers) for the following year; in the account books for Itteringham, the year is divided up into halves with one overseer taking charge for six months. At their discretion, sums of money including rents, were paid out as need arose and at the end of the half year, they levied a rate on the wealthier inhabitants (based on lands, houses and tithes) which was set at the poundage which would raise enough to cover their outgoings or disbursements. All had to be accounted for in detail and the accounts were annually examined and allowed by two justices, although they had no power to alter the rate or expenditure. Of those in the parish John Fish the shopkeeper seems to have been the best at doing accounts and for several years in 1780s was paid for his work along with his draper's bill. Rents could be paid directly to the landlord – in 1787 Pooley had part of his rent (£1 6s 3d) paid straight to Thomas Plaford. The officers were technically unpaid (although there is an entry for 1 guinea in 1787 for serving) and must have taken substantial time – through the 18th century individuals served every 3 or 4 years, up to 9 times in one case.

From the surviving entries Itteringham clearly cared well for its poor and this is confirmed by the comment made in 1795:

> Note: This year the price of wheat set in about 25s per coombe but from the failure of the crops it rapidly advanced to the enormous price of 55s 6d per coombe. Meal sold at 3s 6d per stone, flour 4s 6d, bread 3d per lb and almost all other necessaries of life in proportion advanced one third in their value the distress of the poor was in consequence severely felt throughout the kingdom and in many places they became so extremely clamorous that it required military assistance to keep them in order but to the credit of this little parish, be it remembered, from the willingness of the inhabitants to relieve their poor not one application was made to the magistracy.

### Cottages for the poor

How did they manage? Apart from the rates, the parish had little other income but the gravel pit (see below). Where possible families were assisted to live in their cottages with widows being the most frequently paid for – often continuous rents. But, as we have seen in Chapter 1, early poor houses or almshouses in Itteringham had either been built or had been given to the parish. As commons encroachments they might have been built by anyone at any time with lord of the manor approval at some time. Perhaps the original builder died, his widow was supported by the parish and after her death the cottage was claimed by the overseers in lieu of past rent. The overseers themselves could have had them built to meet their obligation to house the poor of the village. A parallel situation arose in Aylmerton in 1739. The Rector complained that the parish had no poor house and was wasting 45 shillings in renting two dilapidated cottages (in one house) which were not worth the money. He suggested to two of his local gentry that they each provide a tree towards the erection of a Town house for the poor on the common, of two apartments. He calculated that they would pay for themselves in 7 years. One hundred years later one of our Robins clan lived next door to the Aylmerton townhouse on the common.

The cottages on Itteringham Common were known as the Townhouses and the parish retained this land into the 19th century (**27**). In addition the parish could use the row of almshouses later called Church Row (**3**). The townhouses would have been very small timber and thatch hovels and were demolished by the second half of the 19th century. They would have needed regular maintenance and we know that repairs to the townhouses were carried out in the summer of 1739:

September 1739 Richard Shilleta overseer's accounts

| | | |
|---|---|---|
| For Spur-pieces, sills & splents for the Poors House | 4s | |
| for 500 bricks and cariage | 10s | |
| A Load of mudging | 1s | |
| half chauldron of lime | 4s | |
| the lime & clay fetching | 4s | |
| A bushel of hair | 1s | |
| The Bricklayers work & allowance | 11s | |
| ¾ load of straw | 7s | 6d |
| The Thatchers work & allowance | 7s | 1d |
| the Windows mending | | 6d |
| A pound of splenting yarn | 1s | |
| 3 ½ lb of nails | 1s | 4d |
| Carpenters work | 11s | 4d |

On Blickling Common, their townhouses were rebuilt or extended in late summer 1738 with 4,500 red bricks and 300 white 'Pamon'. Glazing was finished by November 1739. Mr Wickes, the overseer and tanner, ordered a new 'penthouse' - a lean-to with a sloping roof - to be added in 1745. Thatched roofs were a constant problem. Itteringham paid for more repairs in the winter of 1752-53:

| | | | |
|---|---|---|---|
| To Christopher Hall for Dawbing work at the Town House 6 days | 7s | | |
| To 9 Spoors [spars] at the Town House | 4s | | |
| To stones and marl fetching | 3s | | |
| To Michael Bullock for Thatching as per Bill | £1 | 5s | 1d |
| 2 cart loads of straw | £1 | | |
| 2 sparr pieces & a piece of Eaveboard | | 1s | |

Sometimes a house repaired by the overseers is described simply by name of the inhabitant. In the summer and autumn of 1784, lime, sand and 1,300 bricks were bought for 'Bird's house', enough for a small lean-to or rebuild of a wall. This may have been one of the Church Row houses. At that time a Thomas Bird was sick and having his rent paid for but an Elizabeth Bird received a weekly payment. Her husband Bartholomew Bird also claimed relief a few months later. Perhaps it was their home that was in need of repair – two of their children, Lydia and Barnard, were buried on the same day in April 1784 in pauper graves. It is less likely to be the house of John Bird who regularly submitted bills for mending the paupers' shoes. Widow Bartram's window was mended in summer of 1787 when she was in need; her son came to stay with her in November and her money increased by 6d so he may have been sick. Apprentices who boarded with their masters were often sent home when unwell; James Barwick left his blacksmith master in Corpusty when ill in December 1801. He stayed at his mother's house in Oulton for 4-5 weeks. For most of the century Itteringham's overseers seemed to make little attempt to 'put the poor to work' (either by paying farmers to hire them or by creating tasks such as preparing weaving materials) but rather to ensure children were clothed and the sick cared for, with an understanding that the able-bodied would return to work as soon as they could. A spinning wheel bought for Widow Bird in 1785 cost 8s 6d, while a spade was 5s.

## The settlement laws

As in every other parish, the officers enforced the settlement laws of 1662. Everyone at risk of falling below the poverty line had to belong to a named parish, either through their place of birth and their father's settlement or through having worked somewhere for sufficient time. As early as 1693, Thomas Robins as overseer, certified that Robert Sutton and his family could call on Itteringham if in need, so Blickling parish officers were happy to let them live there. No parish could afford to be a soft touch; in 1782 overseer John Bell was firm with the parish of Sunderland when they tried to off-load a woman and two children whose sea-going husband, she thought, had been born illegitimately in Itteringham (spelt Itheringham by the overseers). After failing to find the man in the register, Bell (a relative newcomer to the village) had asked around the oldest inhabitants but no-one remembered the name. He then wrote a long reply - Bell's fondness for poetic writing has been noted in Chapter 9 - concluding:

> You may be apprised that we shall not needlessly or hastily encrease the number of our paupers. Such as we know to be legally settled upon us we take care of - And the law itself shall impose no other upon us.

Attracting the vagrant poor would drain the resources meant for the locals, so people were helped and moved on. Those with passes (certificates of character provided by JPs) were given about a shilling in the 1740s - although a woman with child might only get 6d - to help them on the road to Yarmouth or Cromer. By the 1780s a woman and child heading for Cromer still only received a shilling despite the rise in prices. Soldiers and sailors had their own certificates and were usually just given a shilling when in the village but in 1796 one seaman had an extraordinary payment of £9 15s – surely a story there!

In order to decide where an individual could claim settlement, the local justice would ask them about their place of birth, their parentage, where they had worked for a full year or more and whether they had ever rented property worth £10 or more. The examination was written down and kept by the parish as evidence for any later disputes. If settlement was allowed, a certificate would be given enabling the holder to live elsewhere if they wished. Mary Sendall's life history was given in detail before Lord Walpole and William Wiggett Bulwer in October 1776 when she was in her 40s.

Her story demonstrated how frequently young unmarried women moved around. Her mother (Dorothy Sendall) had gone home to give birth so Mary was born in Oulton at the house of Thomas Dewing her grandfather. Mary said she did not know where her father (Martin Sendall) was settled at that time although she knew that he had occupied 'a considerable farm at Cockley'. Failing there, he became an exciseman and when Mary was very young they lived in Gainsborough, Lincolnshire; his job took her father to Redford in Nottinghamshire for six years and then to Malden in Essex where the family stayed for ten years. Mary, who would then have been in her late teens, left home after they had spent six months at Harwich. No more about her parents was noted. On leaving, Mary came to live with her married sister at 'Armingland' (Irmingland) where William Loades and his wife Ann held the large farm at Elmerdale. As Lord Walpole owned this farm, he would have been aware of this part of the narrative. Mary stayed with them about 15 years where she may have helped in the house or on the farm. Now about 33, Mary spent three years with her cousin Bowdle of Castle Acre (probably Hannah Boutell) staying as a relation but then returned to Oulton for six months 'working at her trade of mantua making'. Had she learnt to sew the ladies' cloaks at her cousins? From Oulton she moved to Aylsham for a further six or seven months. In 1768 her sister Ann had to leave Elmerdale when her husband died and she was given a cottage in Itteringham to rent at £4 a year. Mary went to live with Ann and after a year or so, when Ann's servant left, Mary let herself to her sister for a year for £2 wages. She continued the work for another three years until Ann's daughter married and Ann left Itteringham with her. Mary then went to live with her youngest sister Judith Sendall at Thomas Robins's fine Manor House. It was late December 1771 and 27 year-old Judith, who may have been housekeeper to the bachelor Thomas, was then very ill. She died two weeks after Mary arrived and was buried on New Year's Day 1772. Thomas hired Mary for a year at 4 guineas and after that year ended, she had continued there until 10 October 1776, the day before the examination. Why she left is not clear; she had only received about 3 guineas of her wages but could not be precise 'as she thought her money safe in the hands of Mr Robins'. It is possible that another sister, Sarah Sendall, replaced her as Robins's housekeeper at the Manor House until he died in 1782. Sarah Sendall, who lived in part of 98-99 The Street from at least 1785 to her death in 1803, was remembered in the later wills of Thomas's heirs, his sister and brother-in-law, with a generous annuity of £20 which had been paid for some years.

Whatever the reason for Mary's examination - without obvious means she would be chargeable to the parish - Mary's contracts with Robins gave her settlement in Itteringham. The parish may have considered her a reasonable case; although now 51, she had a trade, was literate (as her firm signature showed) and had a good track record. Indeed she did not come to them for help until 1795, when she was 70, after which she remained on weekly collections until she died in 1804. A less fortunate Sendall girl - perhaps another sister - will appear in the next chapter.

Single women who were pregnant would be examined to find out where they were from so that the right parish would be responsible for them. In June 1770 Thomas Plaford of Mere farm, who as the principal inhabitant of the parish of Mannington had to act the role of overseer there, applied to Justice of the Peace William Wiggett

Bulwer for an order to apprehend James Snelling. The constables of Hevingham, where James lived, were to arrest him and bring him to Bulwer to find security to indemnify the parish or else be threatened with trial. Plaford had to ensure that Mary Rust's baby would not be born chargeable to Mannington. Unfortunately this was not the first time for Mary Rust; four years earlier in February 1766 she had come before Bulwer to name John Halett of Buxton as the father of her unborn child. Halett was a husbandman and presumably had spent the summer and harvest period in Mannington where he had 'carnal knowledge [of Mary] several times since July and August'. A few months later Bulwer heard a retrospective claim; Elizabeth Wenn of Welborne said she had given birth at Itteringham in August 1761 to a female bastard child named 'Tomesin'. As her family were of the parish, the child was chargeable to Itteringham; the supposed father was a weaver, Samuel Whalebelly of Mattishall.

Even relatively respectable men found themselves caught up in the system: in 1771 Bulwer had a complaint from the Itteringham parish officers about an illiterate single woman who had 'come to inhabit in the parish not having any legal settlement there and is likely to become chargeable to Iteringham'. On 16th April Bulwer ordered the Itteringham constable to bring Mary Bird before him to be examined. A week later on being examined by Bulwer at his house in Heydon, she said she had let herself to Richard Shilleta the tailor about October 1769 for a year and had received her wages of 2 guineas. The arrangement must have continued because she was still living with him in April 1771. Presumably Mary must have been very pregnant and so had alarmed the overseers. By the time she next appeared before Bulwer - on June 25th - she had been delivered of a female bastard child on 25th May at Shilleta's house in Itteringham. As she was unmarried and both she and her child would have become the parish's responsibility, she was made to declare the father, whom she named as Richard Shilleta of Itteringham. The same day Bulwer signed an order for the constable to bring both Mary and Richard before the justices 'at House of Richard Harriman called the Blackboys in Aylsham on Tues 2 July at 10 am'. Mary was to be further examined and Richard was given notice so 'that he may also be there to make his Defence'. This is an interesting order as it suggests that there may be some attenuating circumstances. Unfortunately the outcome of the pub session has not survived but there was more to the story.

Shilleta was an old man and would die the following year in February 1772. He had been married twice, the second time in 1738 at Edgefield to Mary Bird the widow of Robert Bird, an earlier Itteringham tailor who had died in 1736. Mary was Mary Leak, daughter of the Itteringham and Cawston miller, who had inherited lands in Cawston in 1729. Mary lived with Richard Shilleta until her death in 1769. Whoever the Mary Bird was who turned up in the village the same year, Richard had taken her in. Was young Mary a daughter of his late wife? Perhaps she claimed him as the father with his agreement but the officers suspected it was not true. Whatever the facts, Shilleta willingly gave them a home and the parish was relieved of the problem. When he made his will just before he died, he made generous provision for Mary and her little baby Ann. He had £105 invested of which the interest was to go to Mary every six months to look after Ann until she was 21 when Ann could have the capital. Mary was to take her choice of his household things with which she could furnish herself a house. A few months after Shilleta died, Mary Bird married Nathaniel Hancock, a young journeyman tailor, who had trained at Wells and Heydon. Shilleta had given Hancock a year's contract the year or so before he died so he would have been lodging with them. Might he have been the father? If so perhaps Shilleta had stepped up to help, on the understanding Nathaniel would do the right thing. The Hancocks settled down in the village (Nathaniel was examined by the parish as soon as his wife was pregnant – again) and raised another eight children.

Not always was it so easy for the parish. In February 1795 the overseers examined Sarah Pygal and produced a warrant for Thomas Earle (presumably the father was from another parish) – and then paid out £2 7s 6d for marrying them! As a wife Sarah would take on her husband's settlement so this was a good move. Forty years earlier in 1753 Elizabeth Miller was married off to one John Jones a widower of Holt; the licence and marriage only cost £1 9s then but another £1 was spent on their removal order. In June 1740 William Neal's marriage had been expensively and forcibly arranged to Mary Hill, an Itteringham girl, at a cost of £7 14s 6d. Eighteen months later the parish paid out for Mary's lying-in when baby Peter was born – and shortly afterwards for his coffin. An overseer's note of April 1742 showed Mary still had use of the 'bed and furniture as it now stands' worth 16s. William Neal junior's settlement in 1787 was sufficiently complicated for the parish to pay a guinea for counsel's opinion about his case. He had worked for William Storey of Erpingham between 1772 and 1775 but then hired himself to John Bell in Itteringham for just under a year. He had been living in a small cottage but on getting married he asked for a discharge to avoid serving a whole year. By 1784 they had five children and wished to settle in Erpingham. He and Frances were accepted by Erpingham in October 1787.

Harsh though it seems now, enforcing removal was a practical way of spreading the load; each parish looked after its own and with small populations this was just about workable. Hence the binding of young Bullen out to North Walsham where he would gain a settlement. Some men abandoned their families assuming the parish would pitch in. If not found quickly, the officers would resort to newspaper notices and offer rewards:

> April 1804 Absconded from Wickmere: Michael Ramsdale, of 35 yrs, black hair, Roman nose & dark complexion, 5 ft 5 in tall, leaving his wife and family chargeable to the parish. Overseers John Hook and Jn Beane offer 2 guineas reward and threats to any who harbour him.

Blickling labourer James Knott (or Nott) languished in Aylsham bridewell in 1728 until he signed an undertaking to the churchwarden and overseer not to run away from his wife and four children. In 1769 the Blickling overseer Robert Cooke reported Thomas Harmer a worsted weaver had left his wife and children. In Itteringham 'Mrs Lee' was given 4s in September 1787 when her husband left her and the children. If this was Elizabeth Lee, she had up to five children alive – the last had been born in 1785. 'John Lees' rent of £1 5s was being paid in January 1788 which might suggest he returned although the reference may be to another Lee.

## Clothing and heating

In the early years at least, the children were well clothed. (The term 'cladding the Town children', as used on a Blickling bill, although accurate, sounds less appealing.) There were normally two or three youngsters being cared for at any one time. In 1739 Ann, 'the Girl' Bloom, was fitted out with a hat, a new pair of shoes, a new petticoat and a new pair of Branclets, a shift and an apron. Six months later she had a coat made from three yards of serge and a pair of wool stockings; the following year more shifts, apron and shoes appeared for her. Her old shoes were repaired in 1741 for 6d by John Gay and Goody (Goodwife) Fox, with whom Ann lodged, claimed 6d for making Ann a cap. In 1742 two shifts, an apron, new gown, new petticoat, a handkerchief, a hat and string cost the parish £2 2s 6d for her. As the girl was growing she received a new pair of shoes every other year at 2s 6d (and the old pair were mended). In a later year a rather speculative entry was made for a 'pr shoes for whom they fit 4s 6d'. By 1787 shoes were normally about 4s but in November some cheaper wood-soled shoes were provided – adults 3s, boys 2s 8d. When Ann grew up, others took her place. The Girl Cooper, and the Girl and Boy Forster were kitted out in the 1740s; the Boys Forster, Nap and Towel in the 1750s. The boys had duffield coats, shoes, breeches, stockings and shirts. Nap had 'a best Cote' for the winter of 1750. Girl Forster had the same items as Ann had ten years earlier, though the apron was described as coarse and a pair of pattens was added. Other materials used that year included 'Check & Rushia Cloth ... Ticklingburgh ... Mill Linsey'. Later the Bullen family - there were at least two boys - were clothed in waistcoats, wheelspun hose and shoes and cared for by 'Lydda' Breese (feeding and cleaning) in 1784. The Breese family showed how fragile the finances of small tenant farmers were; they had worked the Mannington estate Wood farm for over 20 years. Once her husband Robert died in 1770, Martha became dependant on the parish and was buried in Itteringham as a pauper in 1784. Lydda may have been her daughter or daughter-in-law. Others received a shilling for taking in washing for an elderly or sick neighbour – Betty Pygal did for 'Cutty' Hall, a regular claimant although not one of the collections widows. Various women sewed: Sendall made shirts in 1754; Ann Newell made shirts for the Boy Bartram in 1786 for 1 shilling; Elizabeth Pratt made 2 shirts for Bullen in 1787 for 1 shilling. Widow Comer was even paid 2s for mending her own children's shoes in 1798. Offering lodgings brought in the odd 6d; when Charles Brett died, his widow took in the girl Comer in January 1797. At no point in the accounts is any hint that Itteringham paupers had to wear the 'P' badge on the right shoulder, as required by law from 1697 to the early 19th century but frequently ignored.

How did they keep warm? Coals were available through the north coast ports and down navigable rivers but for those inland only the wealthy could afford the cost of transporting it by road. Tan, the bark of young oaks, was made into turves for fuel; small wood or faggot wood was bundled up and occasionally ling was still being cut from the heathlands. Widow Hall was given 12 coombs of tan for the winter of 1738-1739 (a coomb was about 4 bushels). This only cost 5s but must have burnt very fast. In 1743 Mary Hase had 5 or 6 coombs each month. Blocks of furze, the most common fuel, were used in 1745; the same year two and a half hundredweight of faggot wood was sent to the use of the poor who were named as John Thorn, James Sparrow, Widow Forster and Widow Hall. The following March, 1746, the overseers paid 15 shillings 'For wagon of Linge, carriage and laying' and 7s 3d for 'Firing for poor at the Common'. For most of the century the firings for the poor were supplied by the tenant of the Bintry tanhouse and small farm, Michael Towne in 1757 and John Read in later years. Was this a fixed contract (between fellow overseers)? Tanners had plenty of scope for firings from tree tops bought for bark. At least there is no hint of the Rector attempting to take a tithe - his cut, as he saw it - on the poor's common furze as Roger Coleman had done in Thompson in 1726. Patrick St Clair, later the Rector of Wolterton, had also raised the idea in Aylmerton until he learnt of his patron's displeasure.

Two hundred furze faggots were cut and supplied for the poor in the winter of 1756-57. 'Old Hardy' was paid 1s for the backbreaking work of cutting furze in 1755; Widow Bullen earned 5s every October in the 1790s for firings that she cut and collected. In 1798 Read billed for £17 but when he was overseer in the summer of 1799, coals were distributed by the bushel throughout April to October, all carefully costed and he put in no bill for 'firing'. Even then the old 'tan and turf' entries still appear as extra for Widow Bird and Widow Bartram. But the following year 1800 Mr Read's bill for firing was £30 17s 6d, a staggering twice as much as usual. Had the coals been an experiment? Had someone, perhaps the blacksmith, supplied them? Coals and 'nuthalls' were regularly used after 1803.

### The collective conscience

The local major landowner was, in addition to paying the poor rates, usually expected to help out. As Church Row never became a parish charity, the original Potts beneficence was forgotten; however Lady Potts's name is remembered for another charity. In the 1830s the Charity Commissioners looked into all the charity lands formerly administered by parishes. In September 1832 the Itteringham officers were summoned to the Black Boys to give evidence to the commissioners about 'certain land ... which in the year 1786 produced 5s per annum'. The final report stated:

> In an old overseer's book there is a memorandum, dated 25th March, 1699 [1700], stating that Thomas Robins and Richard Robins had, with the churchwarden, purchased of Sir Roger Potts a piece of land at Broomhill in Itteringham, containing two acres, and that the said Thomas Robins had paid for the purchase, £18; that the land was purchased for the use of the poor of Itteringham as by a deed of feoffment (the date not mentioned) would appear; and that it had been agreed that the sum of £18 should be raised as follows; viz. "that £8 thereof was a gift of the Lady Potts, late wife of Sir John Potts, deceased, which she gave to the use of the poor, and that £10 should be raised by the overseer, by collecting the same of the said parish, 20s yearly; and that it was also agreed that the overseers should receive the rent of the land, paying out of the same 8s a year as interest of the £8 given by Lady Potts; and that the rest of the rent should be disposed of as the chief inhabitants of Itteringham should think meet; and that it should be lawful for the inhabitants to take gravel upon the said land for repairing the highway.

The church terrier of 1735 confirmed the arrangement was working: 'Also in the parish, better than an acre of land inclosed with a gravel pit in it between lands of Thomas Robins (south and north) and John Bell east, abut on Kings Highway west, now in use of Robert Bird out of the rent whereof the poor have 8 shillings yearly paid by overseers'. The pit produced a helpful amount from the sale of gravel and some marl - 15s was received for gravel in 1743 - but the sum handed out though remained the same despite inflation. Widows were not specifically mentioned in the 18th century. The Charity Commissioners continued:

> We could not discover that there were any deeds now in the parish relating to this land. There is a close, containing two acres, the greater part of which is a gravel pit, used by the inhabitants. The residue is let to Henry Smith, as yearly tenant, at 8s per annum, which appears to be the fair value thereof. The sum of 8s is divided equally amongst eight widows, appointed by the acting overseer.

The same large gravel pit, on the eastern side of the Wolterton Road, claimed the lives of two young boys, Edward Pooley aged 9 and William Smith aged 6 in September 1803. Lady Potts charity is still distributed today.

After the Potts family died out in 1737, Lord Walpole owned both Mannington and Wolterton estates. His assistance was a necessary top-up both to Itteringham and Wickmere parishes which would have had the extra burden of the poor from the defunct Mannington and Wolterton parishes. It seems that the Mannington parish poor system was fairly informal, given the tiny population. Whoever was the senior tenant living in the Hall (or later Mere farm) undertook to support those in need, but this was deemed the financial responsibility of the landlord and the costs were reclaimed against rent. In October 1737 George Copland of the Hall had an allowance against his rent for burying Anne the wife of Robert Wegg. In 1749 he had an offset from his rent to recover from Walpole his outgoings on support for the Mannington poor. He was recompensed for: 2 shirts and 1 [!] new shoe for R Wegg 9s; John Smith at need 5s; Widow Shivers collection £4. In the previous years he had been paying and claiming a collection for the whole year to Robert Wegg of between £5 and £6, and in 1748 he paid £1 3s for shirts britches and a waistcoat for Wegg. When Robert Woods, the new tenant farmer of Mannington Hall came in 1750, the lease stated that Walpole was required to support Robert Wegg for life from being chargeable to Mannington parish, so that Woods had no obligation to fund Wegg's living costs. Money he paid out for Robert Wegg was deducted from his rent. A further small amount of poor rate was also charged against the small Mossymere farm.

Potential employers like Walpole realised the benefit of encouraging apprenticeships: Tom, one of the Bullen boys, was bound as a shoemaker's apprentice to a master in North Walsham in April 1787. Walpole gave 5 guineas for Thomas Crosswell to take him – leaving the overseers only having to pay 2s 6d for the journey and £1 4s 3d to a local solicitor for making the indenture. Boys from Wolterton and Wickmere were also helped: 'boy H Nickels' was bound to Chapman of Corpusty in the summer of 1784 and 'the Boy Burton' to Mr Dugdale in 1787.

Walpole looked out for those in special need too. In June 1776 Captain Collinett of Wickmere was returning home from a visit when he was thrown from his horse and died. His body was found at 4 am the next morning. Ten years on, when 'the boy Collinet' was old enough, Walpole paid for him to have some new clothes and the £5 needed to find him an apprenticeship. After John Hannant's accident (see Chapter 13) Walpole paid his weekly assistance for several years.

In times of special hardship, such as early 1757 when the price of corn had risen steeply, more direct intervention was required. Walpole's steward Ness suggested his master - who was always worried about civil unrest - would be prudent as well as charitable to 'gain some goodwill amongst the lower people'. Horatio died before a decision was made but his son picked up the correspondence immediately. His suggestion was to sell wheat to the 'Poor labourers at 5s per Bushel upon Delivery provided it can be done' as long as a sufficient quantity was reserved for the use of the family. Ness responded encouragingly to his new master saying he approved of the scheme but he tactfully proposed a step further, that of baking the bread for the poor at Wolterton, perhaps to avoid any possible profiteering. Horatio thought it 'a much better method'.

## The Coming of the Union Workhouse

As the century progressed, the growing population together with the effects of war, failing crops and rising prices led first to the Gilbert Act of 1782 and then to the later reforms - the new Poor Law of 1834. Oulton opened a House of Industry in 1792 (as they were permitted to do under the 1782 Act) and this was enlarged for Blickling to join in 1805. Blickling, a much more prosperous parish (their poor rate in 1785 raised over £223) paid £60 to Oulton in 1806 and £154 the next year. Other parishes joined together in order to cope but Itteringham was determined to carry on alone. In 1795, the year when things were very hard, Itteringham's weekly collection list rose from a record high of 20 names at the start of the year to 25 by the end. A massive £155 was given out compared to around £60 ten years earlier and about £80 only two years before. The inhabitants paid up; after the rates were collected there was even £4 to take forward. By 1797 the cost of maintenance reached £157. Now other parishes were enforcing the settlements of their poor and several families were returned to Itteringham; Robert Seely and his wife Mary from Salle and the Alexander family were added to those on relief. The overseers responded by removing Thomas Williams and his 23 year-old wife Winifred to Salle in November 1798. Mr Garnham was paid 5s 'for going after Williams', perhaps ensuring their departure. Thomas had only married local girl Winifred Lee at Itteringham the month before and may have alarmed the officers by showing no intention of taking her back to his parish.

Despite the pressures Itteringham chose not to combine with local parishes to share a workhouse until after 1823. In 1806 the windows at 'the Parish House' were repaired in Itteringham. Even in the 1830s the village continued to care for its own, rarely sending anyone to the little workhouse at Oulton. When the new Union workhouse was finally built at Aylsham in 1849, the old system was at last disbanded. The parish had no choice but to send their folk to the new institution.

## Sources

NRO: Itteringham parish accounts, PD 439/5, 6; Blickling parish accounts PD 434/26; C/Sca 2/178-179; BUL 4/96/37, 42, BUL 4/101, BUL 4/102/1, 8, 24, 25; Itteringham church terriers DN/TER 92/1/1-23

Wolterton archive: 3/1/7; 3/5/4; 3/7/16/1; 8/63

# Chapter 13

## 'Bleeding the Poor People'

*Life expectancy in the past is often quoted as meaning people lived to no great age; of course this is true in the sense that many children died at birth or within the first five years, when most vulnerable to disease. However, those young men who survived working accidents and young women who did not succumb to problems in child-birth, often reached ages which would be quite normal today. Of course many others were not so healthy and needed help. The overseers of each parish were the key to the care the poor received and from the surviving records, Itteringham folk seemed well looked after.*

### Life expectancy

Amazingly, between 1727 and 1845, more than 60 Norfolk people lived to 100 or more. (In 1694 a woman called Amphilus Jarvis died in Hunworth said to be 108.) Ann Robins, mother of the Heydon branch of the family, was nearly 91 when she died in 1706 and still as bright as a button. The local dissenting minister, Abraham Coveney, had 'the perfect enjoyment of all his faculties' at 87 when he died in 1772, no doubt due to a dutiful and abstemious life. Despite his potentially dangerous job, the village blacksmith Robert Jeckyll lived to 92. Oulton's tanner, Thomas Bell, also managed to avoid accident to reach 89 and 8 months in 1721. Henry Blyth, formerly blacksmith at Blickling, and his wife Ann were 83 and 84 respectively when they died in Itteringham at the end of the century. Having money was not a major factor: in Itteringham Matthew Jeary, who had been on poor relief regularly since he was removed from Cawston to the village in 1741, was 85 when he died in 1797. The little old Oulton workhouse, towards the end of its life in 1844, had 18 inmates over the age of 80, three of whom were over 90.

### Nursing

In 1739 Edward Abell fell ill while at Corpusty; the overseers not only paid 13s 6d for his nurse there but more for fetching him home. Unfortunately despite more nursing, and being attended by the doctor, he died. The parish encouraged local women to be carers by paying a few shillings for nursing. 'Nurse Bunn' was paid for nursing Robert Thorpe 1751; Mary Neal (who lost her new baby in 1742) for nursing Widow Thorn 1752, Mary Hall for nursing Widow Thorn 1753, even paying 'Young Goody' Thorn 1s 6d for looking after her mother. But increasingly most nursing was undertaken by neighbouring widows, Widow Reynolds nursed Bartram's wife (probably Mary, wife of Joseph in April 1784) who lost her son James in August; Widow Tubby nursed Woman Bird in April 1785. Ann Thirtle earned 10s for nursing (Mat) Jeary for 10 weeks in 1794; she became a widow two years later. In 1798 she was 'doing for' John Hannant's sick wife. Sarah Harmer 'did for' - looked after - Ark Hurrell's (spelt Harrold) sick wife in 1796-97. A rather modern approach to nursing - based on good diet - seems to have been taken by Harry Harper in Blickling. About 1760 he was paid 10 shillings a week by their overseers for nursing 'John and James' for a month. In addition he charged for 1lb of figs, 2 pints of oatmeal, pearl barley, saffron, nutmeg, soft cakes, 'callerway' seeds, a rabbit, parmatum [perhaps shepherd's purse in place of sperm-whale oil], 3 pints of 'my beer', a loin of pork and various loaves of bread.

Childbirth was of course a critical event, for both mother and baby. A payment of 3s for 'Horse for Pooley's wife in labour July 1787' was probably to fetch the doctor; hopefully it was not to put her on it although there is no register entry for a baptism or burial of a Pooley child in Itteringham! The 'woman Pooley' (Eleanor, known as Nell) was also given 5s 6d for her lying-in when she had baby Elizabeth in 1789. Each case was treated equally – a midwife was sent for when Mary Thirtle had her illegitimate baby Edward on 24th February 1792; she was paid 2s 6d and fetched and sent home at parish expense. Another unwed mother, Easter Thirtle, had her baby son Robert baptised in July 1798 but sadly died the following January leaving the parish to look after him.

## Doctors

Apart from the nursing, doctors were sent for when necessary; on one occasion Thomas Hurrell was paid to fetch the doctor. Their charges varied widely: Ed Abell's doctor was paid 3 guineas in 1739, Mr Dunn 10s 6d for attending M Wenn, Mr Snashall £1 11s 6d for attending John Sendall's wife and Mr Ellis of Aylsham £5 10s for attendance and medicines for her in 1757. Mr Ellis had also been paid £1 11s 6d in 1749 for setting 'the Boy Bunn's arm'. (This may have been Stephen Bunn who was on relief in the 1790s.) Bunn's break must have been a bad one, for 40 years later in 1789 Dr Woodcock was paid only 2s 6d when Samuel Curson broke his arm. Bad or not, poor Samuel was unable to continuing working for Mrs Robins at Matlaske afterwards. As his legal settlement was in Itteringham - from a year he spent with Mr Crosley about 1786 - he joined the village weekly collection. His child lived in Ingworth at the expense of Itteringham overseers during the 1790s. Right up to his death in March 1797 he was given cash help and Lydia Breese looked after the 65 year-old during his last two weeks.

Dr Woodcock, later the regular doctor, charged over £3 for the year 1784. At least the Itteringham overseers seemed to act in the best interest of the patient; in Aylmerton, the poor officer had the stingy rector, Patrick St Clair, watching him. On one occasion he was reprimanded for using an expensive Holt doctor, Mr Legg, to cure a woman's leg instead of just the local apothecary 'honest Hoskins' – a waste of 7 guineas in the rector's view. St Clair, who would later become the Wolterton rector, was of course also a rate-payer in the parish so was looking out for his own bills; on his own daughter, his only child Betty, he did not stint. Subject to fainting fits and ill-health Betty drank asses' milk twice a day. Whether despite or because of her father's mollycoddling, Betty survived her father, married at the age of 46 and lived to 64.

A good idea of the medicines used comes from Walpole's accounts with Erasmus Ellis, the Aylsham surgeon and apothecary who 'cured Richard Ness Anckles' in 1739 for 1 guinea. His annual bills for household remedies were around £2. They included some which sound familiar such as aloes and marshmallow ointment but others that sound rather alarming: oil of turpentine, spirit of Hartshorn, sulphur and antimony. Edward Piggon the other apothecary of Aylsham, who treated the poor of Blickling, had more prosaic if equally unpleasant-sounding items: his bill of 1755 involved plenty of bleeding, 'a blister plaister', vomiting powder, a large bottle of 'Decoction', a 'pot of Electuary' and some unspecified 'bottles of mixture'. The medical profession were less keen on the remedies advertised in the papers: in the 1730s Mrs Joanna Stephens of London had quite a following for 'curing the stone and strangury' although Jonathan Wrench senior, the vicar of Aylsham, found them no help. The claims made in the advertisements were of course rather extreme, for example in *The Ipswich Journal* in June 1806:

> Advert for *Sutton's Specific Pills* Mr Daniel Frostic of Erpingham, near Aylsham, was afflicted by the dropsy in the most dreadful manner, being swelled to a wonderful size for near two years and given over by those who saw him; but by taking one box of the *Specific Pills*, was reduced to his natural size and restored to perfect health, which he has ever since enjoyed.
> Witness to the above John Woolsey 19th February 1806.

For the upper classes, those who could not get to Bath might partake of Bungay Medicinal Waters or travel by sea to have a fortnight at Scarborough. The 'Hott Well' in Bristol was thought the equal of Bath for gout sufferers such as Ashe Windham of Felbrigg. On large estates, permanent staff might be treated well: Horatio Walpole's gardener Bradshaw went to Bath for his 'soares' but unfortunately died on his return. Walpole's steward Ness recommended his employer to take cold baths and drink tar water to cure gout as this had worked well for Ness and Lylestone (the gamekeeper). Walpole also had bad legs, breaking out in a streptococcal skin infection called *erysipelas* in October 1740 but he managed to keep a sense of humour. When, the same month, the collection of fine furniture and a library of books that he had collected in Paris for his new mansion at Wolterton went up in flames in Cley harbour (ironically having survived the journey from Paris to London and then by boat up to Cley), he said he met with 'fire by sea and fire by land' – the common name of his painful red rash being St Anthony's fire.

If the patient was beyond local care, they were sent to hospital. From at least 1768 to 1809, there was a little Hospital House in Wickmere, at modern-day Squallham, which Walpole kept in repair; but this was probably used as a place for the infectious poor. The entries for villagers being sent to hospital more likely relate to the Norwich hospital: in 1784 'Fuller going to Hospital' cost 2s, presumably for travel. In the autumn of 1786 John Hannant cost the parish 5s to get him to hospital. He was obviously badly hurt as he was still there in December when the parish received a letter about him. The overseers paid another 5s to bring Hannant home. During the eight weeks he was in hospital, the 'girl Hannant', presumably his daughter Ann, was given 1s a week. On his return the poor man also was given a pair of crutches and became a recipient of a weekly collection from 1788 so obviously was not able to work again. Hannant could claim settlement here as he had been a hired labourer working for John Read in 1765-67. Although he was in Hackford in 1769, John was working as a labourer in Itteringham again by 1772, when his first wife Ann was accused of stealing a gander from Oulton common the previous Christmas. They had lost their 3 month-old son John in June 1771. Ann was so ill in 1776 that she asked a widowed friend, Elizabeth Randal, to come from Aldborough to look after her. She died in 1780. John Hannant was also receiving weekly relief from Walpole by 1790 and the parish paid part of his rent that year for one of Thomas Robins's old cottages. John Hannant died in December 1798.

His injuries had probably arisen from by being run over by a cart – one of the most common accidents in the 18th century inquest reports. John Davy, despite the efforts of Mr Ellis (12s 6d), died in the winter of 1755-56. As an inquest was held, a fatal accident was probably the cause.

In 1746, following a similar event which caused the death of a man called Coe, Horatio Walpole wrote to Ness with his usual mixture of sympathy and paternalism: 'I am sorry to hear of the death of the poor Carter especially as he has left behind so great a small family, but I cannot forbear observing to you one thing which is often taken notice of by my children that our Carters when their carts are empty, drive like madmen and 'tis no wonder if mischief happens to them. They have no mercy on their horses nor indeed upon themselves. Whether that is the case of Coe, I can't tell but you should give them all warning, to be more sober & cautious with their empty carts.'. No doubt Ness used his discretion as to whether this good advice would be well-received by the local carriers.

Of course there may be many reasons for accidents: Martin Leeder, a labourer of Little Barningham gave evidence in July 1771 about an accident that had left his son James 'grievously wounded and obliged to keep his Bed'. He laid the blame firmly on the driver - a servant of Mr Crow of West Beckham, maltster - who had no-one on foot or on horseback to guide the cart which was being pulled by three or four horses. Being a Friday afternoon, perhaps that too was an empty vehicle. No such blame appeared to attach itself to another fatality, that of John Kidd, age 35, known as the Oulton carrier. His inquest heard on 27th June 1802, that 'his horse having taken fright he was thrown from the cart in which he was travelling along the Norwich to Aylsham Road, near the windmill in the parish of St Clement'. He died at the Norfolk and Norwich Hospital. The verdict was accidental death. Like Coe, John also left his wife with young children who had been born in Itteringham between 1794 and 1798 when they lived in the cottage behind the shop.

Some of those who were permanently on poor relief may have been physically weak from birth, others becoming so. 'Goodman' Sparrow may have been one – he was on permanent relief and his rent was paid from 1739 onwards. James may still have been part of the occasional crew working outside with the Wolterton gardener John Bradshaw in 1740 around the estate. In 1740 Mrs Burman earned 4s 6d for curing a sore on his thigh. Mary Burman had the distinction of being licensed by the Bishop to practice 'Phlebotomy' in Itteringham (not midwifery or surgery) in 1734. This limited her to the art of blood-letting but as this was the most common invasive practice she no doubt made a reasonable living.

## Mental health

Others who were cared for within the parish were the less mentally able. Normally the community would have looked out for the vulnerable inhabitants but if there were acts of aggression, action would be necessary. One such instance concerned Margaret Sendall 'a dangerous lunatick'. In December 1770 local justice William Wiggett Bulwer of Heydon issued an order to the Itteringham constables to bring Margaret to him 'to be dealt with by law'. He was responding to the complaint made three days earlier by Robert Ayton of Itteringham that 'on Saturday night the 1st December about 10 [o/c] at night and again about 2 [o/c] in the morning [she] was guilty of violent breaches of the peace in breaking the windows of the dwelling house of the said Robert Ayton in Iteringham'. Was the unmarried Margaret drunk? Had she and Ayton rowed? Presumably at this time Margaret was given a warning as she remained in the village. Five months later Bulwer issued another, more severe order that 'The Constable on sight of Margaret Sendall is to bring her before [me] to find surety as well for her appearance at next Quarter Session to be held at the Castle and also for her good Behaviour in the meantime'. This time Thomas Robins the gentleman of the Manor House had complained and demanded protection from her. Not only had she broken a window of his house on the previous Monday morning but she had then and 'at several times since threaten to do him bodily mischief'. Why was the 40 year-old bachelor the victim of her anger? The Sendalls were widespread in north Norfolk; Martin the Blickling steward's line came from Irmingland and Cawston and as mentioned in Chapter 12 there was at least one Itteringham branch. Margaret may have been related to the three Sendall sisters who worked for Thomas Robins 3. The paper was endorsed that she was committed on 2nd July but unfortunately no court appearance has been found. Did Margaret's family or friends stand bound for her better behaviour? Was she committed to an asylum, at least for a while? Parishes could apply to Bethlehem asylum (Bedlam) in London or a local private asylum. Whether in prison or madhouse, it was not for long.

At some point before April 1776 Margaret took to living in St Augustine's parish Norwich from where she was removed, only to end up in May in St Martin at Oak from where again she was to be returned to Itteringham. On 23rd August she was found 'wandering abroad and lodging in alehouses' in St Stephen's parish. She could not 'give a good account of herself' and was sent back as a rogue and vagabond, the standard description. By July 1778 she was arrested in St Mary Norwich and taken home by John Tyler who told the Norwich Mayor Roger Kerrison, one of the justices, of her previous history. By now she must have been really behaving erratically, perhaps threateningly, as she was now described as a 'dangerous lunatick' who 'is so far disordered in her senses that it may be dangerous to permit her to go abroad'. Tyler was paid 15s 10d for his and the constable's expenses, 4d of which had been spent on Margaret. Three years later she turned up in Lakenham, south Norwich. Still described as dangerous, she was taken home again by Tyler and the constable. No papers survive after 1781. Did she recover? A Margaret Sendall lived in the village on poor relief - 2s 6d a week - from at least 1784 through the end of the century, joined by Mary Sendall from 1795 until their deaths in 1803 and 1804. The parish was expected to cope with such problems. Perhaps Margaret had recovered enough to be looked after by her relatives or they had found some way of keeping her from roving.

Christopher, the son of Thomas Riseborough and Ann Thorn, who was born about 1803, was living with his parents in Itteringham when in his mid-20s he 'was insane for 2 years'. He recovered sufficiently to return to work in the parish gravel pit but became insane again a year later. His father had told him to 'let blood' when the symptoms started to come back but, in June 1831, Christopher was apprehended in Salle. There he was kept in custody for 6 days before being conveyed to the lunatic asylum at Thorpe which had opened in 1814.

## Smallpox

The scourge of the 18th century was smallpox; it became endemic and, although there were major outbreaks, cases could appear at any time. Of course, other infectious diseases could strike as well and the cause of sickness is not always clear. Patients were treated by medicines and blood-letting; where possible the person was isolated, probably as much from fear as any medical understanding. In Blickling in May 1738 the overseers paid for a horse to carry Thomas Priest's son to 'Burrow where he had the smallpox'; perhaps the move was an attempt to avoid the boy catching the disease. Mary Priest had caught it and was given that cure-all 'a Bottle of Daffeys' while she recovered. In March 1753 the estate gamekeeper at Wolterton, John Lylestone (Horatio called him the gardener) caught it. Horatio Walpole wrote to his steward Ness 'to keep him away from the house and not let any member of the family frequent him or any place where there is smallpox'. Lylestone recovered but a year later in November 1754 had to vacate his house at Mossymere - the remotest property - as the daughter of 'Barton' was getting smallpox. Ness was told by Walpole: 'she can move to Mossymere and Lylestone can come into Wolterton stables and then no connection between my house and Mossimer for fear of accident'. If this was a child of Thomas Barton the Robins's tenant of the Manor House in Itteringham then Walpole was helping the community not just his family, as Barton was not his tenant.

## Local occurrences of smallpox

1714 December: letter concerning the will of John Bond of Wolterton who died of the smallpox. His widow was looking after a household suffering from the same 'distemper'.

1716 Sir Algernon and Dame Frances Potts died within a week of each other and were buried within 2 days.

1727 'the year terrible for Fevers' Hingham church. Mrs St Clair, wife of the Aylmerton rector died.

1734 October Smallpox in the neighbourhood. A mother and son died in Hanworth.

1737-42 Aylsham outbreak.

1738 May Smallpox all round Aldborough, Thurgarton and Hanworth. Joseph, son of Walpole's steward Thomas Bayfield died from the disease. 'The best of the family ... Col Harbord and all laments him - mightily'.

1738 June At Aylmerton smallpox was bad (Clark Rider's school deserted for fear) the Rector buried 5 in one week.

1743 January William Bayly, tanner of Itteringham, and Lydia his wife died quite young – within a week or so of each other

1750 February 27th - March 3rd The Norwich newspapers carried the following announcement:

> Aylsham 'Whereas smallpox has been from some time here, we have now the pleasure to acquaint the Publick that it is entirely ceased and that no Person now has the said distemper nor has had it within the said parish for several weeks past. To the Truth of which we have subscribed our names: Thomas Hawkins, Jonathan Wrench vicar, Francis Mosey, Edmund Jewell churchwarden, James Drake, James Barber overseer, Thomas Curteis, Eras. Ellis and Edward Piggon, surgeons, Thomas Dowell, John Bray'.

1753-54 Itteringham had smallpox – 'Paid for Bleeding the poor People 1s 3d: a bottle of Daffrey's 1s 3d for Thomas Bell and another £2 7s 7d about Thomas Bell in the time of the smallpox and Mary Cooper for nursing 10s'.

1755-56 winter and following summer. Itteringham accounts show Boy Starling, Miles Wenn, Robert Fox's wife in their illness, William Shepherd and his wife having the smallpox, Bird's boy in time of smallpox, William Kendall in time of sickness.

1759 Blickling was again hit by smallpox – one of their poor was lying at Cawston (perhaps removed from the proximity to the Hall). Widow Roberson died despite being nursed.

A number of sufferers survived and many never contracted the disease. Clearly some resistance existed in the body. Inoculation reached East Anglia by 1760 though it was still frowned on but the gentry led the way by having their children injected. In a letter from J Mackerell to William Bulwer at Dalling dated 24th January 1763 he wrote: 'We pray ... for good success in the intended inoculation of your children'. By 5th March there was 'great Pleasure' at the account 'of your Children's perfect Recovery'. Sadly the new treatment sometimes caused blindness or even death but by the end of the century the overseers were regularly paying for poor parents to have their children inoculated. From the Itteringham parish register and overseers' accounts:

| | | |
|---|---|---|
| 1782 December 21st | Edward Howard son of William & Ann died of Small Pox by Inoculation | |
| 1782 December 25th | Walter Wright, son of Thomas & Mary, and Robert Pratt, son of Robert & Elizabeth. Both paupers who died of smallpox were buried on Christmas day | |
| 1796 May | Smallpox noted next to Ann Woods' burial | |
| 1796 June | To James Neighton for smallpox in his family | 6s |
| | Paid Mr Scarlet for inoculation | £1 14s 6d |
| | James Thirtle died in August | |
| 1798 January | Inoculating Comers children | 3s |
| May | Neightons children ill | |
| 1807 | Ann Thirtle for inoculation of child | 2s 6d |
| | Wid Bacon ditto for 2 children | 5s |
| | James Smith ditto | 10s |
| | Thos Burton for inoculation of his children | 5s |
| | Joseph Nickols ditto | 10s |

The disease was not conquered until the discovery of vaccination - using cowpox - was made in 1796.

## Watching and Sitting

When parishioners were nearing death, the parish gave what comforts it could. Mary Cooper was allowed a warming pan (which was returned after her death). In 1787 neighbours were paid for sitting up with terminally ill patients and 'watching' the body after death. The final service was carried out decently and with due attention. Coffins were made by the local carpenter and a proper burial conducted although noted as pauper in the register. Edward Abell's funeral in 1739 had cost the parish 19s, on top of the £6 4s 9d already spent on his care and rent. The earliest full description covers the burials of Robert and his son Thomas Forster at the end of January and early March 1743:

| | | |
|---|---|---|
| Robert Forster's nurses for watching & winding | 5s | |
| His coffin & bearers | 10s | |
| Mary Fox for going of arrands [errands] | 1s | |
| to Clark for the Gravemaking | 2s | |
| pd the Clark his fees | £1 | |
| Wid Forster allowed | 10s | |
| Pd Richard Bunn for the boy Forsters coffin | 6s | |
| for his laying forth & windeing and wooll | 2s | 6d |
| for carrying him to church | 4s | |
| for boy Forsters grave digging | 1s | |

A coffin cost the parish 9s in April 1794 when John Comer died, leaving his wife Mary (nee Colls) to join the widows' list. James Brett the carpenter had a busy time in the three months December 1798 to February 1799 with three coffins to make. The price was now 10s each.

In 1784 James and Ann Thirtle were given 2s to pay for 'burying their child' Noah on 27th June, noted in the register as paupers. Noah was buried on the same day as Rose Foster another pauper; this happened at other times and may have been cheaper to arrange. Others like Cooper and Bartram in 1787 were not buried in Itteringham - at least not registered as such. Edward Abell's funeral may have taken place in Corpusty. The last detailed entry provides the story of Christopher Bullen. The poor widower, who had been on relief for a long time, fell ill. Just before Christmas 1786 he was allowed ½ pint of wine (6 ½ d); at the same time 'Bullen's wife' possibly his daughter-in-law, was also very ill. On 9th January 1787 four persons sat up with her (2s); Ann Thirtle nursed her and minded her, making her a cap, on the 20th. When Christopher was buried on 23rd January, Ann Thirtle, assisted by widow Mary Tubby, earned 2s 6d for laying him out; John Bird dug his grave for 2s 6d. The four bearers who carried his coffin were given 5s beer money. By the summer of 1796 the bearers for James Thirtle, who probably died of smallpox, were still paid 4 shillings with 1 shilling for beer. Bread was added to the beer in March 1787 when Samuel Curson was buried; perhaps the coldness of the day called for some sustenance or maybe it had been for the 'sitters up'. John Lee buried his wife Elizabeth just over a week later at a cost of 10s 6d.

Mary Tubby was a regular helper; she had given lodging to Pooley's wife for 4 weeks in October 1786. To eke out her 18d a week 'widows collection' Mary looked after Sarah Hardy, her sick lodger, for a few weeks (at 6d a week) in the spring of 1788, while sitting making a 6d shirt for Hall. Sarah Hardy went on to lodge with William and Eleanor Pooley where she helped Mrs Pooley in labour with baby Elizabeth in May 1789.

Despite access to medicine and the best physicians, the rich fared little better when it came to the last: Horatio Walpole died on 5th February 1757 'of an excruciating fit of the stone'. George England, the rector of Wolterton died in 1740 after years of severe asthma. For others the last excess may have been the cause: Sir Charles Potts dined and drank well with Edward Paston at Barningham and on rising next morning, died in his chair. Major John Berney drank 'plentifully of Rack punch' at Blickling in 1730 'which put him in the stangury, and he had no passage of Urine afterwards and dyed'.

## Sources

NRO: Poor rates PD 439/5, 6; BUL 1/97 (Sendal) BUL 4/102/15, 18, BUL 4/114; the Itteringham overseers' papers were rediscovered in the church shortly before going to press and are now lodged with the NRO.

Wolterton archive: 8/56, 58, 68 Wickmere hospital (1768 glazing work and 1780 note); shown as belonging to Poor in 1809 estate map and survey in NRO, Acc MJ Sayer 26/2/1970

R W Ketton-Cremer, *Country Neighbourhood*, 1951
Transcript of letter printed p 479 of *See You in Court*
Smallpox, *see* Julian Eve's article 'Epidemic Illness in Aylsham' *Aylsham Local History Society Vol 4 No 10 June 1996* (good on early 20th century outbreaks); also in NAHRG, *The Quarterly*, No 31, 1998
Norwich newspapers

# Chapter 14

## *A Legible Hand*

---

*Despite being a small rural village, Itteringham benefited from a high number of educated residents; a long history of schooling in the village, combined with the promotion of literacy by the non-conformist movement, allowed ordinary men and women to gain useful skills.*

## Schools and schoolmasters

In the late 17th and 18th centuries, young men destined for university were educated at the Grammar schools, particularly those at Holt under Mr Holmes, Scarning under Mr Brett and Norwich. Caius College, Cambridge was a popular choice for Norfolk boys and in 1682 John Empson son of the grocer of Aylsham was admitted. The next day John Parkins (or Perkins) the 17 year-old son of the Itteringham weaver Christopher Parkins joined him. John had been born in Wickmere and educated at Holt. The master at Norwich from 1737 to around 1749 was local clergyman Timothy Bullemur. Coming from a trade background himself in Blickling he taught many Norwich tradesmen's children. At least twenty-four of his pupils over his 12-year tenure, went on to study at Caius College alone. These included 18 year-old Peter Elwin from Booton (1730-98) and William Wiggett of Guestwick, who would later become Mayor and inherit the Heydon estate. Wiggett had also been taught by John Holmes, master of Gresham's school at Holt; Holmes had reversed the decline of the school after his appointment in 1730 and remained there until his death in 1760. Unusually for the time, he was not a cleric but an academic who published many text books, on classics and grammar. One was entitled *The Art of Rhetorick made easy ... to meet the needs of the time when schoolboys are expected to be led, sooth'd and entic'd to their studies ... rather than by force and harsh discipline drove, as in days of yore* (1738). His approach was successful and applauded by his employers, the Worshipful Company of Fishmongers. At the start of the autumn term in 1749 he took the unusual step of advertising in *The Norwich Mercury* refuting rumours he was leaving teaching. Perhaps there had been some confusion with Bullemur's retirement at Norwich. Interestingly, despite the local trend, there is no indication that any of the Itteringham and Heydon Robins families themselves attended university or the inns of court.

Itteringham itself had a long history of providing schooling; in the 1630s Sir John Potts had encouraged his rector Paul Amiraut, who was a licensed teacher, to educate the local boys. At some point a small field on the Mannington estate called 'schoolhouse pightle' may have been charged with providing a small income for a room or a teacher. The earliest known reference to it is from the 18th century but of course the name could be much older. Unfortunately the field was not precisely described, and after Thomas Robins acquired the land from Walpole his amalgamation of small plots into larger closes resulted in the loss of the earlier pightle and furlong names. Although there may have been a period during the decline of the Potts family at the end of the 17th century when education was not being supported, by the time Horatio Walpole bought Mannington a schoolroom of some kind was being used in Itteringham. The pightle name may therefore reflect the building, by rector Thomas Jackson, of the cottage set back at the rear of the shop where at some periods a schoolroom was based (see Chapter 8). Robert Howard had been licensed by the Diocese of Norwich 29th July 1729 to teach in the parish. This allowed him 'to keep a school' which at this time was likely to be a room in a house. Teaching on a village scale would not have been sufficient income and it is likely he was also a tailor. Within five years he had died. Another licence to teach in Itteringham was issued in May 1741, to Ralph Maullum of whom nothing more is known. The next reference does not appear until 1750-51 when Thomas Robins 3 paid the cottage rent 'for the scoolhouse'.

The property is not easy to identify from the rates list after that. John Howard the tailor who was in the cottage in the 1770s may have been the son of the earlier school teacher; he may also have been involved in teaching as two of the witnesses to his will in 1775 were Russell Alger senior and junior (see below). James Duffield was a schoolteacher living in Itteringham in December 1786 as his settlement certificate from Brinton showed. A tenant list of 1798 showed a Miss Dippell (Dyball) as occupying the cottage set back behind the shop, identifiable by its rent being higher than the standard cottages. By 1816 a schoolmaster, Thomas Robins 4, was living here. It would seem that this good-sized cottage was used from about 1710 (and possibly earlier) both as a schoolroom and home for the family of a craftsman.

As we have seen, Walpole assisted the poorer boys to learn a trade by paying for apprenticeships but he also encouraged the education of local children, particularly those from Wolterton and Wickmere. A licensed schoolmaster 'Peter Bussill' had worked in Wickmere from July 1747 but by 1768 Walpole was paying a bill of £33 4s 6d for 'Mr Symonds' schoolmaster. At the end of 1770 Russell 'Edgar' was paid 19s 8d for 'a years schoolgate for Sarah Purdy's boy and books'. This was Russell Alger (or Agar) a schoolmaster (though not apparently licensed by the Bishop) of Barningham. Russell was imprisoned in late 1776 for two months for attempted fraud (see Chapter 8), but Walpole continued to pay him or his son, Russell junior, for teaching the poor children. He received 16s 6d in May 1784 for one years' teaching, one guinea in December 1786 and another in April 1787. The payment was doubled to two guineas in August 1787 and this continued to June 1789. Walpole also contributed to other local schools: in 1782 Reynold Hogg was given his 5 guinea donation to Oulton school. William Hewett, the schoolmaster at 'Albro', received £7 15s for a year's teaching of poor children in March 1787 and March 1788 but only £4 12s 6d in February 1789.

The adult poor were also given some help: Walpole paid a Mrs Booth 1 guinea in March 1787 for teaching the Wickmere poor to spin hemp. This reasonably large sum and the entry for her board with James Lee, the estate rabbit killer, for eight weeks suggests she did a thorough job or did she just spin it out?

By 1833 when the population was 343, Itteringham had three daily schools (but no building), which catered for 60 children of both sexes who were instructed at their parents' expense, except six who were paid for by the rector, the Reverend Robert Walpole. There was also one Sunday school giving free instruction for 20 males and 25 females. The same rector built the schoolhouse in 1846. Sadly this was not soon enough for the chap who wrote the last entry in the overseers' account book in 1848:

| parstage of latters | 10d |
|---|---|
| new Resept Book | 12s |
| Jurney to Pay the Trishury | 2s |

## Men (and women) of letters

Clerics of course were normally the best educated men in the area but perhaps not always. Richard Burrell, the rector of Itteringham and Wolterton until 1721, had an appalling hand.

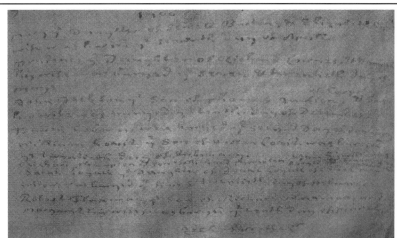

Compare and contrast the untidy hand of the rector Richard Burrell with the fine signature of Clement Robins

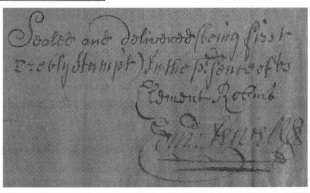

Handwriting of Richard Burrell and Clement Robins

Clement Robins the grocer (who died in 1737) was well-educated and as we have seen, his accounting skills made him ideal as the deacon for a meeting house. He appeared frequently in legal matters, helping his friends and neighbours with wills and deeds. His very fine hand can be seen above, along with that of local Aylsham lawyer Edmund Jewell. The two men assisted Clement's friend Mrs Elizabeth Lightfoot of Hanworth by receiving the repayment of a small loan she had made to a carpenter of Wickmere. We have seen that stewards were also called upon as men of business and in Itteringham tanners and blacksmiths used their education to move up in society. Michael Towne, for example, one can imagine in his office at Bintry farm, seated at the writing desk that had been his father's, keeping his accounts in his excellent hand, the walls decorated with the maps and pictures he had also inherited. An earlier tanner, Matthew Miller of Hunworth who married Lydia Robins, the Itteringham blacksmith's daughter, in 1695 could also write a reasonable hand although his spelling and punctuation were less good. In 1697 he sent a note to Edward Cooper of Edgefield apparently apologising for some mistake and also asking for a favour for a relation:

> Mr Cooper, after my terrible service to you, I retorning you maney thanks for that lat Cines [late kindness] which you gave me ... allow me to bege your pardon for this presumeing to ask another line [?] put your hand upon the behalfe of a servant of youre nave related unto me as for those late of acshons [actions] which he have committed they shall be mad amanes [made amends] by him or me
> no more at present from your friend and servant
>
> Sir, my bisnes being very eagant [urgent] that I could not come

Both girls and boys were encouraged to learn but aspirations for some children were not very high. John Hill, an Oulton farmer who could not write his own name, left instructions in his will in 1768 that his step-grandson Robert Breese 'be put to school til he can read a chapter in the Bible and write a legible hand'. Hill's wife was Hannah Bell daughter of Thomas Bradfield Bell jnr; being from a strong dissenting family, no doubt Hannah was keen on religious education. Susan, the wife of Richard Robins 2, was not only literate but apparently a keen reader as Richard left her 'such and so many of my books as she shall make choice off' in 1743. Mehetebel Leman, as one might expect of a preacher's daughter, owned a bible and hymn book and may have inherited from her father the large work relating to the book of Job. Thomas Jackson, Itteringham and Wolterton's rector, left his grandson Charles 'my great bible in folio' in 1674. His wife Amy was to decide which of his other books, that were in English, 'whether they be of divinity or history', were suitable to be divided between their two grandsons and one granddaughter, Hannah. The rest were to be sold. Both Amy and Hannah therefore were able to read.

Daughters who were to inherit were often raised to be competent in their affairs. As early as 1674, Richard Robins of Heydon, the landed weaver, asked his executor, Thomas Newman the ejected clerk of Heydon, to look after his only daughter Ann. Thomas was to fund her maintenance and education in 'literature as far as she is capable' which Mrs Lucy Jay of Cringleford and Mrs Lucy Barber, who normally lived with Mrs Jay, were to supervise. Mary Barker, the remaining unmarried daughter of William Barker a worsted weaver of Edgefield, had been educated sufficiently to take on her father's mortgage of Mannington Hall. In 1737 when Walpole purchased the estate and paid off the mortgage she became a wealthy woman. Her standard of letter writing was typical for women of the time – very respectful and properly phrased but with poor spelling and punctuation. Her sister had married John Rush, the rector of Baconsthorpe and Itteringham to whom she wrote a brief letter which by chance has survived. Rush's daughter was obviously staying with her aunt:

1730 Nov 28 To Rev Rush, Baconsthorp

'Brother'
I would have come along with the man to night to se you But Durst not venture it Being so Late
But when He come again or the first oppertunity that I Have will wait upon you Be it never so soon

my sisters with neece and self joyn in Due Respets to you Both
your Daughter send Duty to, you and Her mother
and rest your Loveing sister to command

Mary Barker

For other women such as the wives of tradesmen, literacy and numeracy were especially useful. As widows, many took over the family business or became small-time money lenders and mortgagors. In Itteringham's shop, Mrs Fish - Mary Gunton, a gentleman's daughter from Matlaske - played a full role, receipting bills in 1769. Her widowed mother, Rachel Gunton, however, could not sign her own name when she made her will in Wickmere in 1793.

Perhaps the strangest letter is that from Thomas Colles of Briston. Written on 20th January 1720 Colles informed 'your Honour Ash Windham esq at Felbrigg' that he had sent a ratcatcher to him. The man is described thus:

> not pansophical yet famed for distroying ratts, and your worship's sagacity will soon observe his rural demeanour will not give your worship the trouble of a committment as a Conjuror; Butt Begging your pardon Hon Sir I am Credibly Informed upon strict enquiry where he has wrot: that he is an artist and very sanguinary in the premises. I have used Caution that I might not infest rather than serve your worship by sending a pilferer along with the ratcatcher. I hope I am not deceived. Ile assure your worshipp his Carracter is quite otherwise among his Neighbours; if the poor fellow be soe Happy as to be servisable and Meritt yr Esteem it will be of advantage to him.
>
> No doubt and without flattery or fulsome panegyrick I hope you will oblige the sincere Inclinations of yr humble servant with further commands who will take hold of all opportunities when capeable to discharge the obligation and remain

Is this a joke? For a man who cannot spell 'Carracter', he used extraordinary language and correctly spelled pansophical [all-knowing], sagacity, conjuror, sanguinary and panegyrick. All to send a man to catch rats! There were Colles families in the 18th century in Foulsham and Hindolveston and elsewhere, mostly bricklayers. Why should Windham need to go as far as Briston for a ratcatcher for Felbrigg even if the man was an artist?

**Sources**

NRO: DN/SUB/5/5; Microfilm 505 (VSM/1); AYL 953, Mary Barker letter; WKC 7/42/3; MC 1/5; PD 439/7; WAL 529/12, 275x4

Venn, *G & C*
*See You in Court* on Amiraut

# Chapter 15

## *Groves and Pleasure Grounds*

---

*From the late 17th century landowners had become increasingly interested in creating fine gardens and vistas; over several decades the Potts family had planted avenue walks and added decorative gardens immediately around the house at Mannington. At Blickling Hall, the Hobarts, whose former substantial hunting park had been reduced over time, were, by the 1720s, re-designing its old gardens and landscaping new pleasure grounds. As the fashion spread across and down the social scale, more job opportunities for gardeners and plantsmen developed. The Wolterton estate employed its own gardener, who also looked after the woodland walks at Mannington after 1737. The Robins families were unlikely to have afforded a full time gardener but might well have used the services of Itteringham's own jobbing gardeners Richard Thompson and Samuel Saul. Thomas Robins 3 clearly made improvements to the grounds around the manor house, creating large ponds and building the summer house on Broom hill.*

### Wolterton

Horatio Walpole set about major improvements almost immediately after his 1722 purchase of the estate; he was to spend huge sums in landscaping his view down to Wolterton lake, creating garden walks and composing parkland. In some respects, however, the initial vision of a landscaped lake and grounds belonged to the Hall's former owner, James Grey. A letter of 1724 noted that significant fish stocking - '300 tench in the new pond' - had been done some years before Walpole's purchase of the estate. A land deal had been reached with James Grey in 1716 when cousins William Robins of Heydon and Richard Robins of Itteringham had granted Grey a three acre piece of meadow from the old Purdy farm in Itteringham at the bottom of Wood Close. The land was described as having a ditch to the west and a new pond on the east and Grey's other lands to the south, indicating that Grey had already made a new pond, perhaps the small decoy pond at the foot of the main lake. A small wedge-shaped pond is shown on the mid-1720s garden plan, attributed to Charles Bridgeman, now in the Gough Collection in the Bodleian Library but the re-shaping of Grey's pond may never have been carried out. The dried-up outline of the small round pond may still be seen on Google Earth™. The agreement also showed that Grey and Robins had lately constructed a ditch to separate their lands between the existing hedge and Brick kiln close. The deal, completed in 1717, also rationalised the old irregular meadow holdings of Grey, and Thomas and Richard Robins on the parish boundary.

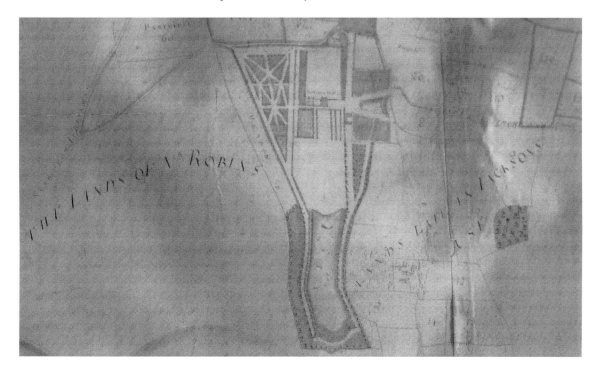

The Thomas Robins estate close to Wolterton Hall and gardens in 1732

After 1720 a small number of neighbourly sales and exchanges with the Robinses of small parcels of land around Wolterton lake enabled Horatio to realise his design for his gardens and park. In May 1726, Walpole gave them 14 acres in 4 closes in Wolterton near Home Close and between the roads to Itteringham. The Robins pieces were only described as 'now in the use of Walpole'. As good neighbours they had already leased the lands that Walpole wanted for his park and gardens near the lake. Whatever changes James Grey had started at the foot of the lake, Walpole's plans were much grander involving a major extension to the lake, tree planting on a large scale and the laying out of extensive areas of gravel walks and lawns nearer the hall.

Thomas Bayfield, the steward, wrote to Walpole about the plans in January 1727:

> I have viewed the brick kiln close nursery and the line to the ditch next the Robins but 30 foot wide from the said ditch, then if they plant a line of young oaks 40 foot from the ditch it will run 10 foot into the young wood (come up) which will broaden the plan of this nursery laid down by Mr Carpenter. Will Brand is sett to work to dig in order to plant out the young setts according to Mr King's direction ... there is a hill in the land which was Mr Richard Robins's that lay very near the head of the new pond and is very good stuff to make the heading of and is agreed by all that taken that away make the ground much more regular and evener.

This letter indicates that the old brick kiln was just to the west of the lake near the parish boundary. Did the presence of old brick earth diggings nearby make it easier for Walpole to enlarge Wolterton lake?

Wolterton Hall and green in 1732

In November 1733, Richard Robins sold Walpole 7 acres in Wolterton meadow, 3 acres of Eastwood meadow and 'land there planted with trees' for £145. At a time when about 20 times the average rent of 10s per acre was the norm, this was a premium price but no doubt reflected the inclusion of some timber. In September 1741, Horatio paid Richard £96 for just over 4 acres of land and meadow on the Wolterton boundary, very close to Walpole's new lake – another expensive purchase, perhaps reflecting how determined Walpole was to have the lands for his garden features. They were to be separated from Robins's remaining lands by a ditch and pale fence.

Plants were bought from various sources including in 1741 11,750 white thorn layers bought from Samuel Saul of Itteringham for £2 12s 11d. Later that year another 15,000 were bought from Philip Jewler and William Mason. No doubt this was for the major work enclosing the park and woods around the lake. Under Henry Turnbull in 1781 there is fleeting evidence in the accounts of fine shrubs being bought from John Mackie whose nursery at Lakenham near Norwich was well known across the county. He also had garden pots and pavements from John Green of Wroxham.

Johnson's pond on Wolterton green was made into yet another fish pond in 1747 – a stewpond for tench. Fencing and paling work was a huge task in the early years and all the work went to Thomas Plaford who was effectively the estate carpenter. In 1755 the men were set to work to dig out the trees in Johnson's orchard, take down the pales and put them all into the ground up against Mr Robins's land.

As Walpole's steward Ness was heavily involved in the continuing creation of the enlarged park around the Hall. As farms and houses were acquired around the green, the park grazing inched ever further out from the Hall. In November 1744 he wrote to explain to Walpole the implications of the planned park:

> I find that the number of acres within the intended paddock will be 216 acres exclusive of the groves and pleasure grounds. And there will also be without the intended paddock:
>
> Viz in your own use 130 acres
> Bells in Hannants use 27 acres
> Hay fenn 20 acres
> In all 177 acres
>
> From the pales at the south east corner of the decoy round as the paddock is intended to be inclosed up to the white gates in the old lane leading to Itteringham will take 750 rod paling which will take 1500 posts 3000 rails 15000 pales. The intended foss from the garden wall to the decoy is 150 rod which may be done at 5s at rod which will cost £37 10s. I am sure that £40 will be the outside that it will cost.

The fence would run along the western side of the gardens from the decoy pond at the foot of the lake. The foss was a fence set in a ha-ha ditch running up the eastern side of the paddock and pleasure grounds, separating them from the old Jackson's farm. The assumption is that the 177 acres outside the paddock was largely controlled directly by Walpole and if mostly used for grazing it would be akin to parkland even though outside the smart paling fence. By April 1746 Ness could write:

> I have finished the park paling from the corner of the decoy as far as the east corner of the orchard belonging to the farm late Greenacres and there left off intending not to proceed any farther there until your Honr comes into the country. And then I began at the corner of Johnsons orchard and carried the paling on thro' the close going to Wayts as far as the upper end of the pithle belonging to the Parsonage house so that I have from thence to the White Gates to do and from the upper end of Greenacre's orchard to the green so that there is about 170 rod to do yet. I have posts enough but I shall want rails and pales for 100 rod that is 400 rails and 4000 pales.

The 1732 estate map locates these properties – Johnson's on the north side of the green, Greenacre having taken over from Bayfield and Nicholas Wayt being in Wickmere Hall. The orchard would have been one of the two fields adjacent to the Bayfield farm. The close towards Wayt was just north of Johnson's and the parsonage pightle was a glebe strip just to the north of the parsonage house. The White Gates were at the north-west corner of the formal walks. In Wolterton parish, these park works were relatively easy to accomplish as properties were acquired. Jackson's farm (now just a cottage) was to the south and east of the Hall; after Jackson died in 1728 his farm was held in-hand. As a result the land to the east of the lake was in Walpole's control and the garden design on that side of the lake was therefore not, as some have argued, materially constrained by the tenant farm.

But on the other side of the Hall at the Itteringham parish boundary, Walpole's extension plans would bring him into conflict with his immediate neighbours, the two Robins families. Although some lands had been sold or exchanged, by the 1740s it is clear that the Robins families were reluctant to cede lands to Walpole at the rate he really wanted (see Chapter 7).

Wolterton in the 1770s showing the curving foss or ha-ha stretching to the east

## Gardeners

Bayfield's letter named 'Will' Brand as the Wolterton gardener in 1727 who was to implement the plan of 'Mr Carpenter'. Brand had witnessed the 1716 deed between Grey and the Robinses, so it is reasonable to assume he was then working for Grey. Walpole had ignored Britiffe's dismissive remarks about the gardener in 1722 and retained the old man's services. Brand clearly had a personal interest in the two little nurseries described by Britiffe in 1722 as 'belonging to Brand the old gardener'. As they were not near the gardens, he was told to rest easy and nothing would be done 'to his prejudice'. Indeed his opinion was sought by Britiffe on how they should be planted. Brand thought only 4 acres should be planted with trees and he offered to make a pond at the end of the grove. He then suggested that 'a walk of Camomoile may lead to it from between the fir trees'.

The garden designers referred to in Bayfield's letter were Joseph Carpenter who ran Brompton Park nurseries, a large and fashionable supplier of plants and planning services to the Royal gardens and others. Although he had died in 1726, Carpenter had been a well known gardener of the time, associated with Charles Bridgeman and William Kent, the more famous major garden and landscape designers. William Kent worked directly for Thomas Ripley, Walpole's architect, and Charles Bridgeman is known to have been involved at Wolterton where plans of the gardens in the 1720s and 1730s are attributed to him. Kent became the King's Master Carpenter when Ripley was promoted from that role to Comptroller of the Royal Works in 1726. Both of course were involved in design work at Houghton and all these men were closely involved with both Sir Robert Walpole and his younger brother Horatio.

The sequence of Horatio's estate gardeners is clear from the accounts. William Brand left or died in early 1732 and John Bradshaw took over around August that year. He was paid on an annual basis at £20 with board wages of a further £3 12s. Bradshaw served at Wolterton for over 18 years. John Lylestone, the gamekeeper, was briefly described as a gardener in July 1739 and again in 1753 when he may have been assisting the ailing Bradshaw. When Ness wrote to tell Walpole of the latter's death in early April 1756, Walpole replied that he assumed Bradshaw would be buried in Wickmere church and he was happy for his funeral costs to be paid. It seems there might have been an issue here since the Wickmere register does not show his burial until early May.

Bradshaw was succeeded by Richard Ness's nephew Richard Jackson – a Yorkshireman like his uncle. Ness's sister Anne had married Anthony Jackson in 1730 in Crambe and their son Richard was baptised a year later at neighbouring Foston-by-Malton, Ness's home parish. Perhaps both uncle and nephew had worked for the same Yorkshire estate to gain early experience. The home of the St Quintin family at Scampston is the most likely estate in the area, just a few miles from Foston. Intriguingly Charles Bridgeman had been responsible for garden design there and Thomas Ripley came from Rillington, immediately next door to Scampston. Another possibility is the Malton estate of Sir Thomas Watson Wentworth (Earl of Malton 1734, Marquess of Rockingham 1746). By the time that Ness proposed his nephew, Jackson was working for the Earl of Exeter at Burghley House in Northamptonshire from whom Walpole had received a personal recommendation:

> Having heard a good character of your nephew Jackson I am disposed to make him my gardener in the room of Bradshaw and therefore I desire you will write to him, if he is willing to serve me, to know upon what terms; I do not care to give above £15 per annum for wages and 5s a week board wages when I am absent; but according to his capacity and behaviour I may give him farther encouragement. Lord Exeter tells me that he works himself in ye gardens which I like extreamly well, and I hope he will continue to doe if he lives with me.
>
> You will let me know his and your intentions upon the proposal as soon as you can conveniently and if he is disposed to serve me, he must however continue to serve his lordship until Mr Lowe can provide his lordship with another gardener and I can accordingly let his lordship know your nephews determination; that all things may be done in a decent manner.

The letter implies that Jackson was already in a fairly senior role at Burghley but that he liked to work in the garden alongside the staff. Brownlow Cecil, the 9th Earl of Exeter, had inherited in 1754 and gave up his seat as MP for Rutland to take the family seat in the House of Lords. Certainly by 1756 he had set about making major changes to the gardens, park and buildings at Burghley with the help of Lancelot 'Capability' Brown. Perhaps Jackson had some exposure to the great designer, which would have enhanced his value in Walpole's eyes. Unfortunately gaps in the Wolterton estate accounts in the 1750s and 1760s mean little more is known of Jackson's time as gardener. Various entries show him paying the gardening team, but these stop in August 1762 when he moved away. It seems likely that Richard had become ill and went to live with his cousin Robert Temple at Tivetshall. Within a year he had died and he was buried in Tivetshall in May 1763.

Towards the end of 1762 Joseph Rumball took over the gardening team. By 1769 Robert Ross was head gardener and in May 1772 he married Jane, probably the daughter of John Lylestone the old gamekeeper. Their wedding was the last recorded in the old Wolterton church. However Ross did not remain long and in May 1776 Joseph Carter, who had succeeded Richard Ness as steward in 1771, paid the gardening team their fortnightly wages himself. This continued into June, but by the second half of that month Henry Turnbull had taken over as leader of the gardening team and was to continue in the job for at least 20 years. It seems likely that both Ross and Turnbull may have been Scottish (the latter possibly son of John Turnbull of Oxnam in Roxborough). An advert for Henry's next of kin was later placed in *The Glasgow Herald* on 30th January 1857:

> The next of kin of Henry Turnbull formerly of Wolterton in Norfolk, gardener or Mary Rutherford his niece who resided with him, may hear something to their advantage [contact Mr Blayney Grays Inn] Henry Turnbull was born about 1732 and went to Wolterton in 1776.

Scotland had acquired such a reputation for innovative and well-educated gardeners that it had been commonplace for the head gardener on an English estate in the 17th or early 18th century to be Scottish. Others set up successful businesses as seedsmen and nurserymen in London and, when asked for advice on finding a gardener, would not hesitate to suggest one of their countrymen. Their apprenticeships trained them not only in botany but also in writing, arithmetic, and their practical knowledge of geometry allowed them to excel at the symmetrical designs then in fashion. By the end of the 18th century English gardeners resented that employers took the practice as normal.

The head gardener was one of the very small group of senior retainers who was paid annual wages and board wages (for food and lodging) and so had some security of tenure. Their basic wages were not, however, significantly above the labourers' daily wages. Walpole's offer of £15 to Jackson was a fairly standard rate although in 1754 one landowner was offering £18 for a Scot who could 'raise Pines (pineapples) and all sorts of melons' in addition to managing the kitchen garden, nurseries, evergreen and forest trees'. He was also to be 'preferably middle aged', a growing preference reflected in the second Horatio's appointment of the 44 year-old Turnbull.

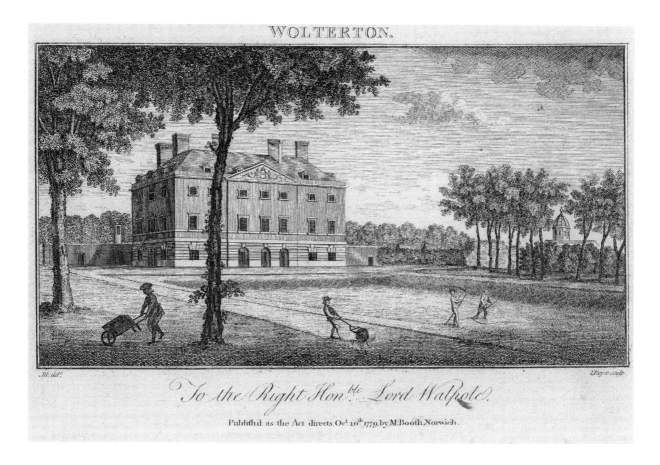

WOLTERTON.

To the Right Hon.ble Lord Walpole.

Publish'd as the Act directs Oct.10th 1779.by M.Booth,Norwich.

**Mowing the lawn at Wolterton in the 1770s**

In the peak periods of work on the major landscape changes the Wolterton estate employed 20 or more local men paid daily wages of 1s or a little more. They worked a full 6 day week. At one point in the winter of 1741-42, so many were employed digging out the lake that even the young Thomas and Richard Robins fleetingly appeared on the list. Apart from very busy periods, it was quite normal for the head gardener to have 6 men working for him throughout the year. In 1738 Bradshaw's team was: Richard Smith, John Wagstaff, James Wright, Richard Lound, the boy (Thomas) King, Robert Hooke. Work on the lawn alone took nearly the whole of June in 1739. In February 1757 Ness wrote to his new boss the second Horatio Walpole giving details of how many men were employed on the estate. There were 27 labourers of whom 5 were under the gardener, 2 more were raking and sweeping leaves, 5 were gravel digging and spreading in the kitchen garden and woodland walks. He added that only the further 6 men planting trees in the meadow bought from Thomas Robins could be laid off when that task was finished in a couple of weeks. The other 5 were doing farming work on the home farm.

Tasks varied from garden creation and maintenance at Wolterton to replanting and weeding the avenue walks around Mannington Hall and draining and clearing its moat in June 1744. Specialists were paid for rat catching and mole trapping. Thomas Aldrich was paid an annual sum for moles in the 1730s whereas in 1747 John Bond seems to have been on piece work – £1 10s for 30 dozen moles caught.

## Itteringham houses

Thomas Robins brought more modest schemes to the village. No doubt in his own way he was emulating the grander plans seen at Wolterton and Blickling as he tried to establish himself locally as a gentleman or even esquire.

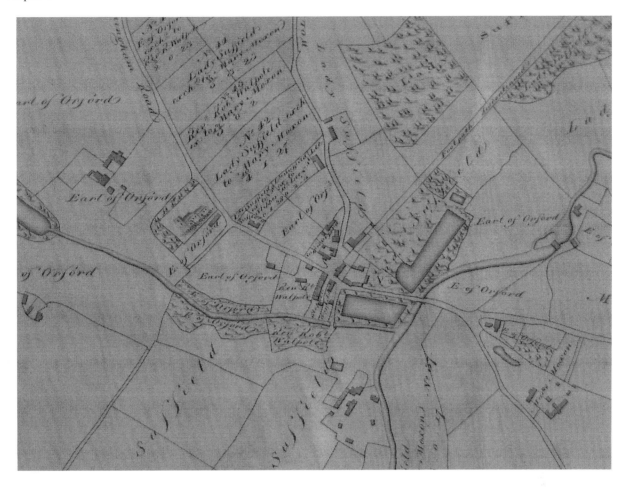

The centre of Itteringham village in 1823 showing the woods and large
ponds by the Manor House and wooded Broom hill

Given the position of his Manor House in the village centre, he had little scope for creating walks but in 1765 Thomas built the summer house on the top of Broom hill, a short stroll from his home. It was well built and probably from the very beginning furnished with a fireplace and flue. Was it visible from his windows in the main parlour? Given the extent of woodland shown in 1823 it seems likely that Robins had created a significant wooded area on Broom hill and in the meadow in front of his house. Repeated references to fishponds when the estate was sold make it almost certain that by 1799 the large ponds on either side of the road had been constructed. Decoratively laid out, they were set in wooded surrounds and were not included in the standard acreage of the farm itself.

Date-stone partly in shadow under the eaves

## Thomas Robins's summer house on Broom hill

His great-uncle Richard Robins 2 had inherited fine grounds, orchards and fish ponds with Itteringham Hall as shown on the 1748 survey. Sadly these were not maintained by Richard Robins 3 as the house fell into disrepair; it was perhaps rather ironic that Richard's grandson, Richard 5 was to become a well-regarded head gardener at Felbrigg Hall in the next century.

**Sources**

NRO: NRS 21027 & 21029, 73x4; WAL 337, 272x6; WAL 524/10, 275x3; WAL 1441/7, 290x3

Wolterton archive: 3/1/1, 5 -7; 3/7/2 &18; 8/4, 5A, 9, 18, 61

Axel Klausmeier's work on Ripley and Wolterton Hall in *NA* 2001 pp 607-30 and in various websites; *ODNB* entries for Bridgeman, Kent and Ripley; Tom Williamson, *The Archaeology of the Landscape park, Garden Design in Norfolk, England, c1680 - 1840*, 1998, pp. 72-80 and 286-291; Peter Willis, *Charles Bridgeman and the English Landscape Garden*, Elysium Press Publishers, 2002; Andrew Eburne, 'Charles Bridgeman and the Gardens of the Robinocracy', *Garden History* vol 31 no 2, 2003

Norfolk County Council Library and Information Service at www.picture.norfolk.gov.uk for images of the two 18th century prints of Wolterton

# Chapter 16

## *Free Liberty to Hunt*

---

*The worst crimes in the countryside were horse-stealing and murder, both carrying the death sentence. Poaching was seen in the same light by most landowners and even legal shooting created endless disputes among neighbours. The loss of a valuable horse, the shooting of a dog, or worse a gamekeeper, were frequent and worrying occurrences.*

## Shooting, gamekeepers and poaching

Shooting and dealing in game were beset with legal constraints in the 18th century and poaching was treated as a serious crime by the landed classes. 'Qualified persons' were allowed to shoot game on their own lands but the threshold for qualification was high. In Itteringham only Horatio Walpole and the two Robins families exceeded the required freehold valuation of £100 and each also had the lord of the manor status that reinforced their rights. Theoretically, qualified men could only shoot on their own land but in practice the only deterrent to shooting elsewhere was a minor prosecution for trespass, itself difficult to bring since the damages threshold was greater than the likely amount of game shot. So in practice qualified men felt they could shoot anywhere and, if their bag was small, this was often tolerated by their peers. In 1707 dealing in game by intermediaries such as victuallers was made illegal in an attempt to restrict illegal shooting. This constraint was widely flouted with both landowners and poachers supplying game covertly. In 1755 a further attempt was made to reduce poaching and even landowners were barred from selling game. Ironically this led to an increase in poaching; the supply from owners not willing to face the risk of prosecution dried up and illegal shooting grew to meet continued demand. The second half of the century saw many poaching incidents and Norfolk had at least its fair share of violent ones with organised gangs poaching at night and fighting back if challenged. The Itteringham area saw a number of significant incidents, some in Blickling and others on Walpole land.

Horatio Walpole, senior and junior were both keen on shooting. Before his death in 1757, Horatio senior had made a massive investment in planting trees and whin cover for birds not only at Mossymere Wood but in plantations around the Mannington and Wolterton estates. Horatio junior maintained the investment and was also a keen shot. Thomas Plaford the estate carpenter was paid for making and mending pheasant houses.

In March 1764 Fletcher Norton the Attorney-General (later Baron Grantley) wrote a formal opinion for Walpole on possible changes to the Game Acts; Walpole was keen to know whether such changes would improve the chances of a successful action against a non-qualified person for being in possession of game birds. He had particular cause for concern, as Norton noted:

> The poachers have lately got into a practice of shooting pheasants by moon light, upon the trees where they perch. In December last Lord Walpole's servants apprehended a fellow, who with 2 or 3 others that escaped, had killed 20 pheasants in this manner in a grove within his park, which were found in bags when they left.

The penalty in the first half of the century was a £5 fine or, if that could not be paid, three months in prison. As poaching became a more profitable business, so this fine became more affordable and less of a deterrent. The 1770 Night Poaching Act increased the penalty for what had always been an illegal practice and one which was always interpreted as a serious form of poaching – clearly gentlemen would not be out shooting at night. Imprisonment became compulsory and fines of up to £50 were imposed. Even though repealed in 1773, the new legislation saw a rise in fines and a greater number of imprisonments. The landed classes had protected their favourite sport but the population as a whole did not see poaching as a significant crime. Indeed some writers argue that it became a focus of class conflict in the 18th and 19th centuries.

### *Gamekeepers*

Gamekeepers had to be officially registered and the names of the estate owners were recorded in the newspapers. Only landed estates - originally manorial land - might employ a keeper. In 1740 John Gay drew up for Walpole the required appointment forms. John Lylestone (as Ness and Walpole called him) was to hold the post for the next 17 years, until three years before his death in October 1760. Little is known about him except that he was working on the estate by 1732 as a waged estate man, earning £5 a quarter, the same rate as the gardener. Between 1738 and 1740 his work included bringing horses from London, meeting 'his master at Newmarket' and going to Hickling for fish. By this time the guns were also within his remit as he regularly purchased the powder and shot. John could not write his name which was spelt 'Lileystone' by Bayfield and initially Lillystone by Ness. He may have been the father of William Lillistone who baptised a daughter Jane in Wickmere in 1763, and possibly of Jane Lillestone who later married the estate gardener. John Lylestone of Wolterton was named in mid-November 1759 as the father of the child Mary Cowper was expecting but the only base child baptised in Itteringham (her parish) in December was Christen Pearson, daughter of Mary 'Cobourn'. If this was the same girl, the child's name suggested a different father. Mary's examination was heard by his employer, Horatio Walpole who would have known the man well. John must either have been the father or was willing to take the responsibility. When John died the following year, Horatio Walpole junior paid for his 'shroud and laying out'; he was buried in Wickmere as Lillistone.

By 1757 Thomas Nelson had taken over as gamekeeper; Thomas had moved into Itteringham with his wife Martha and six children late 1755 from Gunthorpe and may have worked with Lylestone as an assistant. Nelson was followed by the mid-1770s by Sebastian or 'Sib' Daniel. The gamekeepers were retained on an annual salary above the rate paid to day labourers and were kitted out with 'coat and breeches' and powder and shot. It was not until the second half of the 18th century that the dwelling at Mossymere became established as the keeper's cottage. In March 1753 Lylestone was quarantined with smallpox there and by then the area's primary purpose had become shooting rather than farming. The cottage had been given over to the gamekeeper so that he could live beside the prime shooting wood, which being isolated was vulnerable to poachers. After Sib's death in the spring of 1784, Gaunt Williams had become gamekeeper, apparently coming up from London to take the job. In the late 1780s assistance came from William Ward and James Lee, both active in watching for poachers and killing rabbits. James Lee may well have been one of the Itteringham family who later were to own the cottage on Wolterton Road west. In the following century Stephen Barwick, who had come to Itteringham from Oulton in 1793, was to be the first of several of that family who held the post of gamekeeper on the estate.

In 1750 a party of the Gurney family who held the manor of Little Barningham came into Mossymere Wood and shot a number of birds. They were qualified to shoot but not invited in by Walpole. A year later they sent the Bishop of Norwich's gamekeeper to shoot birds on their lands and in Mannington to provide Christmas presents to their trade friends in Norwich. The number of birds shot on both occasions was modest but Walpole was incensed at the number of hen birds killed and the risk to his pheasant numbers that would result. The exchange of strongly worded letters has survived. Ness claimed to have been treated rudely and both sides accused the other of blowing the issue up beyond what was merited. In the end an uneasy truce was arrived at and no doubt the Gurneys were more wary thereafter of shooting on Mannington land. However they had asked Walpole why so many birds seem to be seen early in the year and so few in the shooting season, the implication being that Lylestone was shooting for himself and selling game illegally in Norwich. This hit a raw nerve with Walpole who had seen the number of birds on his lands decline. He instructed Ness to look into matters and warn Lylestone to be more vigilant at his job of protecting the game.

The prime target for legal shooting was pheasant, but no doubt partridge would have been shot and hare coursing was definitely a local sport. In fact pretty much anything would have been fair game, even turkeys as shown in a letter from Walpole to Ness on 23rd March 1768:

> When I left Woolterton some of the wild turkies were strayed to Blickling Park. Nelson said he was in hopes he should be able to get them back again. I should be glad to know whether he has done so for there were no cocks left at home. Mr Bullemur said he would give me one but if I cannot get one from thence as it may not be easy to catch 'em I must send some from hence which must be done soon as the breeding time draws near.

## Poaching gangs

The Wolterton estate accounts for March 1775 show Sib Daniel collecting his wages and ammunition money and also being reimbursed 3 guineas for paying men going out with him after poachers. This was probably a constant effort at this time and not always either safe or successful. After the repeal of the Night Poaching Act the deterrents were not so great. On 25th December 1775, between 11 pm and midnight a number of men armed with guns entered Mossymere Wood. Sebastian Daniel, on hearing their shooting the pheasants, went with assistants to 'enquire who those persons were'. One of them immediately levelled his gun and, without a word, shot the keeper in the left leg. The wound in the thigh was so severe that for a long time his life hung in the balance and it was said that only his saddle saved him from a fatal wound. On the 28th Walpole published an offer of a £50 reward for information leading to a conviction, payable even to an accomplice. The reward would be paid by Joseph Carter of Wolterton, the new estate steward. Walpole gave notice to night-time trespassers that man traps would be set from 1st January in his plantations and woods in Itteringham, Saxthorpe, Wolterton, Mannington and Little Barningham. By 3rd February the reward had been increased to £100, no doubt such a huge sum was necessary to break through the passive support of poaching by the labouring population. This was about five times the annual wages that a day labourer could achieve. But nobody came forward and the reward notification was repeated from time to time over the next two years. Indeed in January 1777 he announced that he had arranged a King's pardon for the accomplices so that the man who shot his keeper could be brought to justice. The reward would be £100 for conviction of the shooter and £20 for each accomplice. He repeated the man trap warning. In 1778 Daniel, recovered and still working, was again drawing cash 'for the use of the watchers'.

Eventually someone found the reward irresistible and five men were committed on January 16th 1779 including John Coxford, aged about 60 and a 'very old offender', who had confessed to being involved. Two months later, the prisoners, all known multiple offenders, were taken from Norwich Castle to Thetford for the Assizes - Coxford, Thomas Bell, Francis Bell, Robert Jacob and Thomas or Joseph Reynolds (a small farmer) - all charged with wounding Sebastian Daniel. Four of the poachers had been armed when they entered Mossymere wood and started shooting pheasants. All were from Oulton, although the ringleader Thomas Bell (alias William Ewing) a shoemaker and labourer had recently moved to East Dereham. A sixth poacher nick-named John Laughland had been married to an Oulton girl who had recently died, but despite his description being circulated he was never caught and he was believed to have left the county, not originally being a Norfolk man. In the event only two were sentenced, as the others confessed and gave evidence. Coxford was held on remand for a further three months, but then released at the next assizes in July having effectively served a three month jail term.

Only Thomas Bell was capitally convicted. On January 20th he was sentenced to death. It was most unusual for a hanging to be carried out unless there had been a murder or manslaughter. The death sentence would often be reprieved by the judge at the closing of the assizes and the offender sent for transportation. Bell was not so lucky. Perhaps Walpole had been particularly vigorous in pursuing the case and pressed behind the scenes for this sentence to make an example to deter others. Saturday 3rd April was the date of his execution and a huge crowd, said to number 20,000, gathered at Castle Hill. The newspaper noted that the pick-pockets had a field day in the crowd. The same newspaper wrote a diatribe against poaching in which they described it as 'the foundation of almost every other crime' and they lambasted respectable people who encouraged poaching by their demand for game to which they were not entitled.

On 20th November 1779 John Coxford signed his mark to a document whereby he claimed £60 of the £100 reward money offered by Horatio Walpole. Coxford said that he and James Allison (at that time both worsted weavers in Bawdeswell) were the first to alert the magistrates about Bell. Coxford and his wife and three children were now of Oulton and the £60 was to be paid directly to the overseers (Thomas Dix, John Barber and William Bell) to provide for his family. Presumably he was no longer able to provide for them.

Horatio Walpole was active in his support for a Norwich-based group of Norfolk gentry led by the Marquis of Townshend who met regularly to consider how to prevent the depredations of poachers. Walpole took legal advice on man traps and spring guns. He was advised not to use them but just to put up notices stating that he had installed them. From a note in the accounts paying Jeckyll the blacksmith to make man traps, it seems Walpole may have been hawkish! From 1775 to the early 1780s various account entries show extra payments to Daniel 'for men going out after poachers' and for mantraps. Information was gathered on night poachers. Gamekeepers led bands of watchers to deter poachers but incidents continued and sometimes game keepers were killed.

In November 1777, John Thomlinson wrote to the Earl of Buckinghamshire with a report on estate affairs at Blickling. He described how Tom Bell the park-keeper had had to deal with a roaming gang of poachers who had tried to take game, shooting as close to the hall as the ice house just across the road from the church. He saw them off, but the poachers threatened to return the next day, which they did. Bell again saw them off by standing firm with his gun and asserting that he would shoot at least one of them dead rather than allow them to take any game. The gun and his spaniels did the trick and the poachers moved on, visiting Gunton and Holt on their travels. They were not caught. This was a gang that came on foot, probably from Norwich, and none of its members could be identified. This may have emboldened them to try again.

Unhappily four years later a Blickling man was killed, as *The Norfolk Chronicle* of 29th December 1781 reported:

> Whereas in the night of Sunday 23rd December instant, 16 or 18 poachers entered the plantations in Blickling belonging to the Earl of Buckingham near adjoining his park and in his own occupation, where they shot 14 or 15 times; and, on the keepers being alarmed and going there with their assistants, the said poachers threatened their lives swearing they would shoot them and did violently assault and most cruelly beat and wound them with their guns and large clubs armed with iron spikes, insomuch that Jacob Blyth, one of the keeper's assistants, is since dead by the wounds which he then received, and the life of James Gibons another of the assistants greatly despaired of, and others of such assistants most dangerously bruised and wounded.
>
> For the discovery and bringing to justice these violent and inhuman offenders, a reward of £100 is hereby offered to any person or persons who shall first make discovery of them so as they may be prosecuted to conviction, by applying to Mr Robert Copeman of Blickling.
>
> NB. One of the poachers appeared to be a very tall stout man, wore a long slop and had with him a rough coated light coloured water spaniel.
>
> NB. It being supposed that some of the poachers may have marks of blows upon them it is therefore earnestly recommended to such persons as live in a neighbourhood where suspected poachers usually dwell to make observation of such as may have received blows or any outward and visible hurts as the same may probably tend to a discovery of the guilty persons.
>
> NB. They left behind them a round hat with a pale blue lining and very bloody, also the broken stocks of 2 guns.

This does not seem much for the local constabulary to go on! But someone immediately spilled the beans and on 5th January 1782 *The Norfolk Chronicle* reported that William Wigget Bulwer JP had already committed to the Castle prison Robert Andrews, alehouse keeper of Horsford, for being involved in the murder of Jacob Blyth assistant to the gamekeeper at Blickling. Within days John Barnard and Samuel Thursby were also charged. At the same time, in an unrelated incident, five noted convicted poachers were apprehended at Lord Townshend's Raynham estate and brought to the Castle 'under a strong guard' to serve three months and pay a fine. The Blickling poachers could not expect such a light sentence for murder.

More incidents followed in 1782. In August Peter Elwin, Isaac Paske and Coulson Bell gave notice that they would prosecute poachers on their Saxthorpe manors and estates (no doubt the latter two also included their Oulton lands) and particularly asked gentlemen not to course or shoot hares there since they were thin on the ground. The Barningham Hall estate warned that man-traps and spring guns had been set to protect their woods and plantations. Despite these warnings, the poachers continued to risk capture. In September two notorious poachers, Die and Nutty alias Cocks, 'were at it in Pond Close' Aylsham and again the following evening at Marsham. They ran off but being well-known in the area and with a handsome reward offered, the newspaper expected them to be arrested even though Nutty was known to disguise himself in women's clothes.

On 11th March 1786 two noted poachers, possibly Die and Nutty, broke out of Aylsham bridewell and only one was quickly re-captured. Later that year there was more trouble at Blickling when on Sunday 31st December 1786 at 4 am a gang of about 14 poachers entered Blickling plantations and fired three shots. The keeper and his watch, in all 15 men, came up on them and 'an engagement ensued'. There were volleys of stones and a watchman was injured. Two guns were fired without shot, but soon after another loaded with shot and one of the watch was wounded. The poachers fled.

In some cases the judge was unsympathetic to the gamekeepers' troubles. In 1761 Robert Thornton was tried for the manslaughter of John Holland while attempting to catch some night shooters at Felbrigg. Unlike the judge the jury believed it was an accident as a note in the assize calendar explained:

> The prosecution of Thornton was cruel and unjust. In following some men shooting by moonlight, he fell & his gun went off & shot Holland. But as the wound went upwards towards the shoulder, it was impossible that the butt of the gun could have been against Thornton's shoulder in an even Country: yet the Judge's malice took pains with the Jury to find the verdict wilful murder. But they having more sense and justice and less malice than the Judge found not Guilty.

## Dogs and horses

Both the Robins families were as keen on hunting as the Walpoles but it was their particular delight in coursing with their greyhounds which brought them repeatedly into conflict with both Walpoles. Thomas Robins's Manor House still has his staircase decoration and dog gate as evidence of his hobby and close scrutiny shows a dog's head atop the cartouche on his gravestone.

Detail from the gravestone of Thomas Robins 3

Staircase decoration in the Manor House

Dog gate in the Manor House

On 25th December 1756, just a short while before his death, the elder Horatio Walpole wrote to Richard Ness, upset that his neighbours had been hare coursing with their dogs on Walpole's land near the Hall:

> I have received yours giving me an account of the behaviour of Mr Hays and Mr Richard Robins with John Bell of Oulton in taking the liberty to come upon my grounds in so destructive a manner. I write by this post to Dr Addison to let Mr Hays know how unkindly I take such an ill usage and desire him in a quick manner to forbear a repetition of it. And you will talk to Richard Robins upon what he has done recently with Bell as what I could never have expected from him. But you will at the same time take a proper notice of it in a quick manner to Mr Thomas Robins and Samuel, hoping they will not continuance their course in acting so un-neighbourly a part towards me. And you will see Mr Bell of Oulton and tell him in my name not to encroach upon my rights any more, because if he does I shall resolve it in a simple manner.

Mr Hays (or Haze) was probably from the Saxthorpe family as Dr Leonard Addison was rector of Cawston and Salle and vicar of Saxthorpe, where he died in 1772. John or Jack Bell was the Robins cousin of Wood farm. Presumably he was a long-time friend of young Richard Robins, being just four years his senior. On 23rd February 1757 Ness wrote to the younger Horatio Walpole, who had just succeeded his father, regarding the same matter. The letter shows tensions within the hitherto mutually supportive Robins clan, with Richard acting increasingly badly:

> Sometime in December last I acquainted my late Lord with Richard Robins and Jack Bell of Oulton coursing in Thomas Partridge's grounds and killing 2 brace of hares. And I had orders to speak to Mr Thomas Robins and Samuel about it and to desire them to talk with Richard and tell him how unkind it was. They both seemed to decline speaking to him and said there was not at that time a good understanding between them, and their speaking to him might make things worse. Some small time afterwards I see Richard Robins and told him, in a very civil manner, that his behaviour in coursing was not consistent with that good neighbourhood that I thought was and might be for his interest to preserve. And if he did not desist from coursing so near the Park I must be obliged, contrary to my inclination, to let his lordship know it. He replied with great warmth that he had a right to course or hunt

within a certain district and he would, when and as often as he pleased. And that I might tell my lord so. I replied: are you in earnest Mr Robins? He swore by G-d he was. I repeated the same question to him three times and his answer was the same. Soon after this the weather set in so as there was no coursing and continued some time that I thought he might have thought better of it; but I find he still continues the same man. Lylestone happened on him yesterday, in John Cubit's farm, and spoke to him and he abused him, he says most shamefully. He says your lordship keeps nothing but a parcel of rogues and that he might come and tell me of it. So I am now satisfied that civility only makes him worse, therefore I could not refrain letting your lordship know it. Mr Thomas Robins behaves, and Samuel, as though they were sincerely disposed to be good neighbours.

The new Horatio Walpole was prepared to give the Robinses a chance to remain on good terms with him but was equally determined to prevent further trouble from Richard. He replied on 1st March:

I have received yours of 23rd and 26th. As to the first relating chiefly to Richard Robins behaviour I am very sorry for it. I would have you tell him in a civil manner how much I am concerned to hear that all the endeavours of my late father took to live with him in a neighbourly and friendly manner were proven so ineffectual. I should be sorry to be a hindrance to any person sporting in a gentleman like way, but it cannot be deemed behaving in a friendly manner to sport close to my Park Gate. For though he is qualified I can bring an action against him for going upon my ground. It is true the damage given in my favour would be a mere trifle but I should have the satisfaction of making him spend some money at law which perhaps would not be so pleasant to him. I hope he will still think the better of it and not force me to extremities. For if he perseveres I am determined to do it, cost what it will. If you think it would have a better effect you might desire Mr Jewell to go over to him. I shall be very willing to satisfy him for his trouble. You may likewise present my compliments to Messrs Thomas and Samuel Robins and tell them I hope we shall always live upon a neighbourly and friendly footing and that nothing shall be wanting on my part to cultivate all means for that purpose. My late father promised T Robins some ducks: he is welcome to what quantity he pleases or anything else I have which can give him any satisfaction.

Tensions with the Robins family, however, continued – at least with Richard. In August 1759 Walpole corresponded with his lawyer Thomas Nuthall seeking advice on his gamekeeper who had shot one of Richard's dogs. Two unaccompanied dogs had been hunting or disturbing game in his park and his gamekeeper had shot at them through the hedge, killing one of them on the land of one of Walpole's tenants where it had also been hunting. Walpole stood up for his gamekeeper saying that the Robins dogs had often been seen hunting in the covers around his park and that they should not have been out unattended before the corn was cut:

He may put collars upon the necks of half the curs in the county and shall I not be at liberty in this case to destroy them?

The issue had as much to do with status and the right to hunt as it did the dogs. Robins asserted what he called his 'paramountship' stemming from his status as lord of the manor. Walpole said he could find no evidence that Robins had a manor, the same argument that had been used earlier over advowson rights despite being in error. Robins argued he could do what he liked wherever he was in his own manor. Walpole asserted that this was an incorrect understanding of the law of trespass by his 'great neighbour'. Nuthall gave his opinion that a lord of a manor could not shoot on the land of one of his own tenants free of the accusation of trespass. But, he added, since Robins had not had a notice to keep his greyhounds off Walpole's tenant's ground he would probably succeed in an action against the keeper for killing the dog. It would have been different just the other side of the hedge on Walpole's park if Walpole had previously given notice.

In contrast, a very genteel dispute occurred between Lord Hobart of Blickling and Mr Gay of Calthorpe in September 1732. Hobart had been wound up by Mr Scott of Aylsham about Mr Gay keeping hounds and he sent a message by his keeper 'desiring him not to come to hunt on his side of the water [River Bure]'. Mr Gay politely bid his service to his Lordship and 'bid the keeper tell him that the best dogs of his pack were at his service, if he pleased, and the rest he would either hang or give away, and would never hunt again rather than displease his honorable neighbour'. Hobart was so pleased with the reply that he went to see Mr Gay and 'gave him free liberty to hunt where he pleased'.

The gentry were not the only landowners who were worried by dogs. In 1769 a complaint was made by two warreners and a farmer from Cawston against three other local men. They wanted the dogs, ferrets and nets with which the weavers were killing their rabbits, seized and destroyed. Hunting dogs were also attractive to thieves. In mid-April 1762, Peter Elwin junior of Saxthorpe reported, succinctly, that a 'bitch of the pointing breed' had been stolen from him. But dogs of course were already also kept as pets and caused distress when lost. In the same week ten years later, the owner of Itteringham's Hill farm, Miss Mary Churchman lost her young greyhound from her home at Mangreen Hall. Given that greyhounds were valuable he might well have been stolen, but the following Saturday the paper carried her hopeful appeal for his return:

> Lost Supposedly strayed out of the yard A young Greyhound Dog a few months old a pale red colour with a white breast Answers to the name of Spring Half a guinea reward for whoever brings him home.

Far more serious than dog-theft, horse-stealing was considered one of the worst possible crimes in the 18th century; repeat offenders would receive the death sentence and were not always reprieved. Newspapers regularly carried such reports over several weeks:

> 1750 December 8th-15th Stolen at a stable on Thursday from Widow Breese of Saxthorpe of Norfolk. A light grey gelding aged 9 years, 14 hands high, a hanging mane and short cut tail. Anyone with tidings of the horse - a reward is offered 'by me Mary Breese'.

Often the theft was part of a larger ring of crimes, carried out by serial criminals. Patrick St Clair of Sustead, soon to be the rector of Wolterton, wrote to Ashe Windham on 14th May 1738 to tell him that 'Will' a son of 'Tom' Gotts (Windham's old carrier) had been apprehended the Friday before at Holt carrying '6 pair of buckskin breeches and pairr of pistols'. Gotts - a 'very dangerous fellow' - was taken before Justice Elwin accused of stealing a mare from Widow Wells at Edgefield and several other robberies. He was convicted at Norwich Assizes on 5th August of several felonies and horse-stealing and sentenced to death. *The Norwich Mercury* described him as about 25 years of age, a smuggler who had deserted several times from the King's service. Two nights before his execution he tried to escape, freed himself from his irons but to no avail. St Clair said 'all our neighbourhood were very afraid of him'. St Clair could not relax though: at the end of December 1738 two chaps on horseback stole 1 guinea from a fellow in a robbery on Cromer Heath, and the same night stole a mare from the stable of Mr Cubitt of Calthorpe. He added 'if they escape we shall not be safe in our houses'.

In 1772 on 15th August Francis Duffield was committed by William Wiggett Bulwer for stealing a black mare, value £12 of Mr Thomas Bell farmer of Cawston but, at the Assizes, the case was not proceeded with, probably because of lack of evidence against Duffield. William Winter and Francis Newham were not so lucky in August 1775 when all the prosecutors - Christopher Youngman, John Clerke, Thomas Windsor, William Clarke, William Wells and John Porter - all turned up to give evidence that the two had stolen a gelding worth £6 from Christopher Youngman and a mare from John Clerke at Erpingham that May. Both were found guilty but had the death penalty replaced by transportation for 14 years. The same fate befell John and William Haynes in August 1784 who were convicted of stealing a chestnut gelding of John Gunton of Wickmere and a brown gelding of a Corpusty farmer. In the summer of 1798 Coulson Bell JP committed a local labourer for stealing 4 shillings worth of items from Thomas Bulwer at Elmerdale farm – 1 iron coulter, 1 hempen rope (a ploughline), 1 iron hake (belonging to the plough). Had David Todd (alias James Todd of 'Armingland' late of Corpusty) stopped there all might have been well, but he also stole a chestnut gelding value £10 from John Goldsmith of Oulton and was sentenced to be hanged. At the following sessions he was reprieved; Todd was lucky, although at the age of 48 his transportation would probably have meant for life.

The crime was so frequent that by the end of the century the landowners in every hundred had formed groups to try to tackle the problem. The Annual meeting of the South Erpingham Hundred Association for Apprehending Horsestealers met at Mr Harriman's The Black Boys in Aylsham.

## Sources

NRO: WAL 1503-1504, 292x5

Wolterton archive: 3/1/1, 3, 6, 7, 9; 3/7/18; 8/58-59, 62, 63A, 64, 65

Articles on shooting and poaching in the *Norfolk Chronicle* and *Norfolk Mercury* and books on shooting and poaching in the 18th century, including: PB Munsche, *Gentlemen and Poachers: the English Game Laws 1671-1831*, 1981; JS Cockburn, *Crime in England 1550-1800*, 1977; T Collins et al, *Encyclopedia of Traditional British Rural Sports*, 2005; JR Short, *Imagined Country: Environment, Culture and Society*, 1991; M Craig, *Cultural Geography*, 1998

RW Ketton-Cremer, 'The Statesman and the Quakers', *NA* vol XXXIV part 4, 1969, on Gurney dispute in 1750, with full transcripts of the letters then in the Wolterton archive.

HMC Report, *Lothian Papers*, p 320

# Chapter 17

## *A Great Day Out*

---

*For the majority of people life equalled work. Six days a week, from sunrise to sunset or later, with church services on Sundays, there was little time for leisure. The home garden plot had to be cultivated, water drawn from the well or pulk and fuel gathered. The gentry and aristocracy had both money and time for social occasions, some of which could be enjoyed by their employees from the sidelines. Even for the workers there were markets and fairs and festivals with all their attractions and gossip.*

## Notable events

News travelled fast and there was always some new tale to be heard and re-told – a great form of entertainment in itself.

### *Holes in the ground*

In 1717 the locality would have been discussing the strange tale of a remarkable incident which took place at Mannington soon after Sir Charles Potts took over the estate following the death of his brother Algernon. The matter was discussed by historians, philosophers and mathematicians of the day.

> An account of the sinking of three oaks into the ground at Mannington in the County of Norfolk communicated by Peter Le Neve esq Norroy King at Arms and Fellow of the Royal Society.
>
> On Tuesday 23rd July of the last year 1717 in the grounds and near the seat of Sir Charles Potts Baronet in the County of Norfolk and parish of Mannington (which lies about mid-way between the market towns of Holt and Aylsham and about seven miles from the coast near Cromer) in the day time, the great oak with the roots and ground about it was seen to subside and sink into the earth and not long after, at about 40 yards distance, two other oaks that were contiguous sunk after the same manner into a much larger pit, being about 33 foot diameter whereas the former is not fully 18. These, as they sunk, fell across so that obstructing each other only the roots of one of them reaches the bottom, whereas the first stands perpendicular.
>
> When the first tree sunk it was observed that the water boiled up in the hole, but upon the sinking of the greater pit that water drained off into it from the former, which now continues dry. The depth thereof to the firm bottom is nine foot three inches and the tree that stands upright in it is 3 foot 8 inches in girth and its trunk about 18 foot long, half of which is now within the pit. In the bottom of the greater pit there is a pool of water about 8 foot diameter, whose surface is 11 foot 3 inches below the ground and the trees that are in the pit are much of the same length with the other but somewhat smaller, the one being in girth 3 foot 5 inches, the other but 2 foot 9 inches.
>
> The soil on which these trees grew is gravelly but the bottom is a quick-sand over a clay upon which there are springs which feed large ponds adjoining to Sir Charles Potts's house at about a quarter of a mile from these holes.
>
> The nature of the soil seems to afford a reasonable conjecture at the cause of this odd accident, which some perhaps may be apt to reckon as a prodigy. The spring running over the clay at the bottom of a bed of very minute sand, such as your quick-sands usually are, may reasonably be supposed in many ages to have washed away the sand and to have thereby excavated a kind of subterraneous lake over which these trees grew. And the force of the winds on the leaves and branches agitating their roots may well have loosened the sand under them and occasioned it to fall in more frequently than elsewhere; whereby in length of time the thin bed of gravel being only left, it might become unable to support its own weight and that of the trees it bore. That this is not a bare conjecture may appear from the boiling up of the water at first in the lesser hole and its standing

in the bigger and lower. And if it shall be found that it was a very windy day whereon this accident happened, it will much add to the probability of this solution.

An accident not unlike this lately happened in Fleet Street London by the defect of the arched roof of a very deep common sewer. The earth gradually falling into the sewer was carried away by it, so as not to obstruct the water; and the continual tremor of the ground occasioned by the constant passing of carts and coaches by degrees shook down the earth so as to leave a very great cavern, the top whereof at length grew so very thin that one day, a weighty cart having just passed by it, a great space of the pavement sunk in, in the middle of the street not without hazard to a coach then driving by.

*Philosophical Transactions* [of The Royal Society] for the months of January February March and April 1718. No. 735 page 766.

To this can be added Francis Blomefield's transcription of the survey by Philip Webster 'Professor of the Mathematicks at Aylsham' on 22nd January 1718, which gave more precise detail and sounds rather like an exam question:

An exact account of the depth of the springs and circumference of the two holes into which the 3 trees sunk:

The distance between the ponds which are by the Hall house of Mannington where Sir Charles now lives and the nearest hole into which the 2 trees sunk is two furlongs thirty three yards

The water in the nearest hole is one foot two inches higher than the water in the ponds

The land at the bank or side of the ponds lies 8 feet 6 inches lower than the land by the side of the holes

From the top of the bank to the water in the nearest of the ponds and biggest hole is 13 feet 3 inches

From the top of the water to the bottom of the loose clay sand is 12 feet two inches, and in this hole where the two trees fell in one fell cross the other and the root of one of the trees is within three feet of the bottom of the loose sand

The circumference of the water in that biggest hole is 22 feet 9 inches

The circumference of the hole above is 32 yards 2 feet 5 inches

The bottom of the spring in the hole is nine feet 6 inches lower than the bottom of the spring in the ponds

One of the oaks which fell into the biggest hole is in girth 3 feet five inches and in length 18 feet one inch

The other tree in the same hole is in girth 2 feet 9 inches and in length 17 feet 5 inches

The distance between the 2 holes is 37 yards 2 feet 7 inches

The circumference of the least hole into which the single tree fell (and stands directly upright as it grew before) is 17 yards one foot 9 inches, there is no water in it but the depth of the hole to a firm bottom is 9 feet 3 inches, the girth of that tree is 3 feet 8 inches and the length 17 feet 11 inches, the root reaching the firm bottom and the tree stands perpendicular

The soil in and about this hole is equal to the other hole, the ground of this being the least hole sunk first and the water boiled up in this but soon after the ground sunk to make the other hole which lies a little more on the declivity of the hill and is deeper the water sunk in this and remains dry since

Today the holes would seem to be the pond known as the scrape and the small pond nearby, lying in the meadow adjacent to Lady's Wood just to the north-north-west of the Hall. Here the stream from Little Barningham and the beck from Barningham Lowes meet. The descriptions do not match the more obvious hole in the gardens around Mannington chapel (no doubt a marl pit) or the larger pit across the lane from the chapel (described on earlier maps as a gravel pit). An even bigger hole appeared in Briston in the summer of 1788 (60 ft across and 27 ft deep). These incidents will not surprise local farmers since holes like this continue to appear in fields and a van-sized hole even opened up in the lane immediately outside the authors' house in the early 1990s.

## Fires and bankruptcy

Fires were a real and ever-present threat in both towns and the country throughout the 18th century. Haystacks, barns, thatched cottages and churches were at risk from lightning, accident and arson. Towns where older timber-framed buildings were still standing close together suffered badly. In Holt on 1st May 1708 three-quarters of the town, including the church, was destroyed in 3 hours. Fakenham lost 26 houses in August 1738, but locals managed to save most of Cawston town when a major fire burnt four houses and part of the church on 23rd May 1783. Foulsham had not been so fortunate in June 1770; 14 buildings were lost when fire caught the general store where gunpowder was being kept; the church was badly damaged and the bells melted from the heat. Some buildings seemed to have been particularly unlucky. Baconsthorpe parsonage had been destroyed by lightning in 1692 only to be burnt down again along with its barns and stable in April 1754. On hearing of the latest disaster locals would have given thanks for being spared; money was often raised for those that lost their livelihoods. The inhabitants of Fakenham - where the loss was computed at £2,000 - raised a petition for relief. They asked only that the poorest sufferers - who had lost £700 - were to be helped. The rest said they were insured or would manage. A rather less sympathetic observer noted that it was not as bad as at first thought 'being only the low mean buildings, that will not cost too much to repair ... the Apothecary's House and the Red Lyon were saved'.

As now, a great day out was going to auctions at houses of the once well-to-do. In the autumn of 1736 a vast crowd of people attended the sale of the bankrupted Edward Paston's goods at Barningham Hall, although it was noticed that no-one from the wealthier estates of 'Blickling, Gunton, Thorpe or Suffield' was there. The top buyers included Mr William Jermy (son of the squire of Bayfield) and Mr Peter Elwin of Booton. Patrick St Clair who lived at Sustead took his daughter and later wrote that there was 'A great deal of china which sold well'. Betty spent £4. The following year, 1737, saw the end of the Potts era at Mannington. Sir Charles Potts's library was sold in Norwich and the heir-at-law Mr Turner's goods were separately picked over at the Hall. St Clair no doubt took Betty to nose through another less fortunate person's belongings of whom he wrote in 1740:

> The pretty Widow of Rev George England, late the rector of Wolterton, Wickmere and Alby is to go into a convent invited by a French lady acquaintance. She is to sell all the furniture of the house at Alby and the books, by auction.

The pretty lady was Veneranda Maria Elizabetha, of Huguenot descent. In her case, the convent was only a stop-gap; she later married a wealthy Huguenot of London and was left £8,000 by a rich female friend.

## Passing distractions

The monotony of daily village life was also punctuated by events and people passing through. National events would be celebrated by the ringing of church bells. In November 1736 the Itteringham churchwardens paid 3 shillings for 'the Ringers at Gunpowder treason'. The arrivals of Walpole and Hobart back in Norfolk were always reported in the newspapers; a flurry of activity for the estate workers and local tradesmen followed. Villagers were expected to show their respects at funerals of their great neighbours, by lining the routes; on a late September Saturday in 1756 the crowd would have seen Augustine Earle of Heydon, George Hobart and others bearing the coffin of the 1st Earl of Buckinghamshire at Blickling. Parades of a different kind - the militia marching - entertained at Holt and North Walsham. Soldiers and sailors were regular travellers through the countryside but Itteringham was given a window on another world when 'Nowles the Barbadoes man' came to the village in 1800. Presumably a sailor, no doubt he regaled the pub with tales of his life before he moved on, with the overseer's generous two shillings in his pocket.

## Markets, fairs and crimes

Market days would have been the highlight of the week, whether buying, selling or visiting. In 1705 Sir John Hobart received a royal grant allowing Aylsham to hold a general market day on Tuesday in addition to its Saturday market. The public houses would have done their best business with deals being made and general socialising taking place. The old hiring fairs were vital to annual labourers who relied on the chance to find work. John Hannant, an illiterate husbandman, used the Aylsham fair to let himself to John Read, the tanner of Itteringham for a year at 6s per week in 1765. He did the same in 1766 at 7s and 1767 at 6s for winter and 7s for summer and 6d hiring money. He was to find himself board and lodgings which he did in Itteringham and continued the full year and had full wages. When he went to work in Hackford, he claimed settlement in Itteringham based on his contracts. The fairs were replaced by petty sessions held for the purpose of hiring servants which, by 1777, were usually taking place in pubs. A boost to the trading activities of the town followed the opening of the Navigation in October 1779. The idea was first discussed at a meeting on 15th December 1772 when Lord Walpole, a firm supporter, took the chair. He was made a commissioner when the act was passed in 1773 along with Lord Buckinghamshire, J Gay, James Curteis and Thomas Robins. (Probably Thomas was of Aylsham, not Itteringham, a son of Jacob Robins.) The new canal allowed the river Bure to be used for transporting heavy goods more cheaply and quickly to the town than by road. Passengers could now go as far as Yarmouth by boat. The work had cost £6,000, way over the estimated price. The road to Aylsham from Norwich was not improved until the turnpike began in 1794.

Less edifying activities also drew onlookers. Aylsham market place was regularly used for public whippings. Often used in minor cases, these were an attempt to shame the criminal in front of his peers while at the same time, deterring others. The Aylsham bridewell, on the corner of Burgh Road and Red Lion Street, prior to its rebuilding in 1787 was very small and held only a few vagrants and the occasional prisoner. With no fireplace, no sewer and no straw it could hardly do otherwise. One 'incorrigible rogue' was sentenced to repeated whippings during his two years in the bridewell: George Armstrong received 40 lashes every six months between 1752 and 1754. The same period saw at least three others, the greatest number of lashes being the 50 each month, for 3 months, given to John Arthur for cutting down the oak trees of a Norwich alderman. On a Tuesday in April 1749, William Cork was whipped for stealing a handkerchief and in January 1771 James Painter was to be 'publicly whipped on the next market day' for stealing a pair of boots at Aylsham. In May 1785 John Pike of Cawston was sentenced to this punishment by the Norwich bench. Four years earlier he had been accused of burgling the house of 'Mr Robins' in Aylsham (possibly Bure House by Millgate Bridge). This time he had been arrested for burgling Berney Bean. Unfortunately the lash did not have the desired effect and in July he was caught yet again for stealing a coat. The sentence was a year in Wymondham bridewell.

Cawston held its 'Great Market' - a general fair - on the last Wednesday in April and a large sheep fair in August. In 1781 the Cawston Sheep Show was advertised as being held at Cawston Woodrow on Wednesday 19th August:

> Plenty of Hurdles, all shall find Civil Usage and a hearty Welcome From their humble servant Richard Andrews.

Horatio Walpole was a good supporter of local suppliers; three years earlier he paid £24 10s for 70 of Holley's lambs at Cawston 'shew'. As with all such events there were those who behaved badly: Peter Scottow an Aylsham chimney sweeper violently assaulted poor Mary Preston at the public fair in Cawston in 1769. She was minding a stall for her master John Howlett of Salle, a labourer who obviously sold provisions to make extra money. Scottow 'pulled the cloth of the stall and threw down the gingerbread, nutts, oranges, cakes and other wares' that were displayed for sale. Scottow was taken before the justice but no doubt Mary, despite being the victim, also was castigated when she got home for the wasted food.

Those returning from major markets had to run the risk of highway robbery. On an April Saturday in 1749, Mr Dewing of Oulton was leaving Norwich about 4 in the afternoon when he was robbed 'upon the Heath at the entrance into Horsford Lane', by two masked highwaymen both on horseback. They made off with over £55 pounds - a great loss but at least Dewing survived. In 1773, Edmund Nurse of Weybourne, miller, also escaped serious injury when he was assaulted by Edward Miller on the Kings Highway near North Walsham. Holding a pistol held to Nurse's breast so he was 'in fear for his life', the robber made off with seven guineas. Drinking and money-making led to other problems as Mr Rump a farmer from Hempstead discovered in 1783. North Walsham's market was held on a Thursday and at the end of the day he was wending his way home with £26 14s 6d on him. The next morning he was found dead at Oulton with his pockets turned inside-out. The inquest jury who 'sat on the body' heard he was thought to have lain there all night and brought in their verdict of accidental death. The person who first saw him was suspected of taking his money and, being threatened with prison, confessed it. As Oulton is not on the obvious route from North Walsham to Hempstead, perhaps Rump had been celebrating his day at market at the Black Boys in Aylsham and had one too many for the road. No doubt all the locals at the bar had their own theories. Drinking, as now, was a popular and dangerous pastime: on 12th March 1784 John Jeckyll, a single man, was buried at Heydon. He also had been found dead in the road, his death 'occasioned by liquor'. Perhaps he was the same 'John Jickell' who was suspected of smuggling in 1771. Robert Manning an excise officer at Heydon claimed that 'a quantity of Run Foreyn Geniva is fraudently held and concealed in the dwelling house or outbuildings in Saxthorpe [*Corpusty deleted*] with intent to defraud'.

It was not just the men who enjoyed their night life and suffered for it the next day. Edward Copeman a farmer of Kerdiston took his servant girl before the local JP in 1769. Jane Griffin had misbehaved herself by staying out the whole night in July - no doubt tempted by the long light warm evenings - without leave. Usually the Justice (here it was William Wiggett Bulwer) would just tick the girl off unless it was a regular offence. Despite risking the sack, servants were often found sneaking out at night or inviting friends into the house when the family were away. The more restrictive their situation - and many had no free time at all - the more likely the temptation to break the rules.

## Evening entertainments

Concerts, such as that of 1761 which featured violin and harpsichord, were held in the Black Boys Assembly Room in Aylsham. When the 'Aylsham Organ' was officially opened in 1769 an evening of music - including French horns - was held there in aid of the organist Mr Neal. In August 1786 *The Norwich Mercury* announced that the Aylsham Subscription concert was to be held in the town shortly. Nor was it necessary to travel to Norwich to see a play: touring companies presented entertainments at the Theatre in Oakfield Road – which was built before 1809. As far back as 1729 the town was visited by the Norwich Company of Comedians from the White Swan in Norwich.

Balls and assemblies diverted the attentions of the wives and daughters of the well-to-do, the biggest being at Norwich. Young women relied on these opportunities to catch admirers; in the middle of the century the Norwich assemblies were graced by the renowned beauties of North Norfolk: Betty St Clair of Aylmerton and Anne Barnes of Northrepps. Anne finally settled on a persistent whalebone merchant called William Russell whom she married in the summer of 1741. He bought and re-furbished the hall at Barningham - lately abandoned by the ruined Edward Paston - for them to live in.

Not to be outdone Holt and Aylsham held assemblies as well. Holt's was monthly on a variable weekday but because the guests were drawn largely from the farming community it was suspended during August and early September to allow for the harvest. The Black Boys was the venue at Aylsham for the subscription assembly held in late summer on Wednesday evenings. Two different gentlemen were named as stewards each year in the advertisements; given their status, this was to elevate the occasion - perhaps above that of Holt - not for any practical organisational reason.

> 1771 September 20th Aylsham Assembly - Earl of Buckingham and Edward Hase esq
> 1772 September 9th Aylsham Assembly - Sir Harbord Harbord Bt and WW Bulwer esq
> 1777 September 17th Aylsham Assembly - Lord Walpole and Sir Harbord Harbord

Lord Walpole paid his subscription (£4 11s in 1775) and attended when he could. While the ladies danced and sought attention, the men did business and gossiped too. At the January assembly at Aylsham in 1758 Horatio junior had chatted with John Repton the excise officer concerning the rumours about local tanner Michael Towne. Horatio of course spent time in London and like most of the aristocracy the families spent weeks or months in Bath or visiting relatives. When in Norfolk there were other parties: Horatio senior's brother, Robert Walpole the Prime Minister, gave wonderful 'Congresses' at Houghton to which all his supporters and neighbours were invited. Lasting 10 days in summer and 20 in November the celebrations were said to be so 'jovial and uproarious' that Lord Townshend retreated from his house at Raynham to Suffolk in November 1732 in disgust.

Local families would have coming-of-age parties especially where the heir was key to the success of the line. Old Robert Doughty of Hanworth Hall invited all his neighbours when his grandson Robert was 21 in October 1738. A great entertainment and a ball was held with 'a great ringing and shooting of popguns'. The boy inherited £16,000 with no conditions but, despite all his grandfather's hopes for the future, by 1744 he and his brother and sister and their uncle were all dead.

## Sport

Perhaps the greatest occasion for enjoyment by all classes, and sometimes for making a little extra money, was created by sporting events. The 18th century was the heyday of all kinds of activities from a game of bowls at the Artichoke in Itteringham to hot-air ballooning in the 1780s. Betting was also very popular with ever more extreme wagers being made in all fields. In the winter The Black Boys held cock-fights which were not finally banned until 1849. One in January 1785 was advertised as being between 'the gentlemen of Aylsham and the gentlemen of Suffolk'. The Aylsham gentlemen took on the Norwich gentlemen on 10th and 11th February 1794 when the cocks fought for '£5 a battle and £20 the odd'. The host Richard Harriman provided a good Ordinary (a celebratory meal) on both days. In 1732 a 'main of cocks' was fought as an additional attraction at one of the great social events of the year for North Norfolk – Holt race-week. On three days, the horses were raced at what is now Holt Country Park and assemblies held in the town on Tuesday and Thursday evenings. All horses had to be entered the day before at the Feathers in Holt or on the day at the starting-post, at double the fee. The range of animals entered would have been rather different from today's finely-bred specimens. To make the race fairer, no horse that had won a Royal plate within the previous two years could take part. Apart from that, it was open to all-comers, for example in 1732 *The Norwich Mercury* notified:

> At Holt upon Tuesday 4th July a Purse of 20 Guineas will be run for, by the best of three Heats, four miles each Heat, by any Horse, mare or Gelding 14 hands to carry nine stone, all above to carry weight for inches, paying one Guinea Entrance , if a Contributor, half a Guinea. On Wednesday the 5th the Town Plate value Ten Guineas will be run for, by Galloways, 14 hands to carry nine stone ... Thursday 6th a Purse of 30 Guineas will be run for, the best of three heats, four miles each Heat, by any Horse Mare or Gelding carrying eleven stone, paying two Guineas entrance, Contributor one Guinea.

Knockabout games of football, cricket and even baseball would have been played by children and young men in villages when time allowed. An opportunity for estate workers to watch a better game occurred at Blickling in August 1787. *The Norwich Mercury* reported on the cricket match in Blickling Park between the Blickling players and those who practiced on Mousehold Heath. The match had 11 men on each side and 2 innings each. Blickling won with a grand total of 143 runs to Norwich's 42. They were described as genteel players, with many spectators watching and bets running high. Major Hobart, on a visit to the Hall, distinguished himself in the game. But the Blickling side brought in 2 particularly good players from Gunton – not what the Norwich men expected.

One sport which anyone - if the weather was clear - could observe was hot-air ballooning which became fashionable in 1784. The previous November thousands had gathered on Mousehold Heath hoping to see a balloon fly. Unfortunately the basket holding a cat, dog and a pigeon could not be seen for the clouds. However a more successful flight rose from Quantrell's Gardens on 16th February 1785 and was soon followed by others in March and June, now manned by James Decker. A special run of the Norwich Post coach left Wells at 4 in the morning and collected passengers from Holt and Aylsham in time to arrive in Norwich to see the ascent. By June the following year flights were taking off from Aylsham as well. The prevailing winds often took the balloons to the south-east and sometimes deposited the fliers in the sea. Decker was flying under the patronage of the 3rd Earl of Orford – George Walpole, Horace Walpole's nephew. (Not to be confused as other writers have done, with Horace's uncle, Horatio Walpole of Wolterton who was never Lord Orford. As George was childless, Horace later became the 4th Earl and on his death the first earldom died out. Horatio's son was later made Earl in a second creation of the title.) George was a whimsical man who became passionate about sport. His enthusiasm for ballooning - he conducted a series of hydrogen balloon flights in Suffolk - led to his widespread patronage of the pastime in Norfolk. When he was watching Decker fly in Norwich he was described by Parson Woodforde as being 'in the most shabby dress'. Horace, that refined gentleman of letters, thought George's behaviour distasteful as so often he did.

## Elections

18<sup>th</sup> century elections were very different from the anonymous box-ticking formality of today. Only men who owned freehold land were able to register and, as their votes were made public, there was great competition between the candidates' camps to acquire support. Norwich was often riotous on election days, with those who could not vote adding their protests to the general hubbub. Contested results, lively crowds and drunkenness often led to violence. Like-minded voters arranged well in advance to cast their votes together, with opposing groups timed well apart:

> January 1715 The clergy who will vote for Sir Ralph & Col Earle will meet on February 18<sup>th</sup> the day of the poll for Knights of the Shire, at the Kings Tavern at 1 o'clock.

> February 1715 The clergy intending to vote for Jacob Astley and Thomas de Grey to meet at Audite Room, in the Close, near Christchurch on Friday 18<sup>th</sup> February about 3 o'clock and go in a body to the poll.

In the countryside, the elections were less visible especially in years when there was no contest; on many occasions the two members for Norfolk had been amicably selected - usually one Whig one Tory - and votes had only been required in 1734 and 1741. North-east Norfolk towns had shown a strong Whig tendency in the 1734 election (only one Tory vote in Cromer, two in Aylsham and three in Holt). However, officially every vote counted and the justices of the peace were supposed to ensure the correct names were registered.

Agents for the candidates would sometimes call on villagers to confirm their eligibility and canvass for their party, much to the amusement of potential voters. A rare notebook has survived for South Erpingham hundred for the election of the two Knights of the Shire to be held on 23<sup>rd</sup> March 1768, the first since 1741. The old allegiances to Tory and Whig were changing; many candidates stood now as independents and the rural voters - influenced by a variety of landlords - were worth cultivating. The two current members, Sir Armine Wodehouse and Thomas de Grey were vigorously opposed by Sir Edward Astley and Wenham Coke (the heir to Holkham). Each voter could vote for two men. The previous December the canvasser had noted the total votes for each candidate promised by the local parishes. Wodehouse, who had been MP since 1737, and de Grey were firm favourites with Itteringham's five freeholders and Wolterton and Wickmere's single voters. In Aylsham, by comparison, three-quarters of the voters promised for Astley and Coke. Overall the hundred was promising to cast 137 votes for Astley, 118 for Coke and only 46 and 52 for Wodehouse and de Grey.

However, there were serious confusions over the eligible names; the official had to try to assess who should be canvassed – some were not sure if they could vote on a life interest in the property, another wondered whether he or his brother had the freehold or only copyhold. No doubt the smallholders enjoyed passing the time offering political opinions and the finer points of their tenure - at length - to the man with the notebook. In Itteringham, tenant farmer Henry Blyth, who had a little land in Blickling, had said he would vote for Coke and Wodehouse but ended up not being included. On another sheet, he is noted as saying both his votes were 'with Miss Churchman', his landlady, and as she would not have been eligible, the agent added 'but I suppose Mr Masters of Walsingham carrys'. Ark (Arch') Hurrell, the shoemaker, who was erroneously given as a blacksmith, gave his promise to Wodehouse and de Grey but did not hold the necessary land value to be registered and was omitted from the printed poll book. Similarly Richard Shilleta offered to vote for the same but was not eligible – either his cottage was below the necessary value or he no longer had the freehold. Robert Jeckyll, the blacksmith who held land in Letheringsett, was noted as having hesitated and was a possible convert to Astley. Of the three who were later listed as having voted - and even then Thomas Robins esq was added in manuscript - Robert Jeckyll and Thomas voted for de Grey and Wodehouse but Richard Robins chose de Grey and Coke. At Wolterton, Walpole's steward Richard Ness, who owned his own land at Thornage and Holt, went with Wodehouse and de Grey as well. Wickmere ended up with two extra voters and all three voted like Ness.

Perhaps the best comments were made by two men in Ingworth. A weaver with some land at Thwaite said he would vote 'As Alderman Ives directs' but Thomas Wright openly told the agent 'his vote is to be sold to highest bidder'. Whether his own choice or not, Wodehouse and de Grey gained his votes on the day. In Heydon and Oulton the tactical voting for one of each pair reflected the overall picture: Astley and de Grey were elected. Such an event, with the opportunity to have a say in national affairs, would have greatly enlivened village life in the winter months of 1767-68.

## The threat of invasion

For hundreds of years, the countryside round the East Anglian coast has been on its guard against invading forces. The 18th century was full of such alarms and the events affected everyone, regardless of social standing, and would have been a constant source of rumour and gossip. Although his estate was several miles inland, Horatio Walpole was always in a state of high anxiety that Wolterton would be attacked. Fortunately several of his letters to his long-suffering steward Richard Ness, have survived. After the bloody battles in Scotland in 1715, the constant fear of the return of the Stuarts, in the shape of James II's son, Charles Edward, was real enough. A local man, Christopher Layer of Booton, who had married into the Elwin family, was executed at Tyburn in 1723 for insurrection in favour of The Great Pretender. An attempt by France to invade Essex in 1744 was only prevented by one of those fortunate storms at sea. In Wickmere that summer, a local tax called 'ammunition money' was collected by Mr Sayer. In early December 1745 the rebels who had landed in Scotland managed to push down as far as Derby, before having to retreat to Scotland. Walpole was obviously convinced they would try again and made known his fears to Ness who replied with a letter which almost sounds tongue-in-cheek:

> 1745 Dec 23 Pray how would yr Honour have me behave provided there should be an Invasion on this coast and the Invader should come to Woolterton. I am persuaded that 50 men would Defend the House against 2000 provided they bring no Cannon with them which they cannot Doe if the Horses be all Driven away.

Walpole was of course in deadly earnest and with fierce fighting continuing in Scotland into the following year, he continued to make detailed preparations. He was so anxious he not only wrote two letters in reply to one of Ness's - dating one with the wrong year - but also repeated himself in the second. He had been pestering the government for cannon defences to be placed on the north Norfolk coast without success and obviously envisaged men having to defend Wolterton, armed with bayonets to engage the rebels in hand to hand combat. Perhaps not surprisingly, given the lack of support for the Jacobites in Norfolk, Westminster preferred to deploy its resources elsewhere despite Walpole's pressure:

> 1746 April 1st I have received yours of 29th past. The Bore of my Guns at Woolterton according to your dimensions is so very small that the Bayonetts made here are infinitely too big for it. I shall send down a Bayonett by Money and I hope Christian and the other smith at Wickmere will be able to make them by the pattern and fitt them to the Guns.

> 1746 [written 1756] April 3rd I have received yours of the 29th past, the bore of the guns at Woolterton is too small for the common bayonets and therefore I suppose they are carbines. Money carrys with him (tho absent tomorrow) one of the Bayonets for the ordinary muskets, and I should be glad you would advise with Christian whether he can make them and of a suitable bore for my guns and what at price [sic] It is impossible to gett any Cannons to place on our Coast; they can't well be spared out of the Tower and the proper persons to attend and use them as occasion may offer, will be a greater expense than the Ordinance board will allow to be at for such an uncertain price.

Ten days later, he was still worrying about what size to order and typically wanted to measure the bore himself:

> 1746 April 13th Money returned home well on Sunday & I learn by him that you tell me that the Bayonett he carryed will fitt all the Guns, now that does not agree with the circle you sent me of the measure round the barrell which I think is much less than that of the Bayonet I sent you and I have directed Bayonets to be made agreeable to that circle but I shall have the bayonett back again this day, I shall be better able to judge of it.

Three days later, at the Battle of Culloden, the rebels were roundly defeated and the Young Pretender fled to France. John Christian, the blacksmith in Calthorpe, may well have missed out on a useful, if eccentric, commission. When the rebels were brought to trial in August, Walpole had tried to get his lawyer Thomas Nuthall chosen to prosecute them but only received a grovelling letter from the Treasury solicitor promising he had talked to the Attorney-General but had been outranked by the Duke of Newcastle who had another man appointed.

The country was of course still at risk; during the Seven Years' war the French planned another invasion in 1759. The British army became embroiled in the American revolution from 1775 to 1783. The government was in need of greater numbers of militia for peace both at home and abroad. After the 1789 revolution in France, Britain was engaged, almost continuously, with first the Republic and then Napoleon for over two decades. Local volunteers were supported by landowners and the poor relief system. During his worries in April 1746 Walpole had written that he had 'ordered one guinea to be payd at Norwich to every soldier & one guinea for every saylor that will enter into his Majesty's land and sea service and an advertisement I suppose will be published ... in the Norwich Mercury signifying my intentions'. His cousin George Walpole, then Lord Orford, made a similar appeal in the *Chronicle* in February 1782 when it was vital to prevent men leaving the militia at the end of their period of service:

> First, or Western Regiment of Norfolk Militia.
> This is to give Notice, that the greatest Part of the Men belonging to the said Regiment (whose Times of Service are nearly expired) have pursuant to the Act of Parliament agreed to serve again as Substitutes for three Years longer. It is therefore hereby earnestly requested that the Gentlemen acting as Deputy Lieutenants in the several Subdivisions do recommend it to all such Persons who chosen by Ballot, and do not serve for themselves, immediately to pay Nine Guineas each to Roger Kerrison, Esq., Banker, in Norwich, for a Substitute, which will be properly sworn and inrolled [sic] for each and every of them at the Regiment.
> By Order of the Right Honourable the Earl of Orford, Colonel of the above said Regiment, [signed] Edward Harcourt, Clerk of the General Norfolk Militia Meetings.

The practice of paying someone to take your place if you were chosen by ballot to join up was quite common; Horatio Walpole paid £3 5s cash to William Burrell as a volunteer for Wolterton in March 1787 and £2 12 6d to Andrew Goodwin in April 1792 as militia substitute for Wolterton. In 1795 Itteringham gave £5 5s to Mr Wegg for John Farrow's substitute, presumably repaying Walpole. In the 1760s competition arose between groups offering insurance against the bother of having to find a substitute or paying the fine. In February 1762, for 10s 6d you could be indemnified for three years by William Baldwin of Holt and John Brereton draper of Briston. They had agents in other towns including Mr Edward Piggon the surgeon at Aylsham and Thomas Dewing at Cawston. Another group of gentlemen were offering the same for only 8 shillings. They then advertised in the newspaper for: 'All clever young fellows willing to serve' who would 'Meet with good Encouragement and have their names entered for that purpose. None but very proper men will be treated with.'. Many of the yearly hired servants, particularly labourers, saw it as an opportunity: John Doughty of Oulton who had worked for William Robins in Aylsham and Mr Sands of Irmingland joined the supplementary militia in 1797. So too did Thomas Field of Corpusty who worked for Joseph Robins in Irmingland – he served for 5 years until 1802. Even those with a good trade took up the challenge: in 1802 William Barwick then an apprentice blacksmith of Corpusty (who lived in Oulton) became a substitute in the East Norfolk militia. Age and size were no barrier either: 59 year-old William Burton, a 5ft 4in worsted weaver served for two years on behalf of Thomas Burton of Itteringham, no doubt a relation. Unfortunately some saw it as easy money. *The Norwich Mercury* for April 1804 reported:

> A Deserter: James Smith of Itteringham, a labourer, of 36 years, 5' 5", dark brown hair, brown eyes, round visage & light complexion, was enrolled the 25 February to serve in the Army of the Reserve, as a Substitute of John Neale of Bessingham but deserted immediately; 5 guineas reward [for apprehending & causing to be detained in prison]. Bessingham March 27 1804.

Desertion was nothing new. Back in 1757 Ness had written to Horatio Walpole, the second baronet, about a deserter called Buck. A year later, in March 1758, he was still at large and had been seen in a gang of poachers. Walpole was anxious that local knowledge should be used to track him down:

> If anything is found out against Buck I am glad of it and hope he will be sent to the Castle as he is [a] deserter. If he should be taken up I wish you would tell Mr Herne that the officers of the regiment would gladly send people in disguise to apprehend him if they thought there was any probability of taking him. But [I] think it is really the business of the constables as they know him to be a deserter and must be best acquainted with his haunts and indeed if possible they should be obliged to do it.

Wives were deserted too; in 1759 Lord Walpole heard Martha Bell's tale. Husband Thomas an Itteringham labourer had joined the Regulars in March 1755, had returned for one night in October but had not been seen since. Martha was now pregnant by John Puxley.

Often the families of the militiamen were left in great need; Itteringham paid the parish officers of Aylsham for the wife of Thomas Gold, a militiaman, for well over a year between 1794 and 1795. In 1798 the parish paid £3 4s 4d for a substitute in the supplementary militia so that the overseer Thomas Dix would not have to serve.

Walpole also spent £1 12s in July 1790 'for Cockades'. At 6d each, he would appear to have bought 64 hat decorations from Peter Copeman of Aylsham. At this time they were probably of black silk (the Hanoverian emblem). That number seems excessive for his own liveried servants so perhaps he was supporting a local regiment. Certainly there was pride in the local volunteers: in 1804, at the height of the Napoleonic threat, the newspaper described Col Harbord's 320 men of the Blickling and Gunton Volunteer Corps of Riflemen (Blickling Rifle Corps for short) as 'a fine body of men' when they marched in Norwich and then to Yarmouth for 14 days on duty.

Among those watching the men practice for the parade might have been 59 year-old Charles Hindry, a tenant of a small Itteringham cottage. Hindry had recently given up a farm in Oulton but he had been brought up in Blickling. At the tender age of 11, around 1756, he had joined the West Norfolk Regiment of Militia as their drummer boy. After travelling for about six years, he returned to Blickling, married at 18 and stayed there for thirty years. No doubt he re-told his tales over the years to other small boys.

## Sources

The story of the holes at Mannington has been summarised by F Blomefield and CS Tomes. The fullest version, used here, is in the notes of Le Neve and Blomefield in NRO: NAS/1/2/6 Mannington. Norfolk Quarter Sessions and microfilm of Marsham papers for Assize Calendars 1753-1796; BUL 4/100, BUL 4/102/21, BUL 4/107

TNA: Norfolk Assizes ASSI 34/42; ASSI 94/531, 637, 1466, 1490, 1491, 1514

Wolterton archive: 8/42, 61, 63, 64, 68, 22/1, library G5 16

R W Ketton-Cremer, *Norfolk Portraits*, 1944; *A Norfolk Gallery*, 1948; *Country Neighbourhood*, 1951
'Norwich Pleasure Gardens', NA Vol XXXV pt III
*The Norfolk & Norwich Remembrancer and Vade Me-Cum*, 1822
Pamela Horn, *Flunkeys and Sculllions: Life below stairs in Georgian England*, 2004 - excellent on all aspects of life in service.
Jermy of Bayfield website
Norwich Newspapers

# Part 5

## THE END OF AN ERA

The Thomas Robins and Richard Robins estates are sold; the family moves away; the male line ends

# Chapter 18

## *Farewell to the Robins: 1*

---

*While their Robins cousins in Norwich (various trades), Cawston (millers and bakers) and Aylsham (farmers and other trades) flourished for many generations, the Robins families in Itteringham died out in the male line. The circumstances however were fascinating, both for the Thomas Robins line in the Manor House and Richard Robins of Itteringham Hall. Their estates, totalling fewer than 580 acres, were sold within a three year period to the Harbords of Blickling and the Walpoles of Wolterton.*

## The end of the Thomas Robins line and his Manor House estate

Thomas Robins 3 died in 1782 unmarried and childless; the blood line was running out. He had only one sister, Mary, who had been baptised in Bradfield Independent meeting house in 1724. She had married William Creasey in March 1749 in Norwich Cathedral Church.

### Mary Robins and the Creasey family

By the time of his burial in Martham in April 1797 at the age of 79, William Creasey esq owned manors and farms in and around Martham and a number of properties in St Peter Mancroft parish in Norwich generating over £430 per year in rents. In addition he and Mary had her mother's property in Tunstead and Sloley, together generating about the same rental value; after her brother's death Mary inherited Thomas's Itteringham estate. As they had substantial property elsewhere, it is very unlikely that the Creaseys ever came to live at the Manor House in Itteringham. Instead they let the property to John Bell from Oulton who, as well as living in the Manor House and running the farm, acted as trustee for the Creaseys when they bought 98-99 The Street in 1785. They kept the estate intact for another 12 years.

In 1798, almost exactly a year after her husband, Mary died at the age of 73 and was also buried in Martham. Mary and William Creasey had no sons to inherit all their wealth, so the property was divided between their four daughters; they each received about £1,000 as dowry and a share of the sale value of the family lands.

One daughter, Diana Creasey, never married and was left her share of property and a disproportionate share of Mary's household goods, furniture, plate, china, jewels, apparel and worked pictures. Of the other three daughters, Jane married Robert Purdy, a Norwich woolcomber in October 1777. They were to inherit the Tunstead property where their eldest son, Robins Purdy, became a farmer succeeded by his son George. In 1786 Ann married John Ewing of Cringleford where William Creasey Ewing was born in 1787. William went on to become a well-known antiquarian – one of the earliest members of the committee of the Norfolk and Norwich Archaeological Society and a contributor of a number of articles to their journal from the late 1840s. His son John William Ewing was a noted nurseryman, both in partnership with the Mackie family at Lakenham and at the Ewing property in Eaton.

Elizabeth Creasey married Joseph Cookson esq of Westminster, an excise man, in 1787 in Great Yarmouth. The son of Thomas Cookson and Sarah Hull who had married in April 1749 in St George Mayfair, Joseph was from a comfortable London family, although being an exciseman was both dangerous and unpopular. In addition to lands left by William, Mary left Elizabeth and Joseph her lands in Mundesley and Gimingham. Elizabeth was also favoured with her mother's gold watch and chain with seal and trinkets on it, her best mourning ring and all the 'family pictures'. Have portraits of the Robins family survived in the possessions of the descendants of Joseph and Elizabeth? Mary also left a quarter share in the residue of her estate to Elizabeth alone, with a specific comment that it was not to be used to pay her husband's present or future debts. This hints at the unhappy marriage of Elizabeth and Joseph.

Cookson, then of St Mary Lambeth, first made his will in 1795 and added a codicil in April 1799 immediately before his death. By the rather mean-spirited original wording he made no provision for his wife, other than leaving her the interest on the £1,000 which he had received from William Creasey on their wedding day. This was only for the lifetime of the Creaseys, after which Joseph bequeathed the capital and its interest to his mother and after her death to his brothers George and Charles Norris Cookson, both then Captains in the Royal Artillery. He 'supposed his wife would be left independent' at her parents' death. The codicil expressed his hope that his wife would not take the third share of his funds to which she was entitled since she 'will have a very ample income'. Instead he wanted the interest on his money to be shared between his own relations. He wrote that his brothers' children would have nothing in the event that their parents died. This was clearly not the case. Both his brothers left wills and George's referred to his pre-1797 marriage settlement and the £5,800 which the couple had received and which was obviously largely still intact at his death in 1835. Charles's will proved in 1830 showed him as of Kenton House in Devon – in a landed estate. Both were Lt-Generals by their death. That Elizabeth and Joseph had an unhappy marriage was recorded on the reverse of the codicil and signed by Joseph:

> I hope my brothers will act with strict justice and liberality towards my wife for tho we have lived very unhappily together in this world I forgive and hope we shall be reunited and together in the enjoyment of everlasting happiness in the world to come in the name and in the merciful mediation of our blessed redeemer Jesus Christ amen. Where I have not been clear and explicit I hope there will be an amicable and generous accommodation on all sides.

Elizabeth made her will in 1818, then of Elkins Row, Bayswater Terrace, and she died in 1825. Needless to say there was no mention of her husband's family. She had no children and left her estate, including her share of the Martham lands, to her nephews William Creasey Ewing and the three Purdy boys – Robins, William and George. Ewing was to be executor (with William Rising) and was favoured with the mourning ring that Mary Creasey had made on the death of her husband and also Elizabeth's secretaire and its library of books. No mention was made of any family portraits, but if Elizabeth had them it seems quite likely that they may have passed to Ewing.

On the other hand Diana too ended up living in London and may have had a hand in sorting out her sister's affairs. She made her own will the year after her sister died and it was proved in 1834. She was of Salisbury Place New Road in Marylebone (not far from her sister's last address) and like her sister asked to be buried in Martham. Her executors were William Creasey Ewing and the Reverend Thomas White Holmes of Martham. Holmes was left her evangelical magazines in trust for his village library (and *White's Directory* of 1845 credits her with leaving the 3% dividends on £400 of consols for clothing and schooling of six poor children there). Her estate was left equally to her four nephews and their children, with one or two singled out for specific minor legacies. No mention was made of family portraits.

In 1797 William Creasey had made his good friends Thomas Wall, a Yarmouth linen draper and Robert Rising a farmer in West Somerton his executors. A year later Thomas Wall was called on again, for Mary's will. As Robert Rising had died just after Creasey, Wall's co-executor was now William Rising of Martham Moregraves, Robert's son.

## Sale of the estate

In 1798 Wall and Rising's major task was to manage the negotiations to sell the Itteringham property for the best price they could raise for the Creasey girls' benefit and to do so with reasonable speed. There were two obvious potential buyers: Horatio Walpole and the heirs of the 2nd Earl of Buckinghamshire. Ten years' earlier, Robert Copeman, the Blickling steward, had approached Creasey to discuss buying the estate. A letter written by Walpole in May 1789 referred to the event but added that Lord Buckinghamshire had told him he was not interested and that Copeman had been 'too quick off the mark'. Wall, knowing of this, gave first refusal to Horatio in August 1798 'at no less than £12,000' a sum he asserted had been offered for the estate ten years previously. Walpole was interested in the estate but hesitant in responding to Wall's description of the property and his valuation. The Blickling estate, now owned by the late Earl's daughter Caroline and her husband William Harbord, was also interested but fearful of showing its hand too early, Colonel Harbord instructed his agent John Dugmore to keep the true identity of the purchaser secret.

Summaries of Wall's 'particular' of the estate, final conveyance papers and some associated letters have survived, describing the extent of the Thomas Robins holdings: the manor of Bintry Hall in Itteringham; the house, tan office and 65 acres of John Read (the tannery and farm in Bintry); the house and its attached shop of John Fish with the 2-acre field at the back; next door the smithy and cottage of Robert Jeckyll and his 2 acre field up the road; 5 cottages split into 13 tenements; and 5 tenements that had formerly been 2 cottages. The capital messuage of Thomas Robins, occupied by Richard Garnham, which with the farm house at Dairy farm amounted to 239 acres and another 17 acres described as lands woods and canals which would have been the meadow in front of the Manor House and the 'park' on Broom hill.

Initially Wall had pitched for more than £12,000 in an estimate of the estate's value based on rents totalling about £400 times more than 30 years – a high multiplier and an overstated rent roll. In an accompanying letter he described the estate as entirely freehold and stressed that it was a manor and that the Manor House itself and timber (worth £800, he said) were not taken into account in his calculation. Only two of the tenants had any protection from ejection or rent increases - Garnham and Read - and their leases were due to expire in 1803 and Michaelmas 1799 respectively. This implied an opportunity to raise rents in the not too distant future.

Correspondence shows that there was in fact stiff competition to buy the estate. The Walpole view of events appears in the correspondence between the now elderly Horatio, Lord Walpole, and his son Colonel Horatio Walpole of Burlington Street London (often away at some military camp or other in East Anglia). They relied heavily on their agent, Thomas Glover Ewen esq of Norwich, who was asked to value the estate for the Walpole family and to advise on what to offer to Thomas Wall who the Walpoles believed was under some pressure to sell the property quickly to pay the legacies.

The letters underline how much Lord Walpole wanted the Robins estates - both contiguous to his park - to add to his Wolterton estate. They also indicate that unfortunately in old age Horatio had inherited his father's micro-managing style, not necessarily to good effect. He and his son, the third Horatio, together with their advisers, mishandled the campaign for the Thomas Robins estate.

On 5th January 1798 Walpole, who complained of having few realisable assets, wrote to his son suggesting he should buy the estate with the legacy recently left him by his cousin Horace Walpole 4th Earl of Orford:

> Dear Hor,
>
> Your being troubled with this letter is occasioned by the renewal of a report that Mrs Creasy the life proprietor of the estate (late Robins) at Itteringham is in a very declining state of health. On her death this property must be sold as I am credibly informed. I flatter myself it will first be offered to this family. I cannot with any certainty ascertain the price which will be asked but I apprehend not less than eleven thousand pounds. It would not be prudent to omit the opportunity of making the purchase if possible tho' the circumstances of the times will I fear create some difficulties, the little money which I have in the funds from the produce of the sale of timber cannot be sold out but at a considerable discount. Unless therefore you continue to find the money which may be wanted on the security of the £10,000 you must receive sooner or later from the executor of Lord Orford the point must be given up.
> I shall feel much hurt at this event, my continuance in this world must of course be short, it therefore concerns me very little. The estate is I believe estimated at £300 per annum and upwards. If you can manage this business to your liking I mean to decline the having any concern whatever in the conduct or direction as to repairs rent etc. If I find it necessary to request any addition for my own convenience I will pay a full and adequate rent. Unless therefore the purchase can be made agreeable to the above plan there must be an end to the business. The assessed taxes, however wise and necessary, with the payments to my children will be a full and sufficient weight upon my shoulders. There is no immediate hurry for an answer, I wish you to give the business full consideration, the real comfort of this place is much concerned in the event.
>
> I am ever yours
>
> Walpole

His son's much worked-on draft reply is folded in with the letter. His tone was formal, even a bit obsequious, yet firm underneath – he would not be pushed by his father into unnecessarily prompt action:

> My dear Lord,
>
> I no longer delay answering your obliging letter lest I appear either inattentive to your lordship or indifferent to the subject itself though there does not appear to me any necessity for immediate decision however prudent it may to keep it under consideration. The estate is not yet offered to sale and whenever it is time must be given for the person wishing to purchase to consider the offer as well as to procure the money and I cannot conceive that was it now on sale the proprietors would expect to be paid for it before Michaelmas next. I think in a former letter upon this subject you believed that a part of the money might remain on the estate [a mortgage on his father's estate is implied] and that you proposed to sell a small detached farm on the Suffolk side of the country the produce of which might be applied

towards the purchase. I believe it would be extremely difficult to borrow so large a sum as £10,000 upon my legacy nor was it paid could I spare the whole of that sum. I am ready to lend your lordship £6,000 out of it, at whatever proportionate rate of interest the estate shall be found to produce. It is far from my wish that your lordship should have any additional burden upon you. I have sufficient experience of your goodness but in all feel the weight of the times and what with the additional taxes and other unforeseen though melancholy events I shall have an expense of at least £600 more than three months ago I had reason to expect.

When Walpole wrote to his son on 22nd July 1798 he said again that he would not intervene further but then proposed a complete negotiating strategy:

Mr Wall of Yarmouth executor to the late Mrs Creasy and agent for the estate at Itteringham has I am informed expressed being surprised that this family have not appeared anxious for the purchase of this estate as the contiguity must be a great object to the possessor of Wolterton. On being told the valuation was too much he answered £12,000 would be accepted but no abatement made of this sum, that he made no doubt he should sell at this price before Michaelmas next at which time the estate must be sold. He said he would give no answer to the applications he has received till this family had refused all further treaty.

I therefore now repeat my firm and final resolution to give up all interference in this business in any shape whatever either as to treating for the purchase or future management of the estate. You are fully acquainted with every inconvenience from the contiguity, experience of 40 years has fully convinced me of the nuisance arising from this property having been in the possession of other hands. I am apprised of the worst [and] can therefore without repining undergo the same vexation for the remainder of my life.

Tho' perhaps it would be imprudent to appear over solicitous yet I think some answer should be given in the course of next month. You may therefore enter into correspondence with Mr Wall as you think proper. Some offer I think must be made on your part the price which is at present asked appears too much, perhaps you may think £10,000 a sufficient offer, you may then consider if this sum is refused how far you would make a further advance. The present rent amounts to £322 1s 3d it will I should think pay the sum of £270 per annum [ie, after taxes and repairs], that I may not exceed I will compute the income at £250 the estate is certainly much out of repair.

I am willing in this case to contribute my assistance as far as I am able with a proviso that my income is not diminished. I will give my consent to the sale of the Pulham estate, a farm on which there is no lease which rents at £110 mostly freehold. I should hope this farm would sell for the sum of £4000 perhaps £5000. There is some timber upon the estates in this vicinity which I should think would amount to £1500 or £2000. There are also the fee farm rents which may be sold, if possible I should wish to reserve these or a part towards the purchase of accidental intermixed property either in this vicinity or elsewhere. I must inform you that Miss Churcham [Mary Churchman, owner of Hill farm] has some lands which are intermixed with this property of Creasy, the quantity is 20 acres. I have often and even very late made my request that she would sell these lands but have not hitherto been successful. These lands we must hope to obtain in due time as it certainly may be inconvenient in the present state.

A great part of the money will be permitted to remain on the estate. Mr Wall's name is Thomas, he lives at Yarmouth is a linen draper and is very artful shrewd sensible fellow. There is I believe upon the estate timber to the amount of £200 or £500 value, since my treaty with them about ten years since there has been sold to the amount of £800 I believe £1000 tis certainly an object. I have therefore I hope explained the whole sufficient for opinion how to act.

I am most affectionately yours

Walpole

PS I have enclosed Mr Wall's particular I have a copy you need not therefore return it to me.

The enclosure summarised the estate as 260a 0r 18p in Garnham's farm and 65a 1r 23p in Read's. Wall assumed an average rent of 20s which would produce £325 10s per annum, with £20 more from Read's tan office, £16 from John Fish's rent at the shop and for his 2a 0r 35p field, £12 from Jeckyll for the smithy and 2a 0r 15p field and £33 12s 6d from the 18 tenements. The estate was just short of 330 acres and it was noted that there was common of just over 116 acres (in which the estate would have some rights). In fact, through Wall's perhaps deliberate exaggeration, this overstated the rents at £407, which shortly afterwards were found by Ewen's work to total £325, with potential to raise them to perhaps £351. However at this stage Wall was suggesting a multiple of 35, thereby hoping to make a top price of £14,245. He did concede that there were £30 of taxes and free rents to deduct from the annual rent roll, which would bring the valuation down by £1,050. Nonetheless Wall's tough early stance in pursuit of £12,000 or above was off-putting to the Walpoles.

On 2nd August 1798 Horatio wrote to his son again, approving of his appointment of Mr Ewen to advise on the deal. Ewen was well spoken of by Nathaniel Kent the experienced land valuer and agricultural commentator:

> I this day received your letter dated yesterday, I approve your employing Mr Ewen he is I am informed a very clear headed sensible man and has been recommended by Kent to Mr Anson in business relating to the raising of farms where Kent wished not to interfere on account of intimate connection and friendship. This estate will I fear not be purchased otherwise than at a high price I think I should stick hard at ten thousand paid. I offered £9000 ten years since tis impossible to determine at present upon a certainty. If you should judge it expedient that Ewen should look over the premises and he will write a letter to Mr Wegg he shall be ready to attend him, I mention his writing to Mr Wegg least I should not be in the way, tho' this is very probable.
>
> A daily post is to be appointed by way of experiment in the course of next week to Aylsham.
>
> I am etc
>
> Walpole

On 19th August Ewen wrote to Colonel Walpole:

> Sir, ... on Friday I went over to Wolterton and very luckily found my Lord Walpole and Mr Wegg both at Home - I looked over the Itteringham estate with a good deal of attention and inclosed I have given you my idea of <u>the marketable price to any indifferent person</u> and I am confident no man will give a greater advance when the leases are out on the two first articles than I have put upon them. Indeed the present tenants, who are both good farmers, told me they would not hire again at any advance, but perhaps we are not to pay much attention to such an assertion. I took but little notice of the timber but I should think that if the estate was stripped as some speculating purchaser might be inclined to do, it would amount to nearly £300. The buildings are extremely numerous and none of them in good repair. They must necessarily therefore cost a large annual sum.
>
> Now Sir, you must be your own judge how far you will go in paying for <u>convenience</u>, for convenient it certainly is and you ought to have it, but I must say where it my case, I would go without it for ever before I would give £12,000 for it. It is a price out of bounds and I will venture to say Mr Wall will not find a Purchaser at that sum or even at 9,000 guineas which I think I understood my Lord Walpole has been offered for it.[sic]
>
> I should be very sorry that any advice of mine should be the means of your losing the estate but were it my case I would decline any further treaty for it ... if however you think I can be of any use in going over to Mr Wall I will do so with pleasure, as soon as I have your instructions.

Ewen's valuation of the properties adds to the description of the estate given in the later sale deeds. The Manor House was 'a small mansion house and offices' with two barns, stables and a number of outhouses. It also had a farm house, with two barns, stables and other outbuildings, confirming that a house had been erected on the Dairy farm site by Thomas Robins. Mr Garnham of the Manor House had provided Ewen with a detailed list of tenants and their rents. His list totalled £325 for the lot, which was much lower than Wall's rather fanciful particular. Garnham's list was likely to be the more accurate as he may have been acting as local rent collector for the Creaseys as well as being their chief tenant:

| Rents | £ | s | d |
|---|---|---|---|
| Richard Garnham | 200 | | |
| John Read | 63 | | |
| John Fish | 16 | | |
| Robert Jeckell | 12 | | |
| Miss Dippell [Dyball] | 4 | | |
| Charles Brett | 2 | 10 | |
| John Newell | 2 | 5 | |
| Samuel Pygall | 2 | | |
| William Alexander | 2 | | |
| Matthew Mitchell | 1 | 11 | 6 |
| Robert Ayton | 2 | 2 | |
| Robert Bruce | 2 | 2 | |
| James Brett | 2 | 12 | 6 |
| Thomas Hurrell | 2 | | |
| Ark Hurrell | 1 | 11 | 6 |
| Sarah Sendall | 1 | 6 | |
| John Hannant | 1 | 16 | |
| John Lee | 1 | 5 | |
| Stephen Bunn | 1 | | |
| John Bird | 1 | | |
| Thomas Bird | 1 | | |
| Dorothy Bird | 1 | 1 | |
| Elizabeth Bruce | 1 | | |
| | | | |
| Total | 325 | 2 | 6 |

For the main 260 acre farm, Ewen reckoned the rent, if on a new lease, was worth just £220 and the smaller farm at Bintry of 65 acres with the farmhouse, tanning office, two barns, stables and other outbuildings, worth a new rent of £70. He judged the total rents to be worth at most £351 per year, or £279 after taxes and an allowance of £42 per year for 'repairs on an average, the buildings being very much out of repair, will cost at least £12 per cent annually'. Ewen took a multiple of 28 years as reasonable and arrived at a total valuation of about £7,900, including £200 for timber.

It seemed for a while that the younger Walpole had been right in his belief that the following Michaelmas would be the deadline and that there was no great urgency in the negotiations, but in the spring he began to worry at the numbers of new enquirers. On 19th April 1799 Ewen wrote to reassure him and to suggest an offer be made:

> Sir ... that curiosity should lead many people to take a view of the Itteringham estate I do not at all wonder at, as Mr Wall's advertisement was a very <u>flowery</u> one. I do not think any of the three persons named as likely to be purchasers and the two from the other side of Fakenham I think likely to be farmers that I know and if so it will not suit them as they want immediate occupation and of course a five years lease will prevent them. As you seem a little alarmed about these people, I have sent a trusty friend to Mr Wall to see how the land lies and if he finds a fair opportunity, he is to make an offer of £8500 and then to fight his way as far short of £9000 as he can and perhaps an offer of £1000 paid down and the rest at Michaelmas would close the business which I hope will be the case. He was not however to exceed £9000 As soon as I receive his report I will forward it to you.

Two days later, he could report, still with some optimism:

> My ambassador to Mr Wall called upon me yesterday and I hope I have done no harm in sending him, as it has brought Mr Wall to acknowledge that he had no judge as to the real value of the estate and also determined him to take the opinion of some person conversant in these matters before he would accept

my friends offer of £9000 and he has promised my friend faithfully that he will not sell to any person whatever before he gave him an answer, unless anyone should come forward and give him £10,000 so I think there is no occasion for you to feel any alarm for the late visitors for I am confident he will not find a better customer than yourself.

When anything further occurs I will trouble you.

Sadly his faith in Wall's promise was misplaced. Just two months later, on 20th June, a rather nervous Ewen wrote from Aylsham to say he had misjudged the situation; the Walpole limit of £9,000 had not been enough and the estate had been sold:

I am extremely sorry to hear at this place what I suppose you may have been acquainted with before, that we have lost the Itteringham estate. I cannot at present learn who is the purchaser but I understand the price of it was from 9,000 guineas to something under 10,000 and my intelligencer says a most enormous sum and more than a thousand pounds beyond its real value.

I feel very sorry indeed for this matter turning out as it has done, fear you [think I] should have misled you, as you were at one time inclined to have given £10,000 for it.

Still hopeful of a successful outcome, he cryptically wrote again on 12th July:

I have learned who is the purchaser of the Itteringham estate but strange as it may appear my mouth is completely sewn up and I must not tell you - however as it may in some measure relieve your mind, I conceive (although I do not know it) that the purchaser must offer it to you, and should such a thing happen you will of course not discover that you thought it possible. Time must of course unfold this riddle very soon and I hope my conception will not prove abortive.

Again he was mistaken. Time revealed that Harbord had clinched the deal and was not of the view that he need offer the estate to Walpole. Harbord, equally determined to acquire the estate, had been better served by his agents over the price. Dugmore's final bill, sent to Colonel Harbord in January 1800, showed that in May 1799 he had made a survey and valuation of the estate, valuing it at £9,327 plus £781 for the timber. Wall, when he learnt of this, reduced his price to £10,750. He stressed that the tenements were under-let, implying that the rents could be readily increased. He insisted on an absolute minimum of 10,000 guineas.

Dugmore noted that the two main farm leases were normal, except for an odd covenant which allowed Garnham to deduct 10% of his produce before calculating the tithe payment – presumably some long standing deal to the benefit of the owner of the estate agreed with one of Itteringham's rectors in the distant past. (From the early 18th century Itteringham church terriers showed a modus of 8 shillings in lieu of tithes from the farm 'anciently called the Manor of Byntree Hall'. Perhaps this arrangement had been incorporated into Garnham's lease as a discount on his tithe.)

By late May, Wall had conceded to talk pounds not guineas with Dugmore and in June 1799 they signed articles of agreement: the Robins/Creasey 329 acre estate (generating almost exactly £1 per acre rent) was sold to Colonel William Assheton Harbord (later Lord Suffield) of Blickling for £9,710, including the timber and allowances for lease oddities – remarkably close to Walpole senior's original view of the realistic market price. Dugmore rather unctuously waved his 1% fee on completion, writing to Harbord to say he thought it was too much and asking Harbord to pay him whatever he thought appropriate for making the deal: 'I cannot help thinking that the result is a very great sum; and I must request, if you are of a similar opinion, that you will make any deductions you think proper, assuring yourself that, whatever you may pay me, it will be most perfectly satisfactory to me'. Curiously, in the same letter, Dugmore referred to making contact with a surgeon in Ormesby named Mr Jeffries who he thought was connected to 'young Robins'. Might this have been a distant relation of Mary Creasey's mother, Mary Jefferies? It appears that they were trying to trace young Richard Story Robins, obviously without much luck. As Richard was about to come into the Itteringham Hall estate in just a few months' time when he reached 21, it is clear that Harbord was hoping to buy all the old Robins property in Itteringham.

The Walpoles must have been hopping mad - certainly with Harbord - but remained calm in writing to each other. On 22nd July 1799 Walpole senior wrote:

Dear Hor,

We have been truly unfortunate in the non acquisition of the estate at Itteringham, it appears to me a most ungracious act, I should not have entertained an idea of attempting to purchase an estate under the like circumstances.

This event has however inclined me much to purchasing in this neighbourhood whenever an opportunity may offer, and I think it not impossible to accomplish this business perhaps in the end with advantage to this family. You know that we have a very extensive property immediately adjoining to that of Mr Coke [at Burnham] that he would I make no doubt give a considerable price even for a part thereof. Some very convenient property will shortly be disposed in this neighbourhood, the late Peter Elwin's [at Saxthorpe] will ere long be offered for sale as Mr Ewen told me the other day. He has promised to inform me as soon as the family have settled the plan. He has in some measure the management of this property either as trustee or executor.

The estate also adjoining to these premises at Itteringham may possibly also be offered for sale within a short time. If possible I think it would be wished to prevent Mr Harbord from coming up by the park pale in every direction. This estate claims a paramountship [manorial lordship] which I have never allowed but in certain person's hands it may give trouble.

I have wrote this much for your consideration, nothing however can be arranged till you have an opportunity of passing some few days in the country, this is left entirely to your option, I shall only add that if you have an inclination to increase your property near home it may be done with less difficulty during my life.

I have only to add that Mr Coke would have purchased the estate at Itteringham, having been informed that it was upon sale he refused to treat thinking this measure would have the appearance of forcing us to change property against our inclinations. This is at least to his credit and does him honour. Mr Kent suggested to Mr Coke this plan.

With best wishes from all here I am yours most affectionately

Walpole

One week later he wrote again regarding the possibility of sale of Burnham land to Wenham Coke of Holkham and the possibility of getting the Saxthorpe estate. He was adamant the Harbords should not enlarge their lands:

... Coke is ignorant [of possible offer of Burnham to him] ... he lodged here one night on his way from the Assizes, he told Lady Walpole that he heard the estate at Itteringham was sold, the purchasing this estate was suggested to him, that he had declined the proposal because it would have the appearance of forcing this family to make an exchange at Burnham and would be a very ungrateful return for the support he had received by my interest in the County.

[He suggests that] Mr Ewen value the Burnham estate and Mr Kent value the estate at Saxthorpe (which I think should not be lost at all events). The Harbord family will smuggle all the estates in the county if possible, these have a large plan for future events ...

I am ever your affectionate

Walpole

As we shall see, Walpole beat Blickling to the Richard Robins estate the following year but continued to covet the lost Thomas Robins estate. Harbord was obviously furious that the Itteringham Hall land, nearer his estate, had gone to Walpole and wrote to say he wanted it. His son's carefully worded letter to Harbord in late October 1802 proposed 'an exchange of lands adjoining the Park at Wolterton'. The proposition seemed a very reasonable one:

Sir

My Lord Walpole received from Mr Ewen your obliging message relative to the exchange of some land adjoining the park at Wolterton and I am concerned that being obliged to go to Town prevents my again waiting upon you on that business. On looking over the farm which Ld W lately purchased of Mr Robins, I do not see any land which appears a desirable object to you, but if there should be any, and you will have the goodness to point them out, every attention will be paid to your proposal. I freely confess that the estate you bought of Mr T Robins's executors on this side of the river is a very desirable object to us, not from its contiguity only but because the River as it ought to be would then become the boundary of the two properties.

If therefore you can be prevailed upon as an act of kindness to part with the land we are perfectly ready to make over to you any manorial or other rights we may have in Itteringham convenient to you, or in the event of Inclosing the Common such allotments as fall to Ld Walpole share will be at your option to purchase.

In short Sir as neither Ld W or myself have any wish to interfere with any plans you may have in agitation either for improving or increasing your estate on the south so we are desirous of making ours as entire as we can on the north of the River, preserving that as the boundary between us. Having thus stated our ideas upon a subject which concerns both families we are ready to attend to any proposal you may at your leisure think fit to suggest should not the above meet your approbation.

... H W

However Harbord did not bother to reply to the first letter and Walpole wrote to Ewen at the beginning of the following year. Ewen's answer implied that Harbord was not interested in giving up the Manor House farm and had come up with feeble excuses. In his last letter dated 16th January 1803 Horatio junior gave up any pretence of diplomatic negotiation:

Sir

We are much obliged to you for the trouble you have taken on our account. I was only anxious to learn whether Col Harbord had received my letter and the subject certainly required consideration [words deleted] the reason Col H now gives for not letting Ld W have Garnhams farm, namely the beauty of the wood (as a prospect from Blickling), is too trifling for anyone to suppose for a moment that it is the only one, and the fear of a stranger getting it would be equally done away [with]. And my letter was sufficiently explicit at least as to a general outcome but I believe the Col wants to get both ends of the stuff of which we have one at present and it will be to our fault if he does. As he sets more value upon the game than we do should a carr Ld W has opposite this wood be any inducement we shall not object to his having it provided the River be turned or [on?] our side. But this is not to be parted with unless he lets us have the whole of his estate on this side of the river ... this letter [much deletion] you may communicate the whole or any part of this to the Col when a convenient opportunity offers ...

most obliged  HW

Horatio later managed to buy the shop and associated cottages, in 1816, from Harbord, then Lord Suffield but no other part of the Thomas Robins estate. By 1822 Blickling's tenants in Itteringham still included some of the earlier families. Richard Garnham remained in the main Manor farm, William Brown had replaced John Read in the tannery, and Henry Hall was now the blacksmith. In the cottages (no longer separately described) were: Joshua Ayton, Elizabeth Bird, John Doyley, Benjamin Hancock, Thomas Hurrell, Thomas Hurrell the younger, Edmund Jeckyll, Itteringham poor overseers, William Pooley, Richard Pygall, Joseph Reynolds and John Chambers.

Since Thomas Robins's day, the smithy and its small cottage, the cottages at Dairy farm and those in the Manor House farmyard and the front of Big Yard have disappeared. The Wolterton Road east house has been rebuilt and extended. The cluster of buildings around the shop is intact and might be somewhat recognisable to Thomas, as would 98-100 The Street. Apart from the shop, his estate remained in Blickling hands and is now part of the National Trust estate.

## Postscript: Summary of schedule of title deeds relating to the Thomas Robins/Creasey estate in Itteringham

Pinning down the exact circumstances of each of the Robins family's acquisitions is not possible: not all Robins family deeds survive and there are no family papers. In particular the purchase by Richard Robins of the Nowers estate cannot be precisely identified. However, enough survives, including some detail in the final sell-off of the family property, to be sure of what they held and roughly when they acquired each parcel. In addition to a spread of lands around the parish, a majority of the houses in the centre of the village in the eighteenth century belonged to the Thomas Robins line including their Manor House. The Richard Robins line did not expand materially out of their base at Itteringham Hall, now White House farm (although they did have a farm in Ingworth and Erpingham near the parish boundary with Calthorpe). The sustained effort to build up the Thomas Robins estate was remarkable as seen in this schedule of the main events:

<u>The main estate</u>

| | |
|---|---|
| 14th Jan 1672 | Deeds Roger Potts esq to Richard Robins blacksmith |
| 26th Sep 1682 | Deed William Grand to Richard Robins |
| 13th Jul 1688 | Probate of will of Richard Robins the elder |
| 28th Jan 1690-91 | Deed Thomas Robins to William Robins and William Robins blacksmith in trust for his daughter Mary |
| 18th Nov 1695 | Acquittance by Mathew Miller tanner of Hunworth of £200 to Lydia his wife, daughter of Richard Robins – witnessed by Robert Rose |
| 29th Dec 1783 | Administration of Thomas Robins estate granted to his sister Mary Creasey 'Mary Creasey, you having been first duly sworn upon the holy evangelists ...' |
| 1-2 Nov 1784 | William Creasey and Mary in trust to Wall and Rising (and subsequent wills of William and Mary Creasey making Wall and Rising executors) |
| Oct 1799 | Estate sold to The Hon William Assheton Harbord of Blickling, Colonel of His Majesty's Regiment of Norfolk Fencible Light Dragoons [volunteers] |

<u>Bintry</u>

| | |
|---|---|
| 14th Oct 1656 | Deed John Gay and Martha and Robert Gay to Luke Gay |
| 27-8th Mar 1689 | Deed Richard Gay to Thomas Robins |
| 20-22nd Apr 1691 | Deed Richard Gay to Thomas Robins |
| 13-14th Feb 1700-01 | Deed in trust Thomas Robins and Mary to the 2 William Robins |

<u>Main estate add-ons</u>

| | |
|---|---|
| Mar & Apr 1696 | Deeds Sir Roger Potts to Thomas Robins (TR acquired the farm near Wolterton parish boundary and paid off various Potts debts) |
| 29th Mar 1697 | Deed Thomas Robins of Heydon to Thomas Robins of Itteringham |
| 17th Feb 1701-02 | Deed Sir Roger Potts to Thomas Robins |
| 27-8th Apr 1697 | Deed John Bell jnr gent & Hester to Thomas Robins – 5 acres in Muckle Meadow Hirne and nearby |

<u>The shop site</u>

| | |
|---|---|
| Dec 1711 – Mar 1712 | Various deeds between Charles Jackson butcher and Aaron Heath butcher conveying the premises to Thomas Robins. CJ and AH both then of Halvergate but CJ heir of CJ late grocer of Itteringham |

<u>Nowers lands</u>

| | |
|---|---|
| 7-8th Jan 1711-12 | Richard and Clement Robins to Thomas Robins – part of Nowers manor |

<u>Wills and exchanges</u>

| | |
|---|---|
| 25-6th Oct 1717 | James Grey esq to Thomas Robins gent – meadows on Wolterton parish boundary |
| 29-30th Jan 1723-24 | Thomas Robins (1) and Thomas (2) his son in trust to Daniel Robins at marriage of Thomas jnr and Mary Jefferies |
| 1725-26 | Will of William Robins |
| 5th May 1726 | Deed Horatio Walpole to William and Richard Robins |

| | |
|---|---|
| 17-18th June 1728 | Deed Richard Robins to Thomas Robins – 14 acres in 4 closes in Wolterton in the fork of the 2 roads near the Stulps, which had been exchanged to RR by Walpole. £250 |
| 1732 | Will of Thomas Robins |
| 12th Apr 1749 | Deed by William Creasey (marriage to Mary Robins sister of Thomas 3) |
| Oct-Nov 1755 | Deeds exchanging lands near Wolterton parish boundary between Thomas Robins 3 and Horatio Walpole - the old Potts/Purdy/Daniel Robins farm, now of 95 acres plus house and barn - creates title for property conveyed to TR 1 by the will of William Robins of Heydon |

**Field behind 98-100 The Street and 100**

| | |
|---|---|
| 28th Apr 1721 | Will of Richard Flaxman |
| 1736, 1738 & 1744 | Deeds Flaxman heirs to Thomas Plaford |
| 8-9th Oct 1753 | Deed Thomas Plaford to Thomas Bond (100) |
| 16-17th May 1763 | Deed Thomas Bond to Thomas Robins (100) |
| 29th Dec 1783 | Administration of Thomas Robins's estate granted to his sister Mary Creasey |
| 1-2 Nov 1784 | William Creasey and Mary in trust to Wall and Rising (and subsequent wills of William and Mary Creasey making Wall and Rising executors) |

**98-99 The Street**

| | |
|---|---|
| 1744 | Thomas Plaford as for the field behind, but retains the cottages in 1753 |
| 15th Oct 1763 | Deed Thomas Plaford to Ark Hurrell and Ark Hurrell mortgage loan from James Thirtle |
| 4-5th Apr 1785 | Deed mortgage redeemed and Hurrell sold to William Creasey (John Bell as Creasey's trustee) |

## Sources

NRO: WAL 1503, 292x5 contains the Walpole letters – most in the folder on the Itteringham estate, but others in the Burnham folder. A little extra punctuation has been applied and some abbreviations removed to make the letters a little easier to a modern eye. The final conveyance, Blickling letters and subsequent sale information are in NRO: NRS 20997, 69x3; MC 3/595 Blickling estate accounts for 1796 to 1801 show 1801 receipts in February and June for the 'Itteringham estate' but the totals include arrears and cannot give an accurate actual rent roll at that time; NRS 15954A-964, 31F7; WAL 334-45, 272x6; C/Sce 2/1/24; C/Sce 1/8; MC 3/340; DN/TER 92/1/1-33; WAL 345, 272x6; NRS 15961, 31F7. For the build-up of the estate: NRO: NRS 20967, 70x6; NRS 20964, 70x6; NRS 20966, 70x6; NRS 15960, 31F7; NRS 15959, 31F7; NRS 25641A, 140x4; WAL 339, 272x6; NRS 20998, 69x3; NRS 21029, 73x4; NRS 20995, 69x3; NRS 20996, 69x3; NRS 15954A, 31F7

Wolterton archive: 8/67

# Chapter 19

## *Farewell to the Robins: 2*

---

*Had Richard Robins 4 not died in his early thirties, the Robins family and Itteringham Hall might have thrived with more sons to carry the name forward. His only son might have stayed on the rails and the fine house might have been restored to its former glory.*

### The end of the Richard Robins line and his Itteringham Hall estate

After Richard 3 of Itteringham Hall died in 1787, the family line was to carry on for a further three generations. His daughter Susannah gave rise to the Leeds family; his eldest son Richard 4 had no great-grandchildren and his youngest Thomas 4 had no male Robins grandchildren. But the lives of these last generations were very different from their weaving and farming ancestors.

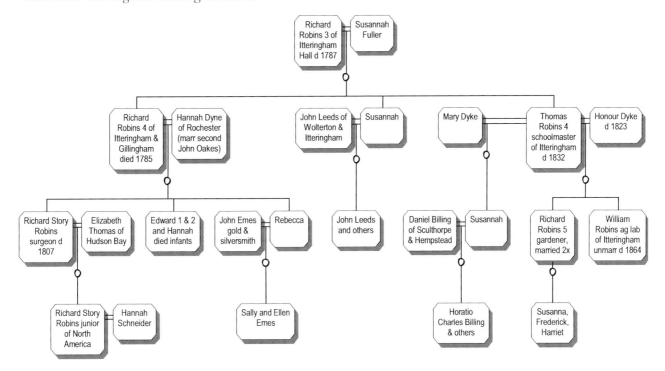

The last line of the Robins family

### Richard Robins 4 and Hannah Dyne

Richard Robins 4, of Itteringham Hall 'gentleman of Itteringham' aged 24, married Hannah Dyne 21, in St Nicholas Rochester Kent in June 1778. Hannah was the daughter of Edward and Elizabeth Dyne of Rochester. Edward Dyne was surgeon to the Royal Navy fleet at Chatham with a private practice in Rochester. He was also a senior alderman and twice mayor of the City of Rochester. He was a respected and comfortably-off man with an eldest son Andrew Hawes Dyne (later called Bradley) a well-connected London and Kent lawyer involved in the management of prison hulks, and a second son Thomas, a landowner living in Gillingham who was also an agent at Chatham for the Naval Commissioners running prison and transportation ships. As Hannah had no obvious connection to Norfolk, how they met remains a mystery but a connection through friends seems likely. Their first born son Richard Story Robins was born in Itteringham on 1st April 1779 and baptised a few days later. The middle name of 'RSR', as he will be known to avoid confusion, is also a mystery. There is no evidence that the Story name came from the Robins or Fuller families, despite it being a name found around this part of Norfolk. Nor was it directly in Hannah's immediate family line: her mother was Elizabeth Hawes and in the previous generation the maiden name was Moyce. The name appears to come from William Story esq of Chatham who was involved as a trustee in Dyne and Robins affairs in the 1780s. William's will left Hannah £200 in 1801 suggesting he may have married into her family. He may have stood as godfather to the boy or his name was chosen in deference to an influential friend.

RSR's earliest years were spent in Itteringham where he may have lived briefly in the increasingly dilapidated Itteringham Hall with his parents and grandparents. With his new family to provide for, Richard 4 leased Mannington Hall farm, one of the Wolterton estate farms, from 1780 for about three years. While there Richard and Hannah's next three children were the last to be baptised in the nearly defunct Wolterton church: Edward in March 1780 (he was buried in Itteringham the same year), Edward Andrew in July 1781 (named for both her father Edward and her elder brother Andrew) who also died and Rebecca born on the 13th and baptised on 18th September 1782.

It seems that during 1783 the young family moved down to Kent, leaving Richard's sister and her husband John Leeds to farm at Wolterton. Maybe Hannah thought she might have more success with her children's health with the support of her affluent father Edward and her brother Thomas. Thomas Dyne and his wife Mary, the only daughter of Peter Fountain esq of London, a well known lawyer of his day, lived in Gillingham. There in 1784 Hannah gave birth to a daughter Hannah, baptised at St Mary Magdalene Gillingham on 2nd October 1784. Sadly little Hannah too did not survive infancy. Worse still, in December 1785, Hannah's husband Richard Robins died at their home in Gillingham and was buried in the Dyne family church of St Nicholas Rochester. For six year-old RSR this must have been a strange time – a new, more comfortable home but the sudden death of his father and his mother's constant grief. Of the strangers who comforted him, uncle Thomas seems to have gained his life-long trust.

Perhaps surprisingly within two years Hannah had returned to Itteringham with little Rebecca to marry again. In August 1787 she married John Oakes the youngest brother of Thomas Oakes junior the tenant of Mannington Hall and its home farm. No doubt the couple had become friends when Hannah and Richard were farming nearby a few years earlier. Hannah now had another seven children in Itteringham – this time six survived to adulthood: Elizabeth, John, Edward, Andrew (died young), Francis, Charles and Benjamin. With Rebecca, and their growing family, it seems likely that John and Hannah Oakes did not live with John's brother in Mannington, but rather that they moved back into Itteringham Hall which they took over on the death in October 1787 of Hannah's father-in-law Richard Robins 3. The hall and estate had been settled on Richard 3 for life in 1783 and was due to come to Richard 4 and his heirs. With his father's death RSR was now the direct heir. Hannah's mother-in-law Susannah moved out to Ingworth. The family settlement deed effectively rescinded Richard 4's will which had left all his real and personal estate to Hannah. But in return she would come into an annuity from the property of £80 per year for life if she outlived her husband; and their daughter Rebecca was to have £1,000 upon marriage. The deed allowed Richard 3 to make a new will but as he did not have the chance, the deed became the binding document giving RSR the inheritance of the estate when he reached 21. RSR's title was further strengthened in June 1794 when a deed was drawn up to pay the legacies that Susanna Robins senior had left in her 1793 will to her other son Thomas and her daughter Susannah Leeds. The deed explicitly confirmed that the estate would pass to RSR at 21.

Hannah and John as we shall see remained at Itteringham Hall until sometime after 1805 when they moved to Burnham Norton; Hannah died not long afterwards and John Oakes remarried Juliana Blyth in 1817.

## Richard Story Robins

While John and Hannah set about bringing up Rebecca Robins and their six Oakes children and attempting to repair the house and farm in Itteringham, the heir Richard Story Robins was left in Rochester to be educated and brought up by his grandfather Edward Dyne. Dyne was a man of substance and both he and his two sons, RSR's uncles, were well-connected. The Dynes were an old-established Kent family from Ashford and elsewhere in the county. Edward carried out his task until his death in 1794, by when RSR was of an age to be apprenticed into a public service role or a trade. RSR's good start in life was further improved by his grandfather's will. While the elder son Andrew Hawes Dyne was main heir, significant sums were left to his son Thomas and his daughter Hannah Oakes. Trustees were to ensure that her two elder children Richard and Rebecca Robins would be brought up and educated from the income of a small trust fund. At 21 they would receive the trust fund but the trustees could use part of Richard's money to enable him to become an apprentice or a clerk in a public office.

The reference to public office almost certainly came from the family's friendship with James Bradley who was Secretary in the Board of Control, had a role in the India Office and who was also involved in the commercial management of prison hulks in Portsmouth and elsewhere. On 9th July 1782 in West Malling, Andrew Hawes Dyne married Frances, James Bradley's sister. Andrew later gave up his legal business to take over his brother-in-law's hulks business and took the Bradley family name in 1800. Having inherited substantially from her brother James, Frances and Andrew moved from West Malling to Gore Court near Sittingbourne. The Bradleys were also important for their naval connections. Through Admiral Parry and William Locker they came to know well Horatio Nelson in his early days as a Lieutenant. The Bradleys and 'Mrs Dyne' (ie Frances) were several times mentioned in surviving letters written by Nelson. These extensive naval links may have had an influence on young RSR's choice of career; he chose his grandfather's profession as a surgeon and in due course joined the Royal Navy. An apprenticeship was arranged for him with his late grandfather's partner John Anthony Barnard Krull of Rochester, a surgeon to the naval hospital at Chatham. Krull was then living in a house owned by the Dynes and the family provided for all necessities of the role and also pocket money for RSR. Unfortunately his life did not go according to plan; how it unfolded was later recorded in a chancery action which survives with all the detail. He was later to claim that he had been ignored and neglected by his family. Hannah refuted that accusation and said she had written to him many times and that John Oakes had called on him in Rochester on two occasions. But Itteringham was a long journey away and certainly RSR at 15 lacked parental influence when he perhaps needed it most. Krull was to tell the family that he thought RSR had regularly gone to visit his two local uncles but eventually he discovered that he had gone out drinking, returning home intoxicated on various occasions. After a bare 18 months, probably in February 1796, Krull terminated the apprenticeship for 'gross misconduct'. It seems that drunkenness, combined with a sustained lack of aptitude and application, was at the heart of the problem rather than anything more improper.

The family rallied round and using their naval contacts found RSR a position on board ship as a surgeon's mate. Krull helped with acquiring the clothing, uniform and equipment RSR needed to take up the role. The not inconsiderable cost of £192 was paid by uncle Andrew from Edward Dyne's estate. Even as a mate, RSR had to provide a chest with his tools and drugs; the chests were locked and sealed on board until the ship sailed in case the surgeons were tempted to sell their own supplies.

## Richard Story Robins in the Navy

Hannah later said that her son became a surgeon's mate in the Navy in July 1796. This may have been the point at which it was agreed that he would join the Navy, but he did not actually join his first ship for another 6 months. Perhaps in the intervening months he had a shore-based role supporting another surgeon. Maybe he was taken under his favourite uncle Thomas's wing. Later there was never a hint of any criticism of uncle Thomas by RSR. Andrew Dyne, his other uncle, said that it was Krull who arranged the job on the *Agamemnon*. Richard Story Robins signed on to the ship's complement of *HMS Agamemnon* on 9th January 1797, giving his place of birth as Norfolk and his age as 19. He was still three months short of his 18th birthday. The lie may have been to cover up that he had only performed a mere 18 months of his apprenticeship under Doctor Krull. Fortunately at this period, the examination for second and third mates was still 'perfunctory' and most were expected to learn on the job. A senior surgeon in 1800 complained that 'his Third mate was so badly educated he could neither understand Latin nor spell the commonest English words ... the First mate is incompetent in his duties and more ignorant than the Third mate ... the Second mate could not perform a simple operation nor make up common medical preparations'.

The *Agamemnon*, a 64 gun 'third rate' ship of the line was launched in 1781 and refitted in the early 1790s as fears about the effects of the French Revolution increased England's state of readiness for war at sea. It was noted for its fleetness and handling. For just over three years until his promotion in the spring of 1796 the *Agamemnon* was under the command of Horatio Nelson and the ship saw action. Although Nelson then left the *Agamemnon*, it remained one of his favourite ships. Suffering severe damage it was sent back to England for a refit and was re-commissioned in late November 1796 at Chatham under the command of Robert Devereux Fancourt. Had Hannah used the family connection to Nelson to find RSR an appointment on the ship or was it down to Krull?

As 'Surgeon's Mate' joining by warrant RSR was on full wages of just over £55 for his first year, working as the assistant to admirably-named Mr James Bones, the ship's new surgeon. Despite this prestigious post RSR did not do well. Although he served for two full years, in the second year he was demoted to 'Surgeon's Third Mate' and his second year full wages, before minor deductions, were only £22. James Bones should have been a good role model; just three years older than RSR he could only have finished his apprenticeship relatively soon before he joined the *Agamemnon* and must have impressed his elders with his skills. When he died he was just 31 and his parents William and Amy Bones erected a memorial stone in Cambridge, their 'testimony of affection [being] a small tribute to exalted merit'.

In his two years on board RSR saw little real action. In mid-March 1797 the *Agamemnon* was still completing its refit and revictualling at anchor in The Nore, the major safe anchorage protected by sandbanks just off Sheerness and just a very short distance from Chatham and Rochester. The *Agamemnon* then sailed to Yarmouth

Roads (a normal anchorage for a North Sea fleet ship) and spent very scarce time at sea until early June, when the ship sailed back to The Nore. However the circumstances of this short trip were quite extraordinary: the *Agamemnon* was briefly under the command of mutineers and sailed under the red flag of mutiny. In the spring of that year the Channel fleet at Spithead had mutinied over pay. Their demands were met and life should have returned to normal. But the mutiny spread quickly to the whole of the North Sea fleet and here it took on wider political undertones with demands for better working conditions, more leave and shares in prizes added to the core demand for more pay. The shadow of the French revolution brought out fears that this mutiny was a real threat to London, exacerbated by the fleet gathering at The Nore and blockading the Thames. There was to be no giving in to the demands of the mutineers' 'delegates' from each ship. Indeed troops were gathered on shore and eventually all the marker buoys in the treacherous shallow waters were removed to prevent the fleet from sailing towards London or making off with the ships to Europe as some threatened. While the *Agamemnon* was not at the forefront of the mutiny, it was fully involved and for much of the eight days or so of action the officers were imprisoned in their quarters by armed men. As the mutiny finally started to crumble the *Agamemnon* was among those where the delegates offered to give up their command to the officers, in this case if Fancourt committed to try to secure them a royal pardon. He agreed, was put back in control and sailed the ship away to moorings in Gravesend Reach. The always terse Captain's log did not record whether any of the *Agamemnon*'s crew were among the nearly 30 delegate ringleaders who were tried and hanged at the yardarm.

After this, life on board returned to its humdrum routine of make-work activity and occasional short exercises at sea. Throughout RSR's time on board there were regular floggings for misdemeanours among the men. Drunkenness was the most frequent cause, followed by disobedience and contempt of officers. This occasionally was described as mutinous. Gambling was occasionally noted. From time to time crewmen, for theft from their fellows, were forced to 'run the gauntlet' as punishment from their own. The surgeon and his team probably did little surgery. Rather, they were general physicians for the 490 crew and marines: patching up the wounds from the lashings and no doubt dealing with those that fell from the rigging – a couple of such deaths were recorded. Venereal disease would also have been rife among the crew – payments to the surgeon for treatment were recorded in the pay books. Other diseases would have been present and the log occasionally noted men being taken off to a hospital or hospital ship. Surprisingly too the medical team would have helped in the delivery of a baby on board – a son to Samuel and Mary Ann Harper delivered in September 1797 while the ship was at sea and named George Agamemnon Harper.

The ship was involved in various trips around the southern North Sea – the log shows positions off the northern Low Countries island of Texel and various positions off the east coast of England from The Nore up to Hull. There is no indication that the *Agamemnon* engaged in battle during this time, but they did take a small Dutch merchant vessel carrying coffee as 'our prize'.

It seems RSR was not a great success on board. Presumably James Bones discovered all too soon that his mate had served little of his apprenticeship and it must be assumed that he was poor at his job, so much so that in June 1798 William Hay joined the ship as Surgeon's 1st Mate. At the end of August a note in the Muster Book shows that RSR made his uncle Thomas Dyne his attorney. Was this because RSR fell seriously ill at this point and someone had to be appointed to receive any wages due in case he died?

However he was not permanently incapacitated by illness. He remained on the ship's complement (ticked as present at every muster) and during November 1798 visited his mother in Itteringham with three men whom she understood to be officers from the *Agamemnon*. Hannah made no mention of his having been ill. This is slightly odd since the Agamemnon's Master's Log showed that on 7th November 1798, moored off Yarmouth, RSR and two other men were sent to sick quarters (probably on shore rather than on the ship). He also came to Itteringham at Christmas time 1798 in the company of a Mr George Hudson. Hudson, the same age as RSR, was another surgeon's mate on the *Agamemnon*. Hannah said she had sent presents of game and turkeys to the officers of the *Agamemnon* while Richard was serving. Was his illness tempered by periods of not drinking? He continued to be recorded apparently as present at all the musters until 6th January 1799 when he was discharged from the ship at Yarmouth. No reason was stated and at best one might assume that the end of his second year was a logical time to part company. Yet the chancery materials make clear that he left the ship not only because he had contracted a 'bad disease' but also because he was dismissed and forced to quit 'owing to his misconduct'. We can only guess that the ship had had enough of his incompetence, and that his drinking had continued while on board. However, the tone hints at a significant misdemeanour. Had RSR technically gone absent without leave while supposedly recuperating on shore? His year's wages were not due until June when they would be paid to his uncle Thomas.

RSR went home to his mother and Hannah nursed him back to health. She then got him a job on *HMS Temeraire*. The *Temeraire*, later the subject of Turner's famous painting *The Fighting Temeraire*, was a 98 gun '2nd rate' ship of the line, built in Chatham and launched in September 1798. It took on its inaugural crew following commissioning at the end of March 1799. On 13th April, Richard signed on (again with inconsistencies over his age) as surgeon's 2nd mate under surgeon Richard Lloyd and Peter Puget, Flag Captain for Admiral James Whitshed. His friend George Hudson had signed on at the start of April as surgeon's first mate (perhaps the key to getting RSR his position) but by August George was promoted to *HMS Vesuvius* an 8-gun bomb vessel. RSR did not last even this long on the *Temeraire*. On 11th June, after just eight weeks, and somewhat unusually noted in the Captain's Log, he was discharged – on 'account of misconduct' according to his uncle. Hannah noted that RSR would have been disgraced for good had she not intervened. Again, this hints at significant misconduct, but nowhere is it recorded precisely what happened. No doubt Hannah still had influential friends in the navy and its medical community to whom she could turn to cover up the truth and to keep trying to get him another position.

After the debacle of a mere eight weeks on the *Temeraire*, 'his friends' (perhaps uncle Thomas, or George Hudson) got him a new posting, this time on yet another North Sea fleet ship, *HMS Monmouth*. He should have gone by water from Chatham to Yarmouth where the *Monmouth* lay. Hannah reported that he then had a handsome supply of pocket money - in mid 1799 he would have received his second year wages from the *Agamemnon*. But instead of going to Yarmouth to join the *Monmouth*, this time RSR went to London, pawned his clothes and got considerably into debt. His naval 'career' was well and truly over. His step-father John Oakes came to London to rescue him, paid off his debts (later noted as over £500) and took the young man back to Norfolk.

## RSR and his inheritance 1799-1800

But Richard did not stay in Itteringham with the Oakes. By early August 1799 he had taken lodgings at the house of Robert Stringer a farmer in Ormesby and he had also taken rooms in Yarmouth. Unknown to his mother, between 5th August 1799 and 6th May 1800 he had built up debts of £197 to Stringer and a further £400 and more in Yarmouth.

By this time, his reputation was widely known. Horatio Walpole senior, having lost the Thomas Robins land to Harbord of Blickling, was watching the Itteringham Hall estate with interest. In writing from Wolterton to his son on 14th August 1799 his words suggested RSR was very ill:

> Dear Hor,
>
> ... I am in much apprehension we may lose the other estate of Robins, at the end of the Water. I am endeavouring to make all possible enquiries, the owner is of age in April, is a very silly dissolute young man and given to drinking, in consequence it is very possible he may die before he comes of age as his health at present is very indifferent. It will then I believe descend to his sister which may perhaps stop the business for the present, you may be assured I will be very attentive on this head and be as private in my search as possible. Our neighbours [Blickling] have long heads are artful in their manoeuvres which must make our success doubtful ...
>
> I am your Walpole

RSR's family described his life as one of idleness and dissipation in lewd company and through his extravagance he was in danger of squandering his whole inheritance. RSR claimed Stringer put him up as an act of humanity in the face of rejection by his family. Rather more believable is the assertion by his family that the young man told everyone that he would soon come into a large estate and that Stringer and the others were simply vultures circling to try to get him indebted to them. Once he inherited they could call in the debts, forcing him to sell his estate at a knock-down price. Indeed Stringer had clearly overcharged him for board and lodging and threatened to arrest him if the debt was not paid.

During this period RSR obviously avoided his family. He was seen once in Aylsham in December 1799 but he went back to Yarmouth without paying them a visit. They found out that he had been there to pawn his clothes. Perhaps he was also visiting his new lawyer, Samuel Jeffrey Shaw of Aylsham whom in December he had hired to look into his affairs and discover what his inheritance would be – prompted to do so by a letter from his uncle Andrew. In a letter of 14th December Shaw wrote to Andrew to say that his client was unacquainted with his own affairs and that it was reasonable for RSR to know what income he would come into and if his estate was encumbered in any way. Shaw assumed, in fact wrongly, that Andrew Dyne was RSR's trustee (his only legal involvement was as executor of Edward Dyne's will). Not long after this Dyne received a letter from another lawyer, Benjamin Kittmer of Little Walsingham, who wrote to say that it was imperative that RSR should be rescued from his situation in Yarmouth. Kittmer was a friend of John Oakes and had first met RSR in December 1798 at Woolmer Cubitt's house in Erpingham. Kittmer's reputation was good and Dyne asked him to act for him in Norfolk, especially since he was himself ill and could not come to Norfolk. He sent him all the family documents by coach.

Walpole, meanwhile, had already visited John Oakes to further his interest and learn the family's intentions. He told Horatio junior on 1st February 1800:

> ... in conforming to your opinion I have spoken to Mr Oakes and explained to him that if this family should succeed in the purchase of the property which he now occupies it was their intention to give him the preference to continue as the tenant. He expressed himself much obliged to me for having thus explained myself on the matter [and] said it was much wished by his connexions that he should become the purchaser. I should much doubt his ability to bring this about tho his wife's relations are I believe in good circumstances and further belong to the profession of the law. He further said Col Harbord was very active in the business and he made no doubt was now at work in procuring emissaries to furnish the heir with such sums as he might want and of course place him under great difficulties to keep out of a goal [sic]. It will therefore I fear be very difficult to counteract a person who is totally indifferent to the opinion of the world on the measure he may take to support his own consequential success and advantage. I expect to see Mr Ewen shortly and shall desire he would occasionally communicate with you as before.

On 15th March 1800 Kittmer and Shaw met up at John Oakes's house to 'settle a plan for the future conduct and benefit' of RSR who was also present. All the papers were shown to RSR and explained by his own lawyer and it was Shaw who suggested that it would be in his best interest if the estate was sold and the money secured to pay him an income for life. All agreed that this was for the best and that the estate should be offered to uncle Andrew Dyne for £7,000. An agreement was drawn up and signed to the effect that if such a sale went through the money should be used to provide for RSR and his sister Rebecca and to sort out arrangements for Oakes to continue to farm the land under a new lease. The lease was to cover 'Nowers manor', the messuage and buildings and the 252 acres of land in Itteringham for 21 years from 5th April 1800 at an annual rent of £220. £1,000 plus interest would be paid to Adam Taylor to discharge his mortgage on the estate. £1,000 would be paid to Hannah to buy out her annuity of £80. A further £1,000 was to be settled on Rebecca, providing her yearly interest when single and the principal on marriage if Hannah agreed to the match. £300 would be used to pay off RSR's current debts and John Oakes agreed to accept just half of the £520 he had paid out to pay off other debts and monies owed to him from the previous period of running the farm. The balance of £3,440 would be invested via trustees to secure RSR an annual income. Dyne agreed to take a mortgage for £4,000 at 5% interest to cover these sums. This was to be loaned by Kittmer his lawyer and John Leeds, the husband of RSR's aunt Susannah. If RSR married and then died his widow would receive £50 per year for life. The principal would pass through to RSR's heirs or if he had none, it would go to Hannah and Rebecca. All this seemed very appropriate and would have yielded RSR a decent income of about £170 per year at the expected 5%.

Shaw wrote on 18th March to Dyne that he was happy with the title to the estate and RSR was 'perfectly willing to join in the plan'. Indeed he said that he could see that RSR's family had all only ever acted in his interests. Dyne agreed to pay £7,000 and undertook to get the formal deeds drawn up for signing in early April once RSR came of age on the 1st of the month. At this stage RSR was still in Yarmouth and the family feared he might sell his estate to those who had got him into debt. He needed to be rescued. On 28th March Hannah finally went to Yarmouth with Mr Siely, a friend of RSR's, to search for him. He was eventually found in 'improper company' and agreed to return to Itteringham with his mother. There he stayed until the end of the month. At the very end of March it was agreed that it would be best for RSR to go to Kent with his mother, well away from his creditors.

So at Andrew Dyne's house between 1st and 8th of April the documents were signed to enact the agreed plan. Thomas Dyne acted as RSR's trustee. Richard, it was later claimed, was well aware of what he was signing and agreed with the plan for his sister and himself. He later argued that he was hustled into the arrangement immediately after his 21st birthday, but discussions had been going on for some time and his own lawyer made sure he knew what was in the deal. For the moment matters seemed to be settled and there is no hint that RSR was at all unhappy with the agreement reached. However, very shortly it became clear that the risk that RSR would be pursued for debts soon after his 21st birthday had been real. He was arrested for debt – he claimed this was for expenses for clothes and pocket money when an apprentice which had remained unpaid by Krull and Andrew. However, his family later accused him of lying about this episode. Dyne reported that RSR had indeed been arrested for debt after April 1800 by a Mr Hall a tailor. But, on trial at Maidstone, it was proved that Hall had received his money from Krull (provided by Dyne) and RSR was acquitted. Not only this but at the start of April, on the 2nd, one Jonas Greenwood had come express from Yarmouth bearing a letter from Robert Colls, miller, of Worstead written the previous day. Robert was one of the sons of Robert Colls of Itteringham.

Kittmer had already saved RSR over £100 by negotiating down the payment of a debt due to Greenwood. Now Greenwood was acting apparently only on behalf of Colls and had a brief to see only RSR. But RSR refused to speak to him and Greenwood read out the Colls letter to Dyne. Colls had learned from a Captain Hearne that RSR was now 21 and intending to sell his estate. In part it read: 'If that is your determination you know what have passed between you and me on that subject. I do not wish you to sell it to injure yourself or family. I have only to request if it is to be sold you give me the refusal of it.'. Even though he went on to say he would pay hundreds more than anyone else, the family strongly suspected Colls of what they called 'tampering' with RSR for some time. They did not believe the offer was an honest one, especially since Colls had little property and had been made bankrupt in 1793. They thought this was all a plot to get RSR to accept a reduced price for the estate.

It seems likely that, after the April 1800 signing of the settlement deeds, RSR eventually went to London. There is no indication that he returned to Norfolk, nor that he stayed with one of his uncles in Kent – although again it is possible that he stayed with his uncle Thomas. More likely the bright lights beckoned where RSR would have had ready access to experienced chancery lawyers. At some point, probably later in 1800, RSR asked uncle Andrew to procure him a commission in a regiment overseas. He said he wanted to travel and be abroad, particularly to get well away from the bad influences on him in England. Dyne used the army agents Messrs Cox and Greenwood who had only three commissions available, two in England and one in Surinam in South America. He paid £315 for the latter since it was the only overseas posting. On 27th April 1801 the trust settlement was amended to withdraw a quarter of RSR's £4,000 to enable Dyne to pay the £315 and to kit him out for this new role. Richard signed a further document asking his trustees to invest any balance in 3% consols to add to his trust income. These documents were all properly signed and executed by the relevant trustees with £700 going to a lawyer acting for RSR. By implication at this stage RSR was still happy with his financial arrangements.

## RSR and the chancery case 1801

But RSR almost certainly did not take up the appointment as an Ensign in the 60th Regiment of Foot. He later complained in chancery that Surinam was a very unhealthy place and the regiment a poor one – 'one of the least eligible regiments'. He accused his uncle of taking this commission simply to bundle RSR out of the country as quickly as possible (and by implication perhaps hoping that he might die out there!). What was the cause of his sudden change of tone and for his entering a bill in chancery by June 1801? The underlying reason for his behaviour was that RSR had discovered that his uncle had decided not to keep the Itteringham estate but had agreed in February 1801 to sell it to Horatio Walpole ... for a substantially greater sum than the £7,000 paid just one year earlier.

Had someone from Itteringham told him about the deal? It is interesting that in his bill of complaint of June 1801 he confirmed his commitment to pay Rebecca his sister her £1,000. Perhaps he had attended her marriage in April - to a London silversmith - and heard talk of his old estate. However he discovered the news, RSR felt he had been badly done by, a feeling no doubt fanned by his so-called friends. The balance of 1801 probably saw RSR in London, briefing his lawyers and extricating himself from his army commission. There are hints in the defence statements that he may have continued to build up debts at this time, implying a continuation of his extravagant habits. As with most chancery actions there were all kinds of false and unlikely red herrings thrown into the mix. He claimed that he had been rushed into the signing of the deeds on his birthday – not very compelling. He talked of a friend at Ormesby, the Reverend Charles Boutell and a letter that was never posted in March 1800 and another letter at the time supposedly written by his lawyer Shaw that said his mother was to give him the estate. As Shaw had written to Dyne that RSR was happy with the deal, all this was a fabrication. (Boutell apparently had been promised the Itteringham living, which considering the right had been sold to Walpole in 1738 was another distraction.) The illogicalities in RSR's case add to the belief that his whole argument that he was unwittingly defrauded was a concoction. His uncle John Leeds, involved in the family meetings, testified that he was in no doubt that RSR understood that the estate was his and that he understood what he signed in April 1800. So how did RSR's case not only continue for two years but result in his favour?

It was the November 1799 letter that did the damage. To try to scare RSR into quitting his Yarmouth lifestyle (as he put it), Andrew Dyne had written at some length to show that RSR was spending money that he did not then have and would not have. But Dyne in fact lied when he asserted that RSR's father had broken the male entail and left the real estate entirely to Hannah and that it was up to her to do with it as she pleased. Dyne's intentions may have been good, but to the court this looked deeply suspicious. Clearly the 1783 family negotiations over Richard 3 and 4's wills and the property settlement had been complicated and the earlier will taken on its own could imply that all went to Hannah. But the settlement took precedence and since that time nothing had been done to change RSR's right to inherit when 21 as long as the annuity to Hannah and dowry to Rebecca were paid. Dyne was dishonest in only citing the will and not the settlement document. He knew the documents well – he was a lawyer and actually had custody of the family papers for many years. Hannah repeatedly said in her chancery answers that her brother had acted from good motives and she had only said to RSR that she waived 'any right to the estate she might have had under the will' – ie, she never said that the estate was hers. She said her son fully understood that the estate was his not hers and signed the April 1800 deeds on that understanding.

RSR argued that not only had his uncle lied about his inheritance to scare him into a settlement, but now he was going to reap the reward by selling the estate to Walpole for more than £9,000, thus making a £2,000 profit in just one year. Dyne was of a wealthy family and there is no indication that Andrew would have had any reason to try to defraud his young nephew RSR, although that is exactly what he was charged with. It looked bad, but Dyne argued his case. The price of land had unexpectedly shot up during the year after the signing. Dyne's basic argument on the estate valuation may well have been right: Richard Robins 3, well before his death in early October 1787, had let the house and estate fall into poor repair – John Oakes described it as the 'bad management of Richard Robins the elder'. By 1800 the family agreed that a fair rent for the new 21 year lease would be £220 – a measure of the extent of the improvements made by Oakes and current intensity of land use. Dyne argued that in 1800 local estates would rent for 16 to 20 shillings per acre and that the new rent sat in the middle of that range. Oakes said good land fetched 17 to 18 shillings – the rent of £220 was full and fair, as had been the old computed rent of £160 when the estate had been in such poor condition. The new rent reflected all the improvements and these had accordingly boosted the sale value of the premises. A 227-acre estate within two miles of this Robins estate had recently sold for just £4,500. This made the original £7,000 price a full one, at 32 times the annual gross rent. Dyne only paid the price because it was to help the family. He would probably have had to spend up to another £1,000 on the farm buildings and would get no return on this for the term of the 21 year lease to Oakes.

But Dyne said that Oakes was an excellent farmer and an enterprising man and was of course well-known to his neighbour Lord Walpole. In fact in January 1801 Walpole, knowing that Oakes wanted to farm on a larger and more profitable scale, on the death of a tenant, offered Oakes the lease of a 500+ acre farm in Burnham Norton. Oakes asked Dyne's advice on what he should do, so soon after the start of his new lease. Both agreed Oakes should take the new farm, which he did.

According to Dyne, only then did he think of selling the Robins estate to Walpole. He denied that he had ever had any approaches from Walpole or that it was ever explicit that Walpole wanted to buy the estate. This was a half-truth - Walpole had approached Oakes, not Dyne. As the land was adjacent to the Wolterton lake and park, no doubt chancery thought this was pretty unlikely. However, it got worse. Walpole offered £9,450 in February 1801, less than a year after the £7,000 transaction, for unencumbered possession. This was contingent on the Oakes lease being cancelled for which Dyne had agreed to pay Oakes £500 although he said the full value was in fact £1,000.

Dyne argued that the increase in price was a reasonable state of affairs. Grain prices had recently shot up (after a famously bad harvest) and with them agricultural profits. Therefore, with estates sold on a multiple of annual value it was only natural for land prices to surge also. He claimed he had just experienced the same thing in a farm of his own in Kent which, over almost exactly the same period, had appreciated from £5,400 to an offer valuing it at £8,000. RSR argued that the true rental value for the Itteringham property should have been £400 (saying the rent of £220 was a fraudulent deal with his mother and step-father) and that, on that basis, the true sale value was £11,000. This of course piled on the pressure on his uncle, with the underlying implication that the fast sale to Walpole was also somehow dubious and designed to accelerate the transaction. Perhaps Dyne's facts and figures would have been more compelling to the court if he had offered to share the windfall with RSR, but at no point was this ever mentioned as even a possibility.

## Horatio Walpole's part in the sale

In all this Walpole was an innocent party, even though a defendant in chancery. His concern had been to act quickly in order to secure the property even though he was worried about financing the purchase. In their earlier correspondence, he and his son had covered familiar ground. Horatio senior offered to sell his Pulham timber to raise £1,000 but added 'I must remind you that I cannot undertake to diminish my income'. As with the Thomas Robins sale, he asked his son to manage the business entirely. His son's reply read:

> My dear Lord
>
> I had flattered myself that the experience of last year would have convinced you of the impolicy of leaving the purchase of Robins estate to me, who not residing in the country have neither servants or others who I can send about and employ as you who live upon the spot can do; I therefore have again to request that you will manage that business yourself.
> To that part of your letter which declares that the loss of income occasioned by this purchase is to fall totally upon me I shall not say a word; if you buy the estate you are certainly at liberty to make whatever deductions you may think proper from the allowance you are so good as to make me.
> ... [Burnham] The marshes have to stay unimproved as it would be the greatest absurdity ... to involve myself in that expence and having no power over the estate, it would (should anything happen to me) be robbing my younger children of a considerable proportion of the very small fortunes which in that case they would inherit.
>
> I am my Dear Lord your most obedient and affectionate
>
> H Walpole

After Walpole and Dyne had shaken on the deal, Walpole wrote again to his son on 2nd March 1801:

> Dear Hor
>
> Husey has told you the estate at Itteringham is agreed for, the next thing to be considered is how to procure the money to pay for it. I shall be able to command from timber etc about £2000 from the estate at Pulham which I have ordered to be sold for £4000. There will remain a deficiency of about £4000. If you do not choose to apply your disposable cash to this purpose we must raise it upon mortgage and Bircham can get us the money, let me have your answer. It is hard at my time of life to have my comforts diminished by a defalcation of income, however I am willing to bear my part, it is therefore my intention that whatever loss of income may be incurred may be divided between us equally. I shall wish to have your answer at Catton on Friday as Mr Bircham will require time.
>
> I am Dear Hor your most affectionate
>
> Walpole

Letters from 1801-04 between Horatio Walpole and his legal advisers, Daniel Jones of Fakenham and WB Fleaney in London and his estate steward, John Bircham, have also survived. These show that by September 1801 it was clear that RSR was not against the sale to Walpole but only challenged the validity of the deeds of April 1801. The lawyers quickly proposed that Walpole should lodge the purchase price with the Accountant General, while waiting for the court to decide from whom the estate would actually be bought – RSR or his uncle. There were no other worries about the title to the estate. In October 1801 a letter advised that John Oakes should not be allowed to take up the Burnham lease until the chancery situation had clarified – presumably because of the proposed payment to him of £500 to surrender the lease of the Itteringham property. Already at that time the lawyers thought that the circumstances of the purchase by Andrew Dyne would be viewed with suspicion by chancery. In the autumn of 1802 Adam Taylor needed repayment of his mortgage money and Walpole's lawyers paid the £1,000 (plus £90 interest), no doubt as a further way of enhancing the probability that they would eventually secure the premises for Walpole. In April 1803 the money was actually paid by Walpole into court,

£7,861 being the balance due. A schedule showed that the £9,450 sale price had grown to £10,039 including interest at 4%. In addition to the payment to Taylor, Walpole's men had paid a cash advance of £1,000 (notional interest of £87 added) to Andrew Bradley (Dyne) in April 1801, by a draft made out directly to Hannah and John Oakes.

On 6th August 1803 Jones wrote to Walpole at Wolterton to tell him that chancery had found in RSR's favour and that the deeds signed so soon after his birthday were to be thrown over. RSR would be entitled to the net funds from the sale to Walpole. A letter had already been written to him 'abroad' to ask him to come to England to sign a recovery and other papers that would give Walpole secure title. By May 1804 it was known that RSR would be back in the country in November that year and Walpole's lawyers now saw no reason for the final acquisition of the property to be delayed past that date – indeed it was now in everyone's interest for the deal to be done and money to be appropriately shared out.

The estate was sold to Walpole as agreed and Dyne was left to negotiate with a chancery judge to recoup what he reasonably could of his outgoings. After the payments to Rebecca, Hannah Oakes and the various mortgage and debt payments, it seems likely that about £4,500 would have been due to RSR in the late summer of 1803 and payable at some point between then and the final completion of the sale to Walpole in November 1804.

It is not clear whether he took this remaining full sum in cash or as an annuity income from it along the lines of the original settlement. In either event he would have been comfortably off and able to pay any new debts he may have built up.

## Richard Story Robins and The Hudson's Bay Company

In the meantime he had finally carried out his plan to travel. After three years of service, naval surgeons were allowed to practice independently, often becoming village surgeons. Although RSR had not completed the full time, surgeons were in demand as the improved pay and conditions in the Navy drew the best to meet the Napoleonic threat. After a year doing little but watch his case grind through chancery, he managed to sign up with The Hudson's Bay Company as a surgeon and was on station in James Bay, Northern Ontario by September 1802. Nowhere could have been more unlike his former life. His patients were the few English staff and their families and the Cree trappers with whom they traded within the palisaded fort.

Eventually word reached him that he had won the chancery action and had to be in London in person to sign the final deeds conveying his estate to Walpole. In September 1804 he left Moose Island to travel to London. He was back in Canada by June 1805. This implies he did not linger in London. It seems likely that he was already by then married and had given up his old ways. The beauty of the cold wilderness of his new home seems to have brought him some happiness.

But before he left London he launched one further attack on his uncle Andrew. At the beginning of June 1805 his lawyers filed his bill of complaint in chancery that alleged his uncle had withheld significant sums that were due to RSR from his grandfather Dyne's will. The Oakes and the Emes (RSR's sister and her husband) had had their share of the residue of the estate and had signed releases to that effect, but RSR claimed he had never received money or even an account of the personal estate from Andrew. This looks like a mean-minded and spiteful little action to try to hurt his uncle. But it almost certainly failed. In February 1806 Dyne (as Andrew Hawes Bradley) submitted an assertive and devastating reply accounting for all the money and even arguing that RSR owed him money! Detailed schedules showed the make-up of his grandfather Dyne's £3,106 personal estate. The Oakes had been paid their £750 worth of bequests. RSR and Rebecca were each due £150 from the residue and Andrew had paid her £200, the extra from his own pocket. But he had already laid out £229 for RSR's use in addition to the £70 for his apprenticeship expenses separately provided for in the will. The £229 included the £192 for kitting him out for sea (Dyne and Krull had earlier gone to arbitration over the apparent high cost of this, so the amount was provable), £25 for an education bill and £11 for an unpaid debt. So RSR owed him just short of £79. Andrew's answer was sufficient to end the matter and nothing further was heard from RSR and his lawyers.

While in Moose (probably in 1804) he married Elizabeth the daughter of John Thomas, the noted 'Chief Factor' or head of station at Moose Fort. John Thomas travelled to England regularly and was there in 1800-1801. Did Elizabeth accompany him? (His other daughter Margaret had previously independently visited England and by her father's death in 1822 she was living in London.) Did RSR meet Elizabeth in London and then follow her to Moose or was it just a chance decision to join the Company, as a means of escaping England, that brought him there? Perhaps John Thomas's visit was in part to try to recruit a surgeon.

Whatever sent him there, RSR's service record in the Company archives shows that he worked as surgeon at Moose Fort (after 1821 known as Moose Factory), Moosonee, until his death in October 1807, where his burial is still marked by a fine tombstone, giving his Itteringham origins. His is noted as one of the earliest local burials of a European – most served a stint for the Company and then returned home. The gravestone (a picture of which can be viewed on the internet) looks to be a later memorial rather than a contemporaneous stone - the use of Moose 'Factory' was not correct in 1807 - and was probably raised by relations after both RSR and his son had died.

Richard and Elizabeth had one son, also named Richard Story Robins, apparently born in 1805. What happened to the money that remained from the sale of the Itteringham estate to Lord Walpole? Had RSR lived off his 'expectations' before he went to Canada? He was not in London long enough to blow it all in the winter of 1804-05. If he returned with most of the money to Moose he might have enjoyed his last couple of years, but little seems to have been left for his widow and her second husband, or his son.

## Richard Story Robins junior

Seven years after his father's death, RSR junior and his mother left Moose Fort. Following a dispute with the local regional head of the Hudson's Bay Company, her father John Thomas took a large retinue in 1814 in a long trek across country. They settled in the Seigneury of Vaudreuil in York County in Montreal District, in an area then known as Cavagnal (now Como, Hudson and Hudson Heights). Here, by the 1820s, there was a significant English community of about 80 families and 400 people, concentrated in one area in the midst of a large French-speaking population. In due course a few larger houses were built amongst the small farms (typically of about 45 acres) that were created out of the woodland by the side of the river Ottawa. Schneider's Inn with its stone wharf for the river boats and a schoolhouse completed the major buildings in the centre of the community that has since become Hudson Heights. Later an Anglican church, St James, was built near the river with impressive views across The Lake of Two Mountains.

John Thomas made a good life there and when he died in 1823 he left decent legacies, in particular to his daughters, as well as land to his sons. The young Richard Story Robins received £50. Elizabeth, now remarried to the merchant James Russell and living nearby at the 'Cascades' (presumably Pointe des Cascades), was particularly favoured as she and her husband were already looking after John's youngest son and residual heir Henry Thomas. In 1820 James Russell was one of the founding group who agreed to build one of the early steamers for local waters. The 80-foot long *Perseverance* powered by steam and sail was launched in 1822. The same year James Russell sold his share to John McKenzie, a partner in the dry goods importing firm (and Montreal retailers) of Hector Russell & Company. Presumably James was part of this company or family too. Had some of the old Robins money gone towards his share of the £910 cost of building the steamer? Was Russell further involved in the development of the steamers locally? Unfortunately, little more seems to be known about James Russell and Elizabeth. It would seem that the money from the Itteringham estate was long gone before Richard reached adulthood.

In Vaudreuil, Richard Story Robins junior grew up to work on the river system. In the early 1830s 'Mr Robins' managed a team of men who looked after the local locks and canals. In 1836 *The Mississoquoi Standard* quoted *The Montreal Herald* describing an incident in which Richard saved James Boyd, a 6 year-old boy, and his father from drowning – his coolness and dexterity in his rowing boat was praised. In 1837 he was promoted from a captaincy of one of the Rideau Canal steamers to command the steamer *Ottawa*, which he ran for several years between Lachine and Carillon – one of 13 steamers operated by the Ottawa and Rideau Forwarding Company. In 1838, 19 year-old Robert Ward Shepherd, one of many who left Norfolk at that time, emigrated from Sheringham where he had been born. Shepherd came to work for 'Captain RS Robins' for 3 years as his assistant and stayed, becoming well known for his work on the Ottawa River. Indeed he credited Robins for giving him advice and encouragement in his early years. Subsequent anecdotes show that Captain Robins was a popular figure on the river and in 1837 he served as a lieutenant in Col Mathison's Loyal Vaudreuil Volunteers during the uprising that year.

In 1836, Richard junior married Hannah Schneider of a local family of German descent involved in the fur trade and known for their home and inn, Schneider's Inn. At their wedding Hannah's father Charles gave them a farm overlooking the river at Hudson Heights, where Richard and Hannah built their house. Part of their land included the old section of St James's Cemetery and in 1841 Robins donated more land to enable the building of a church. The newly appointed Reverend James Pyke (son of a judge who lived in the Vaudreuil English community) described Robins as one of the most active members of the church. Later their house was renamed

Sydenham Cottage, after Lord Sydenham, Governor in Chief of Canada from 1839, a passenger on Captain Robins's steamboat who had commented on the wonderful location up above the Ottawa river – a far cry from the Bure!

Richard Story Robins junior in about the 1850s - the only surviving portrait of a Robins

Sydenham Cottage today

Richard and Hannah had just one child – their daughter Hannah Elizabeth known as Betsy. She was an artistic and talented girl and a sketch by her of the family home survives. Sadly she died in 1848, aged 11 of typhoid contracted from Reverend Pyke, followed by her mother Hannah in 1853. Robins continued to take an active part in the local community and church until he died in 1891, although after his wife and daughter's deaths he is said to have been a shadow of his former self. Relations through the Schneider family lived for a time in Sydenham Cottage and kept the memory alive locally.

## Rebecca Robins

What of little Rebecca Robins who was only three when her father Richard 4 had died in Kent in 1785? Uprooted again, leaving her brother RSR behind with her grandfather and uncle Dyne, she returned with her mother to Itteringham. With her new stepfather John Oakes and six new half-brothers and sisters she grew up in the now run-down Itteringham Hall farm. However Rebecca was given a great chance to better herself. Unlike her brother RSR, she took her opportunities in both hands. Of all the Robinses in this book, she is the only one featured in the *Oxford Dictionary of National Biography*.

### Rebecca Robins and John Emes

At 12, Rebecca received a small legacy of £4 a year from her grandmother Susannah Robins to be paid by her uncle John Leeds towards her maintenance; at 13 she benefited by her grandfather Dyne's will in which he had set up a trust fund for her education. Even more importantly for a girl she had a marriage portion; the family settlement of 1783 had provided £1,000 to be paid when she wed. Added to this, she had expectations when she reached 21 of £40 from Susanna and a share of the trust fund from her grandfather.

How she was educated is not known but she was probably tutored locally at first. In 1799 when aged 16 she appears still to be living at home but Rebecca no doubt would already have been spending time with her Dyne relations in Kent and being groomed for a good match. John Oakes occasionally made business trips to London and she may have travelled with him – a good chance for shopping. At some point she met and fell for John Emes, an artist, engraver and silversmith of London, 20 years her senior. For the reading of the banns she was resident with her uncle Andrew Hawes Dyne (now called Bradley) at his fine house of Gore Court at Tunstall in Kent and from there 'Miss Robins of Itteringham' was married on 7th April 1801 at the fashionable St James's church in Piccadilly London, where John was given as a parishioner. Uncle Andrew was a witness to the marriage which was reported in *The Times* and *The Monthly Magazine*. John Emes was better known as of Paternoster Row near St Paul's (his firm's location was at Amen Corner).

How did the young girl from north Norfolk meet John Emes? Had her wealthy uncle been a patron of the silversmiths? He may have introduced his young 18 year-old niece to the 38 year-old Emes. By 1801 Rebecca's brother of course was living in Kent and London and they seemed to have stayed on good terms – perhaps visiting him produced the connection. After the family's battles in chancery, Rebecca's marriage portion of £1,000 would have been paid to her from RSR's estate within about 3 years of her marriage, possibly sooner. Perhaps this money was invested into the working capital of the firm that Emes had relatively recently taken over from the Chawners. Rebecca's life was now far removed from her village origins. Initially John and Rebecca may have lived with his father, William Emes, the landscape gardener. William had moved from Elvetham Park in Hampshire and between 1801 and 1802 lived at 8 Argyll St, not far from St James's, and next door to the Duke of Argyll. When he became ill he went to live with his daughter Sarah at the Vicarage House in St Giles Cripplegate where he died in 1803.

### Rebecca's business career

Rebecca had two daughters by John Emes. The eldest was born on 11th February and baptised Sally (not Sarah although she was called both later) on 15th March 1805 at St Faith Under St Paul. Ellen was born on 14th November 1807 but not baptised until 13th March 1812, at St Giles Cripplegate. Still living in St Giles were Sarah the sister of John Emes (the wife of the Vicar) and their brother Philip Emes who baptised a son Frederick there in 1808. The delay in baptising Ellen was presumably a result of the sudden death of her father after only seven years of marriage. John Emes was buried on 17th January 1808 at St James's. *The Gentleman's Magazine* noted his death: 'Mr Emes, silversmith of Paternoster Row, going upstairs to bed, he fell down in a fit and expired immediately'. Aged only 46 he left no will, but his inventory taken that June showed he was comfortably off. Rebecca and John's brother William Emes were left as guardians of the two infant children 'Sarah and Ellen', to use the personal estate for their benefit until 21. Emes had £997 cash in Hankey's bank and £200 in shares in Rock Life Insurance Co. His trade stock and tools were valued by his partner Henry Chawner at £9,421. Of the £1,287 worth of household goods, the single largest item was £505 in wine – for trade entertaining or was he just a keen drinker? It has been noted that in 1806-07 Emes made an apparently unique silver wine bottle shade (for protecting the bottle from the warmth of a fire) engraved for a member of the Farrer family of Brayfield Bucks. Had he made one for himself and subsequently sold the item on to a client?

During the few months of sorting out her late husband's estate and reconstructing the business, Rebecca briefly formed a partnership with John's brother William Emes. By the end of 1808, however, she was in partnership with Edward Barnard who had for many years run the production side of the Chawner and Emes firms (with Henry Chawner as silent partner once Emes took over). Emes and Barnard traded successfully under the 'RE/EB' mark, although it does not seem that she played a significant role in the business. In 1829 the partnership was dissolved. In February 1829 the 'Widow Mrs Rebecca Emes' and Henry Chawner sold their stakes in the business to Edward Barnard and his sons, Edward, John and William; Chawner received £10,327 and Rebecca £5,093 - about £250,000 in today's money. The firm continued as a partnership of Barnard and his sons.

## Rebecca's retirement

Despite suggestions by some writers, Rebecca did not remarry – neither to Edward Barnard nor anyone else. After John's death she moved into several fashionable addresses: by April 1812 'Mrs Emes' is listed at 18 Queen Square Bloomsbury. By the start of 1815 she had moved to 5 Charlotte Street near Bedford Square in Bloomsbury, where she stayed for a decade. In the last years of the 1820s she moved along the road to 19 Charlotte Street. With her brothers-in-law William and Philip, Rebecca appeared in a listing in *The Morning Chronicle* of 26th May 1814 as subscribers to a fund to buy an annuity for the by then destitute widow of William Woollett – many years earlier John Emes's painting master. Apart from these references it has proved hard to find documentary references to Rebecca and the girls outside the books of the firm. Her Norfolk life was far behind her; her brother and mother were long dead although her step-father John Oakes did leave Rebecca and her daughters £100 for mourning in 1826. It seems they lived quietly but comfortably off her share of the profits.

Having left her partnership pay-off invested for income, Rebecca had £6,250 in the firm by 1830 and the company books show her receiving interest on a loan each year. Rebecca stayed at Charlotte Street until 1841 with Sarah, Ellen and three female servants. In 1842 they moved to 13 Connaught Square, off the Edgware Road, which was to be her last home. Ironically Rebecca's near neighbour at number 7 for several years in the late 1850s and early 1860s was initially Horatio Walpole, 3rd Earl of Orford and then the 4th Earl, whose country seat was of course Wolterton, the parish where she was born. No doubt they would have made the connection, but would they have known each other socially? Most of her capital was still intact in 1858 when she held £5,062 – about £220,000 today.

Rebecca Emes, 'widow of John Emes goldsmith', died on 17th July 1859, aged 76 in the new parish of St John's Paddington. The cause of death was 'bronchitis suffered for many years'. On 20th July *The Times* reported: 'On the 17th instant at 13 Connaught Square, Rebecca relict of the late John Emes in her 77th year, after a lingering illness borne with great patience and submission'. Had her bronchitis been the cause of her relatively early sale of her share of the business in 1829? The company accounts for 1819 show she received cash 'for dispensary' and regular winter payments of 1 guinea were made afterwards. Local newspapers for this area did not start until 1860, so there is no other source for a more substantial obituary which might have shed light on both Rebecca's illness and her life. Although her estate was valued at under £14,000 - today's value £600,000 - she did not leave a will. The Misses Sally and Ellen Emes in 1859, after their mother's death, held £1,012 each in the loan account. It is assumed that these sums were from Rebecca's holding and that the daughters had withdrawn the rest on her death. Sally Emes died at 13 Connaught Square on 9th June 1862 – a spinster of independent means. Her will, made a month earlier, left everything - her effects were also 'under £14,000' - to her sister Ellen.

Rather surprisingly Ellen Emes spinster, the last of the family at Connaught Square now in her late 50s, was married at St John's Paddington on 6th September 1866. John Havers, surgeon of St George Bloomsbury FRCS, had witnessed Sally's will showing that he had known the family for some years. He was a younger son of Thomas Havers, head of the family which for many generations had owned Thelveton Hall in south Norfolk. Interestingly several earlier members of the Havers family had been goldsmiths – Thomas of St Vedast London (d 1621), Thomas of Norwich (active 1674-1732 and mayor 1708) and his son George in London (d 1750). By the early 1840s John Havers was an eminent and well-connected London surgeon, of 10 Bedford Place, Russell Square. He was a high profile freemason: sometime President of the Board of General Purposes of the United Grand Lodge of England. Although retaining a London house, his favourite home was White Hill, Berkhamsted in Hertfordshire where they lived in a large house and grounds. There he was involved in local school governance from 1871 and he remained actively involved as a senior and influential freemason until his death. Ellen died in Berkhamsted in 1881 followed by John on 20th August 1884 aged 69. Ellen's age at death was given as 70 suggesting John was unaware that she had been born some eight years before him and was in fact 73 when she died. To be fair, she would only have her baptism certificate as a record (which was dated 3½ years after her birth) so she might have believed she was only 70.

Their wills are intriguing. In Ellen's will, made in 1873, she left the first £10,000 to her husband, with bequests of £1,000 each to her step-daughters Dorothy and Annie Havers, her cousin James Clay, Clay's second son Frederic Emes Clay and his youngest Cecil Clay, her cousin Henry Holmes, her goddaughter Ellen Reid and her late sister's goddaughter Fanny Reid. She left a few specific items, which may be traceable today: a clock designed by her father - John Emes - featuring Hercules supporting Atlas to bear the globe, a picture known as the St Giles's Beauty by Burwell and a sketch by Hamilton of Hydra and the water nymphs from Ovid's *Metamorphoses* went to James Clay. Also she left the chest containing her father's, her sister's and her own drawings, plus some scrap books and trinkets, to Ellen and Fanny Reid. This suggests that Rebecca had not been an artist but that Sally and Ellen were. Have the Emes drawings survived in the Reid family?

Ellen's husband's will left an estate deemed to be worth £18,646 (about £900,000 today), presumably half of it being Ellen's money. The main beneficiaries were his two daughters, but his brother Richard Havers of Banbury received £3,000 and was executor. He also left Richard all his silver plate, some of which had belonged to Ellen, a gold snuff box and 'a silver snuff box, inlaid with copper and gold', which he proudly boasted 'I made myself'. Richard also received the contents of his workshop and photographic rooms at White Hill. Havers was clearly a remarkable man of many parts.

Rebecca's daughters may have been quite active in the arts and education; the family were certainly well-off and cultured. Had they heard stories of the draughty old Hall where Rebecca grew up, back in a remote part of Norfolk? Did Ellen know of her cousin, Richard Story Robins junior, sailing steamboats on the Ottawa river? Whether she knew or not, ten years after her death in 1881 their line of the Robins family would come to an end.

## Thomas Robins 4: the schoolmaster

The younger son of Richard Robins 3 of Itteringham Hall, Thomas did not marry as well as his elder brother Richard 4. Born in 1757 he was probably locally educated - enough to become a schoolteacher later - but nothing is known of his early life. He may have lived with his parents at Itteringham Hall until his father died in 1787 although he may have also spent time in Norwich. Not being in line for any inheritance from the family settlement he had to make his own way. He was 'of Itteringham' that same year, when he married for the first time at the age of 30: he and Mary Dyke wed on 10ᵗʰ October 1787 at her church St George Tombland, Norwich. The marriage was witnessed by Elizabeth Dyke - presumably Mary's sister - and William Burgess who themselves married in the same church the following year. It seems at first the marriage was childless but when Mary died in November 1793 she may have been giving birth to a baby girl Susannah. Susannah junior married in 1811 so must have been born around 1793; that she gave one of her daughters the forenames Mary Dyke is reasonable confirmation. At this point Mary and Thomas may have been living in Erpingham not far from his mother Susannah Robins, as that is where Mary was buried. Interestingly Susannah senior had made her will a few months earlier and left money to Thomas's children 'born or to be born' suggesting that she did not yet have a named grandchild. His mother had died about a month before Mary and was also buried at Erpingham. Susannah had made, from her own resources, a good provision for Thomas and Mary (had she lived). £700 was to be invested for Thomas's life to provide him and his children with an income. His children would then inherit the remaining capital at his death.

Thomas fairly soon married again, possibly to Mary's younger sister. On 9ᵗʰ November 1796 Thomas Robins widower of Erpingham married Honour Dyke at St Helen Norwich. Less than a year later, in October 1797, she produced their first son Richard, baptised in Erpingham. She may have had other unsuccessful pregnancies as no other baptisms have been found until the much later baptism in Itteringham in November 1810 of William Robins the son of Thomas and Honour ('late Dyke spinster'). As by then Thomas and Honour were living in Itteringham, it is possible that he had started holding school in the cottage behind the shop. Sold in 1799 to the Blickling estate, the property was purchased from Lord Suffield by Walpole in February 1816 with Thomas Robins 'the schoolmaster' as the sitting tenant. He remained there at least until 1827 and may well have stayed for the rest of his life. Honour Robins died in Itteringham in November 1823 aged 55 and Thomas followed in February 1832 when he was 75.

All three of Thomas's known children survived, two of whom married and had children. Susannah the eldest married Daniel Billing in Itteringham in February 1811. They settled in his home parish of Sculthorpe and baptised five Billing children at the Fakenham Baptist church between 1812 and 1820. The surnames of Robins and Dyke were used as middle names for Richard, William and Mary. In 1841, he and Susannah ('Anne') were farming with their son Horatio, a butcher and daughter Susanna aged 20 living with them. When Daniel died in 1852 he had remarried and was living in Hempstead. Only two of his children were mentioned in his will: Susannah had married William Bastard of Briston and Horatio had fathered an illegitimate son Henry Savory.

William Robins, Thomas 4's younger son, stayed in Itteringham as a general labourer. In February 1831 a one-off entry in the Walpole estate accounts shows William Sparrow and William Robins paid £5 11s 6d to take or collect horses from Newmarket. By his 30s he was an unmarried agricultural labourer lodging in Joshua Ayton's house in Slipper's Yard (now Big Yard). He was buried in Itteringham in November 1864 aged 55 and there is no evidence he ever married or had children. His elder brother Richard Robins 5 however did marry and one of his daughters was to be the last surviving person from the Itteringham families to bear the Robins surname.

## Richard Robins 5: the gardener

Richard Robins 5 was born in Erpingham in October 1797; again little is known about his early life but certainly by 1824 he had married a girl called Sarah. They baptised their daughter Susanna in Itteringham church in August 1824, when Richard was described as a gardener living in Itteringham. They may well have been staying with his widowed father behind the shop at this period. Where he had learnt his trade and met and married Sarah is not known (nor is her maiden name) but he could have trained at any of the local Halls, Blickling, Gunton, Cromer or Wolterton, or even further afield. They may earlier have had a daughter called Sarah but this is not certain. Whatever his start, his skills were evidently sufficient to achieve the post of head gardener at Felbrigg where James Bertram had been gardener in the early 1820s. He held the position, becoming celebrated among his peers, until his death in 1869.

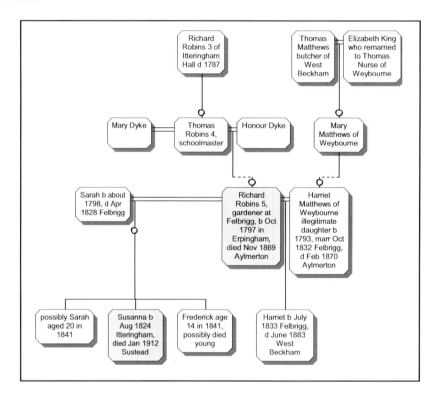

Summary family tree for Richard Robins gardener and Susanna the last Robins

In the 1842 first edition of John Wighton's *The History and Management of Bees* 'Mr Rubens' [sic], gardener to WH Windham esq of Felbrigg, was listed as a subscriber. The 1854 edition of *White's Directory of Norfolk* listed 'Richard Robbins gardener' in Aylmerton. It seems that he had a reputation at the time for growing fine pineapples in the kitchen garden at Felbrigg. In 1841 James Grigor, a nurseryman and botanist from Lakenham, remarked that Mr Robins had done a particularly fine job bringing it to 'a style of excellence which but few gardens present'. The 4-acre walled garden had choice fruit trees which, it was said, bore astonishing crops, including very old Genoa fig and Breda apricot trees. As a head gardener he would have enjoyed a little status on the estate and he would have been provided with board wages or a cottage in addition. He would have paid his men's wages but his own, if similar to Wolterton's rate, were only marginally above those of an agricultural labourer.

His first wife Sarah was buried in Felbrigg churchyard in April 1828 aged only 30. She may have died from complications after the birth of their son Frederick, who must have been born about 1827. No baptism record has been found for him. In October 1832 in Felbrigg, Richard remarried to Harriet Matthews of Aylmerton. Both signed the register with a confident hand. Harriet had come from Weybourne, the only child of her unmarried mother Mary Matthews. Mary was the only daughter of Thomas Matthews a butcher and churchwarden of West Beckham and his wife Elizabeth King. Elizabeth was the daughter of Charles King an Aylmerton farmer. Thomas Matthews died young and Elizabeth remarried to Thomas Nurse of Weybourne – one of a large clan of Nurses in that parish. It seems likely that Elizabeth held on to her first husband's West Beckham property until her death in Weybourne in 1810, when it passed to the still unmarried Mary to provide for her and her daughter Harriet. Three years before her marriage to Richard, 36 year-old Harriet inherited her mother's property. In July 1833, still living in Felbrigg parish, Richard and Harriet baptised their only child Harriet junior.

In 1841 Richard and Harriet were living in Felbrigg with Susanna 15, Frederick 14 and Harriet 7; Sarah Robins aged 20, who may have been Richard's eldest child, was a servant in a large house in nearby Aylmerton. No further trace has been found of Sarah who may have married or moved away. Similarly Frederick vanishes from the records. This was a time of great upheaval in Norfolk with a mass emigration to Canada - one Fredrick Robins went to Ontario to farm but identification is uncertain.

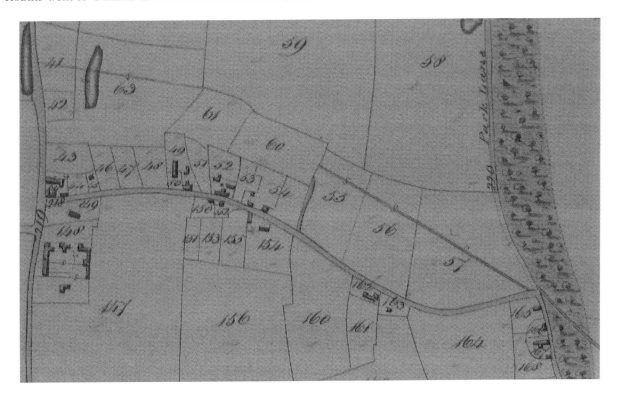

Section of Aylmerton tithe map 1842

Richard and Harriet Robins were then renting a cottage and pightle somewhere in Felbrigg from the Windham estate for a total of £6 but in 1842 they moved to a cottage and garden with the use of a 1 acre arable pightle and a further 2 acres of enclosed pasture on the old Weldon Common in Aylmerton. All were leased from William Howe Windham at a rent of £6 10s and marked as lots 161 and 162 on the Aylmerton tithe map. Next door, immediately to the east, was the tiny townhouse owned by the Aylmerton poor overseers. In 1850 Robins started paying a further £1 for land late of Robert Sharpin (earlier the Felbrigg blacksmith), probably part of his holding of Weldon Common pasture. It seems likely from the map and examination of the building today that his cottage had two rooms up and down – larger than that of a labourer. Subsequently the cottage was turned into two small dwellings and is still there, once known as Meadow View and now Sawmill Cottage (although the townhouse has gone).

The Robinses also had some income from Harriet's old Matthews property in West Beckham which was shown in the Voters List as 'houses and lands' with Richard's tenants being 'Doughty and others'. The West Beckham tithe map of 1845 shows the two cottages on a small plot in The Street, West Beckham, now Chestnut Farm. Richard died on 15th November 1869 aged 72 and was buried in Aylmerton with Harriet following him in February 1870 aged 76. Richard's effects worth less than £100 were granted to daughter Harriet junior.

Richard's daughters Susanna, often called Susan, and Harriet outlived their father by quite some years but their story is not a particularly happy one. Neither married and both appeared to earn a living from dressmaking. In

1861 both were living in Aylmerton with Richard and Harriet but after their parents' deaths they would have lost their home, unable to afford the rent for a large cottage and land. The half-sisters did not seem to stay together. Harriet, a needle worker, went to board in the house of Edmund Hall, a beer-house keeper in Aylmerton and Susan was in a small cottage in Gresham on her own, working as a dressmaker. In 1881 Harriet, an 'unmarried annuitant', was a visitor in the house of the 57 year-old builder George A Jekalls in Victoria Street, Lakenham. Susan(na) was still in Gresham, but now as a visitor in the house of 71 year-old labourer Thomas Nurse – no doubt a cousin via her step-mother's connection to the Nurses. It seems that our Harriet was probably the Harriet Robins who died in June 1883 at the West Beckham Poor House and was buried in the village churchyard. Her given age of 42 is not quite right, but is consistent with her under-stating her age in census returns. Her sister Susan, who may have been of limited capability, had a long and lonely old age. By 1891 she lived in Sustead doing 'general work and char'. Recorded as 'imbecile' by the census enumerator, she could not tell him where or when she was born. In 1911 Susan was an 'old age pensioner', aged 79 and whoever helped her do the return wrongly gave her birth place as Aylmerton and year as 1832. She remained alone at the cottage in Sustead until her death in January 1912 when her death certificate showed cause of death as 'senile decay' at age 80.

As Richard Story Robins junior had died in 1891, with her death all those bearing the surname Robins from the Itteringham families were dead.

## Sources

Unfortunately none of the later Robins wills and deeds have survived. Perhaps they were lost during the chancery suits in which they were recited in detail. As a result, however, there is no surviving detailed description of the Itteringham Hall premises for the whole period of Robins family ownership, although apparently such a schedule was attached to the 1801-04 legal papers.

For Richard Robins:

The parish registers for St Nicholas Rochester are viewable online on Medway Citiark www.medway.ac.uk/library/files/daybyday/October.pdf for Edward Dyne.
Dan Byrnes, *The Blackheath Connection*, a website book – an extremely well researched and footnoted book covering the convict ships to Australia.
There is no reason to believe these Fountains were connected directly to the local Norfolk family of Fountaine and so were not the link between the Robins and Dyne family.
IGI; *The Gentleman's Magazine*, 1826; TJ Pettigrew & HN Nelson, *Memoirs of the Life of Vice-Admiral Lord Viscount Nelson*, 1849

RSR action:

TNA: IR 26/388; IR 26/395. This chapter has been written using the family information contained in chancery items dating from 1801-05: TNA, C 13/589/28, 13/596/25, 13/603/7, 13/624/43 and a lengthy chancery decree in C 33/523

For RSR and Canada:

TNA: Various pay books, muster books, Captain's and Master's log books survive for the Agamemnon for this period: ADM 35/69; 35/1834;  36/12871; 36/13071; 36/14587; 51/152, 51/1123; 51/1194; 51/1228, 52/2633; and introduction to Surgeons Journals. PC 1/43/147; C 33/523 p 925
NRO: AYL 955 Walpole letters; WAL 1503, 292x5

Other sources include: EP Brenton, *The Naval History of Great Britain* ..., Volume 1, 1823; *The Times* Archive Online and a variety of web resources on the Navy of this period. C Lloyd and J Coulter, *Medicine and the Navy 1200-1900 Vol 3 1714-1815*, 1961; J Nichols, *The Gentleman's Magazine*, 1814; JS Clarke & S Jones, *The Naval Chronicle*, 1807; J Burke, *Genealogical and Heraldic History of the Landed Gentry*, 1847; J Burke, *Genealogical and Heraldic History of the Commoners of Great Britain*, 1838; *New Monthly Magazine*, 1816; H Nelson, *The Dispatches and Letters of Vice-Admiral Nelson* ... , 1844. www.gov.mb.ca/chc/archives/hbca; *Moose Factory, an Exploration of Frontier History*, Ontario Heritage Foundation, 2002; *Pioneer Families of Hudson, Volume 1*, an article on Richard Story Robins by Marnie Clarke; John Thompson, *Hudson: the Early Years, up to 1867*, Hudson Historical Society, 2004; E Collard, *The Potter's View of Canada*, 1983; LRE Quin, *Moose Factory Hudson's Bay Company Graveyard*; *Dictionary of Canadian Biography Online*; C Thomas, *History of Argenteuil* ... , 1896; F Mackey, *Steamboat Connections* ... , 2003; Vaudreuil websites; Scot & Siliclone website: T Santa, *Main Road Hudson: Then and Now*, 2002; J

Bouchette, *The British Dominions in North America*, 1831; F Mackey, *Steamboat Connections ...*, 2003 - Mackey in error cites the Captain of 3 river boats (the Commodore Barrie, Bytown and Ottawa) in the 1830s as Redford S Robins instead of Richard; WH Atherton, *Montreal, 1535-1914*, 1914.

For Rebecca Emes:

TNA, PCC Emes will 1803, PROB 11/1398

*Boyle's Fashionable Court Guide*, 1801 & 1802. Although John Emes is known to have been William's son (*ODNB*), it is unclear whether the family had been related to the earlier London goldsmiths named Emes as listed by Sir Ambrose Heal, *The London Goldsmiths 1200-1800*, David & Charles Reprints, 1972.

Judith Bannister, A Postscript to the Barnard Ledgers in *The Proceedings of the Silver Society*, Volume 3 (1983) page 38-9; The Emes daughters' baptisms suggest addresses close to St Paul's. Ellen's place of birth is given as St Paul's Middlesex in 1871 and 'London, Bow' in 1881 which could be St Mary at Bow near St Paul's, Bow to the east or an error.

*The Gentleman's Magazine*, 1808, p 560

*Silver Studies,* The Journal of The Silver Society, Volume 14, p 126

Notes from a website summary at its sale. Deed now in the possession of John Fallon.

*Boyle's Guide*, April 1812, 1815-25, 1826-28, 1829-67; *Royal Blue Book: Fashionable Directory and Parliamentary Guide*, 1829, 1842, 1843

British Library 19th Century Newspapers Online; *ODNB*. Interestingly an Ann Woollett was one of the witnesses to William Emes senior's will when first made in Hampshire in September 1792.

The 1841 census gives her age as 50 whereas she was actually 60 in Sept 1842.

*The Era*, 16th September 1866, 19C BLNO

Havers's first wife was Maria Cory the daughter of William Cory a bank director from Southwark. *The Times* Archive Online and British Library 19th Century Newspapers Online. The census returns for 1841, 1861, 1871 and 1881. Maria was still alive in 1861.

For Thomas Robins 4 and Richard 5:

NRO: WKC 5/257a-260, 400x8; PRDC 2/2/1/87; DN/TA 698; DN/TA 696; DN/TA 813; C/Sca 2/112; WKC 5/261, 400x8; PD 652/44; C/GP 6/167

Wolterton archive: 3/1/9

In 1861 the only likely census entry for William Robins is an unmarried servant aged 58 in the West Beckham household of Samuel Sayers. William was noted as born in Sheringham – had Thomas and Honour once lived there? Since his brother had property in West Beckham, William may have been found a job there. Indeed Samuel Sayers might even have been a tenant of Richard and his heirs.

*The Gardener's Magazine and Register of Rural and Domestic Improvements*, 1841 reviewing James Grigor's *The Eastern Arboretum, or Rural Register of all the remarkable Trees, Seats, Gardens, etc, in the County of Norfolk*; also the book itself on Google Books; *ODNB* entry for Grigor.

The Canadian census 1881 for Adelaide, Middlesex North, Ontario shows Fredrick Robins, a married farmer of English origin, but aged only 48.

Walter Rye, in *North Erpingham*, noted a tombstone at Aylmerton giving Richard died 18th November and his wife, incorrectly, as *Hannah* Elizabeth d 21st January 1870 (stone not found in 2010). National Probate Calendar

# Person and Place Index

No subjects have been indexed except occupations which have been entered as a group. Surnames are grouped together except for major families where individuals have been separately identified. Where no county is given, place-names are in Norfolk; similarly local sites are in Itteringham unless shown otherwise. Page references to the main history of local properties are shown in bold.

Abbot's Wood (Grove), Wolterton 80
Abell, Daniel jnr 137, 139, 142, Daniel snr 47, 68, 123, 142, Edward 181, 186
Addison, Dr Leonard 206
Adey, Mr 147
Alby 133, 141, 146, 213, parish 135
Aldborough (Albro, Alburrow) 3, 91, 108, 111, 113, 116-7, 120, 122, 132, 140, 170, 183, 185, 190, shop 123
Aldhouse, Ann 147, Augustine 123
Aldrich, Thomas 198
Alexander family 179, Willam 228
Alger (Algar, Agar, Edgar), Russell snr and jnr 124, 126, 189-90
Allen, John 156
Alleyn, Hannah 25
Allison, James 203
Almshouses 4, 6, 173
Amiraut, Paul 189
Amis, Elizabeth 123, Hannah 123, Samuel 123
Amiss, - 12
Amyas, John 160
Andrew Thomas messuage and fields 90, 93
Andrews, Richard 214, Robert 204
Anson, Mr 227
Antingham 38-9
Archer, John 137, Thomas 119
Armstrong, George 214
Arthur, John 214
Arundel, Earls of see Howard
Ash Hill farm, Calthorpe see Oak Hill farm
Astley, Jacob 217, Joseph cleric 141, 143, Sir Edward 217, Sir Jacob 84-5
Asty, John cleric 135, Robert cleric 135
Athill family 35, Elizabeth 135, Mary 135, Sarah 147
Atwood, Edward cleric 120, 150
Atwood's house 4, 150
Aylmerton 146, 178, 182, 185, 215, poor house 173, school 185
Aylmerton, Rector of see St Clair, Patrick
Aylsham 3, 18, 24, 27-8, 35, 71, 78, 83, 99-100, 108-9, 112, 116, 120, 123-5, 129, 139, 144-5, 147, 149, 175-6, 179, 182, 185, 189, 191, 204, 207-8, 212, 214-7, 219-20, 223, 227-8, Aylsham Assembly (rooms) 109, 215, bridewell 177, 204, 214, churchyard 148, fair 214, Market Place 124, 214, Aylsham Navigation 214, Rectory 27, theatre 215, turnpike road 214
Aylsham Road 17, 30, 183
Aylsham Union workhouse 179
Ayton, Joshua 231, Richard 56, Robert 183, 228
Bacon, Francis JP 100
Bacon, Matthew 4, Sarah 159, Widow 186
Baconsthorpe 24, 36, 91, 104-5, 112, 128, 140, 143, 145, 191, manor 135, parish 135, parsonage 145, 213, smithy 24, 104

Baker, John of Gayton 43, Thomas of Yorkshire 43
Balderston, Elizabeth 129
Baldwin, John 126, Mary 148, William 219
Barbados 213
Barber, James 185, John 203, Lucy 168-9, 191
Bardwell, John 120
Barker family 145, Mary 145, 191, William 191
Barker's farmstead 90, 92
Barnard, John 49, 204
Barnes, Anne 215, John 12
Barnham, James 82-5
Barningham 91, 126, 130, 187, 190, Hall 204, 213, 215, Lowes 12, 213
Barningham Road 14, 47, 65, 116, 128, 130, 155, 157
Barns family of Yorkshire 42, Frances ('Francis') 42
Barton, - 184, Thomas 86, 88, 103, 184
Barton's pightle 87
Bartram, - 186, Boy 177, James 61, 181, Joseph 181, Mary 181, Widow 174, 178
Barwick, James 174, Stephen 202, William 219
Bateley, Widow 100-1, William 100
Bateman, Edward 48, 119
Bath 120, 126, 182, 215
Bawdeswell 203
Baxter, Elizabeth 120, John 30, Jonathan 30, 78, 114-5, Robert 78
Bayfield 146, 213
Bayfield (Bayfeild), Thomas 10, 15-6, 38-9, 48, 52-3, 143, 161, 163, 185, 194, 196, 202
Bayfield, Henry 10, 38, 80, 123, 195, Joseph 185, Mary 87, Rachel 150, William 38, 150
Bayly (Baly, Bayley) family 107, 137, Elizabeth snr and jnr 107, Lydia 107, 185, Thomas 107, William snr 66, 107, 127, William jnr 107, 185
Beall (Beale or Bell), Anne 23
Bean, Berney 214
Beane, John 12, 66, 177
Bear (Bare), Mr 85
Beaumont, William 100
Beckham 124
Beer House farm, Cawston 89
Beeston Regis 145
Bell family 5, 21, 24-30, 67, 69, 120, 133-4, 137, 142, 148, 155, 159, family tree 26
Bell, Alice 26, 30, 70
Bell, Anne 120
Bell, Barbara 27, 159
Bell, Bridget 117, 137, 170
Bell, Coulson snr 126, 149, jnr 204, 208
Bell, Daniel 28-9, 129
Bell, Edmund (d 1636) 26-7, 68
Bell, Edmund of Matlaske 27
Bell, Edmund s of 'Tanner' Bell snr 120
Bell, Edmund tanner 26, 137

Gore Court, Tunstall, Kent 236, 247

Gotts, Thomas 208, William 208

Grand, Helen 100, Thomas 100-1

Grange, - 10

Gravel pit, close, field 46, 65, 87, 150, 178, 184

Graver, Cornelius 14, 16, 64-5, 67, 167, John 78

Graver's Close 64

Great Ellingham 106, 110, 132

Great Snoring 105

Great Walsingham 111

Great Witchingham 127

Great Yarmouth 30, 59, 104, 108, 137, 140, 146, 149, 175, 214, 220, 223-4, 239, 241-2, Old Meeting 134, Yarmouth Roads 237

Green farm, Oulton 26-7, **29**, 148

Green, George 125, John 195, John cleric 140, Mary 123, 149, Richard snr and jnr 123

Greenacre, - 195, Ann 129, Edmund 38-9, 42, Thomas 129

Greenwood, Jonas 241

Gresham 99, 131, 252

Gresham, Edward 107-8

Gresham's School 189

Grey family 146, Anne 10, Deborah 10, Elizabeth 9, James 9-10, 193-4, 196, Penelope 9-10, 36

Griffin, Jane 215

Griffiths, Dr Elizabeth 45

Griggs, James 108-11

Grigor, James 250

Grimstone, Mr of Yorkshire 42

Groom, John 125

Guestwick 25, 59, 134, 137, 140-1, 143, 147, 189

Guestwick Meeting House 25, 27, 135, 137, 139, meeting 140, 143

Guist

Gunthorpe 9, 107, 110-1, 202

Gunton 57, 145, 203, 216, 220, estate 213

Gunton, Dennis 10, 124, Henry 10, John 208, Mary 124, 192, Rachel 192

Gurney family 202

Hackford 111, 145, 183, 214

Halett, John 176

Hall, Christopher 174, Cutty 177, Edmund 252, Henry 105, 231, Mary 181, Mr 241, Peter 99, 105, Widow 177, William 99, 105

Halvergate 121

Halving lands 14

Hammond, Francis 110

Hamond, Horace cleric 146

Hancock, Benjamin 231, Mary 176, Nathaniel 176

Hannant, - 195, Ann snr and jnr 183, John jnr 183, John snr 129, 179, 181-3, 214, 228, Thomas 67, 70

Hansey Close 78

Hanworth 106, 137, 140, 146, 185, 191, Hall 215

Happisburgh 59

Hapton, Suffolk 147

Harbord family of Gunton 35, 223

Harbord, Caroline Lady Suffield 78-9, 224

Harbord, Col Harbord 145, 185

Harbord, Col William Assheton 2nd Lord Suffield 30, 105, 119, 220, 224, 229-31, 239-40, 249

Harbord, Rebecca 145

Harbord, Sir Harbord 1st Lord Suffield 57, 147, 215

Harbord, Sir William see Morden, William

Harcourt, Edward 219

Hardiman, John 79

Hardwin, Anne 120

Hardy, Old 178, Sarah 187, Valentine 113

Harley, William cleric 131

Harmer, Sarah 181, Thomas 177

Harper, George Agamemnon 238, Harry 181, Mary Ann 238, Samuel 238

Harriman, Richard 176, 208, 216

Harrison, Cornelius cleric 62, Ruth 119

Harts Yard 101, 112

Harvey, Benn cleric 146, Ness 43

Harwich, Essex 175

Hase, Edward 215, Mary 177

Hastings manor, Hindringham 90

Hastings, Mary 134

Havers, Annie 249, Dorothy 249, Ellen 248-9, George 248, John 248-9, Richard 249, Thomas 248

Hawes, Elizabeth 235

Hawkings (Haukings), Thomas 36

Hawkins, Thomas 185

Hay Fen, Wolterton/Calthorpe 195

Hay, William 238

Haynes, John 208, William 208

Hays (Haze), Mr 206, Mrs 53

Heacham 23

Headley, Henry cleric 141

Heare (Hare), Anne 25

Hearne, Capt 241

Heath, Aaron 121

Heigham 107, 128

Hemmings family 75-6

Hempstead 125, 143, 214-5, 249

Hepworth, Suffolk 132

Herne, Mr 219

Herring, Archbishop 145, Dr William snr and jnr cleric 145

Hethersett 21, 23

Hevingham 99, 128, 176

Hewett, William 190

Heydon 21-3, 25, 30, 45, 50, 57, 89, 91, 99-101, 105, 125, 135, 139, 145-7, 176, 183, 189, 191, 213, 215, 217, church 147, Hall 108, parish 134, smithy 104

Hickling 14, 202

Hill farm 3, 5, 17, 19, 45, 64, 66, **75-7**, 85, 89, 101, 118, 165, 208, 226

Hill, Hannah 191, John 191, Mary 176, Richard 13

Hilton, John 45

Hindolveston 110, 192

Hindringham 76, 90-1, 107-10

Hindry, Charles 220

Hingham 185

HMS Agamemnon 237-8

HMS Monmouth 239

HMS Temeraire 239

HMS Vesuvius 239

Hobart (Hubbard) family 17, 193, 213, George 213, John esq 100, Major (1787) 216, Sir Henry 4th Baronet 131, 135, Sir John 2nd Baronet 131

Hobart, Sir John 1st Earl of Buckinghamshire 35, 72, 80, 91, 146, 159, 207, 213, 214

Hobart, Sir John 2nd Earl of Buckinghamshire 18, 28-9, 35, 148, 203-4, 214-5, 224

Hoddy, William 130

Hogg, Reynold cleric 147, 190

Holkham 230, Hall and estate 39, 42, 217

Holl, Augustine 91, Katherine 91

Holland, John 204

Holley, - 214

Holmes, Henry 249, John 145, 189, Nathaniel cleric 137, 141, Thomas White cleric 224

Holt 108, 110, 129, 145-7, 149, 176, 182, 189, 203, 208, 213, 215-7, 219, Country Park 216

Holt Road 67-8, 72

Home Close, Wolterton 194

Hook Hall farm, Calthorpe 10, 51

Hook, John 177

Hooke, Edmund 83, 85, Mary 125, Robert 198

Hooker, Joseph snr and jnr 149, Sir William Jackson 149

Horse marsh 49

Horsestealer 208

Horsford 77, 204, heath 214

Horsford Lane, Norwich 214

Horstead 59, 99, 114

Hoskins, Mr 182

Hospital farm, Calthorpe 10, 53

Hospital House, Wickmere 182

Houghton family 90, family of Gunthorpe 9, Gregory 9, Richard 9-10, 90, 132, Robert 9, 75, 90

Houghton Hall 36, 39, 196, 215

Hoveton 145

Howard, Ann 124, 186, Edward 186, John 124, Mary 124, 171, Robert 124, 127, 171, 189, William 124, 186

Howard, Dukes of Norfolk 90

Howlett, John 214

Hubbards Herne 91

Hudson Heights, Montreal 245

Hudson, George 238-9

Hull, Sarah 223

Hull, Yorkshire 140

Hunworth 91, 101, 107, 110, 134, 143, 181, 191

Hurrell (Harrold), Ann 125, Ark (Arch) 107-8, 111, 125, 128, 181, 217, 228, Thomas jnr 128, 181, 228, 231, Thomas snr 6-7, 125, 128, 160, 231, Thomas of Wickmere 125

Ingham 149

Ingworth 78, 89, 91-3, 182, 217, 236

Ipswich, Suffolk 147

Irmingland (Armingland) 21, 35, 45, 47, 56, 67-8, 91, 140, 142, 146-7, 159, 175, 184, 208, 219, church 67-8

Irmingland Hall 28, 35, 45, 69, 126, 134-5, 137, 147, 159

Irmingland meeting 91, 135, 137

Itteringham advowson 132, 143, 145, church 66, 70, 80, 88 105, churchyard 49, 107, 114, 115, 124, 140, 148, glebe 12, 47, 144, Parsonage Cottage 5, House 144, 150

Itteringham Common 4-7, 17, 19, 49, 72, 125, 157, **159-60**, 173, 177, 231, (nos 89 and 90) 7

Itteringham Hall 4-5, 12, 19, 49, 56, 61, 70, 75-6, 80, 84, 89-94, 129-30, 137, 139-40, 165, 200, 223, 229-30, 232, 235-6, 239, 245, 247, 249

Itteringham mill 12-4, 19, **112-5**, 123, mill cottage and house 5, pightle 78

Itteringham parish 6, 9-19, 45, 50, 62, 72, 75, 89, 132-3, 143, 145, 147, 173-9, 181, 195, 229, poor 111, 173-9, 186, 231, poor houses (town houses) 5-7, 116, 159-60, 173-4, 179

Itteringham shop 5, 19, 62, **120-3**, 125, 192, 224, 231

Itteringham smithy 5, 19, 99-101, 104-5, 112, 156, 227

Itteringham tannery 5, 19, 66, 101, 106-7, 111-2, 231

Itteringham village 3-7, 58, 64, 67, 69, 99-100, 105, 112, 156-7, 189-90, 199, 232, alehouse 118, bowling green 5, heath 30, open field 79, 100-1, population 6, pound 117, school 190, schoolroom 124, watermill on the Cut 65, west field 65-6

Ives, Alderman 217, Clement 61, James 61

Jack Bell's Grove, Oulton 28

Jackson family 123, 137, - 10, 48, Amy 120-1, 191, Anne 43, Anthony 43, 197, Charles jnr 121, Charles snr 104, 121, 191, Hannah 191, Mary 21, 64, 76, Richard 113, Richard (d 1728) 10, 167, 195, Richard cleric 121, Richard of Yorkshire 197, Robert jnr 13, 64, 76, 165-6, Robert snr 3, 61, 64, 66, 76, 121, 165, Susan 61, Thomas 61, Thomas cleric 4, 64, 120, 132, 150, 165, 189, 191, William 3, 42-3, 120

Jackson's farm, Wolterton 195

Jacob, Robert 203

James Bay, Northern Ontario 244

Jarvis family 26, 69, Amphilus 181, John 12, 66, William 69, 105

Jay, John 38, 56, Lucy 168-9, 191

Jeary, Matthew 181

Jeckyll (Jeckell, Jickell) family 105, Agnes 105, Edmund 105, 113, 231, Francis 105, John 215, Lucy 105, Mary 105, Robert 105, 181, 203, 217, 224, 227-8, Sarah 105

Jefferies, Dr John 101, 140, Jane 101, 124, 140, Mary 80, 101, 229

Jeffery, Thomas cleric 140

Jeffries, Mr 229

Jekalls, George A 252

Jempson, James 3

Jermy, Alice 146, William 213

Jessopp, Frances 120, Thomas 120

Jewell, Edmund 27-8, 71, 82-3, 87, 93, 109, 111, 146, 185, 190-1, 207

Jewler, Philip 195

John's Bridge (Water) 47, 49, 91-2, 112

Johnson family 4, 157, Ann 11, Clement 125, Judith snr and jnr 99, Thomas 99, 131, Tobias 3

Johnson's Close 46-7, pightle 87

Johnson's meadow 91

Johnson's orchard and pond, Wolterton 195

Jolly (Jolle, Gelley), John 66, Thomas 140

Jones, Daniel 243-4, Elizabeth 176, John 176

Keeper's Cottage, Mossymere 12, 14, 62-4, 202

Keeper's Cottage, Wolterton 10, 167

Kendall family 62, Henry 62, Susan 13, William 56, 62, 185

Kensey, Henry 62

Kent, Elizabeth 77, Nathaniel 227, 230, William 196

Kenton House, Devon 224

Kerdiston 38, 67, 215

Kerrison, Roger 184, 219

Schoolhouse pightle 87, 189

Scott, Dr Joseph Nicolls cleric 149, Francis JP 123, Martha 149, Mary 68, Mr of Aylsham 207, Mr of Norwich cleric 140-1, Samuel 111, Sarah 111, Thomas cleric 29, 147, 149

Scottow 23

Scottow, Peter 214

Sculthorpe 159, 249

Seely, Mary 179, Robert 179

Selth, Roger 106

Sendall (Sandell, Sandle, Sendale) family 35, 184, Ann 69, 175, Dorothy 175, Jane 35, John 35, 72, 182, Judith 175, Margaret 183, Martin (exciseman) 175, Martin jnr 35, Martin snr 35, 184, Mary 175, 184, Mary (d 1747) 35, Sarah 128-9, 175, 228

Sewell, Adam 128, John 125, 128, Mary 128

Sexton, Richard 45-7, 68, junior 47, Thomas 46, William 46

Sharpin, Robert 251

Sharrington 110

Shaw, Samuel Jeffrey 239, 241

Sheldrake, John 137, William 137

Shepherd, Robert Ward 245, William 185

Sheppey, Kent 147

Sheringham 49, 61, 245

Shilleta (Shelladay), Mary, 176, Richard 124, 128, 150, 156, 174, 176, 217

Shivers, widow 179

Shop (sheep) Close 100

Shop Pightle 78

Sibbs, Abigail 133, John cleric 145, Richard (17th C cleric) 133, Richard 133, 145, Robert cleric 133, Sarah 145

Siely, Mr 240

Silvergate, Blickling 35, 119, 133

Simpson, Francis 43, Hannah 43, John 43, Simon 42-3

Sims, Edmund 125

Skelton, John 115

Skinner family tree 76, Mary 76, Richard 76, Thomas 64, 75

Skoulding, James 108-10

Slipper family 155, 157, James 157, Mary 157

Slipper's Yard 250

Sloley 223

Sluice Close, Irmingland 68

Sly, Robert snr and jnr 127, William 107, 127

Smallburgh 101

Smith of Irmingland family tree 136, Dame Alice 45, Sir Owen 45

Smith, Edward 159, Henry 178, James 112, 172, 186, 219, John 12, 118, 179, John of Norwich 30, Mary 68, Mrs 118, Richard 10, 198, Sarah 112, Sir James Edward 57, 147, William 178

Snashall, Mr 182

Snelling, James 176

Snellings farm, Wickmere 52

Soame, Henry 12

Sotherton, Thomas 85

South Erpingham hundred 208, 217

Southrepps 59, 61, 111, 134-5, 137, meeting 140

Spa Beck, Lane, meadow, Irmingland 68, 119, 137

Sparrow, James 177, 183, William 250

Spink, William 49, 130

Springall, Ebenezer 137, 140, Joshua 137

Spufford, Margaret 3

Spurrell, - 14, William 52

Squallham 10, 12, 182

Stagg, - 62, Minns 63

Stalham 144-5

Starkes, Agnes 21, 25

Starling, Boy 185, Elizabeth 69, Martha 14, 69, Simon 14, 69

Stavers, Mary 126

Stephens, Joanna 182

Steward family 87, 140, arms 87-8, Mary 140, Susannah 140, Thomas cleric 140

Stiffkey 90

Stockings, John 29

Stody 36, 110

Stokely, Andrew 111

Stokesby 146

Storey, William 176

Story, William 235

Stowmarket, Suffolk 149

Stringer, Robert 239

Stulps, the 9, 14, 80-1, plantation 14

Sturbridge fair, Cambridge 108

Suckling, Benjamin cleric 147, Maurice 147

Suffield 213

Suffield, Lord see Harbord

Summer house 200

Summers, Thomas 123

Sunnyside 7

Surinam, South America 241

Sustead 127, 145-6, 169, 208, 213, 252, parish 133

Sutton, - 10, Robert 174

Swaffham 126

Swannington 126

Swanton Novers 169

Swardeston 77

Sydenham Cottage, Hudson Heights, Montreal 246

Sykes, John cleric 147

Symonds (Symond), William 12, 52, Mr 190

Taylor, Adam 240, 243-4

Temple, Elizabeth 43, Mary 43, Richard Ness 43, Robert 42, 197, Thomas 43

The Artichoke Inn 5, 12, 19, 116, 118-9, 123, 129, 216 and see The Walpole Arms

The Bell Inn, Oulton 159

The Black Boys Inn, Aylsham 176, 178, 208, 215-6

The Buckinghamshire Arms (The Blickling Arms), Blickling 119

The Bull Inn, Norwich 141, 143

The Cockpit, Whitehall London 40, 144

The Cut 65-6, 101, 112, 157, 167

The Feathers, Holt 147, 216

The Half Moon, Briston 108, 110

The Hudson's Bay Company 244-5

The Linnaean Society 57, 147

The Long House 72

The Maid's Head, Norwich 110

The National Trust 158, 231

The Nore 237-8

The Old Forge, Saxthorpe Road 159